W9-DBH-162

QUESTIONING AFRICAN CINEMA

University of Minnesota Press   /   Minneapolis   London

QUESTIONING AFRICAN CINEMA
conversations with filmmakers

Nwachukwu Frank Ukadike

Foreword by Teshome H. Gabriel

The University of Minnesota Press gratefully acknowledges permission to reprint the following. The interview with Chief Eddie Ugbomah originally appeared as "Towards an African Cinema: Chief Eddie Ugbomah, Nigeria's Leading Independent Director Discusses Film, Finances, and the Obsolescence of the Jungle-Melodrama," *Transition* 63 (1994): 150–63; copyright 1994 W. E. B. Du Bois Institute and Duke University Press; reprinted with permission. The interview with Flora Gomes originally appeared as "In Guinea-Bissau, Cinema Trickles Down: An Interview with Flora Gomes," *Research in African Literatures* 26, no. 3 (fall 1995): 179–85; copyright 1995 Indiana University Press; reprinted with permission of Indiana University Press. The interview with Djibril Diop Mambety originally appeared as "The Hyena's Last Laugh: A Conversation with Djibril Diop Mambety," *Transition* 78 (1999): 136–53; copyright 1999 W. E. B. Du Bois Institute and Duke University Press; reprinted with permission.

Published by the University of Minnesota Press
111 Third Avenue South, Suite 290
Minneapolis, MN 55401-2520
http://www.upress.umn.edu

Library of Congress Cataloging-in-Publication Data

Ukadike, Nwachukwu Frank.
   Questioning African cinema : conversations with filmmakers /
Nwachukwu Frank Ukadike.
      p. cm
   ISBN 0-8166-4004-1 (alk. paper) — ISBN 0-8166-4005-X (pbk. : alk. paper)
   1. Motion pictures—Africa. 2. Motion picture producers and directors—Africa—Interviews.
I. Title.
   PN1993.5.A35 U45 2002
   791.43'096—dc21

                                                    2001008023

Printed in the United States of America on acid-free paper

The University of Minnesota is an equal-opportunity educator and employer.

12 11 10 09 08 07 06 05 04 03 02   10 9 8 7 6 5 4 3 2 1

For all those who stand against injustice

Contents

PART II. VISION AND TRENDS

PART III. BOUNDARIES AND TRAJECTORIES

Foreword
A Cinema in Transition, a Cinema of Change
Teshome H. Gabriel

The art of the skillful question puts the questioner in a stance of opposition to conventional wisdom and provides a framework for the development of new insights, new methods, new ways of seeing and thinking. In this volume, Professor N. Frank Ukadike certainly asks the pertinent questions, eliciting responses that speak to the nature of African cinema and African culture more generally. Yet, as Ukadike suggests in the book's title, African cinema is itself a matter of questions and questioning, an ongoing questioning that never merely accepts the supposed givens of African reality. In many ways, Ukadike's questions in this book are in part, but probe deeper into, the questions that African cinema and filmmakers have asked and continue to ask: questions about the relationship of contemporary African life to Africa's past, to its traditions; questions about the political and ideological institutions imposed by colonial rule and maintained by postcolonial power structures; questions about the roles of men and women in African society; questions about the importance of language and oral narratives, and about the ways in which myths and mythmaking are recast by cinema, as in the case of Safi Faye's most recent film, *Mossane*. Yet the questions that Ukadike asks, like the questions that African cinema asks, are not eternal questions. Indeed, they serve to disrupt the perception—so common in Western representations of Africa—of an unchanging, monolithic Africa. Neither Africa nor African cinema can be reduced to a fixed, eternal essence. To say that African cinema is a questioning cinema is also to say that it continually moves and changes.

African cinema connects the past and the future of Africa. In making this connection, it often employs a nonlinear structure, moving from one time frame to another, so that sometimes the past resides in the present, and sometimes the future is in the present. To many Western observers, these films may seem to be rooted in the past, and, in a sense, that is so. But these links to the past are, as Deleuze and Guattari have suggested, more a matter of rhizomes than of taproots. History and tradition in Africa, and particularly in African cinema, are the equivalent not of oak trees, but of grasslands; they provide sustenance for a way of life, but they also spread across the land in a complex, interwoven pattern. This complexity allows for movement, for change. It also means that if traditions are sometimes destroyed in one area, they grow back. Connections are reasserted; history reemerges. This decentralized but insistent sense of connection helps to explain the survival of African culture in the face of repeated degradations. African cinema as well draws its strength from this web of traditions.

African cinema, then, does not simply follow a single path. As the filmmakers interviewed in this volume have demonstrated, there are many strands, many threads within it. And these strands are themselves interwoven into intricate patterns, creating an immense tapestry in which one can discern images of the past mingling with those of the present and foreshadowing the future. If Africans and African cinema are highly regarded for their storytelling abilities, they do not, as in the Western conception of history, tell one triumphal—or tragic—story. As in the oral narratives of the griot, to which African cinema has often been compared, stories tend to bend back upon themselves, to circle as they circulate, so that their fabric contains many interlocking stories and permutations of stories, as is beautifully illustrated in Gaston Kaboré's *Wend Kuuni* (God's gift), and Idrissa Ouedraogo's *Yaaba* and *Tilai*. Sometimes legends are combined; at other times, they are spun into separate strands. Yet, in this process of weaving and interweaving, which continues to underlie Western notions of "textuality," everything is inevitably connected. Nothing in African cultures can be seen simply as separate from the whole, from the larger patterns. Every image is part of a larger story, a larger film in the making, as is made obvious in such internationally acclaimed works as Kwaw Ansah's *Heritage . . . Africa*, Med Hondo's *Sarraounia*, and Haile Gerima's *Sankofa*.

In this sense, the stories that are woven into African cinema are concerned not simply with the retelling of myths and folklore, with the recording of history; they are part of a collective effort at mythmaking. Mythmaking involves creating new stories from out of the old. Here, Souleymane Cissé's *Yeelen* (Brightness) serves as an excellent example. Yet what people sometimes forget when they speak of stories and narratives is that, in Africa at least, stories are also a matter of images. Narrative, in an African context, has always been visual—has always been, one might say, cinematic. The stories of African tradition are built of layers upon layers of figures, of metaphors and analogies, of sly references to political and social events and institutions. These figures and images may point to many references, may have many interconnected meanings, as for example in Salem Mekuria's moving documentary *Deluge*. Putting these images together becomes an adventure in visual thinking, a way of imagining a different reality, a different future.

The interweaving that forms African culture and African cinema also involves a sense of community or collectivity that does not mesh easily with Western notions of the sovereign individual, individual freedoms, and consumer choice. African films, as many commentators have noted, do not place the same stress on the role of the individual that Hollywood and European films do. African cinema, like African culture, is based in the social and political experience of Africa's peoples. By the same token, we should not, despite the fact that it is possible to view African filmmakers in the tradition of the Euro-American auteur, make the mistake of seeing African films merely as products of individual genius. As the filmmakers often point out in their conversations recorded in this volume, filmmaking in Africa is generally a highly collective endeavor. There is, moreover, a strong sense of community among the quite varied filmmakers whose views are collected here. They all recognize themselves as part of a larger picture, as playing roles in a momentous epic that continues, even now, to unfold. African cinema, in this sense, projects itself beyond individual films and filmmakers, beyond even the boundaries of languages and nations.

The future of African cinema, however, cannot be divorced from the pragmatic questions of filmmaking in a context where there is little financial or institutional support. African filmmakers have almost always labored under economic and political conditions that are at best inhospitable and often completely hostile. Issues of economics appear frequently in these conversations, and questions of materialism and Western-style capitalism also form important subtexts in many of the films discussed here. These questions are illustrated in Djibril Diop Mambety's remarks during his last interview with Professor Ukadike: "I will make *Malaika*, the third part of the trilogy about the power of craziness. The first two were *Touki-Bouki* and *Hyènes*. Then I will consult God about the state of the world." Sadly, Diop Mambety, hailed by some as the "African Dionysus," died of cancer before he was able to complete his trilogy on "human greed and the power of insanity," which, according to him, have "betrayed African independence for the false hopes of Western materialism."

As a scholar of African cinema, Ukadike brings a depth of knowledge and an intimate understanding of the African situation to this book. It is his understanding that allows a space and a context for the filmmakers to speak and for a genuine dialogue to take place. His questions are often probing, inviting responses that are at times visceral, always intellectually stimulating, and often profound. There is, in fact, a remarkable sense of spontaneity and freshness in these conversations: unlike in many standard-format interviews, one never gets the feeling that old issues and set answers are being rehearsed yet again. Like the questioning involved in African cinema itself, the questioning here is productive, generative; the exchanges between Ukadike and the filmmakers produce offspring, in the form of new ideas, new ways of thinking about the questions at hand.

The figure of offspring is an apt one in this context: both Ukadike and the filmmakers are intensely concerned not only with the history of African cinema, but with its future, its potential. As has been the case with oral narratives and legends in Africa, African cinema is continually figured as an inheritance for future generations, as a valuable archive of memory, knowledge, and wisdom that is to be preserved, handed down, repeated, reinterpreted. Here, cinema, and thinking about cinema, becomes a gift to the future.

Preface

The views expressed in this book might be controversial, but as anyone familiar with African films will recognize, they reflect the audacious ways in which film has been used to dissect Africa's issues.[1] My work on this project has been both rewarding and frustrating. Some of the filmmakers I interviewed supported this project wholeheartedly and believe, as I do, that the critic and the filmmaker can work toward the same goal: that of developing a creative and competitive cinema with a rich body of scholarship around it. Their responses to my questions were often exhaustive and extended the discourse far beyond my expectation. But a few of the filmmakers consider critics to be their nemeses and are suspicious of even the most genuine intentions. (How was I to respond, for example, to a prominent African filmmaker who pointed out to me, "You make a living out of African cinema, and yet you criticize it?")

Interacting with people of varying interests and beliefs was inspiring as well as challenging. In addition, unforeseen circumstances dictated to whom I would or would not speak, how long the conversations lasted, and how much information filmmakers were willing to divulge. Many times, to save the project from collapsing (because some of the filmmakers I wanted to feature were either inaccessible or skeptical of my project), I was compelled to act decisively regarding the filmmakers to be featured. Occasionally, I found my disappointment was a blessing in disguise! For example, the granddaddy of African cinema, the veteran filmmaker Ousmane Sembene, is conspicuously missing from the table of contents despite all efforts I made to interview him.[2] I consider the absence of this filmmaker to be relatively unimportant, given that he and his work are already well publicized and interviews he has given are fully documented; in addition, the lack of a Sembene interview created a vacuum for an unknown but progressive young filmmaker to fill.

Similarly, there were a few cases in which individuals agreed to be interviewed, but getting them to talk was tantamount to passing a camel's head through the eye of a needle. The brevity of some of the chapters here attests to this difficulty and reflects the kind of arrogance and nonchalance that nearly derailed the project. It also partially limited my ability to probe more deeply, not into the general African cinematic discourse, which the other contributors pursued relentlessly, but into the issues that their own films provoke.

The driving motivation of this project has been my zeal to discuss pertinent issues that could lead to a fuller understanding of African film practice—issues that I either had to leave out of or was unable to explore fully in my book *Black African Cinema* and that I believe only the filmmakers can address. I mapped out these issues carefully for individual filmmakers, and to accomplish our agenda it was sometimes necessary that I assert authorial voice to shape the discourse. Sometimes, I had to intervene at some level in order to get to the heart of the matter under discussion. I believe that these interventions were justified and were not intrusive or editorializing. My goal was to initiate discourse on African cinematic practices that will provoke other discourses, and I hope the reader will find that I have succeeded in this goal.

N. Frank Ukadike
March 2001

Notes

1. For discussion of African films and other ideological ramifications, see my book *Black African Cinema* (Berkeley: University of California Press, 1994).

2. In responding to my request for an interview dated January 17, 1994, Sembene wrote: "Cher Monsieur, Je suis en possession de votre lettre du 7 Décembre 1993. Malheureusement, je n'accorde plus d'interviews. Mes travaux en cours me 'mangent' tous mes moments. Je vous demande de ne pas insister. Veuillez agréer, Cher Monsieur, l'expression de mes sentiments les meilleurs. SEMBENE Ousmane" [Dear Sir, I have received your letter dated 7 December 1993. Unfortunately, I no longer give interviews. My work takes up all my time. I ask you not to insist. Please accept, sir, my best wishes. SEMBENE Ousmane] (my translation).

Acknowledgments

Since the publication of my book *Black African Cinema* in 1994, the widening scope of African cinematic practices has compelled me to look for new ways of examining unexplored issues in African film practice. These are issues that demand in-depth discussion and that, I believe, are best synthesized from the perspectives of the filmmakers. I would like to thank all of the filmmakers featured in this compendium for dedicating their time and thought and for providing diverse and incisive perspectives on contentious issues in contemporary African cinema.

My gratitude goes to Dr. Jude Akudinobi and Fr. Thomas Ebong for their encouragement and brotherly bond, especially during trying moments in the course of this project. I am also grateful to my colleagues and staff at the Department of Communication, Tulane University, for granting me a collegial and congenial atmosphere devoid of insanity while I completed my work on the manuscript.

Further thanks are due to the Rockefeller Foundation for awarding the fellowship that allowed me to stay in the pristine setting of the foundation's Study Center in Bellagio, Italy, where some of the chapters in this volume were edited. I would like to express my gratitude to the editors and staff of the University of Minnesota Press for their assistance in the final realization of this project. Thanks are due also to the publishers of *Research in African Literatures* and *Transition: An International Review* for their permission to reprint previously published interviews. Last, but not least, many thanks go to my family for their support and understanding.

Introduction

African cinema is at last infiltrating the world market with major works of indigenous cultures that explore and adapt their oral and literary traditions to the articulation of a new film language. This book clarifies the notion of African cinema by providing a matrix of convergent and divergent perspectives through interviews with film directors about the evolution of African filmmaking. It identifies the specific sociopolitical, cultural, economic, and pedagogical issues that influence the production, reception, and discourse of films while at the same time serving as a compendium of "alternative" approaches in African cinematic trends.

The project features interviews with key personalities of African cinema, covering three and a half decades of African film practice. Twenty filmmakers, drawn from Burkina Faso, Cameroon, Congo, Ethiopia, Ghana, Guinea-Bissau, Mali, Mauritania, Nigeria, Senegal, and South Africa, are interviewed. There are now in these countries significant cinematic practices that justify a project of this nature, and, by featuring many directors, I hope to identify the various trends that constitute those practices that are situated within a common bond, geographically, historically, socially, or politically. Through interviews with pioneers Souleymane Cissé, Med Hondo, and Kwaw Ansah, renowned feature filmmakers Djibril Diop Mambety, Haile Gerima, and Safi Faye, and award-winning newcomers Idrissa Ouedraogo, Cheick Oumar Sissoko, and Jean-Pierre Bekolo, among others, I strive to set individual achievement against the backdrop of the often complex historical, social, political, economic, and state practices that affect the production of films in Africa.

Included also are conversations that foreground acting, distribution and exhibition, history, theory and criticism, video-based television production, and television's relationship to independent film. Through my exploration of these trends with the filmmakers, this project surveys the evolution of African cinema, the ambiguities of ethnographic films, and the politics and problems of seeing Africa through African lenses. The book also examines thematic diversity, stylistic configuration, the role of cultural codes in patterns of signification, and all the contextual factors hindering development as well as various accomplishments. My overall goal is to offer the most comprehensive discussion to date of African filmmakers and the cinematic trends they have initiated.

Since its inception in the 1960s, African cinema has undergone a radical transformation. Initially a product of the sociopolitical upheavals of late colonialism, its recent phase is marked by aesthetic and ideological diversity. Encircled by the constraints of production, exhibition, and distribution, but maintaining an urgent cultural agenda, it has struggled to assert distinct indigenous voices representative of African experiences. In this volume I intend to assess those voices and analyze the conditions of their production and reception.

The earliest films made by the pioneers of African cinema were deliberately didactic and overtly political. The primary goals were to use the medium to inform, to educate, and to project authentic visions of Africa and its peoples as well as to assist in reversing the demeaning stereotypical images of Africa found in dominant representations of the continent. Considering that this cinema was born out of oppression and resistance—coming only after the independence of the producing countries—the prevailing mood of nationalism propelled filmmakers to link cinema with national development. Simply put, the pioneers developed a cinema grounded in the belief that the film medium could speak for the people while also being an impetus for social change. However, faced with the social, political, cultural, and economic challenges and contradictions endemic to postcolonial Africa, and with the arrival of the second generation of African filmmakers, African film practices had to go through an inevitable reorientation. What was once strictly documentation on educational and political levels has become more of a diversified art form that is not only constantly changing but confronting dissension within its own domain. This dissension revolves around individual/collective prerogatives—the value of juxtaposing innovative modes of filmmaking with traditional paradigms to enable profound levels of imagination, so as to keep the art form forever changing with the constantly evolving African world and aesthetic sphere. Although the pioneering films tell important stories, their points of view and their originality in general are what make them uniquely African. The points of view taken by the younger directors break the mold of traditional paradigms and allow new "revolutionary" forms of expression and interrogative models of narrative patterns and aesthetic orientations to proliferate, thus challenging entrenched notions of cinematic orthodoxy.

Connected with this imperative is an urgency to explore the variety of cultural productions in Africa, taking into consideration the hybrid nature of these films, which combine direct political commentary and indirect work on cultural and cinematic codes. The interviews presented here explore questions of power relations, ideology, identity and collectivity, and especially aesthetics within the larger context of the development of national cinemas in a transnational era. As a whole, this book addresses the impact of politics on film styles and on video and television culture, while reciprocally delineating the role of cultural codes of cinematic expression in patterns of signification. The discourse also traces African cinema's preoccupation with culture and history, its influence on various aesthetic developments, and the widening scope of African cinematic representational patterns. It is here that the discourse conceptualizes what really constitutes African film language. Given that all of the filmmakers featured here acknowledge their narrative techniques' indebtedness to oral tradition, another pertinent question that arises is, What is the impact of oral tradition on individual narrative strategies? Is there a unified stance on narrative strategies among African filmmakers? How can we use the experiences of the filmmakers sampled to illustrate the thematic and aesthetic diversity of African cinema in relation to film form, history, and culture/context? How can we draw upon the filmmakers' knowledge of cultural contexts, codes and subcodes, and symbols and meanings in African cinema to express and inform our own knowledge of film? Finally, this volume contributes to the ongoing debate about the (in)adequacy of contemporary critical methodologies for dealing with African cinema.

The main structuring principle I have applied in this book emphasizes the filmmakers and their practices; this represents a marked departure from the scant attention previously given African filmmakers' self-expression in professional journals and magazines. The diversity of textual expression found in African cinema and the increasing mass appeal these films have for both local and academic audiences necessitate the widening of opportunities for filmmakers, teachers, students, critics, and audiences to experience African films and the creation of educational contexts that can facilitate understanding, exchange, and cultural bridge building. By giving a number of filmmakers from across Africa the opportunity to discuss their works in this book, I hope to provide a multicultural, multi-ideological, synchronic, and diachronic view of African cinema.

This volume builds upon the only two other books published to date that attempt to synthesize Africa's film practices from African perspectives: Manthia Diawara's *African Cinema: Politics and Culture* (Bloomington: Indiana University Press, 1992) and my own *Black African Cinema* (Berkeley: University of California Press, 1994). It is an especially significant follow-up to *Black African Cinema* (which explores the history, theory, and practices of black African cinema), in that it probes geopolitical, socioeconomic, and ideological influences deeply through conversations with the filmmakers themselves. This line of inquiry was tangential in the books cited above. In this book I seek to rectify this lapse by exploring the contentious issues that academic writing often finds too challenging or too controversial to explore. As candidly discussed by the filmmakers, these issues offer the reader firsthand knowledge of the plurality as well as the deeper meaning of the African continent's cinema. Similarly, among other books on African cinema, such as *African Experiences of Cinema*, edited by Imruh Bakari and Mbye B. Cham (London: British Film Institute, 1996), and *Arab and African Film Making*, by Lizbeth Malkmus and Roy Armes (London: Zed, 1991), only Françoise Pfaff's *Twenty-five Black African Filmmakers: A Critical Study with Filmography and Bio-bibliography* (Westport, Conn.: Greenwood, 1988) highlights the achievements of individual filmmakers by allowing them to speak out. However, unlike this volume, Pfaff's book (given when it was published) does not probe most of the specific issues and developments that can contribute to an understanding of the present situation.

Over the years, African cinema has undergone a radical transformation, widening its scope and offering an expanded definition of African womanhood and a reassessment of the notion of anthropology. For example, how has the image of African women emerged in this cinema to reflect women's contributions to the continent's emancipatory projects, the Diasporan cultural productions, and, centrally, to global feminist perspectives? I examine such representational patterns and the issues they deal with through interviews with two prominent female filmmakers, Safi Faye of Senegal and Salem Mekuria of Ethiopia. Furthermore, how has African cinema become a privileged medium of anthropological attention, one that in itself deviates from the culturally distant and biased gaze that is typical of ethnographic film practice? It is here that this project links the views of female filmmakers with those of their male counterparts, including the dissenting views of two young filmmakers, Jean-Pierre Bekolo of Cameroon and Ramadan Suleman of South Africa, to address the larger problems of the politics of representation and of the depiction of African experiences on film.

This book emphasizes the cultural dynamics of African traditions in order to give the reader a broader understanding of African cinema as a cultural art form informed not only by ideological determinants but by the concern to foster the film medium as a pedagogical tool for enlightenment. As the table of contents indicates, the book is divided into three parts, and each filmmaker is assigned an individual chapter. A complete filmography of each filmmaker's endeavors provides a fitting conclusion to each chapter.

Part I highlights the works of "pioneer" filmmakers as geared toward the awakening of African consciousness to the continent's social, political, and economic realities and the commitment of cinema as a powerful and valuable tool for communication and education.[1] The discussion in each chapter foregrounds processes of production and synthesizes the motivations and ideologies that structure each film. The crucial issues of production, distribution, and exhibition are analyzed placing African films within their historical, political, social, and economic contexts.

Part II contains conversations with members of the "new generation" of African filmmakers, who, like the pioneers, also see Africa's need for an aware and assertive cinema that reflects Africa's cultural, sociopolitical, and economic realities.[2] This quest for autonomy is matched by compelling experimentation and enables us to appreciate African cinema as innovative and diverse. However, owing to the unresolved problems

of distribution and exhibition in the 1980s and 1990s, filmmakers are now striv-
ing to build cinema as an industry by focusing on an entertainment function for films,
eschewing the heavy-handed didacticism of the 1960s and 1970s. Many of the films
produced under this new aegis still remain indebted to the nationalistic concerns of
the pioneering years, with some of the filmmakers using inventiveness to affirm their
own voices on the prerogatives of African production codes. Continuing with the
issues addressed in part I, the interviews in part II address the place of African
cinema in relation to world cinema, coproduction among African countries, and oral
tradition, with its quintessential impact on narrative patterns/styles.

In the third chapter in part II, I pay homage to Djibril Diop Mambety of Senegal, who died on July 23, 1998, at the age of fifty-three. The interview that appears
here, which was his last, was granted to me a few months before his death. He was a
director, actor, composer, poet, and orator, and was loved and admired by critics and
audiences as one of Africa's greatest auteurs.

In part III, the central themes, among others, are the evolving aesthetics of
African cinema and the effects of culture, politics, and socioeconomic issues on production, thematic concerns, and narrative styles. Reinforcing the discussion of these
issues in the previous sections, the interviews in part III bring to light some controversies, such as the digressional tendencies among younger filmmakers, exemplified
by Jean-Pierre Bekolo and Ramadan Suleman, who argue for the overhauling and
dismantling of the pioneer traditions of filmmaking, and King Ampaw, who does not
favor African governments' subsidization of filmmaking. Haile Gerima, who might
well also qualify as a pioneer, is featured in this part because his reflections on African
and black cinema in general offer thought-provoking counterarguments in support of
the pioneers. Also in this section, Salem Mekuria and Jean-Marie Teno are acknowl-
edged for having popularized the African documentary tradition.

I should note here that in my interviews with the filmmakers, I posed certain
questions to all as a way of ascertaining commonalities and differences among them
concerning their opinions on specific issues. As the interviews reveal, although all of
the filmmakers share a common goal—that of promoting the use of African cinema
as a mobilizing force and as a tool for enlightenment—they have widely varying beliefs
regarding the nature of African cinema, film aesthetics, and methods of representation.

Notes

1. As used in this book, the term *pioneer* reflects in some cases the pioneering status of
individuals within specific countries rather than any continental chronology of seniority.

2. As used here, the generic term *new generation* has nothing to do with age; rather, it
refers to the period marking individuals' entrance into filmmaking.

PART I
THE TRADITION:
PIONEERING, INVENTION, AND INTERVENTION

Kwaw Ansah (Ghana)

A man of many talents, Kwaw Ansah is an artist, theater designer, dramatist, and music composer turned filmmaker; he is also the most important individual in Ghanaian cinema. He has expressed enormous gratitude for his success and development as a filmmaker to his father, a trained photographer. Although his father wanted him to engage in his own trade of photography, the young Ansah, having discovered his talent in drawing and painting, had other options. After he had completed his secondary school education, he found employment with the United African Company, a Unilever firm in Ghana. There he acquired basic training in textile design. However, he soon abandoned this occupation to further his education. From 1961 to 1963, he was enrolled at the Regent Street London Polytechnic, where he obtained a diploma in theater design. Following his education in England, he studied in the United States, graduating from the American Academy of Dramatic Arts and the American Music and Drama Academy. As a playwright, he produced several notable works, including *The Adoption* (1964) and *Mother's Tears* (1967). *The Adoption* was produced off-Broadway at the Hermon Theater, and then at the Macmillan Theater, Columbia University, New York. *Mother's Tears* played to enthusiastic crowds at the Drama Studio, Arts Center and the National Theater, Accra, where it met with instant success.

Having completed his education overseas, Ansah returned to Ghana as a multi-talented artist, ready to test his practical skills. He worked as a production assistant and set designer for the Ghana Film Industry Corporation and later joined Lintas Advertising Agency as a film and radio producer, producing series of short films, including documentaries and television commercials. In 1971, Ansah established Target Advertising Services Limited, a successful advertising agency that is now an

3

affiliate of Saatchi & Saatchi worldwide conglomerate. The agency is now called Target Saatchi & Saatchi Limited. In 1977, Ansah established a film production company called Film Africa Limited, based in Accra. To date, Film Africa Limited has produced a number of major films, including such international award winners as *Love Brewed in the African Pot* (1980), *Heritage ... Africa,* (1988), and *Crossroads of People, Crossroads of Trade* (1995). The company has also produced numerous TV commercials and documentaries for its sister company, Target Saatchi & Saatchi.

Kwaw Ansah continues to expand the media map of Ghana. Against this background and accomplishments, he has set up TV Africa, an independent television station that was incorporated on November 17, 1995. The station will, as he puts it, "play an effective role in the development of communications as a major instrument for nation building, and as an integral part of, and a vital element in, the socioeconomic development process."

In this interview, the director makes his position clear, reflecting on a wide array of issues concerning African cinematic practices. Although he does not believe that African film should be devoid of politics, he does, unlike a number of African filmmakers, identify with the commercial and industrial aspect of filmmaking, and thus does not reject the integral role of entertainment in film.

Portions of this interview were conducted at the Pan-African Festival of Film and Television of Ouagadougou in 1995 and in Ghana in July 1996 and August 1997.

As a prolific and well-known Ghanaian filmmaker, tell me how your filmmaking career began.

I come from a family of photographers. My father was a professional photographer, and so it was passed down to all the children, including the women. Although we had to take regular-paying jobs to pay school fees, whatever job we took, we still had photography in our minds. My father's interest in cinema started as far back as 1951, when he purchased 16mm projectors and started exhibiting both silent and sound films. My brothers and sisters and I helped out and also became interested in the business. During school vacations we traveled to various cities and villages with mobile cinema equipment exhibiting films. That was how I first became involved in the film business.

Obviously these films you exhibited were colonial films, Hollywood and British films, that did not pertain to African culture. Did that absence of African specificity inspire you to start thinking about cinematic image in relation to African history and African culture?

Definitely. All Africans have been affected one way or another by the invasion of Hollywood movies. When we were kids, we all identified with the heroes in cowboy and other films, and wanted to be like them. When I was young and growing up, black people in films always played the buffoon roles, and the white people were portrayed as superior; of course, we all enjoyed it. We laughed at the black people. When they rolled their eyes and ran away from the little mouse that they saw, we all clapped. When there was movie with white and black people on safari in the jungle, everybody sighed with grief when an enemy arrow happened to kill a white person. But when we saw thousands of black people being mowed down, we all cheered. This illustrates clearly how powerful the film medium is. Those images were created to elicit that kind of response from the African audience. I must say, as a youth I had not matured sufficiently to discern between negative and positive portrayal and the film-maker's ideology. It wasn't until I grew up and began to reassess the image of black people in alien films that I began to realize that I was laughing at myself! I was laughing at my own people being killed and caricatured. Seeing my own values so badly mutilated and my person so dehumanized, I realized film is by all means a powerful medium. Also, considering my interest from infancy, I felt the only way to repair the damage done to the black race through the film medium is to use the same medium to combat those stereotypes.

Your best-known work is Love Brewed in the African Pot. *How did you come up with this concept?*

Love Brewed in the African Pot stemmed from basic African problems—class distinctions, interethnic marriages, and, of course, social-standing disparities, which have broken apart many couples and families. I have not had the experience personally, but I have seen people who really love each other have their dreams shattered due to class differences and family intervention. This problem usually arises if one of the partners is a member of a prominent, elite, or middle-class family which tends to measure a person's worth by his or her family's material background. What he or she is capable of contributing to the relationship is secondary or nonexistent to the preference for class materialism. Because this is a common problem even outside of Africa, and because everyone experiences love and/or marital problems, I felt that it was important to work with a love story that would appeal to everybody. I wanted this film to be successful, but I never thought that *Love Brewed in the African Pot* would be so popular or would break so many box-office records on the African continent. Perhaps it is the way I approached the universal subject of love.

You have certainly been influenced by different filmmaking techniques throughout your career. To which approach is Love Brewed *indebted?*

Let me start by saying that Africans did not invent cinema; therefore, influences can be acquired from many sources. But basically, what is important is the filmmaker's approach. We all develop our own styles. You may have three or four people analyzing a particular circumstance, but the product of this analysis is bound to reflect each individual's reactions to the subject matter. Naturally, how you approach issues may be affected by your training, the people you are studying, and, of course, the environment. But all the same, it is each artist's way of thinking and approach that really shapes the structure of your film. I studied in America, and I have been to Hollywood. Even though it is possible to say America (I have used some of their gimmicks in one way or another), along with my education, and the people and places I have visited, has had an influence on me, developing my own style predominated over the other forces.

What are those Hollywood influences and gimmicks?

To tell the story in a way that people will follow and enjoy it; to be the least academic as possible. Let the message be simple and digestible.

A francophone African film critic dismissed all films from the anglophone as amateurish. How would you respond to this criticism?

I would laugh. Even though anglophone filmmakers are not as prolific as the francophone, I would not think quantity necessarily translates to quality. Ghana, for instance, has been in the industry for forty-two years now. The first film school in sub-Saharan Africa was established in Ghana in 1945, with pioneer students from Ghana, Nigeria, Sierra Leone, and Gambia. Our problem has been that British neocolonial assimilation has not been as complete as French neocolonial assimilation. The French made their colonies more a part of them than the British did. Also I think the French, being very cultural, were more interested in molding their subjects, so to speak, to follow a certain pattern, a pattern which might not have reawakened people's consciousness. I must say that we in the anglophone countries must be blessed for not having received such "gracious" support from our colonial master! This makes us original thinkers—independent film thinkers. As you can see, most of the films that come from the anglophone, few though they might seem, mostly address issues that are pertinent to our development.

Some Ghanaian television programs have made use of popular existing high-culture aspects of society to create shows with traditional narrative structures. Did those programs influence you as you drafted the scenario for your first film?

No, I do not think so. I have a feeling that those things can be very poisonous and I would not depend much on them. They are made to satisfy a particular audience and its way of receiving things. I cannot do the same thing for Africa. I think we must tell our stories to reflect our well-being and our own people, and not just go out to copy those things we see on television—those that do not really tell our stories. They are just fantastic spectacles which I do not think are really worth copying.

Popular comedy, caustic satire, and oral narrative paradigms sustained the popular TV program Osofo Dadzie *for more than two and a half decades and Ghanaians love it.*

It is simply because the approach of *Osofo Dadzie* is similar to our way of life.

Did you exhibit Love Brewed in the African Pot *throughout Africa or just in anglophone African countries?*

The film was exhibited only in the English-speaking African countries, because the cost of dubbing into French is quite expensive. Even in the anglophone we are constrained. Unlike the French colonial master, who has always made postproduction facilities available for his subjects, the British colonial master did not provide the anglophone such facilities. In Britain the price of dubbing is no less than twenty-five thousand pounds sterling. No African filmmaker can afford to pay that price. Distributors are not willing to invest in postproduction. They would prefer the filmmaker to do all the work so that they can get their share of the profits.

Are exhibition and distribution of African films going to remain a perennial problem throughout Africa, since most theaters are owned by Indians or Lebanese?

Luckily in Ghana, during President Nkrumah's regime quite a number of theater houses were nationalized by the government. Locally, theaters were quite competitive. Usually, the Lebanese and the Indians would disregard African films, so when *Love Brewed in the African Pot* was released, I was not surprised that they were not interested in distributing the film. They would rather distribute kung fu films and Indian musical melodramas. However, when the foreign distributors realized that the government-owned theaters showing local films were consistently selling out shows and that they were losing money, they could not help but negotiate on our own terms. Also, another interesting experience occurred when I took the film to Kenya. The authorities at the Kenya Film Corporation said to me, "Well, African films, what are they about? They address the same issues: drumming, dancing, juju and all that." Although they had not seen the film itself, they started making false assumptions. I was persistent and gave the film to them for a trial run. When *Love Brewed in the African Pot* started showing in Kenya, the James Bond film *For Your Eyes Only* had recently been released there. For three months there were endless lines of people waiting to see the film while Twentieth Century Fox struggled for patronage. They had to convince the Kenya Film Corporation to withdraw it for a while so they could make money. That was the beginning, and *Love Brewed* went on and broke box-office records in Zimbabwe and Zambia.

Nigeria created a problem for you, though.

I had a rather unfortunate experience in Nigeria. The National Theater of Nigeria agreed to distribute the film. We had a beautiful premiere with Chief Abiola as the guest of honor. When I met him, he said to me, "I am sorry, but I have very little time to watch films. Even though I am the guest of honor, I do not think I can stay through this film. I will sit in for fifteen minutes and then I will have to leave because we have an unexpected change of schedule." But, surprisingly, Chief Abiola sat through the film. Afterward, he came down to congratulate me and the leading actor, who was also present, and said, "My brother, you kept me here. You have done well. I will donate five thousand naira to the National Theater." After the premiere, the film started in the National Theater and was doing very well. During the first week, we made about thirty-six thousand naira, which was quite a lot of money at that time. We used the profits from the first week's run to pay for the advertising expenses. The second week brought us the rewards that we all expected and we made even more money. Then, unfortunately, a Nigerian filmmaker, Eddie Ugbomah, wrote to the *Punch*, a Nigerian daily, a biting criticism pertaining to *Love Brewed in the African Pot*. He stated that the first time a Ghanaian film showed in Nigeria it received enormous attention and was given a special premiere, which is contrary to the lukewarm reception Nigerian films receive. What is more, he wrote that my leading actor had been put in the presidential seat in the theater, which was absolutely false. He also claimed that millions of naira had been transferred to my bank account in London, at a time when I had not even received a kobo. I was fed up with false accusations and decided that if this was how I was going to be treated in Nigeria, that it was time to stop the screening of the film and go home. So that is the story of *Love Brewed in the African Pot* in Nigeria.

After the success of Love Brewed *why did you wait eight years to make your second feature-length film*, Heritage . . . Africa?

This illustrates the fact that in African countries film has yet to be considered a viable project. The banks have always regarded filmmaking as a very risky investment. Despite how successful one is, financial houses, who have been our main source of support, are hesitant to give loans to filmmakers. One would have expected after having paid back the loan on *Love Brewed* it would have been easier to obtain another loan, but I had to go through the same rigorous process. I feel that (of course, our government is addressing this issue seriously) if a film finance fund, with less stringent conditions attached, were to be created it would encourage anglophone filmmakers to produce more films. Assuming that every filmmaker produces one feature-length film every two years, the production of anglophone films and the film industry in general would prosper.

Heritage . . . Africa *has won several awards, including two, on separate occasions, at FESPACO [the Pan-African Festival of Film and Television of Ouagadougou], which is quite unusual. How will this special recognition affect your future work?*

I must say that winning the Institute of Black People's award yesterday was so overwhelming because, in the first place, this is the same film that won the Grand Prix two years ago, and it had won the OAU [Organization of African Unity] Prize, and the same institute's prize two years ago. It came as a surprise when the judges felt they had to reaffirm that this film addresses important issues of the African Diaspora. To have received a trophy plus five hundred thousand CFA was quite an overwhelming experience. This also encourages me very much, because I believe that if I make a film and the film is accepted outside Africa, but rejected by my own people, it has failed.

That films get rejected in Africa when they are overwhelmingly appreciated everywhere else is problematic. How has Heritage . . . Africa *performed in Africa in terms of distribution, exhibition, and audience response?*

In Africa it has moved very slowly, simply because of its political message. Unfortunately, most of the theater houses in Africa are owned by Lebanese or Indians insensitive to our aspirations. They are only interested in procuring huge profits from films brought from India. But I am not going to let their actions deter my ambition. Also, there seems to be some concerted effort to downplay films from Africa which have very strong political messages. This discrimination is very much alive and, fortunately, we are battling it. For instance, I am very happy that the new high commissioner for Nigeria, His Excellency Olu Otunla, after seeing the film said to me, "My God, this film has got to come to Nigeria. We must learn about past experiences. We have to overcome all these things because it is a subject that most of us must address." So he is feverishly working toward that. Already there has been a Nigerian cultural delegation visiting Ghana which has discussed making this film part of the program, and we are working to have it open in Nigeria very soon.

Heritage . . . Africa *weaves a number of themes that encompass historical, social, and political matters in relation to evolutionary change. Would you please expand on film and evolutionary change in relation to* Heritage . . . Africa?

In regard to evolutionary change, Africa basically has been raped as far as its values are concerned. I think that the basic problem facing the African today is lack of faith, which is something very relative to one's heart. It is your well-being, it is culturally based. For instance, take religion. We have been made to believe that whatever our ancestors bequeathed to us is heathen. You go to any African society today and put on a white collar and call yourself a priest and you will be revered. But in Africa today, it is not common to find educated people like you who will stand in public to, say, perform the ritual act of pouring libation. I am sure there are people who would say, "No, Frank, you can't be serious. You can't do that." Compared to our cultures, the Japanese are doing so well because they have their image right in front of them, Buddha. The Indians respect Hinduism, and their representative, Krishna. The Europeans have got Jesus Christ. Through whom do we reach our God? This fate is very much connected with life, which is why there are people who choose to die for their religion if it is tampered with. But we have been corrupted in such a way that we laugh at our own values; and yet religion is fundamental in sustaining African values.

There is an evolution that is taking place in Africa—if we do not address the issue of culture which is derived from one's faith, we will never be able to build a meaningful society. You cannot rely solely on foreign premise to build a solid foundation, nor make any progress if the platform upon which national agenda is constructed is not indigenous. If the people understand the meaning of this national agenda, they will have no fears in participating in its implementation. But if the agenda is based on abstract alien ideology, it is likely to be questioned. But if we draw upon our own values and try to make a progressive leap into the future, knowing that the path is ours, I think we can really be very prosperous. In this sense the evolution taking place will benefit our generations to come.

This film is replete with political messages that range from colonialism to neocolonialism. I would like to mention two examples in particular. First is your explanation of the way an original Ghanaian name, Bosomefi, was transformed to Bossomfield. Second are the scenes you created with schoolchildren trying to register for colonial school. This scene reminds me of when I was growing up in those days, and it makes me wonder in what ways this film relates to your childhood experience.

I count myself lucky to have lived through this kind of colonial experience. I remember when I was first sent to school to be registered, the teacher felt that I was too small. A test was used to determine who was admitted into colonial school. One had to stretch one's right hand across one's head and touch one's left ear. An alternative method was to judge by one's height. There was a measurement on the wall, and in order to qualify one had to be at least as tall as that line. This was unfair because not everyone will be tall or have long arms to reach one's ear, especially at such a young age. I do not know who created this ridiculous colonial measurement, but it left a legacy for determining which Africans were tall enough to register for elementary school. In those days it was not uncommon to find twelve-year-old boys in the first grade, boys who could have finished their elementary school by then if such a criterion was not imposed. It is interesting to see how much things have changed; these days it is common for both men and women to acquire their first degrees by the time they are nineteen or twenty. They are able to achieve this despite the length of their hands or their heights. So I think it is a personal experience. This is why the film vividly accounts for such experiences.

The film is also heavily influenced by cultural codes such as the invocation of a powerful cultural symbol, the family heirloom. You use the heirloom in an intriguing sequence at the end of the film in which Bossomfield does not grasp the heirloom to take it back to tradition.

As you well know, Bossomfield represents the past and present. What the film attempts to do is to create an awareness of the evil machination of colonialism. Bossomfield, at least, becomes aware of his folly before his death. That it is his encounter with the colonial government that leads to his death is proof of that; it illustrates that even in his lifetime, he could not achieve what was necessary to transform Africa from colonial oppression. He would, however, be born again with a kind of nationalistic valor, because it was wished that he retrieve the heirloom so that the symbolic Mother Africa forgives him. In the film, Bossomfield's mother was outraged that her son gave away the heirloom to the British colonial officer, who in turn sent it to the queen. His mother warned him that he would never have peace unless the family heirloom was retrieved. The film was left open-ended because we could not offer resolution. To do so would have suggested that the problems had been solved while they are not. The way it ended is a reminder of what is historically and culturally important to Africa. Simply put, Africa must retrieve its own.

The film was well acted. Were there any professionally trained actors in this movie?

A number of the leading actors are professionally trained, but I do not think that it is always trained actors who can give you the best performance. There are people who are naturally good as actors, and I encountered several while doing this film. For instance, Buchnor, who played the leading role so well and won the award for best actor at FESPACO, is not a trained actor. He did not go to acting school, but he was perfect for that role. Buchnor is a member of my staff in Film Africa. I searched all over the place for someone to play Bossomfield to no avail. I had Buchnor read the part of Bossomfield during auditions for the other characters. Then, one day, one of the ladies in my office said, "Well, don't you think Buchnor is Bossomfield?" He was a young man then, and I had never pictured him in the role of Bossomfield. I later realized that, with the use of makeup and a mustache, he might be able to play the role of Bossomfield. Every morning after doing the normal official duties, Buchnor and I would discuss his role in my office. We worked on his character for nearly six months and it registered. On the whole he is quite a good actor.

How did you construct the dialogue for the mother in the film? It was so moving and inspiring.

Basically, I have never scoffed at my culture. I have always believed in the traditional way of doing things. At first, I wrote that part in English, and then translated it to Akan. I made sure the person who was translating understood the story and used the rich idiomatic expressions that our people use. In Africa, most things are said in proverbs. A word to the wise is enough in the African context. I am sure the same thing happens in Nigeria. If you go to your village and your grandmother or mother wants to test your level of intelligence, she confronts you from time to time with proverbs and asks you, "What did I say?" to reflect on tradition or to come back home, as we say it. The implication is that if you are tutored to understand the idiomatic expressions of your own people, there is the possibility of growing up wiser than the elite tutored in the English tradition.

The caning in the film! Don't you think that was too drastic?

I do not know what age group you represent, but during our time, zealous teachers went around gathering the names of students who did not attend church or were seen indulging in fetishes or other activities that were considered un-Christian, and the punishment was more drastic than the ones shown in the film. There were some people who were so badly caned that for weeks afterward they could not go to school, and when they finally came they hardly could sit in their seats. The cause of death, for those people that died, was attributed to witchcraft. But who knows if most deaths were not due to tetanus as a result of caning in schools? I think pupils who attended the German Presbyterian schools suffered the most. It was so harsh. In some cases pupils' fingers were pricked with pins so harshly that for months they could not write properly. So I do not think the scene was drastic at all.

Heritage is well made and it would be well received abroad. Given the recent recognition you have received, what efforts are you making to distribute the film to other countries?

I have received requests from foreign distributors, but I am not rushing to have my films shown in America simply because one should have them shown in America. Some distributors come with ridiculous propositions that are unacceptable. The usual scenario is, "We even have Ousmane Sembene's film here. We paid three thousand dollars a year." In their terms all African films should be treated the same. In fact, *Heritage* nets more than three thousand dollars in one day if screened in Ghana or anywhere in Africa. So why would I give it away to American distributors? This does not mean that I do not intend to use an American distributor, but the terms of agreement must be reasonable. I do not favor the situation where the distributor who's cheating me pretends that he is doing me a favor.

Scholars in the United States frequently call me to ask about renting Heritage . . . Africa for use in their classrooms. They say that it is a wonderful film, which must be distributed in America and everywhere.

Frank, I must say that the most difficult aspect of this industry is distribution. It isn't that I haven't tried to solve this problem. I have been bitten more than once and it is very painful. Which filmmaker does not want his film seen? Of course, we need money to make films. After *Heritage . . . Africa* was made, it was interesting that so many people expressed an interest in distributing this film in the United States. They felt that it would do well in the movie theaters. Unfortunately, the distribution cartels have not come up with any reasonable propositions. Our negotiating has made me wonder if it is really necessary to have the film shown in the United States at all. One of the people interested in distributing the film is Akbah Mohammed, who had been informed of the film through my government; I also think his boss, Minister

Louis Farrakhan, had seen the film. When Mohammed came to meet me, he said, "Brother man, my brothers should see it." He arranged to premiere the film in Harlem. It played there to large, enthusiastic audiences. After about two months Mohammed came to meet me in Accra and we signed a contract. The Ghanaian government was aware of the deal. The proceeds from the film were to be channeled through a bank in London, the Ghana Commercial Bank. On another occasion Mohammed came back to me and said, "Mr. Ansah, I am sure that you would want some money from this film very quickly. And I have come to you to give you your money." He opened his briefcase and brought out a traveler's check and signed over two hundred dollars to me. I was astonished and furious but well composed. I told him that nothing pains me in this world more than when a black person tries to cheat another black person. I had no choice but to ask him to get out of my office with his two hundred dollars. Ayuko Babu, another American distributor, came to negotiate with me. It was not easy. He had been chasing me for three years and prevailed by using influential people who are close to me. I gave him the benefit of the doubt and Ayuko Babu took *Heritage* to the United States. After four years, he returned to tell me that the film had only made about three thousand dollars, when I can make the same amount of money in Ghana or Nigeria in one day. To complicate the matter, he even made an unauthorized video copy. That's piracy. I asked to have my film returned. It arrived just as I was about to leave Ghana for Burkina Faso. These are the type of problems we encounter from distributors who come with their grand designs that cannot really promote African films. Distributors think that FESPACO and other African film festivals are the easiest and cheapest ways to acquire African films. They use our films to enrich themselves. And then after the festival, the distributors vanish.

Crossroads of People, Crossroads of Trade is a wonderful work; surely something deep down in your heart must have inspired the making of this video.

I would say even though *Crossroads* is a short documentary, it consumed more of my time than *Heritage . . . Africa*. Initially this video was supposed to be a simple historical account of the way of life of a people. By people, I mean Ghanaians before the coming of the Europeans, which ushered in the slave trade, forced emigration of our people to the so-called New World, building trading posts, and the struggle for emancipation and independence. As I researched this history, I became more and more emotional and totally committed to creating powerful images that would realistically explain our experiences. The end result is stunning. I'm convinced that the Smithsonian Institution and MUCIA [the Midwest Universities Consortium for International Activities], who initiated this project, probably did not expect me to go that far. If this film had originated from outside Africa, the history of the people would have been written differently. But my concern was to show how Africa was raped, how it lost so much of its wealth to retrogressive foreign ideologies that precluded the continent from genuine development. What I mean is that before the coming of the

Europeans, Africa was developing on its own, and however primitive our beginnings were, if Africans had properly guarded their traditions and not carelessly allowed alien ways of life to proliferate, I am sure that our own development would have been much more meaningful. One of the central themes I pursued in the video is the confusion in the Black Diaspora and why we are not making enough progress as a race. There are some people who believe that we did not revere our traditions enough to defend them at all costs. Others argue that it is only possible to have a meaningful development when those developments are based on the traditions and the roots of the people. It makes sense. As you could see from my other works, this issue has always touched my heart. I felt I should really spend some time to try and eradicate some of the misconceptions about black people. This film is not just about Ghana, it is about Africa and wherever the white man invaded. It is about colonialism and the undermining of a people's culture. The depiction of how blacks have been subjugated has always been a serious issue for me.

How did you condense such a tremendous amount of historical information into forty-five minutes? It is more than an encyclopedia.

The process of making *Crossroads* was very time-consuming. I felt that someone had to document this important history, and we consulted with several experts in various African disciplines. It was an unprecedented challenge which we wholeheartedly confronted. So for every step we took we had to make sure that we were on the right track, therefore it required a considerable amount of explanatory, filmic, and video techniques. To put these images together, we consulted a content committee, made up of intellectuals, from time to time in order to tell an authentic story with the utmost accuracy. On the whole it was a team effort. Of course for the final product, we had to structure all the ideas that we gathered from various sources in a coherent way.

In an environment like this, did you receive criticism from supper intellectuals, as they might be called?

They were surprised we were able to use still pictures in such a framework to tell a very moving story. The consultants drawn from our universities who served on our content committee were happy even though it was clear that I did not depend solely on the information they gave me. Whatever they said from their intellectual perspective I cross-checked with the old people of the villages. They provided us with invaluable information, which we incorporated into the video. For instance, you could see how certain cultures have been preserved. We had to go to the hinterlands to seek out grandmothers who still preserved those early cultures. Listening to some of the elders meant getting firsthand information.

In what other places did you do your research that helped to connect the story with the Black Diaspora?

Apart from the University of Ghana, I spent quite some time at the Schomburg Center for Research in Black Culture in New York City to research the topic. The information I gathered on Ghana and Nigeria was fantastic. I was really amazed to discover the tremendous amount of history that we didn't know about and that also helped a great deal. Luckily, there were African American facilitators who were working with me from the Smithsonian Institution who themselves felt that this is a story that could not be haphazardly assembled but needed in-depth treatment. They worked very hard trying to uncover new material, written or pictorial, that would help document the Diasporan history and culture. I exceeded the budget for the film by over 60 percent, but the satisfaction of being able to make that documentary was more important to me than the amount of money that was going to be realized from this project.

What is the situation of the financing and general support of cinema in Ghana today?

The Ghana Film Guild is working seriously and, of course, in collaboration with the government to deal with the issue of funding. Filmmaking is capital-intensive, and many African countries have not come to grasp the importance of the industry. As far as the governments are concerned, the film industry is a secondary concern. In Ghana, even with the recognition of *Heritage . . . Africa*, the government has not done much. However, there is an interesting story. A company in Britain was interested in providing about one million pounds sterling on the grounds that I would agree to alter the story, because my script was written from an African viewpoint. If I had agreed to their proposal, the film would not only have been funded by the organization but they also would have forced me to use well-known popular stars. In other words, they wanted to dilute the story and its effects and bring in stars who would consume the very money they invested in the film. But when my government heard of their proposal it was rejected outright. This is what caused the Ghanaian authorities to become involved, making it possible for me to obtain bank loans. They were in favor of retaining the original story. If the government had not come to my rescue at that crucial time, I might have been forced to alter the story to satisfy the funding agencies. Whether I would have been able to maintain the original story after I received the money is another issue I have not considered.

What percentage of the film's budget did the government of Ghana provide?

It was the government's intervention that helped in securing the bank loans, which I'm obligated to pay back. After *Heritage . . . Africa* was released, the government started to consider the best help that could be rendered to help in repayment of the loan. They are still deliberating.

You have said that you do not want to distort African history or African culture because of foreign money. Yet coproduction seems to be what has increased the level of Ghanaian film production in the late eighties. Is this something that you would recommend?

Coproduction is not a bad idea. I have never spoken against coproduction. If coproduction means having to sell my birthright and having to tell my own story the way other people want me to, then I do not think it is worth it. I am not in the film industry to sell out or just make money and use my people as tools. Film has a very positive role to play in the developmental process of Africa and that is cardinal to me. I do not hate coproduction. It could be a great relief if the intention of the coproducer correlates with my aspirations. So I am not against coproduction at all.

Your film Heritage ... Africa *could be termed as the OAU of African cinema because of the combination of the characters and technicians used, some from Ghana and some from other African countries. Was this intentional?*

No, let's face it—there are certain areas in filmmaking in which we are not competent, and if we really want to make a film of good quality, we must eschew this parochial thinking that everything has got to be home based. We must learn what we do not know. Fortunately, for my two feature films I was able to use a Ghanaian cameraman who was quite good, but if there is an area which needs the importation of foreign expertise, I don't have a problem with that. The main thing is to get the story told and told effectively. That is what we are looking for. So that kind of coproduction is healthy.

How does the above strategy affect the film language? Do you think there can be an African film language?

Heritage ... Africa, for instance, was made in English and if shown in this format in the francophone it may not communicate to the audience as effectively. But because the imagery is so strong and the story itself is familiar and very relevant to the people who are watching it, despite the language the characters speak, the francophone audience is able to understand what is happening on screen. A film has its own language, be it African or whatever. The people you address with this film must be able to identify with it, and once that is done, our language should not be a barrier. I would have wished, for instance, to do a film in my own mother tongue, but then there are commercial constraints. Unlike Nigeria, where you have large ethnic groupings, it is very uneconomical for me to make a film in Fante or Twi because there is a limited audience that can understand the language. This is regrettable in the sense that in *Heritage ... Africa*, the actress who played Mother Africa was at ease and very natural. After four months of rehearsal her performance became impeccable because of her familiarity with the language. I wish I could produce a film in my own language, but the economic restraints pose a big problem.

What is the impact of foreign films on Ghanaian film culture?

It has been overwhelming. But then, when you have such a low output of films, you cannot really satisfy the demand or be competitive. It is normal, though unfortunate, to entertain African audiences with foreign films whose images are devoid of African values. However, our people are no fools. You cannot underestimate them. Because the audience laugh while watching those images does not necessarily mean that they are pleased with the images or sanction the methods of representation.

What is your opinion regarding FESPACO?

With regard to FESPACO, I am beginning to feel that years of effort by filmmakers to give a true Pan-African meaning to the festival have not yielded much fruit. It has regrettably been sliding back to the francophone status quo.

It looks like video production has killed celluloid filmmaking in Ghana and Nigeria.

I would not consider the proliferation of video as spelling the doom of film, especially where English-speaking Africa is concerned. It's only a poor man's stopgap measure. We must continue telling our stories even when money is hard to come by. Don't forget that we in the English-speaking African countries are not as lucky as our brothers in the French-speaking African countries, whose former colonial master created a film-supporting mechanism from which filmmakers can source funding for a film idea (so long as the idea is nonpolitical against the former master). Film or celluloid is expensive, and ideally that's the format by which I would prefer telling my story, but realistically no African filmmaker on his own can afford celluloid as things stand now. And neither can we wait for our mismanaged economies to be revamped before telling our stories.

Filmography

Love Brewed in the African Pot, 1980
Heritage . . . Africa, 1988
Harvest at 17, 1991
Crossroads of People, Crossroads of Trade, 1995

Souleymane Cissé (Mali)

Born in Bamako, the capital city of Mali, Souleymane Cissé, a pioneer in the development of Malian cinema, is one of Africa's most acclaimed filmmakers. He discovered the cinema at the early age of six when his brothers took him to a theater; he was so enchanted with the motion picture that he then went unaccompanied to many films, to the dismay of his parents. He became interested in the art of making films in 1962 after seeing a film about the brutal treatment and murder of Patrice Lumumba, the former prime minister of Congo.

In the 1960s, Cissé joined the ranks of other Africans offered full scholarships to study in the Soviet Union. From 1963 to 1969 he studied filmmaking at the VGIK, the State Institute of Cinema in Moscow. There he had the opportunity to be taught by the Soviet Union's eminent filmmaker, Mark Donskoi, whose former African film students included Ousmane Sembene and Sarah Maldoror.

In 1969, Cissé returned to Mali and was hired to work as film director by the Service Cinématographique du Ministére de l'Information du Mali (SCINFOMA), where he produced more than thirty newsreels and several documentary films dealing with Malian issues. It was not until 1972 that the young director shot his first independently produced fiction film, *Cinq jours d'une vie* (Five days in a life). With the funding he received from the French Ministry of Cooperation, Cissé was able to make his first feature-length film, *Den Muso* (The young girl, 1975). This film is the first Malian film to be proscribed; it was not released until four years after it was made, due to legal entanglements. This first feature is imbued with creative excitement and stylistic complexity, and Cissé's next feature films, *Baara* (Work, 1978), *Finyé* (The wind, 1982), and *Yeelen* (Brightness, 1987) confirmed his mastery of cinematic conventions. Indeed, all of the films mentioned above have captivated audiences all over

19

the world. In fact, *Baara* enjoyed immense popular success in Africa and Europe, becoming the first African film shown, in 1982, on prime-time French television. *Finyé* captured the 1983 FESPACO's grand prize, the Étalon de Yennega, and *Yeelen* has played at the Samuel Goldwyn Theaters in Los Angeles, at the public theater in New York City, and at numerous other theaters in the United States. It is also one of the first African films to be released on video.

Although Cissé claims to still be searching for an original form or style of expression—an acceptable film language—his film *Yeelen*, described by a British critic as "the best African cinema ever made," seems to have satisfied this quest. Imbued with unprecedented creativity, it won the Jury Prize at the Cannes Film Festival in 1987. Unfortunately, when *Waati* premiered at the 1997 FESPACO it received a lukewarm response from critics. Although it is an ambitious film set in South Africa, Côte d'Ivoire, Mali, and Namibia, it is aesthetically superfluous and overdramatized; one cannot help but see it as three films in one. I interviewed Cissé at the 1997 FESPACO, where the atmosphere was chilly as a result of the unfavorable response to *Waati* from the disappointed audience and the corpus of international critics who expected *Waati* to replicate the magic of *Yeelen*. The interview was conducted in French. (Most of the interviews in this volume that were conducted in French have been translated by Kathryn Lauten.)

In this interview, Cissé reflects on contemporary issues pertaining to the development of his film style, refusing to comment on all other issues.

You have been working from the pioneering phase of African cinema to now. Please tell us about your experiences with filmmaking. You once said that one must be crazy to think about making films in Africa. Do you still subscribe to that view?

If there were a better term today to describe it, I would use it. We still face the same problems as in the beginning of African film history. I said it many times before that making film in Africa belongs to the realm of a miracle. Most African filmmakers still have to be involved with every aspect of the process when working to realize a film. There are still no adequate production facilities in black Africa. We still rely on going to Europe to process films, to do postproduction work and sometimes import camera and sound technicians. It is costly; it drains one's energy and the meager funds available to produce a film. In essence, nothing has changed except, in some significant ways, the developments which have taken place in the areas of coproduction between African states. Apart from sharing production costs, this cooperation also offers us the opportunity to compare notes, discuss our strategies, and, above all, ensure that our films are able to be shown in the coproducing countries. There is also another aspect of coproduction that has its pros and cons. While it is not necessary to detail everything now, I will state that because of the surging interest in African films in all of Europe and America—correct me if I am wrong—there are now serious negotiations going on with regard to prospects for coproductions between Europe and Africa, or the U.S. and Africa. Some coproduction agreements have been finalized and production already started.

Your style has advanced over the years. Why did you move away from didactic films to making films exploring artistic possibilities to the fullest?

My style has not changed. It is the story that has changed because I deal with different issues under different situations. In terms of aesthetic and poetic dimensions, the same manner of approaching the topic and narrative construction applies to all of my films.

But in each film, the language seems to change. For example, what in Yeelen *is different from* Finyé?

You must understand that human life changes. It has to grow up and go through stages. If the films were all similar, that would no longer be cinema. My own experiences in life cannot be said to be the experiences of others. There are certain changes or transformations during a lifetime that force one to rethink one's ways of doing things, one's goals—to approach issues differently in order to arrive at, if not a new meaning, a new synthesis. It is all right if that synthesis amounts to what you might term a different style in my film language. If *Yeelen* is different from *Finyé* and *Baara*, it may be because of the above reasons, certain impulses driving each creation. The change of style may also be deliberate. After I made *Finyé* and *Baara*, I was labeled a political filmmaker, some said my films are too didactic. But an artist should have the freedom to experiment with theme, content, and narrative strategy. As my own experiences have shown, what you narrate may also put you into trouble. Sometimes, in order to survive a hostile environment one is forced, not necessarily to disarm, but to construct a narrative that is not too political nor devoid of pungent criticism of the system.

Which audience do you aspire to reach?

When one makes a film, it is for people who are used to going to see films and who understand them. I don't think I can say that I aim to reach any specific group. It is the film itself that determines that. My films have found their audience in the francophone, South Africa, and we continue to explore various ways of expanding the market. As it is, African films are more widely seen in metropolitan capitals of Europe, the U.S., and Asia than in African cities. That needs to change.

Yeelen *has been praised for its relentless exploitation of the cinematic device; it has also been pointed out that it is difficult to understand the film's story because of its complicated structure. There are so many motifs that a viewer has to see from an African perspective to understand the structure of the film. What is your position regarding the use of film as a cultural tool in the dissemination of issues particular to Africa?*

If it is possible to explore artistic possibilities in trying to move *Yeelen*'s narrative to a deeper level, what is the problem doing it? Filming *Yeelen* was an extraordinary lesson for me. It was a discovery of a new thing that I knew existed but which I had not experienced in real life. And discovering the ritual scenes was like taking part in the activities; it was like an initiation for me. This is one aspect of Malian culture—and there are many cultures in Mali—just as there are numerous aspects of other cultures in Africa. Because of this, certain elements and codes resonating from a particular culture may influence film form and film style. I had a unique fascination with the culture I was discovering, which also meant for me looking intensely to be able to interpret what was going on. It also enabled me to find the creative device I felt was appropriate in the dissemination of this important information. As I have stated before, it is this discovery which compelled me to reveal, and in this revelation the content dictated the form and the strategy with which to shape the film style. *Yeelen* is embedded in deep cultural codes. It is possible that meanings may not be easily accessible—even to Malians not initiated into the Komo cult. However, the film tries to interpret the rituals; the rich imagery and symbolism are carefully depicted to achieve a specific goal and significance, which is to invite the spectator to seek for the deeper meaning which transcends the literary meaning of what the entire film signifies. *Yeelen* compels spectators to ask questions about the secrets of the Komo, makes you an active observer, and provokes discussion and participation. This, I hope, paves the way to uncovering the deeper meaning. It is possible for Malians who have heard the songs of the secret rituals on the radio to understand the film more than the uninitiated Western spectator. For me, each film has its own identity and personality. Consequently, each film represents a certain history. One film cannot resemble another, just as different people cannot be the same.

You show many practices of the Komo that only an initiate can understand. What is the significance of the symbolism that you bring into the film?

I chose to do a story on a secret society. I tried to reveal the language of this society to the viewers. It is clear that it was a fiction, and I cannot transgress that as if I was doing a love story. If the audience did not understand, it is because it is the first time they encountered a deep culture in a society they did not know. If the audience knew the problems and the cultures of others, the incomprehension would have been diminished. This kind of history cannot be treated as it would be in Hollywood. Otherwise it would not have its own originality.

How did you get access to this secret worshiping when you are a Muslim? How did you initiate the research into the Komo cult?

The fact of being religious does not hinder someone from discovering the world that surrounds him. Religion is not an identity. It is a belief, a form of knowledge. What is transmitted is an identity of an ethnic group that existed before the penetration of Islam. I don't understand the problem, because I am, above all, Malian. I know at what moment in history Islam came in, so I don't see this as a problem or frustration. I must say that my experience in researching and filming the Komo ritual was overwhelming and rejuvenating in many ways. I consider it exceptional to have witnessed the rituals performed, from the vantage point of a novice. It took the usual process of negotiating as in location scouting or the process of obtaining permission to film certain events. But the Komo is more than an event: I put forward to the members my project, my interest in the rituals, etc., and explained to them what I wanted to accomplish. I was glad they cooperated because it is an aspect of culture never before documented on film. And when the filming of the ritual began, we discovered it to be an exercise of hypnotizing dimension.

Some people have misinterpreted this film to be your own commentary on a system that you do not think is relevant today.

It's too bad for those people. I don't play that game. It's an American game. I am not going to justify myself in the eyes of American university scholars, only to Malian eyes such as the Bambara. But I would like for those who speak that way to come to Mali so we can see together and discuss together and so that they touch with their own fingers the reality. If they say that this tradition is no longer valid, why do they keep talking of Egypt, the pharaohs, and pyramids? Where does the source of civilization come from? One must not be elementary in such questioning and denigrating of culture. It is especially those who call themselves African specialists who say they have the key to African cultures. They need only keep that key for heaven that awaits them.

I do not subscribe to that idea, but I want to use this opportunity to clarify some misconceptions about the film.

I know that well. But that has not stopped *Yeelen* from having its impact, which continues to this present day. It is not a dated film; it is based on the evolution of human beings and their cultures. It is because of this that the end of the film takes place without any commentary. If people stop at problems of tradition or such, it means they did not understand the film. That is too bad.

Is there an explanation as to why in Yeelen *and, most recently,* Waati *animal symbolism keeps recurring?*

What I regret is that when people make films in the United States with animals, nobody asks any questions. But when we do it in Africa, everyone asks why.

Because we know that there are animal tales that make sense in our tradition. We believe in some of those tales. And in Yeelen *and* Waati *you make a specific commentary in regard to animal symbolism, such as with the lion, elephant, goats, and dogs.*

That's true everywhere. In the United States there are tales with animals. You have the eagle that represents something fundamental and the lion that is the emblem of certain societies. It didn't just happen; there are reasons for using such symbols. I think simply that each time you develop things, people have to make an effort to decode them. I am a creator of images; I feel things and find a way to fit them into my narratives. These things must give more than what I alone would give. A film does not need to be commented on or you take away its universal aspects. You cannot pluck away at a film like a chicken. I will not make commentaries on my films but rather I will leave that to the critics. They all encompass ideas and feelings that came out of my guts. I cannot, like someone just selling peanuts, throw out ideas. It goes beyond that.

The multinational, multiracial crew used in Waati *is unprecedented in the history of African cinema.*

The multinational, multicultural talents and crew reflect my ambition of moving cinema beyond the borders of Mali or Africa, to work with people across the globe, and use the medium to communicate with audiences. *Waati* brought together people from Mali, Côte d'Ivoire, France, Guinea, Italy, South Africa, Russia, and America. It was filmed on locations in Côte d'Ivoire, Mali, Namibia, and South Africa. I have been told that the greatest attribute of this film is the freedom allowed the characters to use indigenous African languages in the regions the film was set. The question of language has been a major concern for African filmmakers, and I have been a strong advocate of the need to respect the languages of various people. Over the years, I have realized that people feel more comfortable and are more fluent in the delivery of dialogues in their mother tongues, besides that it renders authentic the manner in which certain issues are portrayed and communicated. As in the other West African countries we filmed, in South Africa, characters spoke Zulu, Afrikaans, English, pidgin English, and so on. My purpose is to let the actors convey their emotions naturally and convincingly, not as in Hollywood films when an American actor tries to speak like an African in a bastardized accent simply because the producers do not want to offer an African role to an African.

Why was Waati *set in South Africa?*

The film could have been done anywhere. I thought that it should be done in South Africa because it is on the African continent. It would be better there than doing it in the United States. I preferred South Africa because it is the least-known country, the youngest independent country in Africa today. But the story could have happened anywhere.

It seems to me that the demise of apartheid and the jubilant mood that ushered South Africa into the community of free African nations influenced your decision.

Partially correct! The script was written in 1988, before President Nelson Mandela was released from jail. However, after Mandela's release, I went to South Africa in 1990. I saw the new South Africa as it was emerging, and for me it was possible to reflect on the past to assess the present. But from the film you can see a broader spectrum of African reality—how the problems in one region affect the other countries within the continent. It is also about the future. After my visit to South Africa I was convinced that this film must be made there. I made some changes to incorporate new developments into the script without altering the original structure.

Toward the end of the film, the whole question of forgiveness would be difficult for anyone to tackle. Now, however, we are starting to hear about people making confessions about the killing of Steve Biko, Chris Hani, and others, and the other atrocities committed during the apartheid era. It reminds me of that last scene, which makes me think that you have a clear vision of how people feel about the oppression in South Africa during apartheid, and a vision of the current mood. How do you feel now, with the inquiries of the Truth and Reconciliation Commission going on in South Africa, where some people, but not everyone, are beginning to be encouraged to look forward by forgiving the past?

That makes me laugh, because even today, there are still crimes from World War II that haven't been tried. *Waati* is like a book. It is our memory. Each time there is a need, we will open up this book and look at it. People can refuse to talk about it today, but the memory is there. The issues are resurrected because they exist in our memory and will stay there. It is all for the better if there is reconciliation. Let us hope that there is reconciliation around the whole planet and that people of all races would pay less attention to what races they belong so that man emerges victorious. It is in this objective that I made this film. This film is not a bitter film, but an understanding one, so that people can mutually pardon each other and tell each other the truth. It is only with this spirit of forgiveness that we can function. We have to give time to South Africans to take care of their problems, and it is for that reason that the film is called *Waati*, which means time. Time will show a reason for this, even if I am no longer here.

What significance do you give to all the symbols and the academic lessons illustrated by performance of masks, juxtaposition of traditional ritual with contemporary dances, and the other symbolic images, such as the Rasta?

The passage of the Rasta has a rather spiritual vision, and because they have some deep beliefs in themselves the Rastafarians are rather misunderstood. They are completely put aside, and thus there is a parallel in the system that happened in South

Africa between the social levels, that is to say between the blacks and the whites. And the symbol of the family of Nandi [the lead actress] is also the symbol of the Rasta, which is the lion. Thus somewhere there was a coming together of the two. They have a fundamental dimension of accepting things and of seeing justice in another manner that the other does not want to believe. That is why they are a people completely set apart, which is what pushes them to do things like drugs. They are rejected. For Nandi, who goes to West Africa, the masks are for educating her. In this education, in West Africa, masks have an important place. At some universities there are sections for African civilization. Nandi wanted to know and understand Africa as well as herself, so from this moment on she is able to get a base education that allows her to understand the situation and to tell herself that racism is a moment in their history, and it will go away. With that, her heart and her soul become something different. Without this part, she would not have had this strong soul to be able to decide to return to South Africa, which is not the case among many who go away to study and choose instead to remain in their newfound comfort and not return home.

What are the technical problems you encounter making your films?

All the general problems associated with filmmaking in Africa. In making *Yeelen*, for example, we lacked adequate facilities in every aspect. And when this sort of thing happens, you are forced to rely on improvisations. We had not enough light to illuminate all the scenes—handicapped not only in terms of determining the right aperture for exposing the film, but of maneuverability of the camera for desired effects. For *Waati*, I think that I will give only an overview. It was, for example, difficult to work with a team that was half Russian and half French. That was my first problem. It was so horrible that it was necessary to stop the first filming. Second was the misunderstanding that started from the beginning and followed the second team. Finally everything was stopped for this and also for financial reasons. At one point my partner said we would have to stop because there was no more money. At that point I had to either stop or find a solution on how to complete the filming. The team of about forty to forty-five people was ready to get on a plane and leave. At six in the morning I went to see my assistant and explained the problem. He remained seated and said we would find a solution. I had to let the team leave and I stayed in Bamako. I managed to get the necessary money to make the film. The history of this film is filled with these types of anecdotes. Each film has its own problems or similar difficulties. One has to be sure to have a good production structure to be able to make a film. In each case, you give away all your time and energy in order to surmount the anguish from accumulated problems, many of them unpredictable.

You spoke about these same problems many years ago. Why do they still exist today?

In our states there should be structures such that cinema is considered an economic industry and that those in power allow a system where businessmen can integrate themselves into the furthering of this industry. As long as that is not done, we will have to live with the situation as it is now. We have partners, those who finance the films, and who have their own ideas about what African cinema should be and should not be. We have our own ideas about what we want to do, and in the end we find ourselves cornered by these differences. If you don't want to follow the sponsor's ideas, they stop you, just exactly like what happened with *Waati*. But since I am the author, creator, and director of this film, I took everything into my control. After that, everything went well. We went to South Africa and filmed in six weeks without any problems. After the experience, I concluded that if I must make another film I must also be the producer.

Why was Waati *not shown at the fourteenth FESPACO? And what are your plans for its distribution?*

Waati was finished in April 1995, after the 1995 FESPACO. I couldn't have presented it at the last FESPACO. But despite that, I am glad that this question came up. Many people have said that Souleymane Cissé refused to have anything to do with FESPACO. Let me state in the strongest language that I have only the highest respect for the festival. I know that I have given a part of myself for this festival. If I can participate in FESPACO in any way, I must. I presented my films here, and I want FESPACO to rise to a higher level. That is my hope for FESPACO. As for the other question on distribution, we established on January 14, 1997, in Bamako an organization whose goal is to provide for the sixteen countries of West Africa a means of distribution so that all African and European films can be seen by the people of this part of Africa. As you well know, there are few theaters for this. Thankfully, at Ouagadougou there are some good ones. At Bamako there are almost no more theaters. In Côte d'Ivoire, the few theaters that remain have become cathedrals. In Senegal, the theaters are closing to become shops. In Guinea, the theaters are falling in. Given this situation, we thought it our duty to take this on. "We" means the professionals, the creators, and the operators. Our inclusive act wants to have everyone involved who wants to see this industry established and prosper in our countries: distributors, creators, filmmakers, journalists, cameramen, everyone. I do not think this organization can be compared to FEPACI [the Pan-African Federation of Film-makers]. They have similar but different objectives. It will help to reinforce FEPACI. We do not want to destroy FEPACI. FEPACI must be reinforced with a lot of action. Cinema must be a place that pulls people in and a place of interest. If we do not want to eternally be beggars, we have to put to work our human resources such as intelligence, so that we can get out of this crisis. It is not a closed professional society. It is open for everyone. We want to open up viable possibilities for the cinema so we can begin to see it as an industry that is very complex and which needs people with business management background. Our problem is one of management. As long as this training is not done, and its effects are not situated in a grounded legalistic and economic system, it will not work. Now a minister of finance will not even speak to a filmmaker, because he does not see the possibility of an "economy of image." This economic reality is evident in developed countries, or at least the United States, where the film industry ranks second in the entire economic structure. Now everyone is mad at the United States, but it is because it succeeded in imposing its supremacy with images.

Is this all because you have felt the risk of no longer having the financial support of a sponsor, because they are tired of financing African cinema?

If I tell you how I made my first film, it will be clear that we must try to create structures appropriate to our own means, and make films that will ensure our determination of getting rid of dependency. This is missing because there is no legal structure.

Earlier you spoke about forgiveness; will you forgive the South African juror at Cannes who blocked Waati's chances of winning any award on the pretext that the story of the film was "not updated"?

Yes. In this world, there are always people who want to have a monopoly. That is the case with Nadine Gordimer. I have nothing against this woman. But she must keep in mind that the world turns. That means that life does not stop on earth but it goes beyond. Everyone has the right to express him- or herself. When people express themselves, I do not see how one can condemn it to the extent of saying that this is not South Africa. No, nobody has the monopoly on South Africa. Nobody! She has the right to say what she has to say, but everyone has the right to make films on what they think, on a particular subject.

Filmography

L'homme et les idoles (Man and idols), 1965
L'aspirant (The aspirant), 1968
Sources d'inspiration (Sources of Inspiration), 1968
Degal à Dialloube (Degal at Dialloube), 1970
Fête du Sanké (The Sanke celebration), 1971
Cinq jours d'une vie (Five days in a life), 1972
Dixième anniversaire de l'OUA (Tenth anniversary of the Organization of African Unity), 1973
Den Muso (The young girl), 1975
Baara (Work), 1978
Finyé (The wind), 1982
Yeelen (Brightness), 1987
Waati (Time), 1995

Safi Faye (Senegal)

Born in Senegal, Safi Faye was the first woman of sub-Saharan African to make a feature-length film, *Kaddu beykat*, in 1975. She enrolled at the École Pratique des Hautes Études (Sorbonne) to study ethnology and at the Louis Lumière Film School in 1972. In 1975, Faye continued her studies in ethnology at the Sorbonne and obtained a diploma. Combining filmmaking with educational pursuit, this relentlessly hardworking woman obtained a doctorate degree in ethnology from the University of Paris VII in 1979. As she states in her interview, it was her findings from the research she did with her own people, the Serer peasants, that engendered the themes of two of her films, *Fad'jal* (Come and work) and *Goob na nu* (The harvest is in), both made in 1979. However, her initiation into the cinematographic world started with a brief acting experience in the 1970 film *Petit à petit ou les lettres persanes 1968* (Little by little, or the 1968 Persian letters), directed by the French ethnographic filmmaker Jean Rouch. Since she made her first short, *La passante* (The passerby), in 1972, she has realized ten documentary films about African cultural, economic, and political experiences and three feature-length films: *Kaddu beykat* (Letter from the village, 1975), which was shown at the Cannes Film Festival and won the Georges Sadoul Prize as well as winning the award of the international critics of the Festival of Berlin and a special award at the fifth Pan-African Festival of Film and Television of Ouagadougou in Burkina Faso; *Fad'jal* (1979), which was featured at the Cannes Film Festival as the first black African film in official selection; and *Mossane* (1996), which was featured as the official selection at the Cannes Film Festival and was also invited for a second screening at Cannes in 1997.

Described by Françoise Pfaff as a "strong-minded and outspoken yet amiable woman possessing a keen sense of humor," Safi Faye believes that a film's structure must bear the signature of the filmmaker. Although she is careful not to criticize her counterparts in other African film practice, she does allude to the differences separating her from them in matters of technique and ideology.

I would like to thank Dr. Awam Amkpa for his help with the second part of this interview during the fifteenth FESPACO in Ouagadougou in 1997. This interview was conducted in French and translated by Kathryn Lauten.

You are the first black woman to make a commercially distributed feature film?

Yes, *Kaddu beykat* was made in 1975 and it is my first feature-length film. The film is one hour and forty-five minutes long. I experimented with both content and narrative style, and you can find in it a mixture of fiction and documentary styles.

You have made history, then, in being the first black woman to make a feature-length film.

Actually, I am the first black woman to make any films—I did a short film in 1972. The title of the film is *La Passante*, and it is only ten minutes long. Am I the only woman, the only active black woman in feature filmmaking in Africa today? Surely I am not! A lot has changed.

How many feature films have you made to date?

My first real feature film is *Mossane*, which was completed recently; and it is also a fiction film. Before that, I made two other features, both mixtures of fiction and documentary. They are *Kaddu beykat* [Letter from the village, 1975] and *Fad'jal* [Come and work, 1979], which was one of the films selected for the 1979 Cannes Film Festival. I have made many short films and several feature-length films that juxtapose fiction with documentary, as I stated before, but *Mossane* is completely fiction.

Kaddu beykat is a very powerful film that deals with economic, historical, social, and political situations. It is also an ethnographic film and makes a powerful critique of the Senegalese system. What inspired you to make this film?

As a young woman I was very enthusiastic about documenting the lives of the peasant community, the farmers, where I come from. I wanted to film their preoccupations, to tell their stories. They live in this world like any other people; they are happy, maybe, but not often. In their society, they can live only if they can cultivate their lands. But they face two handicaps—the problem of inadequate rainfall, which causes drought, and that of government exploitation. I felt I must tell their stories my own way—through film. When I was doing my fieldwork and examinations in ethnology for my second degree at the university, I gathered a lot of research materials and resources in the community. When I began to work on my findings, I found that, following all discussions of political problems, people were also very interested in talking about ethnology. When I completed that study, I put aside the information on economic problems and used only my ethnologic themes, for example, the "primitive" (read: traditional) religions before Catholicism and Islam. That was the theme of my thesis. One day I realized that I could use all the sociological and economical information I had gathered to make a film. So I created a little fictional love story between a man and a woman who could not be married and happy because of the worsening economic situation in their country. That was the beginning of *Kaddu beykat,* which does not quite mean "Letter from the village," as has been translated in some sources, but rather *paroles,* or "words of the farmers." I did, however, introduce a letter into this film to show the world and to emphasize what their lives are really like.

You just mentioned your training as an ethnologist and anthropologist. That shows in all of your films through your careful observation and how you apply your research. Your films are different from Western ethnographic films about Africa. In making your films, how do you stay back to let the action happen uninterrupted and to let the camera capture that action? That is one of the greatest attributes that makes your films so powerful.

Actually, it is difficult to say. Maybe it is my kind of writing, or my sensibility. Each filmmaker has his own sensibility. For me a film has to have a particular structure or distinctive hallmark. Sometimes it is hard to explain how that structure was realized or how the entire film was made. Ideas come in a flash and so does the creative impulse that drives the whole initiative. It also depends on the circumstances surrounding the making of the film. I may be reacting this way because I had to fight a lot to save my last film, *Mossane,* and now I have no more ideas. I am afraid to make films again. Before I had a lot of ideas. I am sure, though, that all the films I made happened because I admired and liked the people and like to show that via the film medium.

You are a member of the village so you are looking from inside as opposed to other people who look from the outside, at what they call "exotic cultures." That is the difference that separates your films from, for example, the films of Jean Rouch.

Yes, but also other African filmmakers could make films like me, but they are preoccupied more with cities and towns than the places of their origins. I don't like the city.

Your film Kaddu beykat *concerns society. You made an honest assessment of the society, but the film was banned in Senegal. Why?*

It is because of how the farmers told their stories. They said it was true that governments cheat on them when they come to buy their produce. The government was embarrassed and did not like being exposed. So the criticism made the government censors intimidate me by ordering me to cut two segments of the film. One segment is the sequence where the children played. In one scene the children narrate how they saw the government officials arrive to collect money from their parents. For some parents, this is a humiliating experience, and when the government officials arrive to harass them they would ask the children to leave home and go elsewhere to play. Another part they asked me to cut concerns what happens when the government buys the goods from the peasants. They pay a certain compensation for the cash crops bought, but it is only when the farmer returns home that he finds out from others that the government took advantage of his lack of education and gave him less than the agreed-upon amount. The censors insisted that I eliminate these two sequences but I refused to comply. I make my films alone without government money, and I find it unacceptable to comply with government censors who want to cut my film so as to cover the atrocities they have committed against their own people. I believe in the stories my people told me and for me, that is the main issue. But this is all in the past, because for my last film never before has the government of Senegal put up so much money to support an independent production. It shows how people and governments can change.

When I met with you at the 1995 Pan-African Festival of Film and Television of Ouaga-
dougou, your first time at the festival, you said you stopped in Senegal on your way
to Ouagadougou to receive an award. So the government finally recognized you after so
many years?

Yes, the award coincided with the preparations for the Women's Meeting in China, which started in Senegal. They had to congratulate one woman, and it was I. The year 1995 marked the first time that I attended FESPACO. I had not participated since its inception because of the choices I had to make—to be a filmmaker, yes; to be a mother, yes; to pursue my work on anthropological studies, yes. And if I want to support my daughter who is now studying at a university in England, I have to be careful regarding how I manage my affairs. All these things control my life. I want to succeed at the choices I make. If I do these three things at the same time, I must elim-inate certain things such as festivals and many other activities, which is why for twenty years I never attended any festivals. It was my choice not to attend FESPACO. But in 1995 I received a special invitation to attend FESPACO and to receive a mer-itorious award given to me by the Organization of African Filmmakers, which I was mandated to accept. It was a great honor.

How do you do everything you do—so well? To combine motherhood with your other
jobs? The problem of shooting films and doing postproduction work must be very diffi-
cult for you.

Yes, it is. If I cannot do all the things that I plan to do, I am never satisfied. And I want to be satisfied. I try to be satisfied. For me there is no confusion making movies and all the rest. I am not lost inside. I always manage to find a way out. When my daughter was three years old, she could read because I devoted a lot of time to teaching her. I was a trained teacher in Senegal before I left my country for a temporary absence. It also worked to my daughter's advantage because she was always taking first place in her classes. Similarly, when I make films I also try my best to accomplish certain goals. I must state that choosing to make films before any other black woman was easy for me. First I studied at a very prestigious film school, Louis Lumière, in Paris. After I received my diploma I realized that I had some expectations and I said to myself, "I'll try." Suddenly a black woman is making films. At that time it was less difficult because there were a lot of possibilities. I got a lot of attention and admiration because I was the first woman of my time to use the camera. The only film where I had problems is *Mossane*. But before that I always got an immediate yes to my requests for funding.

What is the problem you had with Mossane? *I know it took a long time to make this film, and you were very angry about your working relationships when I asked you about it at the 1995 FESPACO.*

I don't know if it is necessary to give the whole story. Anything can happen at any point during one's lifetime. When I decided to make the film, which I conceived as my biggest film, it was because I was convinced I could do it competently. But something happened and the film did not materialize according to plan. I got enough money—about seven million French francs—to make the film; however, the total amount was eight million. I raised almost all of this money single-handedly. The financiers liked the project and provided the funds. They were also confident that I could handle the project well. However, it is not always possible to make films and also do all of the accounting. So I entrusted that aspect of the production to a Frenchman who was not honest. He took my money, my rights, and the rights of everyone who funded the production. What saved the film—and I will never forget it—is that I shot every part of the film in record time in 1990. For that I am happy because if I worked like other African filmmakers who would shoot some sequences today, then wait six months to shoot more, and then another six months to shoot the rest, I would not have been able to complete the film. How could I have completed the film with the actress? She was fourteen years old when we shot the film, and by the time everything was done, because of the delay caused by the litigation, she was twenty when the film was released. I finally got my rights back in 1995. I don't want to dwell on what happened. I am happy that the film turned out to be good. I am satisfied with it. But it was a lot of work, not an easy task working day and night on one project in the middle of other life problems. When so much work goes into a film, it shows in the final product.

Your films pay meticulous attention to womanhood; how you foreground women's lives and how, through the characters, the viewer experiences vignettes of culture attests to women's contributions to society. I know you have said that your films are not only about women but about all of society.

No, no! Because women alone cannot live in Africa. Women live in a community, and I cannot eliminate the community. This is a reflection on me: I cannot live without my people. I cannot separate out an individual. But this is typical of African cultures. You cannot live alone; you can't do it because a big family, a big community, is all around you.

In Ferid Boughedir's Camera d'Afrique: Twenty Years of African Cinema, *you talked about your filmmaking experience while holding a Muslim prayer bead.*

I don't remember that, but I am a Muslim; my father is a Muslim, his brother is a Catholic, and his uncle is an animist. All of the religions can live together—the most important thing is belief in one's faith.

I think you are a bridge uniting all these differences. As a woman, carrying a camera, going to a village to film, how do you coordinate all of the things you do?

Because I know what I am doing. When you cannot get what you want, it is because you do not know where you are going. Before I say, "Shoot," I know where I am going, and I do it very quickly. It is just the way I approach my work.

What inspired Mossane*? And what were you trying to achieve?*

"Love" is what I say to everyone who asks me this question. I wanted the most beautiful woman to be an African girl. In this case the girl is fourteen years old; she is pure, she is innocent, and she looks as if she does not belong to this world—because she is too beautiful. The entire world loves her, including her brother. She is so pure and beautiful, but she cannot stay in this world because the spirits who died or departed long ago will come back to take her. The beginning point was a legend affirming that every two centuries a young girl is born whose beauty is such that she can only know fatal destiny. Mossane belongs to this group of people.

Is this taken from a real story?

No, I created everything. It is a fictional story.

The way you treated her brother's sexual advances toward her was not exoticized. That was cleverly integrated into the narrative.

It is because I like punctuation in my films. The film is about Mossane, which means "beauty." All of those things happening in the plot are punctuation, nothing else. And when you have those points of punctuation, you don't have to make the story about those points. My story follows Mossane's development as an individual who is lovable. I love her. I created this character. Her brother could also be in love with her, like I can be in love with her, because she is supernatural, ethereal. The point I make is that anybody, woman or man, can love her. I wanted to get that point across.

Her death was tragic, and if she is so much loved, do you think it is justified that she died a violent death?

Yes, like I said before, she is supernatural. She does not belong on this earth. Nobody knows why she is so supernatural. She has parents all right but she is still unique in this world. Nobody can touch her. Somehow she is inaccessible, and I like inaccessible beings. That comes also from my experience as an ethnologist.

She dies when she is kept from marrying the person she loves. Is this a criticism of society? Are you suggesting that the practice of arranged marriages is outdated in Africa?

Everybody is free to make his own interpretation of the film. For me, I say that she doesn't belong to this world, and nobody can touch her. She has her destiny. I remember that in my script, I wrote that she is going to follow Fara the student, and when the university reopens she attempts to meet him. The obstacle separating them is the river. She has to cross the river alone, but spirits live in the water, it is believed in my country, and a spirit took her to another destination. My sense of creativity, though, is to let the audience imagine what the images signify. It is not necessary to make everything explicit for the audience. They have to think. Creativity invites such thinking; that is why I create.

Is that why you didn't quite show clearly how she died? We are left to assume many things, such as whether she drowned on her own or whether someone murdered her.

Traveling alone, she heard some voices—voices of the spirits, which frightened her. She drifted into the woods and began to cry. In my conception it is the spirit that took her, because this girl didn't belong in this world. She had to go back with the spirit to become a member of the spirit world. And maybe she will come back one day looking for the most beautiful man on earth.

Another interesting way you present culture is in your depiction of black sexuality. You depicted the lovemaking sequence in a way unusual for African films. I liked how it was shot, but it may be too controversial for some Africans, including your colleagues.

Some people may see the lovemaking scene as too explicit. I do not think there is anything unusual. Every married man and woman makes love at home. When things are beautiful, when the body is beautiful—and, yes, Mossane is beautiful—I show them as beautiful. As if it is expected to happen, and the audience knows it will happen, why can't the couple be shown having intercourse? When I chose to present such a scene I aspired to present it as beautiful and as pleasing as possible. The president of my country saw the premiere of the film in Dakar and he told me that people make love and that there is nothing wrong in depicting lovemaking in films, especially regarding how I constructed the scene.

The scene was well shot. The lighting and the serene atmosphere contributed to its splendor. What kind of a crew do you use? Do you use African technicians?

The technical crew is all German. I made my name in Germany before France. I lived for a long time in Germany, teaching at the university and so forth. When I wrote my script and sent it to my financiers in Germany, they immediately suggested that Jürgen Jürges [Fassbinder's acclaimed cameraman, considered one of the best of his generation] should film *Mossane*. After he became interested in the story, Jürges pointed out to me that both of our daughters were thirteen years old, and we could put all of our affection for our children on *Mossane*. That comment contributed greatly to the harmony of our working relationship. We filmed the little girl like a genie to inject into the character all of the mysterious aspects you can only see in a child at this age. A child changes a lot between thirteen and fifteen years old. You can experience those characteristics in Mossane throughout the film.

Do you think African cinema is in a crisis?

I think it is difficult to make films now. I am no longer ready to make a film like *Mossane*. It is my last big film, because I do not want to be destroyed anymore. If something bad should happen to me, my child will lose everything. I was very depressed over this film because of a number of bad experiences culminating in a series of financial and legal disagreements. It was like a dream for seven years as I waited and waited for the justice system to rescue me. If I didn't have my whole family, my community with me during this painful period, I would have perished. They were the ones who knew how sad I was during those years and they were the ones who gave me the encouragement to keep going. I am sure I could not have taken all of those pains alone. They too shared a little part of that sadness. They saved me.

Have you shown Mossane *in a public theater?*

No. It was shown at the Cannes Film Festival for two consecutive years, but I still have a lot of production costs left to pay. I need money to pay for postproduction, including the costs of making internegative and interpositive prints, as well as some other expenses. At this time, we have only two prints made. *Mossane* has not made me financially solvent as yet, as there is also a lot of lab work to pay for. I am expecting to settle all the bills and to be able to make more copies for distribution. However, Trigon-Film in Switzerland, who contributed to the production fund, organized a commercial screening of the film in November 1996 that is still going on to this present day [September 12, 1997]. I was there to present it. To make it worthwhile commercializing the film, Trigon paid to make three copies. My distributor in Africa is Ousmane Sembene, who is really great. He promised to begin the distribution and exhibition in October 1997. The German exhibition will also begin in October.

Would you consider putting Mossane *on video to sell it to universities in the United States?*

I don't know. I won't rush into anything, because this film has made me afraid. I had planned for the shooting of this film to be completed in 1991, and it wasn't until 1996 the film was ready for screening. Destiny is at work, maybe. Perhaps it is better for me to wait. People can inquire about the film or offer proposals for acquisition, but I will exercise some degree of restraint. Remember that I created the story and invented the spirits; nobody can see spirits or represent spirits, so when you show them in a film, maybe the spirit will find a way to bring something good for the future. For me, spirits do not belong to this world, and if they come, heads must bow.

Yes, but a spirit can also make us ascend to a level we didn't think possible before.

Yes, I agree! I think that the spirit that I venerated in my film gave me back my rights.

Because of the energy and time of putting this film together, there must be a way to find a channel of distribution for it. You know Haile Gerima. His film Sankofa *made a lot of money because he organized its distribution through the help of many people. The film showed in major cities, and after that, he put it on video. I bought a copy myself. I think that strategy could also work in your case.*

I am optimistic that *Mossane* could make money because it is a nice film. Yes, I know Haile Gerima. His distribution company, Mypheduh Films, distributes my film *Kaddu beykat* in the United States.

I tried to rent Kaddu beykat *some time ago but I was told that the print is in bad shape. That is one of the reasons I suggested having* Mossane *and the other films you made on video.*

You are making a good proposal but I have to clear impending debts. I was glad that after the rough cut was shown to some guests last December [1995] it was predicted that this film would go to Cannes, and it did. For that and other reasons, I think I should wait for the right distributor to handle the film. I will not give the film to any distributor without getting a twenty-thousand-dollar deposit up front. I need this money to pay the bills. I am only asking for a fair amount. All of my films are still out there in distribution—some of them twenty years after they have been made, and I am sure *Mossane* will be universal and eternal. For that, I can wait.

How was it received at the Cannes Film Festival?

Mossane was received as the official selection of the Cannes Film Festival and for its world premiere. I was elated. I went to the Cannes Film Festival with my daughter, and she witnessed the whole thing. She saw her mother destroy what I would call the myth of the stupidity of filmmaking. For me it was a special occasion and a special occasion for the government of Senegal, who sent high-level government officials to witness this event. The government was glad that my film made it as Senegal's official entry to the festival. The president gave me his full support. Ousmane Sembene threw in his weight, too.

What is your source of influence?

I don't have a specific influence. I work from my own sensation. I like to be alone. I like silence. It is only my child who cannot disturb me, but other people can disturb me.

What do you think about African cinema?

I cannot talk about that. Sometimes when there is an African film showing, I pay my way to experience the film. If I happen to meet the filmmaker, I don't admit I saw the film because I don't want him to ask me what I think about it. I think there are some differences demarcating my work from theirs. It could be that I have great self-confidence.

What do think about FESPACO?

I do not normally go to FESPACO. The first time I participated was in 1995 and the second time was this year, and only because Sembene told me, "You must show your film, you must put your film in competition." As you know, I prefer to be alone; I don't belong to any group. For me, three days here at FESPACO is enough. If I could have changed my ticket today I would have left, but I was told it was not possible to change it. I like the generosity of the organizers. I appreciate that, but I don't like festivals. I do not envy the structure of the organization of FESPACO. In short, I don't like festivals except in some exceptional circumstances.

You display a lot of rituals—matrimonial rituals, dances, ghosts, and sensuous feasts of young women—in the film that people who do not know much about Senegalese culture may not understand.

It is interesting how people marvel about all the things happening in this film. When I showed it in Paris and invited my former professors of anthropology and ethnology to see the film, they admired the creative imagination involved in the realization of those images. Of course, they understood them to be fictional images which I invented, but some people think the story was real. One of the professors said to me,

"Ms. Safi, you know this is the origin of myths. In twenty years, people will still say this is the myth of Safi Faye." All the same, the images are not realistic.

This is again what is unique about your film structure. You have a unique way of juxtaposing fiction with documentary to create the kind of myth you are talking about.

Yes, you are correct. But if you make films and you cannot create, then you must stop making films.

Doesn't that describe some of the problems we are seeing in African films?

I am not competent to comment generally on the issue because I don't see a lot of African films, but I think that in any one film a new image must be created. As they said in Cannes in reference to my spirits, never before has a person created on film this kind of vision of humans. Critics also admired the music, the warm and lively colors, and the sensuous nature of the film. For me, the head must think and create. If not, you are like any other filmmaker.

I saw that a number of agencies, including television, were involved in funding the project. Doesn't it bother you that when the film is shown on television that you may not be able to control piracy, especially since it has not been widely distributed commercially?

The film will be shown on Channel 4 in England, Arte in France, ZDF TV in Germany—all of whom financed the film, along with some other television networks. On the question of piracy and illegal duplication, I have a lawyer and a contract, but it is true that no television station can control satellite broadcasts. Regarding my earlier problems, the mistake I made was that I did not have a lawyer when I first started the production. At the time I was advised that it was not necessary to hire a lawyer because it would be too costly. Actually that would have meant hiring three lawyers, each of them taking charge of the legal questions that might have arisen in France, Germany, and Senegal, respectively. I learned my lesson. If I had lawyers from the beginning, I would not have had the problems I had for these past five or six years. But I learned a lot from these mistakes and from this film. When there is so much money involved, as with this project, there is a tendency that your trusted associate will try to steal from you. I will never make that kind of mistake again.

This kind of affirmation is frequently heard among African filmmakers. Often they say they will never make films again because of bad experiences they had and the problem of working as an independent. But because of their reputation, they are forced to make more films. So I am hoping that pressure will come one day to say that the woman who made this beautiful film, Mossane, *cannot stop making films. She must be given full support.*

I will tell such a person to bring the money, take control of the legal aspects, give me my rights, and I will prepare the film's scenario and shoot it. All the people who gave me money to make *Mossane* know me, and they know my work. I am grateful to them all. I am not planning to start looking for money for a new film, because money is dangerous. The more you find the money, the more a lot of people will come behind you and, believe it, you may not know who the unscrupulous individuals are.

I talked to you before about Selbé, *which is doing very well in the United States.*

The film was commissioned. It was coproduced by UNICEF and Faust Films Production [Munich]. I directed it and it does not belong to me. People tell me I did a good job on that film, and I do get payment from it. Everybody likes *Selbé*. It won a special prize at the 1983 Leipzig Festival in Germany. The people who commissioned it wanted a woman filmmaker to make the film.

I still think you must try to explore distribution possibilities in North America.

I say, let *Mossane* have its own way. I can't say I want this or want that, but I can't continue to suffer. I believe that after six years of uncertainty the time has now come for me to reap the fruits of my labor. For me, in my head, *Mossane* is done, and you don't know how happy I am.

Filmography

La Passante (The passerby), 1972/5
Kaddu beykat/ Lettre paysanne (Letter from the village), 1975
Fad'jal/Arrive, travaille (Come and work), 1979
Goob na nu (The harvest is in), 1979
Trois ans et cinq mois (Three years five months), 1979
Man sa ya/Moi, ta mere (I, your mother), 1980
Les âmes au soleil (Souls under the sun), 1981
Selbé et tant d'autres (Selbe: One among many), 1982
Ambassades nourricières (Food missions), 1984
Elsie Haas, femme peintre et cineaste d'Haïti (Elsie Haas: Haitian painter and filmmaker), 1985
Racines noires (Black roots), 1985
Tesito, 1989
Mossane, 1996

Gadalla Gubara (Sudan)

Mainly because the cinema of Sudan is one of the least developed in Africa, film-making by the government and by Sudanese individuals is rarely discussed. It was, for me, a significant discovery when, by chance, at the 1995 Pan-African Festival of Film and Television of Ouagadougou, I came in contact with Gadalla Gubara, who, as this interview reveals, is probably the oldest pioneer of African cinema. This slender man of average height, clad in an immaculate white robe and matching turban, stood out among the crowd and immediately drew my attention as someone from the Maghreb region. He was in the company of friends when I heard him make illuminating comments about the festival and cinema in Africa. This made me think of him as an important dignitary in the African film business.

After I introduced myself and asked if he would relate his connection with the festival, Gubara revealed himself as the holder of the official title of assistant secretary (eastern region) of the Pan-African Federation of Filmmakers. However, he claimed to be the first African to handle a motion picture camera (reluctantly changed to "the first black African to handle the camera," after I reminded him of Algeria's Felix Mesguich, one of Louis Lumière's first cameramen to film in North Africa, around 1896). That made me consider him and his story indispensable to the African cinematic discourse. When I requested an interview, he accepted my proposal heartily. The interview took place in my room at the famous Hotel Independence in Ouagadougou. I consider Gubara's views to be among the most provocative, incisive, and candid assessments of the development of cinema in African. Offering a rare perspective with unusual courage and candor, his reflections touch upon a wide array of issues, ranging from the dissension within FEPACI and the contradictions of FESPACO to French cultural colonization, with its hegemonic policies, to the cinema's relationship (or lack thereof) to development, culture, and politics.

Gubara's interest in cinema began with his military career during World War II, when he worked with the British troops as signal officer. His job was to project films for the Sudanese infantrymen enlisted in the British Army, who were reportedly very impressed with war films. In 1950, he made *Song of Khartoum*, which, according to him, is the first color film made by a black African. The film captures the beauty of Khartoum, the capital city of Sudan, in a narrative embroidered with historical and geographic detail. That same year, he received a brief training in filmmaking in England, and in 1960 he attended the University of Southern California for training in film business.

Immediately after Sudan achieved independence in 1957, Gubara was appointed the head of the Sudanese Film Unit, which had formerly been under British colonial administration. The new government was highly interested in the use of film for public enlightenment. It was, therefore, Gubara's task to produce a fortnightly news-reel and other documentary films shot in 35mm and in black and white. During his tenure, he produced more than forty documentary films funded by the state. One of his best-known documentary films is *Independence* (1957), which chronicles the history of Sudan and shows the hoisting of the Sudanese national flag as the British surrender power to the new government. In 1984, he made a feature film called *Tajoog*, the story of an Arab community whose people are known for their resilience and tra-ditionalism. Although resources for filmmaking are almost nonexistent in his country, Gubara remains optimistic, noting that "there is a prosperous future for cinema [in Africa] in spite of everything."

You are one of the founding fathers of African cinema. Hearing from you is a pleasure, and I never expected to meet this kind of fortune in Burkina Faso. Tell me about your experiences in pioneering African cinema.

First of all, I started my career as an officer in the army as a pilot. In 1950 I went to England to acquire training in film. In 1960, I attended the University of Southern California, where I received my training in film business. When I returned to Sudan I was appointed the head of the government motion picture department. It was there that I made about forty documentary films about Sudan. I am proud to say that I am the first African cameraman. I am the first, because I started using the camera to film in 1946—exactly fifty years ago.

When you say the first African to be a cameraman, you are not including North Africans like Felix Mesguich, one of Louis Lumière's first cameramen.

No, those people are French. They are French in their blood, in thinking, and living. At that time there was no cinema in Africa. Films were made by the French, British, and Germans, so I was lucky to find work. I wanted to make a feature film in Sudan.

At that time there was no equipment to make a feature film, so I built a studio equipped with 35mm camera, a 16mm camera, sound recording, and mixing facilities. I did not establish a laboratory, because I believed it was not viable in a country where there is not much film production. I used to send my films to England for processing. I also made one feature film, which is a love story called *Tajoog*, 1984. Tajoog is the name of the most beautiful girl in the Homran ethnic group. It is one of Sudan's Arab communities that maintain their tradition.

Can you tell me about the earlier films you made?

Most of my films were documentary films about Sudan. The British colonizers were in Sudan at that time and they wanted to document their activities. They had an agricultural scheme for cultivating cotton so I made a film about that. I also made a film, called *Independence*, about the history of Sudan and the hoisting of the flag for independence. The film is set in a beautiful scenery and shows the British conceding power to Sudanese. After the release of *Independence*, films started to be made regularly in Sudan, but now we have very little industry, unlike in West Africa. West Africa advanced in film production because of French benevolence, as you know the French like to force their culture on the francophone Africans. They try to encourage francophone filmmakers to make films, but who is behind the ideas, the whole process of production? The French use francophone directors to make films that promote French influence. For example, if one makes films in the French language it is a success for France. It is true that the French underwrite francophone film production, but they are obligated because of their quest to replace African culture with French culture.

Do you see any solution to this French hegemony?

The organization of African filmmakers [FEPACI] could make decisions that would help this situation, but unfortunately we are deterred because we do not have enough money. FEPACI must create a company to distribute African films. If the films are well distributed, it is possible to make a profit to invest in the making of new films. But if there is no effective distribution, then there is no profit and the industry will stagnate. However, if we are going to create an African distribution company, then we must convince our governments to give African films a chance to be shown on African television channels. We are also considering asking for the quota system. Under this system, if we consumed a certain number of foreign films, then those foreign countries should show a certain number of our films. For example, if we show one hundred French films, France must show at least two or three African films. Otherwise their films would no longer be allowed in our countries. With these numbers, we are not advocating protectionism, but the survival of the African film industry.

Talk about film exhibition and distribution has been going on for many years and nothing has happened. What makes you optimistic?

I am optimistic now, because I think African filmmakers have begun to be serious about certain issues. We have learned a lot, but we still have this financial problem. Even our production is not controlled by Africans; it is dominated by the French. Unless we are able to sell and distribute our films, we cannot fund the production of our own films. Therefore, the problem continues. It is up to our governments to support African filmmakers' efforts to make films for Africa.

Given the economic problems in the African continent, do you think that governments will give the film industry priority?

We do not want the government to take control of our film industries, but to initiate and to give incentives to those involved with the film business. For example, I think the government should eliminate import duties on film materials and equipment. It should encourage or participate in the building of new cinema houses and the renovation of existing ones. If we have a large number of cinema theaters, it will help to distribute the films and boost cinema audiences. The government should give money to those who make good films and not spend it on decorations and awards. This happened at the 1995 FESPACO in Ouagadougou, Burkina Faso. Some of the filmmakers were decorated by the president. Honoring them is a good idea, but why not provide them with money which could be invested in new films. We are not interested in glittering medals, because they do not serve a purpose. It feels good to have one on your chest, but if the pocket is empty, the marginal filmmaker cannot afford to make films.

Without French money, most African films would not be produced today. We probably would not have FESPACO. We do know, as you rightly pointed out, that there are strings attached to all this foreign aid, including French benevolence. Can FESPACO be liberated to make it what it is supposed to be—a Pan-African affair, when French money supports it? This is a question that is especially bothering anglophone filmmakers, audiences, and critics.

About 80 percent of what the French government paid to stage FESPACO was spent on the French, rather than on Africans. For example, books and literature promoting the festival were printed and paid for in Paris. The money comes to Africa not in cash but in the form of airline tickets and hotel accommodations provided for foreigners. We do not need these millions of foreigners coming here. For example, it is almost impossible for an African to find accommodation in this hotel [Hotel Independence], where the major events of FESPACO take place. If you check, you will find that only about 20 percent of the hotel guests are Africans. The rest are tourists or guests invited by FESPACO. Why invite people to come here and then pay for their tickets and lodging? I feel that we can organize successful festivals that serve our interests if we plan them properly. We can spend wisely. Of the hundreds of people in this hotel, only a handful are cinematographers—in fact less than fifteen! The rest of the occupants are tourists who have come to have fun and have no involvement with the cinema. Although the French spend money on FESPACO, very little is spent on Africans. From time to time, the French might encourage an African to make a film, but the majority of those films are made on the platform of French identity, not on the African identity. We must make films that show we believe in ourselves, our nationality, and our aesthetic criteria. If we do not emphasize this, and we apishly remain a follower of France, England, or the United States, we will never progress.

I have always thought there is something wrong with the system. I have traveled all over the world, and have never seen where any organization invites an audience, pays their tickets, gives them free food, free accommodations, goes to the airport to collect them, and takes them to their hotels, and so on, like FESPACO does. I just cannot understand it when only a few Africans are given that kind of red-carpet treatment. How is it that foreign distributors who distribute African films and cheat African filmmakers are given all these free amenities to attend FESPACO?

Yes, it is crazy but this is the policy of colonization. It is created in spite of us and certainly not for us. It is very dangerous indeed. Most of the administrators in charge of cinema in Africa are either pro-British, pro-French, or pro-German because they have got the money and they give it to those who follow them. I understand that all these revelations might put me in a critical position, but my stance on these issues is in the interest of Africa and her cinema.

Although Africans like to see foreign films, they also like to see films made by, for, and about them. But as you know, the film industry is called film industry and art, not art and industry. Industry is first because to make a film you must have money. If you want to create a play, you do not need a large sum of money, because people can get together and stage a play outside, where it costs nothing. But to make a film you must have money for the cameraman, actors, raw film stock, a laboratory, the soundman, etc. The foreigners who support African cinema have the cash, but they use it to stifle the growth of Africa's film industry in order to ensure lack of competition from African filmmakers.

When Italy started to make good films, the Americans brought all the good directors and actors like Fellini, Sophia Loren, and others to the United States and gave them contracts. It is because they wanted to kill the Italian industry. Now the French are doing the same to Africa. If a new talent emerges, he or she is likely to be lured to France and to possibly be indoctrinated. The filmmaker is offered a position and funds so he can work under their supervision. This is one way of killing the African film industry. But I am sure if we stand together and if we understand and trust ourselves and our ability, we can make good films. This aspiration cannot be fulfilled, however, if we do not have a distribution company, and if we do not acquire dubbing studios for our films.

Here at FESPACO there are several books about African cinema on display: *Cinema in Africa, Cinema in Sudan, Cinema in Algeria,* etc. They are very expensive to produce, but how many Africans read these books? We want to make films, Algerian films, Sudanese films, films to bring Africans together. That would be better than these books. Most of these books were printed in France and America, so the money goes back to their foreign publishers. The cinema is a big mafia, and it is not easy to penetrate this network unless we rethink how we do things, try to make films with our own means, distribute them, and prevent the importing of foreign films. If we import, we must impose a custom duty of no less than 50 percent on the box-office income on foreign films to be put in a special account to be spent on African filmmaking.

French funds support francophone filmmaking, and in most cases they also supply the technicians. If one looks at the films screened at this festival [1995] critically, one discovers that the few good ones we have are very good and the bad ones are very bad. It is pitiful how much camera work has deteriorated from the pioneering stage of African cinema.

We are seeing African films made by the French. In this festival, I have seen the French film *50 Years of the French Occupation* or something with ambiguous content. What did they show? They showed hospitals, French doctors, and services they gave to Africans, but what they have taken from us was not shown. They forced our soldiers to fight for them in two world wars. They made us slaves to work in their industries. We have paid more than we have received. They pretend to have saved us, loved us, and liked us, because they want to make use of us. They succeeded. The purpose of this film is to make the people who saw the film believe that the French are good people. The French may argue that they helped in the development of African countries. But it is not development, they are more concerned for their well-being, the sustenance of hegemony, by milking Africa dry. However, I hope things will be better in the future, because the African has begun to wake up. There is movement toward the improvement of African lives, and the younger generation is beginning to reinforce this inclination. A day will come when we realize a lasting progress providing we, as elders, try to open our minds to new understandings to emerge before it is too late.

This kind of criticism is in the interest of Africa—not only of African cinema, but of African people. FESPACO reveals a dichotomy between the anglophone and the francophone. For instance, the francophone complain that the festival is too French; even at important meetings the movies are not subtitled, nor do they provide interpreters. In fact, some of the anglophone people I have talked to have said that they are not going to go see the films anymore. Why see a film they cannot understand?

Yes, I told you once, the French did not want the anglophone to get involved with FESPACO, but they forced themselves in anyway. When we started FEPACI, Lionel

Ngakane, of South Africa, who was then living in exile, and I were the first members from English-speaking African countries. Now there are eleven members, including Kenya, Sudan, Ethiopia, Uganda, Zimbabwe, Namibia, Nigeria, and Ghana. Eleven is a great improvement, and it will only get better when South Africa joins the group. South Africa is a very strong country now, especially in cinema; it is more advanced than any other English-speaking country. It is understandable why France would like to control the affairs of FESPACO. From the planning stages, they co-opted for the French language, French culture, French understanding, how to eat French, to drink beer the French way, maybe even to make love the French way, to be French. With the relationship between the British and the anglophone, we find the opposite.

The British wanted the anglophone to be perpetual slaves, but the French wanted their African subjects to be French and forget about their identity. Even the hotels, the Silimande in Burkina Faso, for example, is owned by a French company. Even after independence they still want Africans to act French. They want African men and women to become loose so as to obliterate their identity and honor. They want Africans to keep looking to France as a role model through the media—films, radio, television, education, etc. I see the cinema as a dangerous medium to drive Africans into cultural, political, and economic oblivion. I say dangerous because it is not necessary to know how to read or write to understand the film language. Film images have the power to mislead. If the only images shown are French, then eventually you will forget your identity and begin to adopt French ways. North Africa is a typical example. Many of its people now hate the Islamic movement because France has convinced them that the movement is very dangerous, fundamentalist, and must be destroyed. The Islamic movement said that the French are dangerous, and that they did not want them. France contends it is fighting the Islamic movement not because it hates Muslims but the Islamic movement itself. Now it seems that the North Africans have discovered their mistake, which is their adoption of the French culture instead of maintaining their own identity. North Africans speak French better than Arabic or any other language, and that is what the French like. Look at the books exhibited here in FESPACO, they are all in French. Nothing is written in a Burkina or any other African language. We must open our eyes and develop a means of resistance.

Do you think French will continue to dominate African culture, politics . . . ?

I will tell you why I think that today we are better off than yesterday. Now we can express our own views and say what we want concerning our problems. For example, today in FESPACO we had a discussion about the dubbing of African films. We realize the marginal status of our films, caused by the problem of distribution and exhibition. Even our films made in English cannot be freely shown in the United States because of the monopoly of the American film industry by Hollywood. Where else can we show our films? The Arab market is bigger than any other market in the world, however, the Indians are also monopolizing the film market in those countries. Why should Indian films prosper at the expense of indigenous African films? If the problem is how to communicate with diverse ethnic groups, why not have subtitles in Arabic, English, or French? About 95 percent of the films are in French, which means that we are cheating ourselves if we embark upon dubbing. In essence we would be dubbing to our own languages. It makes more sense to make films in a native African language and then dub to a foreign language.

In a recent interview in one of the Nigerian dailies a FESPACO official stated that nothing could make FESPACO move from Ouagadougou to any other African capital, because FESPACO is the Pan-African Festival of Film and Television of Ougadougou. This official used the Cannes Film Festival and other stationary festivals as an argument for why FESPACO should remain permanently in Ouagadougou. Do you think FESPACO should remain permanently in Ouagadougou?

I think FESPACO should be moved to another country every four years. Once you take the initiative to host one festival then it becomes easier to coordinate a second one. By that time, you have learned to raise money not only for the festival but also for the improvement of theaters and accommodations for guests. Before the war there used to be a festival in Mogadishu, Somalia. Because it is a Pan-African affair, it makes sense to rotate the hosting of FESPACO. It would be progressive to allow other African countries to experience this festival. If we were to have one in Kenya, it would give the anglophone countries the incentive to get more English-speaking people involved. The French will not agree to this, of course, but it is up to us to debate the issue in FEPACI meetings. I believe that we shall succeed, but let us not forget our financial impediment. Film festivals can be held anywhere, even on the moon, providing you have the appropriate funds. France is willing to pay any amount to keep this festival in Ouagadougou. That is detrimental to FEPACI's aspirations and for those filmmakers who support intrastate rotation of the festival. If FEPACI decides to move FESPACO, then it must be moved. But the French people do not want FEPACI members to be overcome by English-speaking members. If you advertise a festival in Ethiopia and provide money for telexes, tickets, food, and other subsidies, as is done in Ouagadougou, people will come. If I were to receive a free ticket to attend a film festival in Ethiopia I would go, even if there were only five or six cinemas there. As long as there was a market and an opportunity to promote my films I would go. Without money, African cinema cannot be promoted. Right now, France has got the money and the will, and the French are very anxious to expand their culture.

But FESPACO also gets money from other European countries . . .

The European Union does not know what is going on. France is the strongest force behind FESPACO, as it is its largest sponsor. France encourages Europe and other countries to participate. For example, France invites participants from Belgium and

Holland, filmmakers from Brazil, etc. Why wouldn't these people attend FESPACO when every amenity is made available to them?

What do you think of the quality of African films shown in FESPACO 1995?

Terrible! Not good from any point of view. Except for those films done in cooperation with France, the films are poorly photographed and edited and lack coherent narrative structures. With the former, there is an appreciable standard and quality, in most cases because of the work of French cameramen. African filmmakers must devote more effort to making films that the audience can relate to on an emotional level. A few years ago, *Heritage ... Africa*, a film by Ghanaian Kwaw Ansah was released, and it is one of the best films I have ever seen. However, films of this caliber are the exception rather than the norm.

That raises another question concerning the criteria FESPACO uses to award prizes to films.

These prizes are just like any other film festival prizes. For example, in the United States there is the Oscar. Critics have argued that the prizes are rarely given to the deserving film. These prizes may be awarded based upon political and ideological factors, similar to a mafia organization. If the political agenda of the director conflicts with that of the establishment, he could be deprived of an award. This also applies to FESPACO in Burkina Faso. In any of FESPACO's categories, the awarding of prizes depends on the mafia—the people who select the winning films. These films are chosen because of unethical political forces rather than the quality of their directing or photography.

Let us turn away from FESPACO for a moment and turn to Sudan, film and development, the situation of filmmaking in Africa today.

Let me broaden the topic. I was in Iran about a month ago. Iran has a very good high-tech film industry. They make about seventy quality films a year based on the Islamic faith. I am part of a group trying to form an Islamic Film Federation for the Muslim countries. The purpose of this organization is to make films that will address issues affecting not only Muslims but all peoples. Topics include the indictment of alcoholism and other evils. Hopefully more countries will support this federation. The organization now has a mandate. Some of the culturally oriented films made by Iranians have won prizes at the Berlin and Cannes film festivals. The Chinese are also making entertainment films that address their cultures and societies. Also, the Indians are making entertaining comedy films that are penetrating Africa constantly. This is very dangerous because there aren't any African issues emphasized in these films. The irony is that Africans are indoctrinated because they want to be entertained and the Indians have succeeded in this venture.

Again we have come back to a problem whose cause is the lack of a system of distri-bution. Heritage . . . Africa *has not been seen in Nigeria, Sudan, and many other African countries. African actors and actresses aren't known by the African audience. How do we cultivate an African film culture when we do not have enough films and don't even know who played in the films already in existence?*

Yes, it is a continuous cycle. We must start, first of all, by making quality films and finding the money to support production. America, Italy, Germany, and France have a long history of filmmaking. They have built a star system. It is not surprising that people will go see a film simply because the French actor Alain Delon is in it. The French film industry invested large amounts of time and money to create Alain Delon. The American film industry did the same with Marilyn Monroe. My experi-ence studying in the United States proved to me that cinema is a big industry which creates star actors and actresses. We have good actors in Africa, but nobody knows them because they are not promoted, as in America. There are no newspaper articles or television interviews about them; nothing. It is amazing to find pictures of foreign film stars in FEPACI books, when there are no pictures of African actors and actresses. I have not seen a picture of well-known actresses from Burkina, Cameroon, or Ghana. In my opinion, Africans must do more to promote our own.

When cinema started in Africa, the pioneers were not interested in using professional actors. They wanted people to play themselves and portray their experiences in realis-tic ways. Are you in favor of developing a star system for Africa?

Yes, definitely, because cinema is show business. Making realistic films is good, but the use of professional dancers, singers, and actors will make the film more effective. We must definitely develop the star system in Africa. In India, they have the star sys-tem. Many Indian actors and actresses have achieved international fame. In Africa, there are many talented actors, musicians, dancers, and griots. It is up to us to utilize these talents in the development of African cinema. Although they may not possess experience in film acting, their other talents can carry them to the top of the film industry. Even though she was the prime minister of England, when Margaret Thatcher appeared on television for the first time, the experts told her how to do her hair, what to wear, and how to act in front of the camera. The same is true of other world leaders such as Bill Clinton, Richard Nixon, and even Ronald Reagan, who is an actor. To pose for the camera is a very difficult task. Not everybody can act, but if you can appear photogenic, then the viewing audience will accept you.

Under the star system, a story is usually perceived from an individual standpoint as opposed to Africa, where even if a film is centered on an individual character the story is considered a representation of society as a whole. Isn't this collective stance the one favored by the pioneers of African cinema, including you?

I do not think so. As I said, the cinema is a show business created to fulfill certain functions. If a film was being made about farmers and there was a question of whether to use a professional actor or an actual farmer, then I would use the professional actor. Although using a real farmer would give a realistic quality to the film, a professional actor would be a better choice because of him having been trained to be at ease in front of the camera. Why do we add music to the film? Because we want to create a mood, make a statement, and enhance the impact of the film. The use of professional actors can aid in reaching a wider audience. If I want to make a film to be distributed in the United States, England, or any other country, it would be recommended to use a professional actor. A qualified actor knows the job and can be part of the creative team that will enable the film to be successful. A good director is also essential. It is the director who tells the actor which emotions each scene is supposed to evoke in the audience and how to achieve it. In Africa, there are a few talented directors. Others pass themselves off as good directors, but in actuality they are more like shadows of French directors and technicians. The French and other foreign directors want to assert enormous control over African directors. It is becoming more and more difficult to find independent directors, not even Ousmane Sembene himself is truly independent. If Sembene fails to find the necessary support (usually from France), he cannot make films. Most of his films are made using French technicians. In my opinion, Ousmane Sembene is an ordinary individual but he has been overly publicized by the French and other foreign presses where he is considered an icon and the greatest African filmmaker; this is a great myth.

It is possible with time to transform a neophyte to a professional great actor of high caliber. As we say in Africa, "Practice makes perfect." What makes American films the best in the world is the amount of work done behind the scenes polishing the acting. And if you have money after the film is made it is widely advertised to appeal to the audience. But in the African film industry, the name Ousmane Sembene generates excitement. Who is Ousmane Sembene? He is just like any other person, but the press has idolized him so much that he has become what they want him to be, the dominant figure in African cinema. The thing that separates him from other directors is that he follows a trend approved by his sponsors. For any other aspiring filmmaker not to follow this trend means relinquishing his or her authority to another subservient filmmaker.

Let me just add that Ousmane Sembene is a rebel even to his French financiers. While working on his films, he has respected his African identity and incorporated political messages, unapproved by the French, into his films. What is your comment regarding film and politics? Do you think that film and politics should be interwoven?

All films are political. They all proffer certain kinds of ideology; they carry messages from diverse viewpoints, about life experiences. A film about the history of Sudan carries with it a message, but it may be portrayed in various ways. Any film carries a message, political or not; it is left up to the filmmaker to decide which method to use.

What do you think of the new generation of African filmmakers?

I believe that 90 percent of the African directors now are still under the pressure of the French, whether they like it or not. Even now you cannot make a film without going to France to process it, develop it, and do the sound mixing. It means you cannot get away from France. You cannot make a film as an individual without relying, in part, on France. The irony is that there is no longer a French empire, but there are cultural institutions of the government of France specializing in hegemony. There are qualified intellectual Africans who go to work in France, and they know how to play without compromising the Africanity of their films. The cinematheque opened yesterday in Ouagadougou by the French was created, by all indications, to preserve the films made by the French. This film library, paid for by the French people, was opened by the French Ministry of Culture. One of the primary concerns is to preserve their films, so even if Africans make new films the old French films will always remain there to teach us how great France is. I have seen the list of films in the archives and most of them are the old African films with French actors and actresses processed in Parisian laboratories. These are their films. When the archives were opened by the French we all celebrated. It is sad because in reality it is not ours; it is pure manipulation. This revelation might mean that I won't be allowed into France anymore.

Have you ever thought of having a retrospective of your films? Until you talked to me today, I did not know that you had made forty documentaries in addition to your feature films. How many feature films have you made?

I made my first films for the British, because at that time I was ignorant about the philosophy of the British. The films made by the British were to portray their greatness. But after I made about ten to twenty films I began to realize I should make films focusing on the Sudanese experience. The first of these films were documentaries. Documentary films are very educational. They carry important messages if they are well done, especially if the sight and sound are well integrated. The new government of Sudan is now trying to make documentary films. The country is more than a million square miles—the size of England, France, Italy, Portugal, and Germany combined. Yet it only has twenty-six million inhabitants, hence the government wants to use the documentaries to bring the Sudanese together and to show exactly what is available in different areas of the country. There are people working in industries, agricultural sectors, civil service, and all walks of life. With the documentary, the government wants to be able to show the various societal contributions that allow Sudan to be self-sufficient.

I stress self-sufficiency because America did not give us a chance to import anything for the last five years. They blocked every channel available because American policy makers labeled Sudan a terrorist nation. The fact is, today we don't need American aid to survive. They sent us a big boat full of wheat, for at that time, the Western newspapers reported there was a huge famine in Sudan. Our government rejected this offer not because we did not need it but because government officials wanted the people to cultivate their own food. Sudan has enough land and enough water. The credo was and still is, "If you want to eat, produce your own. If not, die of hunger." Now we have an abundance of wheat and sugar. We even have enough to export to Arab countries, because we learned to depend on ourselves. That could be true in cinema as well. We must depend on ourselves and our ability to make good films.

Video production is proliferating in Africa, especially in the anglophone. Is this a positive trend?

Yes, video production is just a trend that will dissolve in a short time. There is a prosperous future for cinema in spite of everything. There are still people who like to take their families out to the cinema at least once a week or twice a month. The future lies in the cinema but unfortunately favors big productions. People would rather go to a theater than stay home to see films like *Gandhi* and other blockbuster films. The cinema not only offers entertainment, but it also provides viewers an opportunity to interact with fellow moviegoers. I still maintain that the cinema is the future. The film I made in 1946, during the struggle for independence of Sudan, is still shown on Sudanese television. If I had shot it in video, it would have probably been destroyed by now. It was filmed in black-and-white 35mm, and we made a print that is still in good condition. For posterity, film is the right medium. Television is good but may not be ideal for preserving important works. A good film can be shown anywhere in the world where there is an audience. Furthermore, the cinema will turn actors and actresses into stars. There are many well-known television actors and actresses, but they have no international fame like their big-screen counterparts. Those famous actors who appeared on television ten years ago have now vanished due either to lost or disintegrated videotape or a lack of interest by the contemporary audience. Africans must build more cinema theaters because that is what helps to maintain a viable film industry. In Iran, they have more than 150 cinema houses. The industry is progressing because they have a loyal audience who make it possible to recuperate money invested in production, which in turn is invested in the making of new films.

You are right! We cannot talk about a viable film industry without considering the role of the audience and reception. I do not know about the situation in Sudan, but here, in Ouagadougou, on Channel 4 you receive CNN. If you press 6, you receive a French television station. In Ghana and Nigeria, there is MNET, an affiliated foreign cable company that transmits BBC, CNN, BPOW, SKY TV, MTV programming. We talk about African film and distribution, yet satellite broadcasts are another form of competition to African cinema.

The government in Sudan does not allow private individuals to own satellite dishes, although there are still discussions going on about this topic. But the government has satellite dishes, and they select programs that are suitable for Sudan. They show about two hours of programs, relevant segments of world news and documentaries, from satellite dishes each day. The government is very strict about broadcasting foreign programs. Before I left for FESPACO, they were debating whether to ban satellite dishes altogether. Until we are able to improve our own television and film industry, we must try to continue to prevent an influx of foreign ideas or programs that are of no benefit to our people. The Arabs now have their own satellite called ArabSat. They try to make programs in the Arabic language that can compete with any other program. We are very happy about this.

Do you know any other African country that has taken such an initiative as Sudan did in combating this cultural colonialism aided by satellite dishes?

Yes, I think Egypt began to take action, because they also have good programs. The emirate has Arabic programs broadcast from eight to nine hours daily. If I could receive, for example, a Burkina television program, I would prefer watching it instead of the French or British programming which may not emphasize Africa and her people. The problem is that the French already taught former colonies to embrace the French language and culture. It is not like in Sudan, where very few speak English. In the francophone countries, they speak and act French. They are West African people but they follow the trends of the West. They are followers of the French ideology which their presidents and policy makers emulate. I know that speaking the truth can be dangerous. The relation of the francophone with the West is an African problem, and my thoughts reflect the African tradition of speaking the truth.

What is your plan for the future? Do you still plan to make more films and continue to express your opinions through the film medium?

I am planning to make a film about Elmhadi. Elmhadi is the great man who created the new Sudan. He is well-known in Sudanese history. Gordon of England was killed by Elmhadi. Later, Elmhadi was killed by the British who came back to wage war against Sudan. The film is not only about this hero but also about a big event in history when in one hour he and his army destroyed the invaders, who consisted of sixty thousand well-equipped soldiers. Now it is our duty to try to make films about our people to remind the younger generation how the sacrifices of their grandfathers made our nation great. If we show how France came to occupy this country we must also provide them with the knowledge of the people who fought against them in the struggle for freedom. If this is accurately depicted it will create a new awareness in the young generation, who will understand how their country evolved and will be able to take pride in it. My plan is to remind my countrymen that we are a great people. The Americans tried to attack Sudan, but when they read the history of Sudan and saw we were good fighters, they withdrew. They knew that if they came they would be destroyed under any circumstances unless they used nuclear weapons. To make a film of this kind will illustrate the untiring efforts or our departed leaders—how they stood strong to build Sudan.

Filmography

Song of Khartoum, 1950
Independence, 1957
Tajoog, 1984

Med Hondo (Mauritania)

Med Hondo (whose full name is Mohamed Abid Hondo) is one of Africa's most prolific filmmakers. He is also considered a pioneer, not because of his age, but because he started his filmmaking career in the 1960s, the decade marking the birth of African cinema. He was born to a Senegalese father and a Mauritanian mother in the village of Ain Ouled Beni Mathar, in the Atar region of Mauritania. From 1954 to 1958, the young Med lived in Rabat, Morocco, where he pursued training at a hotel management school. After graduation, he emigrated to France in 1958, hoping to find a well-paying job as a chef. But in France he discovered that he and the other North African Arab and black African immigrants were not welcome and that a college diploma did not guarantee any of them jobs in their respective disciplines. To survive, Hondo worked at many menial jobs in Marseilles and in Paris, always paid less than his French counterparts. During this period, he also explored other avenues. He took drama courses and studied under the well-known French stage and screen actress Françoise Rosay. His ultimate goal was to use theater acting and stage directing to publicize black theatrical performers in France, who, according to him, had no place in mainstream French theater because of racism and discrimination.

In 1966, Hondo established his own theater group called Shango, named after the Yoruba god of thunder. The group performed in cultural centers and small theaters but fell short of achieving the goal of using this brand of alternative theater to win French audiences. This tradition would later be used to promote the works of playwrights of the Black Diaspora, including Aimé Césaire of Martinique, African American playwrights such as Imamu Baraka, and other African and South American playwrights. But to Hondo's great surprise, the French were not receptive to black-oriented alternative theater. He discovered that black theater was marginalized in the same manner that blacks are marginalized in other sectors of the French economy. However, Hondo later found himself playing minor roles on French TV series and in such films as *Un homme de trop* (Shock troops, 1967), directed by Costa-Gavras; *A Walk with Love and Death* (1969), directed by John Huston; and *Tante Zita* (1968), directed by Robert Enrico. Having been initiated into films, Hondo was determined to acquire more skills; he worked his way up and eventually served as an assistant director on various film sets. This was how he learned to make films. Although he had no formal training in filmmaking, Hondo has distinguished himself as a creative filmmaker with an unusual talent. He has won many awards and has demonstrated through his works that he is one of the best film directors Africa and the world have produced. What he could not accomplish fully through the theater, Hondo finds in filmmaking—self-expression and the ability to say the things he wants to say in an unrestricted manner. Thus, in all his films, Hondo explores the predicament of African peoples, using a combative, innovative style coupled with theoretical conviction.

Hondo's personal experience of the subjugation and displacement faced by Arab and black African migrant workers in France has been the propelling force behind his filmic approach. His style of capturing those images is, he contends, a reflection of his anger—his reaction to the societal injustices that have rendered a group of people humiliated and helpless, injustices that he would like to see abolished. Similarly, his pointed attacks on the perpetrators of such injustices and his sharp criticism of French imperialism and African leaders have accorded him in some circles the status of a radical, a stigma that has not helped him in his efforts to distribute and exhibit his films, both in France and in Africa. In this interview, this ebullient director talks candidly about the development and underdevelopment of Africa and African cinema. He deals with issues ranging from African leaders, who, according to Hondo, refuse to understand the importance of cinema as an integral component of development, to African filmmakers, who, he says, must avoid mimicking retrogressive alien conventions. Hondo is an advocate of Pan-African structures in cinema. He rejects the conventions of commercial Western cinema and other escapist films, arguing for an African alternative film language that he sees as deriving from African culture and patterns of oral tradition. At the 1987 FESPACO, Hondo's epic film *Sarraounia* won the festival's grand prize, the Étalon de Yennega.

I would like to thank John Williams for his help with the first part of this interview, which was conducted during an African film series that Jim Kitses and I coordinated at San Francisco State University, April 27–30, 1990.

Most feature films made in Africa, except those made in Nigeria, that have made it to the Western film festivals are coproductions financed primarily by foreign sources. How do you perceive the problem of financing in African film production?

The financing of African cinema depends on the politics, leaders, economic and social development of each country in Africa, and reflects the contradictions of the politics in Africa. Africa is not united or fully developed. Although African countries are now independent, foreign countries still control the international commerce and monetary systems of African countries. This situation is helped and accepted by the majority of African leaders.

Our presidents and ministers do not pay adequate attention to our culture or cinema. African leaders are apprehensive about supporting the motion picture industry because they are afraid that cinema would be used by filmmakers to manipulate political situations. Filmmakers have to deal with this fear and decide to be with or against the government. Of course, contradictions also exist among filmmakers. Africa's filmmakers do not all have the same education, will, courage, or dignity. Some African filmmakers make films just to be rich. They want to raise money to have a very good life and to be a part of the so-called bourgeoisie. The real bourgeoisie, however, do not exist in Africa. Western European countries, such as France, subsidize African films for economic and political reasons. They give money to influence filmmakers and have the postproduction of the films done in Paris. Ninety-nine percent of African films are processed in the laboratories in Paris, which helps the economy of France. In Africa, we have no economic, technical, or distribution structures. Those are the contradictions that surround the filmmaking industry and the problem that filmmakers are trying to resolve.

I always try to express in my films my vision of the world as an African and my dignity as a human being and an African. Like any other filmmaker, I have to go to France, Germany, England, or Africa to raise money. I am in the same swimming pool as other African filmmakers, but I do not allow the people providing the funds to interfere with my projects or the profound meanings in my films. Prohibiting the interference is very difficult—very, very difficult to accomplish.

I will return to the revolutionary aspects of your films, but, first, what are other problems faced by Africans trying to raise money to make their films? What kinds of ordeals do they endure?

Africa is not independent. Africa does not create what it wants and what the African people need—clothes, food, culture, and education. Everything is imposed on us from the outside and through the collaboration of some insiders—traitors who do not think about their own people. These traitors do not think about the past, present, or the future. They do not think about how to feed the peasants or how Africa could advance politically, economically, and culturally as other civilized or developed societies. This type of treachery is further demonstrated by how these African cohorts have formed the habit of siphoning billions and billions of dollars from their countries. This money was stolen from their own people and could have been used for genuine developments in Africa. These traitors do not believe in Africa. They are there just to make money. If the situation demands their forced removal from positions of power, they do not care, for they have amassed enough wealth to live comfortably in exile with their families. The main reason why African filmmakers have to turn to foreigners to raise money is that African countries have no film funding structure, no general policy on culture, and no specific policy on cinema. There are different reactions to this situation from filmmakers. Some filmmakers treat our culture like folklore to please Westerners. They are dishonest, because they debase African cultures to satisfy the fantasies of the Westerners. These filmmakers also could be regarded as traitors. I am not casting judgment on anybody; rather, I prefer to talk about the common situation that prevails. As you know, the socioeconomic situation creates a culture, and culture by itself is dynamic. If culture is not dynamic, as Frantz Fanon, Amilcar Cabral, and others have pointed out, but is popularized, folklorizing it is also a treasonable felony that has been committed against the people.

In the 1980s, Africa witnessed its worst economic predicament as almost every African country was mortgaged to the International Monetary Fund. For instance, in 1985, the exchange rate for the Ghanaian cedis was 2.75 to one U.S. dollar, but, in 1997 rose to 1,850 cedis per dollar. Given this situation, it is almost impossible to imagine how anybody would try to make a film in Ghana. Ghana, however, actually increased its feature film production in the 1980s, mostly through coproduction and production on video. Does this mean that only coproduction will save African cinema?

For twenty years, we tried to prove that coproduction among African countries is the most important thing for African cinema. The way to save Africa's cinema is to promote coproductions among several countries and to distribute the films in several countries. This is not solely for the purpose of recuperating production costs but also to improve the education of people. As you know, many African people do not know much about their neighboring countries. For example, there is a border between Ghana and Burkina Faso. This artificial boundary makes people not to realize that at the other side of the borders are their own people. Film is an integral arm of development. Even thieves in Africa steal to raise money to go to the cinema. African filmmakers have been saying for more than twenty years that, if one produces a film in Mauritania, for example, making any profit from such a small and disorganized market is not possible. The most important thing now is to design a system of change by involving the collective, filmmaker, and government.

Sometimes our governments do not even understand where their interests lie. When a foreigner comes from outside and provides an African government with a lot of money to make films about its country, the government accepts the money not knowing the subject of the film. Too often, the subject matter insults the recipient country. But this kind of domination, as in the example you gave about Ghana, is the same in my country. The Mauritanian national currency, the ouguiya, is valueless in the international monetary market. It faces constant devaluation, dropping in value daily. How can Africa survive if it cannot create and protect its own production independently as it sees fit? It is a pity that African societies are disorganized and that African cinema is following the same path.

Foreign funding and coproduction provide for the exposure of African films in Asia, Europe, and the United States, through metropolitan cinematheques, international film festivals, or television (as in Europe). However, many African films do not make it to the international circles for exhibition because they were not coproduced by the powers who dictate which films will be shown internationally. Another problem is that there are no outside sources to help advertise the films. Do you know of significant films that are not known abroad because of this problem? And how serious is this problem in terms of repressing significant African films?

This happens in Europe, and I think in America as well. For your film to be distributed you must find some producer who will agree to invest in your film. We must see the issues in concrete terms and understand that cinema is like buying seats. You have to occupy the space available—monopolize it, for when you occupy the seats with your film, this means that those seats are not available to any other films. Also, if you do not have powerful promoters who understand the business of film, your film could very well rest forever in the closet. In general, that is the situation in Europe, the U.S., and, I think, all over the world.

I experienced the same problem with *Sarraounia*. But our efforts were also thwarted by other contradictions, too. For example, African filmmakers will often encounter dishonest people claiming to be distributors. When they come to negotiate, they say, "Give me your film for free. I will distribute it and make a lot of money for you." But the profits never materialize! The enemies in your own society are often your worst exploiters.

The first time *Soleil O* was screened in the U.S., as you know, it won a lot of prizes. New Yorker Films approached me and offered to distribute the film. At that time I knew nothing about distribution, so I went to talk to Ousmane Sembene, who said he knew Don Talbot and that he considered him an honest man. He added that whenever Mr. Talbot acquired his films, he was always paid. Since New Yorker Films distributes all of Sembene's films, I did not hesitate to sign a contract with the company, allowing it to acquire *Soleil O*. But I have not received from them one red cent, ever. They also tried to sell the film to the Canadians without my knowledge. By chance I caught them before the contract was signed, because someone I knew told me that my film was going to be shown on Canadian TV. I was shocked; no organization in Canada had been given the rights to distribute the film. Upon further inquiry, I was told that it was Don Talbot of New Yorker Films who authorized the screening of *Soleil O* in Canada. When I called him up for explanation, he told me that it was a mistake made by his secretary! That was my first experience, and it was a bad one.

Then I met Angela Davis, who named many places where the film has been shown. Larry Clark and many other people, including Spike Lee, told me they had seen *Soleil O*, commenting on how good a film it is. My response to them all was, "Thank you, but I have received no payment for these showings, not even a penny." If someone were to approach me today about putting my film on the market in the

United States via film festivals, special screenings, etc., my reply will be, "Good, but for how much?"

Most often, however, what I hear from such exhibitors is that they are operating a nonprofit organization and, therefore, have a limited budget. This is funny, because when I was making the films none of them provided Med Hondo with any funds. I depend on my salary to produce my films. And today my whole life is inundated with debts. It is a situation of poverty and misery. But I am not complaining; I am only trying to explain a situation. Nor am I asking for charity or for someone to bail me out. If someone wants to coproduce with African filmmakers, we are ready to work with them in a normal system, one in which we create the subject and have the power to make the final cut. The final cut should remain the filmmaker's decision and not the producer's. Our desire is simply to construct images that reflect our consciousness, our struggles. But we are open to coproduction, and we hope to find coproducers to work with, as well as people who are willing to distribute our films in the normal way. I am sure that for these films there is an audience. The public exists.

This claim is substantiated with my experience in Washington, D.C., Philadelphia, Atlanta, and Chicago, where people filled the theaters to see my film. After the screenings the majority of them—black and white—would stay for discussion, which sometimes extended indefinitely. They wanted to speak about the images, the issues they provoke. I was amazed—people would approach me, captivated. I mean, the public exists. On some other occasions admirers have put money into my pocket or presented me with some gifts like we do in Africa. They would tell me, "Keep this. It is a token of love. How can we help? What can we do?" They were deeply touched by the film.

What film was this?

Sarraounia. The screenings of this film and my other films convinced me that the audiences exist everywhere for African films. But for me, to work with someone, the person must act in his own interests, not just to help African cinema. I do not like that word, *help.*

Because it is paternalistic?

I need people to work with, and this is different from needing help. To coproduce for each person's interest—his interest and mine—is the only way to help our people, and for that person to help with his money. But these kinds of people, though I am sure they exist, are very hard to find.

What were the funding problems and lessons you learned with Sarraounia?

It took me seven years to raise money and to shoot *Sarraounia.* I began with a contract between Niger and my production company. Together with Abdoulaye Mamani—the author of *Sarraounia*, the novel we adapted to film—I spoke with the government representatives, and this led to the signing of a contract involving coproduction between Mauritania, Niger, and myself. When we were to begin shooting, however, we ran into many bureaucratic problems having to do with the military, politicians, and various ideologues, who stopped us from shooting the film. I was told that the authorities did not want the film shot in the country. Even today, I do not know why I was prevented from shooting the film in Niger. My lawyer, who is himself an African, tried to resolve the problem in an African way. He explained to the authorities that I had already labored many years on this film. He asked a lot of questions to find out if I had done anything that infuriated the government or the community as a whole. The answer was no. What then was the problem? We wanted to understand their points of view. Still nothing happened. I tried to meet with the former president, who is now dead, to ask him to intervene. Still nothing happened. One day, during FESPACO, I had the opportunity of being invited to the State House for a drink by the head of state, Captain Thomas Sankara of Burkina Faso. I had known this charismatic man from the time when he was the secretary of state for culture. I had some drinks with him and we talked. As usual, he liked to talk. He told me that he had heard about the problems I was having with our "brothers on the other side"—referring to Niger. "Yes," I said to him, "I have problems with them but I can't explain them since I do not know what they are." I was elated when he said to me, "As you know, we have no money to offer you, but you can shoot the film here in Burkina Faso." Upon hearing that, I felt like God had descended upon me, upon Africa. So, when I left FESPACO, I went to raise the money I lost from the botched Niger partnership. The Burkinabe minister of information wrote letters to the minister of culture and foreign affairs in France, and together they tried to raise money for this film.

At one point, the Centre National du Cinéma [CNC] in France tried to stop me from making the film. They demanded that, before shooting commenced, I raise an additional one million francs to increase the film's budget. I protested. My budget was three million francs and I told them that I did not need to add another one million francs to make the film. The authorities at the CNC insisted that I must raise the extra one million francs before I could begin. I went back to the savior who had redeemed me before, Captain Sankara, and requested immediate intervention. He did just that! A loan was hurriedly arranged through the Ministry of Finance because, in his view, this film must be made. Despite all the conflicts and problems, I shot the film. It was at this point that I realized that it is still difficult to operate effectively even in one's own cultural backyard.

The problems did not end there! When the film was completed and ready to be released, I found a distributor in France who paid some money up front to distribute the film. In the contract we signed, it was stipulated that the film was to open in fourteen theaters. The first day of its premiere, I noticed the film was showing in only five theaters, and I began to worry. After two weeks, they threw out the film. The distributors economically censored it. I got a lawyer to look into the case, but the film was already assassinated, practically speaking, in France. However, the film was shown in six countries in Africa with much success, and in London. But with these limited showings, I did not recover the money invested into the film. Out of my fifty million CFA debt to Burkina Faso, I paid back only ten million. I have, even today, forty million CFA left to pay for that loan. That is my experience making and distributing *Sarrounia*.

You have to understand that the French, generally speaking, hate Africans, and they do not want people to talk about colonialism and neocolonialism. They censor people who talk about the atrocities they committed, their brutality during the decades of colonization. As you know, there are very few films made by France on Vietnam, Algeria, or other African countries it colonized for the same reasons. They officially censor dissenting views. In the brochure I gave you, there is a protest statement signed by many French filmmakers and critics who agreed it was scandalous the way *Sarraounia* was censored in France. Constantin Costa-Gavras and many other influential people who signed this document did so because they believed that *Sarraounia* is an incredibly important film. They contended that it was a scandal that this film was censored, and as a protest, Bertrand led a group of sympathizers who wanted to organize a special public showing of the film to give other critics an opportunity to sign the protest note. But the CNC refused to release the film, stating that there were a lot of problems with the film which needed to be resolved before it could be released for general viewing. Even within the CNC, not every member accepted that excuse. As one of them put it, "I thought I knew my country, but the way they are handling this film is unbelievable!" This individual asked me if I had violated the rules of the CNC. I told him I had done nothing wrong.

I think that all of these disappointments are normal. They remind us about the need to focus on national and continental problems in Africa. Until we implement certain demands relevant to our development, the situation will not change. If the situation does not change, the future filmmaker in the belly of his mother is going to face similar problems. This is the African reality we face and must address.

Your films deal with important themes concerning the experiences of the Black Diaspora, but each film uses a different style to address the issues. You are relentless in your artistic endeavor, and because of your combative style, you have been called a Marxist, revolutionary filmmaker. Yet your films are partly funded through foreign sources, sometimes through the "establishment," the perpetrators of imperialism that your films attack. How do you retain your integrity without allowing your funding sources to dictate what you do?

It is consciousness. The more liberal the French people are, the more I have to be radical. Their systems continue to work against Africans, history, and humanity, and this is terrible. They have so much power and money to influence the development and underdevelopment of Africa. I do not accept the notion that any money the French government gives to or invests in Africa is to "help" Africa. My consciousness prevents me from compromising on issues affecting Africa's interests and needs. I always say to myself, "Be careful." And in dealing with a specific individual I remind myself to ask, "Who is he? What does he want?" To keep up with trends in history, I read books, and I try to maintain my so-called dignity, and my vision of the world. If I should lose my dignity and my vision of the world, it means I am done for. Anyone with the privilege today of creating images of Africa must do so with consciousness of the meaning of those images. This consciousness guides me not only to speak the truth but also to remain part of that truth. I have never called myself a revolutionary, or a Marxist, an activist maybe, but for some people it is easier to put me in a box to marginalize me, to avoid engaging in debates with me, and to avoid seeing or accepting the reality I present.

I believe I have something to give back to African people. I am a Mauritanian, but first of all, I am an African. My ancestors, as yours, in the performance of their duty, faced danger and experienced all sorts of insults and exploitation when they fought to liberate us. I cannot betray them. I consider myself to be, along with them, part of the entire history of Africa.

Above all, I am an African. Even if I have problems in my own country, I feel at home in every African country. I know about forty-two countries in Africa and, in each of them, nobody has ever prevented me from entering or said, "You are not at home." Believe me, if that were to happen to me I would piss on the face of whoever said so. I am at home in any African country. Some film scholars have labeled my work as "cinema of exile" because I operate from France, but this does not concern me. I live seven or eight months a year in France because I have to work and feed my family. They think I am in exile? That is their problem. I am not in exile, not at all. There are many people inside Africa who are more in exile than I; they are those traitors who usurp our rights. I am not in exile and I am not a traitor. I am still an African, and I live with my memory.

On the question of style, I am always amazed when people complicate the issues of style and content. In the West, Europe in particular, there are the separate notions of content and a style. I have never understood this because, for example, if we shoot here in this little room, the style derives from the environment: how and where the camera is positioned, how the images are realized and made to convey meanings—this culminates in a style of representation. If we went and shot a film in Arizona it is possible that the desert, the landscape in general, will impact on the construction of a different style. The style is given, of course, by the content, the script, what the filmmaker wants to say, and also the concrete space where he or she is shooting. That is why, for me, the theme and content dictates the style of presentation. For me, style derives from content. For a filmmaker sitting in his home, at his desk to say, "I am going to create a new style" is absurd. That is why I try to be profoundly involved with the content, with human beings, because the most important raw material is the man, the woman, the child, all human beings. I try to be with them, to understand them and their environments, and it is this that tells me where to position my camera and what to say with the images I capture. These are the elements that dictate my style. It is true that my films are different from one another. Even the general meanings are not the same, but they mirror the past and the present, and both can be used to project the future.

Did Hollywood offer you a couple of million dollars to make West Indies?

In 1973 or 1974, I was in New York, and some African Americans suggested that I should meet some Warner Bros. executives about *West Indies*. They told me there was a very nice man there, so I went. This man was very honest. He and his colleagues read the script in two days, and they came up with a contract. They agreed to produce the film with one million dollars and offered to assign production staff and so forth. They also suggested some changes in my script to make it "Hollywood." The changes would have affected the middle and the end of the film as well as the music. It was then that I realized they had a different version of the film than the one I proposed. I did not like the changes they suggested. I told them I respect their ideas, but that the changes they proposed did not do justice to the actual history of Africa that I was trying to reconstruct. "I need money," I told them, "but I must refuse your money, because I am not able to put your story in my film." It is not that I refused to accept Hollywood money to make *West Indies*. No. It is very specific in each case, but the point is that if I cannot impose my ideas on Hollywood executives, why should they impose theirs on me? If I want my films to retain the authenticity of history, I had to find money by myself. However, if in the future, Hollywood producers become a little bit curious and want to explore Africa from an African perspective, or they want to explore new themes, they can contact me. I will receive them with pleasure—under certain conditions, of course.

We have seen African films that have done fairly well worldwide. These films tend to depart from the didactic phase of the pioneering period. The new African film is inundated with hybrid cinematic styles, incorporating comedy, satire, and African cultural motifs, all geared toward economic viability. Is African cinema losing the educational role it assigned itself? How have these changes affected the African film language? In short, where is African cinema going?

African films comprise maybe 1, 2, or 3 percent of the films that are shown in normal distribution in Europe, and this is considered exceptional. On European television, very few African films are shown. In France, for example, it is very rare to see an African film. Of course, the film which pleases Westerners is sometimes shown in theaters, but only as a means for them to assuage their consciences. They pretend to be helping African cinema, whereas, in concrete terms, all the money they spend for partial funding, including advertisement and publicity, is minuscule in comparison to the promotion budgets of their own films. Another problem is that the general French education on Africa is mystified, which is why the people sometimes do not understand when an African presents African issues from a perspective different from known official French accounts. Prospective producers who are in the position to invest in African films were all educated in the same manner. They were born and educated into colonial mind-sets, so what do you expect? If an African filmmaker approaches such people with a script in the hope of securing funds to produce a film, the norm is to begin to assign the characters in the film with ridiculous roles. They would want the characters to smile, play, or dance—doing the Uncle Tom thing. Most of the producers are literally blind to African issues, and they put the education they had in the past between the film you propose and their colonial mind-set. Therefore, the role of cinema in Africa must be to function as an educational arm for development, for culture and history. The audience must be educated to know us as we are. If we do not know our past, how can we build our future? In the past Mozambique, Angola, and Algeria tried to build dynamic, honest, and dignified societies, but there are very few countries that realize the power with which film and audiovisual images can aid development. Africa must, therefore, unite to create its own internal products and markets.

Why have a lot of intellectuals and brilliant people left Africa? Is it because their brains can only function outside Africa? I do not think so. At home, the governments maintain repressive machineries—the police and the military that intimidate and beat up people every day for no reason and deny them fundamental human rights. Coupled with economic quagmire, this is the typical environment in which we make films. This situation is intolerable. It is the reason why we have outsiders who pretend to love Africa simply because the Africa they love is the one that exists outside of the continent. They do not want to change how they know Africa. They like how they think of Africa. The challenge is how to change their antiquated mentality.

In Europe, for example, even though African filmmakers are oppressed and live a difficult life, they are still privileged, if for no other reasons, in that they can say what our people cannot say in their respective countries. The African filmmaker is somehow an orphan because he is marginalized both outside and inside Africa. Sometimes the government is afraid of filmmakers but cannot do them any harm because of the repercussions of such an action. Can you imagine an African government jailing Ousmane Sembene or Cheick Oumar Sissoko for making films? I do not think that they want to deal with the international backlash such an action would generate. That is the kind of contradiction in which the filmmakers must resolve their political, economic, and ideological problems. This is why if the situation does not change within ten years we may not have anything left to call African cinema.

I have seen many films made by African filmmakers in the 1980s which are really insulting to the continent. I can only see those filmmakers as selling their souls but, as a filmmaker, I do not want to attack them. When you understand the situation they are living in, it is easy to understand that the lack of national policy on culture, generally, is perhaps responsible for the situations which enslave these filmmakers. But we have to know who is primarily responsible for their predicament. It is not the filmmakers themselves, or their audiences, but a combination of all the factors enumerated above. For example, when you catch a man in the street stealing an orange or an egg from a merchant just to have something to eat, there are two ways to react. One is to beat him up and put him in jail, and the other is to understand the reason why the person stole in order to be fed. Sometimes filmmakers sell themselves just to make a film and survive, or, put it in another way, because they belong to a profession called filmmaking. We have to understand that situation. This situation must change, and not only in one or two countries, but in the whole of Africa.

That is true. Do you consider it the filmmaker's responsibility to stick to his or her own political, aesthetic, and moral convictions, even if it means less financial support for his or her films? To which would you give priority, personal convictions or funding the film, since in Africa it is often one or the other?

I do not have a general stance on that; however, I try to be practical. Sometimes you can make a film for very little money. Some films, like *Sarraounia*, need a lot of money. There is an obligation to make such historical films, because of the truth inherent in the story. But you may need people, horses, elaborate sets, for example, a recreation of a queen's palace, etc. You also have to be very careful of the content so as not to be a traitor to the history, to the story, or to yourself. I have no general advice for other filmmakers on how to make films. It is their responsibility. Each filmmaker is responsible for his own work, and people who are critics, essayists, philosophers, and teachers have to analyze more profoundly the dilemmas facing the filmmakers. We should establish cinematheques all over, so we can screen and discuss our films, scrutinize and understand the differences between people, and elaborate on and share our own memories in filmmaking and film viewing. But it is too early to start comparing filmmakers. They are at present operating in war zones because of the difficult situations in which they find themselves. Even if some of the films may not be good, we must appreciate the militant aspects of the filmmaker's endeavor. They deserve credit because to beat the odds and create African images from an African perspective to a world audience is a positive engagement. If there are too many problems, contradictions, and confusion, it becomes impossible to lead a normal life. Sometimes it is a nightmare.

The subject of images of Africa interests me greatly. As in filmmaking, African writers have addressed this topic.

Yes, but that reflects yet another problem because those essays, by prolific African geniuses, whether published in the U.S., England, Nigeria, Ghana, Mozambique, Sudan, Egypt, or Ethiopia, are not accessible to the majority of Africans because they are not translated into African languages. That also reflects the nature of our domination. When a wonderful literary treatise is written in Portuguese, Arabic, or French and is not readily accessible to our people, it is domination. With the French language, for example, approximately 5 percent of the people in Africa speak it, and those who speak it live with it. Therefore, I would still argue that there is not as much interaction with the literary texts as there is in the use of films.

Let us consider now your own images. In my view, Sarraounia *is the most ambitious African film ever made. How was it conceived? The opening sequence and the queen's palace is magnificent. How did you do it?*

First and foremost, filmmaking demands a lot of work. Abdoulaye Mamani, who wrote the book I adapted for the film, is a friend of mine. I have known him as some-one who is involved in the African political and social struggle. As soon as the book was published, he gave me a copy. He is what I would call a progressive individual, and has sacrificed his life for the interests of the African people. He exposed in his book the true African life, something very few Africans know about as a result of colonialism's assault on their civilizations and cultures. This book captured my attention, and I decided to set aside all other pursuits and projects to make this book into film. I began work by doing research with older people residing in Niger while Mamani continued with his writing. We talked with the inhabitants who knew the history. We spent about one and a half years just meeting with people in towns and villages all over the country, talking about Sarraounia, and also meeting the Sarraounia of today. The film made use of a small cast. There are only about ten very small houses, and one Sarraounia; the tradition has been preserved in memory as it is maintained in history. Of course, the Sarraounia of today is not a queen as in the past, because the situation has changed. However, we went and talked with her, and with the people, to obtain the vital information we needed before shooting in order to be respectful to the traditions and customs of the people. We were very concerned with historical accuracy. That kind of work takes a lot of time. I went with Mamani and Abdul, a Mauritanian friend who works with me, to the national libraries to research official reports and archival materials. We were amazed that, as far back as the nineteenth century, everything was documented in writing. After the gathering of the primary data, we left Niger and I proceeded to write the script.

Regarding the beginning of the film, I tried to blend a cloudy blue sky with a sky filled with blood. I do not think every viewer understands this symbolism. My aim was to introduce how eight French military officers used twelve hundred native Africans to kill their brothers and sisters. This is how I made the opening sequence, to reflect that bloody day. It is a strong metaphor which some people only understand from an aesthetic innovation perspective. I used extra-long and super-wide-angle shots to highlight the vast space that has been occupied and turned into a bloody atmosphere by the invading forces of France. This type of situation continues till this very day under new masters. Enemies within, our own brothers, have now occupied that space now vacated by the colonialists. Through them, it is easy for the foreign enemies to penetrate our frontiers and continue their subjugation and manipulation of the entire population. During colonial times the enemies were inside us; in the neocolonial present they pretend to have remained outside our territories, but in fact they are strongly wired to the enemies within via electronic media. This means of domination is even faster and more devastating than the gun or the bomb for, in a twinkle of an eye, any African president could be easily contacted via the telephone and told what he and his ministers should do. And this opening sequence is meant to prepare the audience for all of the issues and connotations the film evokes.

We built the queen's palace to replicate the Sudano-Sahelian architectural design of the old Sarraounia palace. This type of architecture still exists in Mali. Perhaps one of my motivations to replicate the queen's palace was that that Sahelian style architecture is what my grandfather used to build. The new Sarraounia gave me a lot of information regarding how to build the palace and to which directions those holes should face, and how to shape them. I could see her accounts resurrect from memory, and memory at times can be very fresh. In Burkina Faso and other neighboring countries, the story of Sarraounia is also well-known. But I think it is the Hausas who know more about Sarraounia than, for example, the Senegalese, Mauritanians, or Malians.

With all the necessary information at hand, we embarked on the arduous task of historical reconstruction. The cost of building the palace was about one million French francs. After the filming ended, I did not want to destroy the palace because of its similarity with the actual palaces that were built in the past. I decided that the best tribute to pay to the people was to hand over the palace to the government of Burkina Faso for posterity, for the memory of the film and for Queen Sarraounia. The location of the palace is about twenty kilometers east of Bobo-Dioulasso.

Certain interesting things happened during the period of research and scouting for location. One day, when I was building the palace, the chief of the village came to me and asked why I had chosen this particular location at which to build the palace. I told him of our research which led us to conclude that his village was the best place to build it. It was then the chief revealed to me that a series of colonial battles were fought around there, and that the real village was situated at the very location at which we built Sarraounia's palace. People around us were startled when he said the village had been there. I had not known the actual village existed there when I made the decision to build the palace there; we did not know we would be so accurate. Another memorable coincidence worth recalling was when I went to the north to meet with the Tuareg people. When I expressed interest in a location for our tents, the chief of the Tuaregs told me this was the actual location where two fierce battles against the French were fought, and that more than one hundred people lost their lives there. It was uplifting for me and my crew that we were at the place of real history.

Are you working now with a new "content" that would shape your next film project?

You and I cannot discuss the new project because in this country [the United States], as in Europe, some ideas are stolen. However, I can tell you that I am working with an incredible story of black people, with some major connections to African Americans. This project is a spy thriller and was written by a Frenchman, but, of course, concerns Africa. I plan to engage major superstars to make this film. All I can say at this point in time is that it is an incredible story of black people, somewhere in the world. I tried to raise money in France, and it was all but impossible as I am extremely marginalized there because of my views. I am perceived as a revolutionary African, Marxist, and communist.

The idea sounds good and it is a shame that your philosophy is sometimes misunderstood.

Having an international cast shows that I am not against the people who have previously suggested to me the importance of working together with other people. It is important to prove that such a special alliance could work harmoniously in Mali, or any other part of Africa. Furthermore, we are not against so-called white money, but we reserve the right to refuse charity, because we have our materials in our own hands. We wish to continue working with the materials at our disposal. If after all the effort there are no adequate funds or a distributor for the film, there is no problem. I believe I have presented the yardstick with which to measure the successes and failures of African films. I am not complaining to anybody. The U.S. is not my country, but I am hoping for commerce and good relations between our peoples. I believe the time has come for the people of the U.S. to know a little bit more about Africa and its people, its cinema, and the history of the entire continent. I am open to any progressive agenda. I would like outsiders to engage me in meaningful dialogue, to have a better understanding of my work and philosophy. But if they prefer not to do so, no problem. I will continue to do my best with my small force, my small strength.

Do you have any final comment that you would like to make or words of wisdom you would like to lend to the new generation of aspiring African filmmakers regarding coproduction, funding, exhibition, or distribution?

I receive a lot of letters, and I meet a lot of people who want to be filmmakers. I try to avoid them. My initial reaction is to tell them that I am not capable of such advice. I cannot advise people because I think that much of filmmaking is a myth. A lot of people think that filmmaking is a fast route to becoming rich. There are so many myths about cinema, because people do not know much about the structure of the film industry—production, distribution, and exhibition, and, more importantly, the meaning of African cinema. In this regard, I do not see myself as an educator.

I cannot give advice, but I do know that it is very difficult to be a successful filmmaker. I would like to state that any African aspiring to be a filmmaker must understand that it means to hang in the balance with one's own life. If you are prepared to deal with that—to live with that kind of uncertainty—then proceed without hesitation. I do not like to project this kind of philosophy because each film-maker's experience is different. In my country, Mauritania, a lot of young people come to me and say, "I want to be a filmmaker like you." I respond, "Like me? Oh, you are going to suffer. Do you want to suffer? I have no car and I do not have the luxury of going to nightclubs to dance and drink expensive wines and whiskeys. I live on old things. I have no money." Dismayed, some would retort, "What? You have no money?" "No," I would repeat, "I have no money." There is a discrepancy between my life as described in an article about me in the *New York Times*, for example, and the reality of my everyday life. But for the aspiring filmmakers, this message is dif-ficult to digest because in their minds, Med Hondo is a rich man. I cannot tell these youngsters what to do or what not to do because, most of the time, they have made up their minds.

People like you, the academicians, are more useful to the aspiring filmmakers because you can explain better the contradictions of films, filmmaking, and film prac-tices. It is not easy, but we have to find new words to describe the situation of African cinema. However, my suggestion is, if you want to be a filmmaker go ahead, but always remember that there is going to be a very, very difficult battle ahead. It is a nightmare. In the process of becoming a filmmaker, you are going to have your fam-ily turn against you—your government, the outsiders, the Westerners, men, women, everybody will be against you. Is it possible to survive if everybody is against you? If you can live with this, go ahead. In the end you may have a wonderful experience. That is the only advice I can offer.

Filmography

Soleil O (O sun), 1969
Les Bicots-nègres vos voisins (Arabs and niggers, your neighbors), 1973
Nous aurons toute la mort pour dormir (We'll sleep when we die), 1977
Polisario, un people en armes (Polisario, a people in arms), 1979
West Indies, 1979
Sarraounia, 1986
Lumière noire (Black light), 1995
Watani: Un monde sans mal (Watani: A world without evil), 1997

Lionel Ngakane (South Africa)

Lionel Ngakane is one of the pioneers of African cinema and a founding member of the Pan-African Federation of Filmmakers. He grew up in Pretoria, South Africa. After 1950, he lived in exile in Britain until he was able to return to South Africa in 1993 following the release of African National Congress (ANC) leader Nelson Mandela. The liberation of Mandela in 1990 signaled a political change that ultimately led to the demise of apartheid and the birth of an independent South Africa nation in 1994. Throughout his years in exile as a filmmaker, Ngakane pursued his ultimate ambition of making films that would explain the inhuman conditions forced on his people by the apartheid regime in South Africa. His first film, a documentary titled *Vukani Awake* (1962), deals with man's inhumanity to man, depicting the evils of apartheid and the predicament of black people in South Africa. However, Ngakane could not function as a filmmaker as much as he had hoped while in exile, for competition was stiff and, moreover, the atmosphere in Britain was not conducive to success for a black filmmaker. He soon realized that despite the awards he had received for his second film, *Jemima and Johnny* (1966), he could not be recognized as a filmmaker in Britain. As a revolutionary, Ngakane continued to be very active in the political wing of the ANC and also maintained strong ties with FEPACI—an organization that he helped to found and to which he devoted a lot of energy, working for the development of African cinema. Today, he is the first FEPACI regional secretary for the southern region. Ngakane recently received an honarary doctoral degree (D.Litt.) from the University of Natal.

In his roles as a filmmaker and the FEPACI regional secretary, Ngakane believes that one of his duties in South Africa is to dismantle the established white cinema of the apartheid regime and to create in its place a national film industry that reflects the diversity of peoples in South Africa. He has made it clear that he aims to make the media accessible to blacks and to members of other communities who have long been marginalized by the apartheid system. He also plans to use his films to encourage other filmmakers to promote black history and to foreground the oppressive machinations of apartheid.

When this interview was conducted at the 1993 FESPACO, Ngakane was still living in exile in London. He returned to South Africa in 1994, following the demise of apartheid. Because many events have taken place in the cinema scene, he has asked me to draw readers' attention to several recent developments. The first of these is the Southern African Newcomers Competition, an event that is open to new directors from all countries of the Southern African Development Community (SADC), which includes South Africa, Zimbabwe, Botswana, Lesotho, Swaziland, Namibia, Angola, and Mozambique. The second development of note is that Ramadan Suleman has emerged as the first black in the new South Africa to make a feature film, titled *Fools* (1997). Following this, New Directions, under the auspices of MNET, has produced two feature films, *Chikin Biznis* (1997) and *Sexy Girls* (1998), as well as a host of independently produced shorts. And finally, the Cape Town Film Market, now called Sithengi, is growing. Sithengi is a yearly event that is organized to provide filmmakers with the opportunity to pitch their scripts and projects to international film companies, TV stations, and producers. (I would like to thank Professor Keyan Tomaselli for providing me with the preceding information.)

How did your filmmaking career begin?

I came to filmmaking by chance. When I was young in South Africa I was a journalist, and I met a film producer who thought I should play a part in the film *Cry, the Beloved Country*. He employed me as his personal assistant. During the preparation and making of the film, I had to go to England. It was there he encouraged me to return to England to become a film director. In those days, there were hardly any African film directors, and that inspired me. I could not afford formal film training, so I had to learn on my own. I bought a 16mm camera and experimented with it until I was bold enough to make my first documentary film.

Where was this first film made, and what is the title?

My documentary film was called *Vukani Awake*, and I made it in 1962. I shot some of the scenes in South Africa when I was visiting. The film is a political documentary on South Africa interspersed with library footage. I'm glad that I still have available a print of this film, as I do of all my work.

What is it like working in exile and trying to make a documentary film that pertains to your people?

I do not think it is difficult as long as you have enough money. But in those days, things were different, I shot this film without involving anybody. Since I used a lot of library footage, it was a very cheap film to make. It is not like now, when if you wanted to make the same documentary, it would cost a lot of money, and then the filmmaker would have to scramble to find exhibition channels.

If I am correct, your next film was a powerful film called Jemima and Johnny, *which was inspired by the sporadic race riots in Britain.*

Yes, I lived in an area called Notting Hill, where there were some of these riots. As a result, I decided to make this film. Also, I wanted to make a film with children after having seen a film called *Red Balloon*, which I used to love very much. I used children to express my point of view on racism.

Why did you use black and white for the film? Was it because you were doing a film about racism and black-and-white relations?

It was a choice between doing it in black and white or doing it in color. For this subject I honestly believed that it would be much more dramatic in black and white than in color. Color makes everything beautiful. Even a slum looks beautiful in color. Black and white is stark and it is dramatic. That is why I decided to do it in black and white, and it works, I think.

I would imagine that Jemima and Johnny *is a film that would have an enormous impact, especially in apartheid South Africa. Has it been shown in that country?*

It could not have been shown in the last few years because of apartheid. It was shown in South Africa for the first time, however, in 1994, at the Durban Film Festival. I presented a copy to the organizers, which I asked them to use as they wished.

What is the reaction to this film by the black, Asian, colored, and white populations in South Africa?

Apparently it was a success, but I was not there, at the screenings. Now that I am aware that the reactions were very good, I will go to South Africa and hear from the people themselves.

You have made other films since Jemima and Johnny. *What are these films about?*

I made one called *Once upon a Time*, which was a sponsored film about the wedding of Avital, the son of the president of Liberia, to the adopted daughter of Felix Houphouet-Boigny, the president of Côte d'Ivoire. Then I made some other documentaries. I made a documentary about human rights in Holland. I have made documentaries sponsored by the federal government of Nigeria. One is called *Nigerian*

Transition and is about the political and economic situation in Nigeria at that time. I have worked on various other feature films, and I have written scripts.

What is your position regarding the political and cultural use of film as a tool for liberation and decolonization?

There were some films made during the years when the African National Congress was exiled. But now we South African filmmakers have been training people in order to build an alternative cinema infrastructure in South Africa. There is a lot we need to do. We have to organize the importation of films, the distribution of films, the training of people, etc., and that takes a lot of money. We hope that the international community will in some way assist us in this pursuit.

The ANC did not do enough regarding the use of film to explain the political struggles against apartheid. Mozambique and Angola used films successfully in explaining the situation to their citizens and to the outside world. After independence, they also embarked upon the use of film to educate the masses about the revolution. I know there are financial constraints, but could you comment on why the ANC was unable to use the film medium to explain their struggles to the outside world?

There are several things to be taken into consideration. First and foremost was that we did not have many black filmmakers. As time went on, more people started getting trained and after their education was completed, they faced the problem of lack of equipment, funding, etc. We did not have the money to make the type of films along the lines you suggested. However, we got quite a large library of films made by the International Defensenique, whose films are really widely distributed although probably people do not know about these films. The International Defensenique has a big library of films on South Africa, both the ones that they made and those made by other people. These films are being recirculated, although they might not have been to the United States. Don't forget that for a long time in the United States, members of the ANC were considered terrorists. It was not easy to penetrate America to say to people, "Look, we want to make films," or, "We have these films. Can you disseminate them?" There were small groups that did, maybe, but basically we were portrayed as terrorists and communists, and that made things difficult for us.

Sarafina is a powerful South African musical with political messages, but isn't the documentary film Sarafina *a wasted opportunity, since it failed to expose apartheid to a wider public as the play* Sarafina *did to its Broadway audience?*

You noticed when you asked me about the films I made, there was not even one feature film. The reason is that feature films cost a lot of money, and we did not have the money to make a feature film on *Sarafina*. In any case, the ANC, if it did have the money, would rather use it for making documentaries on several subjects, rather than put all the meager resources into a feature film. It might be a place for a collaborative effort, but in terms of making a feature film, it was out of the reach of the ANC.

But Hollywood sponsored this documentary. Sarafina *was already very popular so there were a number of sponsors ready to offer money. Why did the producers of* Sarafina *decide to make a documentary about the actors instead of* Sarafina *itself?*

Because the producers of *Sarafina* are not filmmakers. Mbogeni Ngema, the creator of *Sarafina* [the play], is a good playwright and dramatist. He is a very good theater man, one of the best black theater producers in South Africa. Therefore, the making of the film out of *Sarafina* would not be his strength. There are many films I would like to make on South Africa, and I have written two scripts. But the moment one talks about having a script that deals with South Africa, the responses from potential financiers are usually, "Oh, it is political. It is this, it is that." It happens all the time. Simply put, film financiers do not want to get involved with any script that they regard as political. Feature-length films are expensive to make, and before one embarks upon such a project, one must make sure that there is a distribution outlet for it.

What is the present situation regarding black South African film production?

At the moment, we have a kind of video workshop; we are not making films in South Africa yet. As far as I know, there are no black South African filmmakers at the moment, although that will soon change. Meanwhile, most of the universities have film departments, but no black Africans have been trained in them. The urgency now is to train people in all the disciplines of cinema and to set in motion a distribution infrastructure, as I said earlier. Soweto has about two million people but only two cinema theaters. Only two; think about it! Other towns and cities have got one, maybe, or none at all. We have to try and persuade our black entrepreneurs to help build cinema theaters in our townships and to help establish effective distribution infrastructures. Along with that would be the training of film technicians. However, acquiring formal education in film is not enough, because after three years of courses, the graduates need to have the experience that will prepare them for the industry. There is the formal training and there is the on-the-job training. The existing film companies must contribute to on-the-job training by offering internships to the benefit of the young graduates.

I would like to turn the discussion to a general one, the aesthetics of African cinema. As one of the pioneers of African cinema, how would you describe the evolution of African cinema in relation to quality, to your experiences with what is happening here, at FESPACO 1993?

If you look at most of the films, with the exception of a few, the quality reflects the experience of the people and the lack of funds to invest in the production of films.

The filmmaker, in almost all cases, is the producer, scriptwriter, everything! To me, the worst thing that can happen in filmmaking is that you have one person who is jack-of-all-trades. But what has happened in the last twenty years of African cinema is quite remarkable. We have now filmmakers who have matured by working on their own. Although not enough, there is some money from organizations in France, Germany, television companies, NGOs [nongovernmental organizations], and governments to improve the quality of films. For instance, filmmakers are beginning to use African cinematographers. People are beginning to think about creative uses of sound in film, which hitherto was a secondary concern. But what is very encouraging is the professionalism of African technicians, who are increasing in number. For instance, in Algeria there are technicians that are as good as anybody in the world. Ousmane Sembene uses African technicians as much as possible. The film I am planning now is going to make use of African technicians of high quality. We have to! The reason why we have to encourage quality productions is that African audiences are accustomed to watching films from abroad, and if we present them with tons of mediocre films we are not going to motivate them to pay and see African films. This is a matter of concern to all of us, every African filmmaker.

The French seem to be more interested in the development of African cinema than the British. Is there any particular reason for this?

We were told the other day at this conference that the French make about 140 films a year. The British make about twenty. The British government is not really committed to our cultures to the extent that the French are with their former African colonies. For the French, culture is a very important thing, and that is why they have the Ministry of Culture. They take culture seriously, and their attitude has been extended to the francophone countries. The British are not interested in the promotion of African culture, which explains why no money from the Commonwealth Secretariat goes to the production of African films. Not a penny is spent in Kenya, Tanzania, or any of the former British colonies to train people or to help in the provision of infrastructure for film production.

Do you think that FESPACO 1993 has emphasized quantity over quality, and, more generally, is there any future for African cinema?

One main aim of FESPACO is to encourage people to make films. Every young filmmaker wants his film to be shown at FESPACO, because it is not going to be seen elsewhere since we do not have a distribution system yet in Africa. In this regard we encourage a greater output of films. If FESPACO is an exclusive arena to showcase only the best filmmakers' works, then it goes contrary to our aspirations. It means that we are consciously creating a black Cannes festival, and we do not want to create African Cannes but the FESPACO of Ouagadougou. FESPACO is the festival that encourages development of cinema on the continent.

Your second question was whether there is a future in African cinema. Yes! There is a future if we get the distribution of our films organized. If we can get our films distributed in Africa, it is possible to have a viable film industry. This would mean that when we make films they would be seen by the audience and the profits accrued from the screening can then be invested into new films. What use is it after fighting so hard to raise money to make a film, and it does not get shown? That is discouraging. It also makes it impossible for filmmakers to go to the same funding source and request money. To solve this problem I believe that governments have to be involved, even if it means creating new legislation. Legislation could mandate that the cinema owners have to show a certain number of African films. I stress again that if we control distribution, we can have a viable African film industry.

The issue you brought up reminds me of the situation in Ghana when, according to Kwaw Ansah, distributors refused to handle Heritage ... Africa. *After this film was shown in government theaters and some other theaters, and drew audiences from theaters that show foreign films, it was only then that distributors realized that a well-made African film could be competitive and widely distributed.*

That is so true! If the audience like the films, which they do when they have the opportunity to see African films, there is always a yearning for more of such films. Yes, the aliens who dominate the exhibition/distribution business, and who specialize in kung fu and Indian films because these films guarantee them profits, will undoubtedly realize that it is possible for them to make more money by showing good African films. But the distributors are not yet convinced, they are not committed to African cinema, and it seems that they have to be forced to comply; they are just vampires who want to suck only blood. From their perspective, film distribution is a business and as far as making profits are concerned, it does not matter to them if African films are marginalized. Equally important also is that we must not only target foreign markets. Yes, we would like our films to be shown abroad, but the films are basically made for the people of the continent. The films are first for our people, and if other people are interested in our films, that is also good.

Since the evolution of African cinema a variety of films have been produced and filmmakers have been addressing issues in diverse ways and styles. Do you perceive the possibility for an autonomous African film language?

It is like envisaging the possibility for a unified European film language. Can it be possible? The problem we have here is that people in the West still perceive Africa as one country and not the very large continent it is, which comprises many countries and different cultures. We must also be aware that from the village to the city, ethnic and cultural backgrounds are different. A Nigerian is as different from a Kenyan as a Japanese is different from a Chinese. So there cannot be an African film language, and it should not be regarded as such.

What is cinema for you? Is it a means of expression, politics, culture, or art?

For me, personally, I believe in a committed cinema. I want to address issues affecting mankind. I want to educate the African. I want to inform the African. But even so, I want to entertain the African. You can deal with politics, or social subjects, or economics and be entertaining. That is the mix I want. I do not want to make meaningless films. There have been one or two African films that have been absolutely frivolous in terms of sex, and they have been rejected in Africa completely. I am glad that at least we still have that sense of morality in our cultures. We all know that Africa is in a developing stage. The filmmakers should play their role in the development process, but it does not mean that they do not have to entertain.

The depiction in films of African cultures relating to sex and nudity is an important issue. As you stated earlier, there are few African films that treat sex and nudity in a manner conducive for overseas promotion while risking their outright rejection in African countries. However, in the absence of adequate funding, is it too premature to be concerned about the practice becoming a trend, and filmmakers capitalizing on it for profit? What kind of impact is it likely to make on the development of African cinema?

The overwhelming majority, but with a few exceptions, of African filmmakers still have a sense of responsibility as far as culture is concerned. But I think we have to be careful, because we have been fighting such things as the French mandating the use of a French producer when they make money available to an African filmmaker. This measure gives the French producer an undue influence and power to control the processes of production. This producer may be the one, for commercial or political reasons, who dictates which image is to be inserted here and there in the film's structure. This type of control can debase and tarnish our films. I think what we need now is to have our own producers who can understand the goals and aspirations of African filmmakers. As I plan my next film, I am faced with this dilemma too. My intention is to engage the best African producer to coproduce with me. We will have discussions, yes, we may differ in our opinions and that is all right too, but we will not fail to understand the basic requirements for accomplishing our task. To this end, what is certain is that we will agree not to intersperse our film structure with sex/nude scenes, or with naked dancers for the simple reason of selling the film and appeasing audiences in France, Britain, Germany, and the United States of America. We also have to get away from the exotic, because that also debases our cultural heritage, or whatever you want to call it.

It is possible to have your own producer if you are working outside of the French domain. But how about the francophone African filmmakers who rely on French benevolence to produce their films? Do you think it is possible for them to have African producers, when Africans are not providing the money?

This came up in the discussions members of FEPACI had here at this conference with potential production partners from the United States, Canada, and France. I think that the French arrogance regarding the manner in which they impose their own producers on African filmmakers is going to end. There is no question about it, because Africans are developing uncompromising attitudes toward combating all forms of hegemony. The time has come for the French to understand that Africans mean business.

What do you mean when you state that filmmakers should reject the exotic? Are you referring to some of the films showing here in FESPACO? Some African critics have observed that there are too many films showing here that are set in the bushes—films that, if made by foreigners, would have been accused of paying ultimate attention to African exoticism instead of the general developments that have occurred in contemporary Africa. These are, however, the types of films that get exhibited overseas because of their so-called anthropological values. Are you worried that because of French funding which makes the realization of such films possible this may become a trend?

No, not really! You have to think of one important fact, and that is that 80 percent of our population on the continent live in the rural areas. A lot of the films deal with the problems of those people: the problems of alienation, the problems of poverty in the village, problems about migration to the cities, and the clash of cultures between the traditional and the new ways of life. I see sometimes how people live in the village, with their strong moral codes, and then I go to the city where the same people who left the villages have, within two years, lost respect of the values they once upheld. They have appropriated the values of the city, values which may not be the best. A lot of people, like Idrissa Ouedraogo of Burkina Faso for instance, are dealing with those kind of problems. Ousmane Sembene has dealt with those problems, and he has dealt with the colonial problems as well as corruption of governments.

We must take into consideration that all of us go back from wherever we live to visit our villages, which may be considered rural areas. My grandfather lives in a typical African village. Even my mother and father live in the typical African village. Your grandfather probably lived in the typical African village. There are problems there that have got to be resolved—problems of making a living, of development, and so on. And what is the government doing about those problems? Regarding how to represent those aspects of life, I think it is a question of how a filmmaker treats a subject. A film could be set in a village and be a good one to watch. It may be considered good because of how the filmmaker is able to depict the problems of the village as well as the beautiful things about village life. Every time I go to the village, I am fascinated by how honesty, respect for the elders and for the womenfolk are still held intact. Above all, the villages are still providing the safe haven for African kids to grow. These are things that belong in the cities, too, but may no longer be as strongly adhered to because of the problems of modern urbanity.

A film set in the rural areas that highlights issues associated with village life can be used to educate the city audiences so they may appreciate the realities and contradictions of life situations. From this perspective, I do not regard a lot of the films we are referring to as exotic. If these films are situated within the African audience, which is who we are really making these films for, they are very relevant to their lives. It may be argued that some Africans react to such films positively because they identify with the subject matter. I can see with you why watching these type of films outside of Africa would pose a different kind of problem, especially for the African audience, who prefer filmmakers to move away from ethnographic cliché to deal more with contemporary developments which are not shown in Western news media. Well, everywhere, there are good and bad filmmakers.

Glad you said it, and since you are one of the good filmmakers, I hope you have future plans for cinematic projects.

I have three possible documentaries, really important ones, and one feature film in the planning stage. The script for the feature is complete, and I am raising some money toward its production. I have to calculate how much I have now, because funds have been coming so fast in the last three weeks. My immediate task is to go back to London and sit down and examine how we have been doing and make plans on how to proceed. I am hoping to shoot about two-fifths of the feature film in Britain and three-fifths in Burkina Faso.

Do you plan to use African collaborators in terms of funding sources, actors, and technicians?

Tunisia and Algeria are involved, and I am hoping to get Burkina Faso involved, so three African countries may be coproducing the film. I do not want money from them, but I want facilities, which is equivalent to money. I cannot expect Burkina Faso to provide money, but it can give me soldiers, houses, and transportation, which they have. I hope that will be their investment. Algeria can give me all the equipment and the technicians needed. Tunisia has a functioning laboratory, editing facilities, and, maybe, all the postproduction facility.

What about money to make the film? How are you raising your money, considering funding has been a major problem for African filmmakers? And after that, how do you plan to deal with the distribution problems?

When the decision makers in funding agencies read one's script, that helps a great deal. If they like the script, then they can be persuaded to fund its production. It also helps to know the appropriate agencies to contact and the techniques for presenting your script. This strategy reflects the methods I have used to get things organized. For instance, I have now qualified for funding from the French sector. This is probably the first time a nonfrancophone filmmaker will be funded by the French. It may be because my film has got a big francophone input, which makes it qualify for French financial assistance.

What will be your role in a free South Africa regarding the development of the South African film industry?

All I can say is that I would like to contribute in any way I can, using my experience in Africa, because I have been involved in developing African cinema since about 1969. My experience could be useful, and I am very anxious that we develop South African cinema expeditiously. An alternative cinema is urgently needed to fill the void. I say an alternative cinema because there is an established cinema in South Africa which does not address the general concerns of blacks or the progressive peoples of South Africa. It is from this perspective that the creation of an alternative cinema is a possibility. It is one way of making the media accessible to the communities that have been marginalized for so long. However, let us hope that it may not be necessary to go the alternative route, and that the authorities in the established cinema industry are prepared for a change—to dismantle all hegemonic inclinations. We are looking forward to creating a new cinema industry that will recognize and tolerate the multi-ethnic and the multicultural structure of the postapartheid South African nation. Going that way, we would have one cinema structure in the country.

Filmography

Vukani Awake, 1962
Jemima and Johnny, 1966
Once upon a Time, 1975
Nelson Mandela: The Struggle Is My Life, 1985
Canariv, 1988
Nigerian Transition, 1989

Chief Eddie Ugbomah (Nigeria)

Chief Eddie Ugbomah was trained in England, where he majored in journalism and drama and later in film and television production at the London School of Television Production. He worked for some time at the British Broadcasting Corporation (BBC) and the Independent Television Network (ITN), and as an actor he appeared in such films as *Doctor No*, *Guns of Batasi*, and *Sharpeville Massacre*. At one time, he ran the first all-black theater company, the Afro-Caribbean Drama Group. A man of many talents, Ugbomah also worked as a model in London and Paris and as a promoter of music concerts featuring such artists as Millicent Small, Chubby Checker, B. B. King, and Soul Messengers, to name a few. Upon returning to Nigeria, and having established himself as a reputable director, he served as chairman of the Nigerian Film Corporation (NFC) from 1988 to 1991. He used his tenure in office to promote several innovative agendas, including the establishment of a film laboratory and other activities on which he proudly elaborates in the following discussion.

He is a well-known and vocal critic of those establishments he ceaselessly blames for not giving adequate encouragement to the development of African film industries. Believing that raising funds in Nigeria to make movies is almost an impossibility, for example, he reveals that throughout his career he has been forced to participate in all aspects of production and exhibition of his films so as to cut down on production costs. At times, to maintain uninterrupted production, he has invested his own money in his films rather than "waste [his] time lobbying, begging for funding to make another film."

Chief Eddie Ugbomah has emerged as the most prominent independent filmmaker in Nigeria. His rise is not due merely to the fact that he has made more films than his contemporaries; Ugbomah has the proven ability to survive the test of

Nigeria's austere economic times. His career spans three problematic decades of Nigeria's history: the buoyant "boom years" of the 1970s, the economic stagnation of the 1980s, and the entrenchment of poverty in the 1990s. Where many of his peers have failed, Ugbomah and his production company, Edifosa Films, have produced a number of feature-length films without turning to outside funding agencies. From 1977, when he launched his filmmaking career with the release of *The Rise and Fall of Dr. Oyenusi*, to the present, the director has produced thirteen celluloid feature-length films and two feature-length works shot on video. Unlike the films of any other Nigerian filmmaker, all of Ugbomah's films are inspired by current events; as he puts it, "They are statement films about societal issues"—issues he fearlessly depicts. Typical examples include armed robbery and the menace to society represented by men of the underworld in *The Rise and Fall of Dr. Oyenusi* (1977), the pillaging of Africa's art objects by British colonizers in *The Mask* (1979), Nigeria's predicament caused by the oil boom of the 1970s in *Oil Doom* (1979), and the assassination of one of Nigeria's presidents in *The Death of a Black President* (1983). For Ugbomah, filmmaking continues to be a passion and, at the age of sixty, he has no plans to retire anytime soon. He is currently developing and shooting three scripts, which he says are almost ready to go to production despite all odds.

Ugbomah envisions a thriving African film industry that requires no assistance from external sources. This insistence, as well as his demotic flair and socially committed art, makes him a uniquely compelling antiestablishment figure in African film. It has also put him on a collision course with Nigeria's political hierarchy, his fellow filmmakers, and African filmmakers in general. Ugbomah is Nigeria's most outspoken and most controversial filmmaker. This interview was conducted at the National Theater in Lagos in 1992.

You have made more feature films than any other black African filmmaker. How do you overcome the financial problems that plague African filmmaking?

The most important thing is that I have relied on my personal finances, money I made while in England and when I came back home. I invest all the earnings from my films in new projects. In this way I have been able to overcome the major crises and financial headaches of making films in Nigeria.

How is your situation different from that of less prolific African filmmakers, who complain that their films do not yield enough earnings to invest in new projects?

I am able to minimize my costs because I've been trained in most aspects of film production. I am one of those people who participates in the production, acting, directing, and writing of his or her own films. This strategy allows me to cut four people from my budget. Secondly, unlike most Nigerian filmmakers today, I do not have a huge family of sixteen wives and a hundred children, so that is great savings. Additionally, my nonostentatious lifestyle allows me to reinvest my profits into my next project.

Getting funding from entrepreneurs or the government is quite difficult. I would rather reinvest my money than waste my time lobbying, begging for funding to make another film. We do not have entrepreneurs in Nigeria willing to invest in the film industry. There are no foundations or banks that fund film production.

What are you trying to accomplish as a filmmaker?

I am a committed filmmaker. I know the power of communication, the harm foreign films have done to our society. I see how the various African cultures are gradually disappearing before the onslaught of foreign influences. What I am interested in is film and its impact on society, in the context of enormous, visible changes taking place in our society. I produce films for television and the cinema; sometimes I support stage productions. Most of my films deal with current events and are statement films about societal issues.

I also believe that there is no reason that the Nigerian film industry should not be lucrative. There is a large audience demand for entertainment. We do, however, have one big disadvantage. Foreign films have ruined the audience's appetite for African films. Africans have become addicted to violence, to what they have come to expect from Hollywood and other escapist, alien films. Furthermore, most academicians who call themselves filmmakers wait until they can get foundation funding to make art documentaries, not commercial features. I think it is important in Nigeria today that we use film to entertain people while informing them. For the Nigerian film industry to survive, our films must make money.

How do you manage the responsibilities of your many roles—producer, director, editor, exhibitor . . .

I do what is necessary to survive. I have to live with smaller budgets, so I assume those duties for myself. It is not an enviable position, it's too stressful and it affects the end product. But if you are committed to a profession, you just have to do what is necessary to survive. Since there is a shortage of skilled technicians, you find you have to get involved in all aspects of production in order to ensure that things get done the way you want them to.

Many francophone filmmakers receive technical and financial aid from the French Ministry of Cooperation. Can you comment on this, as well as on other financial aid that is provided to African filmmakers?

Francophone filmmaking is not a commercial enterprise. The filmmakers are subsidized either by their own governments or by France; many of the experimental or art films they produce are not released. The difference between anglophone and francophone filmmakers is that the latter do not spend their own money to make films. Even before a francophone film is completed it has already made money from the foundation that is funding it. For me, I invest my hard-earned money. I deny myself a Rolls-Royce and Mercedes-Benz in order to make films.

In Nigeria and Ghana we make commercial films. Nigeria has a massive market—it is a country of about one hundred million people. In order to make a profit, a Nigerian filmmaker has to capture only a fraction of that population, say one million people paying ten naira each to see a film. We do not endorse extravagant filmmaking, we do not have to spend twenty million dollars to make a film in Nigeria. We can afford to be independent.

At the same time, we do not want to compete with Hollywood filmmakers who can spend fifteen million dollars on a film and are covered by insurance, so that if it flops the filmmaker can borrow money again to make yet another film. We have no such privilege. Nigerian filmmakers cannot afford to produce movies like *Terminator, Basic Instinct, Deep Cover,* or *Lethal Weapon.* These films are very bad for Third World societies who want to preserve their own cultures.

In October of 1991 we proposed a law to the Ministry of Justice which would have required theaters to show African films for at least four days a week, and imported films only three days. It shouldn't be impossible to run African films four days of the week. But sadly, ever since independence in 1960, governmental policy has hindered the development of a viable national film industry. For example, the government uses the Federal Film Unit exclusively to produce self-aggrandizing documentary films that nobody sees.

Nigerian filmmakers are free agents. We do not have to clear our scripts with foreign sponsors or anybody before we shoot a film. Although, since we invest our own money in our films, we do consider the criteria of the Nigerian censorship board.

This brings us to another problem. Where francophone filmmakers are subsidized by foundations and governments, anglophone filmmakers are subject to heavy taxation. This is killing us. The Nigerian government is not investing this money into independent film production. Furthermore, every state has the power to determine its own taxes on admission fees, what they call "entertainment taxes." We have been fighting this outrageous system of taxation to no avail. So filmmaking in the francophone world does not involve the same personal risk that it does in the anglophone, where a filmmaker like Kwaw Ansah had to borrow twenty-two million cedis from about four syndicated banks to make a film.

Only after intensive lobbying did the Nigerian government agree to build a film industry, the Nigerian Film Corporation. They have now built a color laboratory, but who is using this 88-million-naira lab now? Nobody—because the government has not been able to convince investors that film is profitable. The NFC ought to be run as an economically viable enterprise, which means appointing a reliable management staff, among other things. The government should also establish a commercial bank that would lend money to filmmakers.

African filmmakers have been fighting for a long time to get African governments to subsidize or sponsor film production. But how can that goal be achieved when African governments have mortgaged African economies to the International Monetary Fund and the World Bank, when many African countries are struggling to feed their people? When governments are concerned with feeding their populations, do you think African governments are going to commit their resources to film production?

This is where people make a mistake. When there is frustration, depression, that is when entertainment pays the most. This is when you have to use entertainment to cool down people's tempers. Now is the most promising time to invest in the film industry. In Nigeria we used to charge a three-naira or five-naira cover fee, but because of the depression, we now charge fifteen naira. And yet the theaters are over-crowded. In a country of nearly one hundred million, there are not even two million video machines. The masses still want to see movies, they want to go out. The government has to invest in communication and entertainment now, so it can communicate and address the people's concerns. The media have enormous educational and propaganda potential. The government can use the media to tell the people to buy Nigerian, to be proud of Nigeria. It can communicate that it is cheaper to grow their own rice rather than importing it. Through movies, we can start eliminating those canker worms, tribalism and religion, as I did in my film *Apalara*. Those are the kinds of things you can achieve through the power of the image. Economic depression should not be an obstacle to the development of the film industry.

Despite the fact that you have made so many films, you are not well-known outside of West Africa. Why is that?

People don't realize that the film industry is a powerful medium protected by governments in Europe and America. It is big money. The industry will do everything it can to frustrate a Third World filmmaker. They condemn films that do not conform to Hollywood formulas. So why should I waste my time? There is an enormous African market to explore. Why should I pay thirty-five thousand naira to fly to America to campaign for the distribution of my films only to discover it is a futile endeavor? I have made thirteen movies and I am happy about it, and I am not worried about whether they are distributed outside Africa. In America, even if I do find a theater to screen my film, the owner expects to keep most of the proceeds from the screening. They show my films and refuse to charge admission. At Howard University I had to pay to show my film.

Have you considered showing your films at the Pan-African Festival of Film and Television of Ouagadougou? African films are discovered by distributors from all over the world who go there to view African films. When I was in FESPACO in 1991, only one filmmaker from the anglophone countries, Kwaw Ansah, came to show his film,

Heritage . . . Africa, which won an award. Wouldn't FESPACO be a good place to show your films?

FESPACO is a francophone business, and for the past six years only francophone films have won the three major awards. The year Kwaw Ansah won, the anglophone filmmakers had met before the award and agreed that if anglophone films were not duly recognized we would not return to FESPACO. Yes, *Heritage . . . Africa* was awarded the grand prize, which it deserved. But anglophone filmmakers go to FESPACO merely to promote Pan-Africanism, not to advertise or sell their films. Some anglophones do go—Ade Love, Babasala, and Ogunde have all shown their films at FESPACO. But for me to go and sit in FESPACO, where only French is spoken twenty-four hours a day—it's too frustrating. I do not know of one film that managed to be distributed internationally after having won the coveted FESPACO grand prize.

There are African films, such as Yaaba, *that have received much international attention.*

They may be screened internationally, at the New York Film Festival, the San Francisco Film Festival, or in Montreal, where audiences applaud them, but after the festivals, do they get international distribution? What is crucial at this point in the development of African cinema is for Africa to create a united front to confront the problem of distribution. Individual effort simply is not enough. We must seek a united effort to promote African films outside of Africa. The Nigerian government should engage in publicity or propaganda or whatever. Judging from the few places that I have shown my films, there is a demand, people are inquisitive, they want to see Africa from a new perspective. The days of Tarzan are gone.

You have emphasized film and entertainment. How do you integrate film and politics?

This is a very delicate issue. Filmmakers have to be very subtle about bringing their political perspective into their work. It is imperative that they do not push it down people's throats. Look at the popular Nigerian television programs, like *The Village Headmaster* or *The Masquerade*, which use comedy and satire to make political statements. These programs are entertaining, but while people look at them and laugh, they also understand the political message. My film *Oil Doom* applied the same strategy to warn Nigeria that the oil boom would one day end in doom. Film is a powerful political tool. It is very powerful because you really do not have to receive any special education in order to understand the image and its political implications. There are a lot of filmmakers now in Nigeria who use film as a medium for political criticism. So also are playwrights who have become filmmakers: Baba Ogunde, our famous playwright, dramatist, and filmmaker, uses his plays, some of them adapted to film, as political tools. You really cannot separate film from politics. During the Nigerian-Biafra war, the Biafran leader, Chief Odumegwu Ojukwu, effectively employed the media as a weapon of propaganda, constantly drawing the world's attention to the genocide against his people. So powerful was his manipulation of the media that images of rotting bodies were broadcast all over the world. Filmmakers could be considered harbingers of change. Sometimes they can make and unmake with their stories.

Could you comment on your first feature, The Rise and Fall of Dr. Oyenusi, *and its depiction of contemporary urban problems?*

The Rise and Fall of Dr. Oyenusi was made when armed robbery was just beginning to flourish in Lagos. It was a film I made to show that crime does not pay and to show that most of these criminals have the support of "godfathers," influential individuals with links to the armed forces. I exposed a lot of these political intricacies, all the tricks and maneuvers, and at the same time I entertained people with the film. People have asked why I did not make a film about Zik, Awolowo, or Balewa. I did not make a film about them because these individuals are what I call "Biro-armed robbers." The fact that these figures do not carry guns and shoot people does not mean that their crimes are any less destructive than those of the armed robbers in my film. This film is a reflection of national consciousness, the dichotomy between the oppressed and the oppressor. That is why I made a film about Oyenusi's life and how he was living in glamour at the expense of his victims. But what was his end? Was it worth it? That was the question I wanted to ask, and the answer is that crime does not pay.

You exhibited courage and audacity in the production of The Rise and Fall of Dr. Oyenusi. *What are the trials, dangers, and obstacles involved in making such a gangster movie in Nigeria?*

The problems I had were not only due to the fact that it is a gangster movie. I have gone through hell making all of my films. Making *The Rise and Fall of Dr. Oyenusi* was no harder than making *The Death of a Black President,* or *The Mask,* or even *The Boy Is Good.* I cannot tell how many times my life has been threatened for exposing societal ills. There is even a script, *The Jennifer Connection,* for which I nearly got killed. We were going to shoot this film about a young girl and her connection with drug barons. As soon as it was announced that I was looking for five million naira to make this film, I was targeted by the drug lords. But this time I was not willing to gamble with my life because I had had enough of people's threats. I had to jettison the whole idea. This predicament has destroyed all too many African film pioneers. A lot of trained Nigerian academics and technicians who would have made important contributions to Nigerian cinema have been forced to abandon filmmaking. Also, corruption has taken its toll. Francis Oladele, who made *Things Fall Apart,* was loaned four million naira to make a film called *The Eye of the Man.* Instead of making the film, Oladele sank the money into a farm. This misuse of funds has set a bad precedent, causing the government to abandon about twelve such loans that were earmarked for filmmaking.

I myself have since changed course and adopted the Yoruba film tradition. Since this tradition is oriented toward cultural plays and dramas and remains largely apolitical, a filmmaker is spared the danger of making enemies. The Yoruba theater/film genre does not satisfy my creative impulse, but I have been making money from it. My last four Yoruba-language films have been big box-office hits. It is very frustrating that the quest for survival has forced me to relinquish my original style of filmmaking.

Nigerian cinema seems to be a derivative of the Yoruba traveling theater, what might be called "theater on the screen" . . .

What the Yorubas have been able to do through their mentor, Ogunde, was to just lift the stage onto celluloid. Because this tradition originated in the popular Yoruba theater, there is a ready-made audience. There are ready-made stars and ready-made stories. Since cinematic aesthetics are secondary to the popularity of the actors, the filmmaker does not need to advertise much. The only people with cinema, stage, and art culture are the Yorubas. Unfortunately, mediocre dramatists will now stage anything, film it, and take it to the hinterlands to show an unquestioning Yoruba audience. The industry is still alive not because of the production quality, but because of the huge, enthusiastic audience.

Still, this process should not simply be condemned. Producers are bound to make mistakes. But some of them will make innovations that will map new territories for African cinema. We cannot wait for Oliver Stone to come and shoot an epic in Lagos. We have to continue producing to sustain the audience's interest and to keep the film industry growing, however gradually.

Do you see the Yoruba film/theater genre reaching international film markets and functioning as a vehicle for the exportation of Nigeria's cultural heritage? Do you see Yoruba films competing with other well-made films?

Absolutely. The world today is waiting for African films. I would argue that audiences throughout the world are tired of the *Terminator, Lethal Weapon* genre. If we had the means to launch extravagant productions, Africa would take Hollywood by surprise. That means taking Hollywood technology to Africa, shooting films relevant to Africa. Not jokes like *Allan Quatermain, King Solomon's Mines,* or *Out of Africa,* to name a few. We don't need more jungle melodrama, where zebras and tigers run up and down on-screen. The kinds of films that would have a meaningful impact are what we are interested in—epics depicting, for example, the Benin Massacre, the origin of the Oduduwa Dynasty, the true story of the Yoruba people, and many other African stories of epic proportion that remain untold.

But what about aesthetics? While the Yoruba theater is known for its excellence all over the world, some critics argue that most of these Yoruba films look no different from

Hollywood-style jungle melodrama. In the words of one critic, they are not cinematic enough. They are not the sort of artworks that make people proud to say, this is an African aesthetic.

I would argue the opposite. I am proud and happy that Africans are finally appreciating African films. Most Africans do not appreciate the African aesthetic. You never see an African dip his hands in his pocket and buy a painting for two thousand dollars. The filmmakers are lucky that the ordinary citizen appreciates films and comes to watch them. There are many trained filmmakers who can make films better than Hollywood directors, but they do not have Hollywood money. I keep saying it: money and technology. If I had Hollywood money I'd shoot a film that would go to Hollywood or to the Cannes Film Festival and win. Hollywood films have neither substance nor story line, they have only flying helicopters and missiles exploding. I can fill this vacuum with African culture and captivate audiences.

The Mask is an important film. What statement were you trying to make and to whom is the statement directed?

The Mask was made primarily as a way of getting even with Britain. In 1976-77, Nigeria hosted the World Black Festival of Arts and Culture (FESTAC). We wanted to use the famous Bini mask as the emblem of FESTAC. But the mask was in the possession of the British. They claimed it was their own, forgetting that the mask had been stolen from Benin City by the British. The most outrageous statement made by the British authorities was that the mask would not be safe in Nigeria, and that it was also too fragile to be returned to Nigeria. Even when the Nigerian government offered Britain ten million pounds to buy back the mask, they still refused to let us have it. So in the face of this British intransigence, I made a film which suggested that if the Nigerian government cannot legally retrieve the mask, they should take it back the way it was taken by the British. The implication was that three hundred billion pounds' worth of the British Museum would be destroyed in the process; they did not take kindly to that. The British summoned the Nigerian ambassador to discuss the issue. I am very proud to this day that I made that film because it did send shock waves through the British government.

The British media were unsympathetic, condemning *The Mask* as a rough film. They never thought it was possible for a Nigerian to be bold enough to shoot a film inside the British Museum, let alone indicate how the mask could be retrieved. Philosophically, *The Mask* devastated the mind of the British critic. Anytime Africans fight for their rights the West automatically claims they are communists, Marxists, revolutionaries, etc. But direct and sometimes forceful confrontation is the only language the British, still in their colonial mentality, can understand.

When The Mask *was released, some critics thought that it was rough. But if you look at the history of Third World cinema, Latin American cinema, it is not necessarily the film's "aesthetic" quality that matters, but rather the message and its historical and cultural specificity.*

That is exactly my policy, I create my films in the service of my people. I want to see the result of this "rough" film. I want to know if people have listened to the message, if things have changed or if I have educated my people. But I have to tread a fine line because films which are too provocative risk being banned.

Perhaps the most controversial of your films is still The Death of a Black President. *The title alone is enough to galvanize or to provoke even the most quiescent observer. Can you talk about the inspiration, what you hoped to accomplish, the reflection on society?*

The Death of a Black President, like most of my films, was inspired by an actual event. This is a film that focuses on our former president, Murtala Muhammed, who, unfortunately, did not live long enough for Nigerians to know who he really was. During the two hundred days he lived as president, Nigeria changed. People began to feel they belonged to the society, irrespective of hierarchical divisions. This sense of belonging connoted a new awareness of their rights as human beings. But this euphoria dissipated abruptly with Murtala Muhammed's assassination. He was killed because he was of that rare breed, a dynamic Third World leader who Western powers feared would free his country from dependency. His policies were considered anti-British, anti-Western. A stooge, Colonel Dimka, his own friend, killed him. This has become a pattern marking the downfall of African leaders. This was how Patrice Lumumba, Kwame Nkrumah, Thomas Sankara, and many more were killed. These were African leaders who took a stand to defend African interests.

Murtala Muhammed openly supported liberation movements in Angola, Mozambique, and Zimbabwe. We all remember, for example, when Britain was not fully supportive of Zimbabwean independence, how Murtala nationalized two British companies in Nigeria, British Petroleum and ESSO, as a signal that favoritism toward the white minority population in Zimbabwe would not be tolerated. This bold move determined the outcome of the Lancaster Talks in London, which led to the independence of Zimbabwe. His dynamism was unprecedented, and this is exactly what Western imperial governments felt compelled to extinguish. The assassination of African leaders who have refused to be puppets of the West has been orchestrated through blackmail, bribery, and collaboration with the leaders' close, and sometimes most trusted, associates. The film immortalizes this great leader, Murtala Muhammed, for his works, his failures, and his achievements—his place in history. He was almost like a dictator, yes, a dictator, and today Africa needs a dictator, not necessarily Western-style democracy. We need a leader who prioritizes the interests of the people as opposed to exploiting the people under the guise of democracy. Africa needs leaders, not rulers. To this I will add that General Idiagbon, Muhammed's chief of staff, his right-hand man, who embraced his agenda, will remain as one of Nigeria's best leaders, but we did not give him a chance to lead.

You played a leading role in The Death of a Black President, *as in many of your films. What motivated you to play General Odongo, who is really a fictional version of General Gowon?*

Well, first off, we look alike. I am trained as an actor. And again, most Nigerians did not want to partake in the film. I had to bring in an all-foreign crew and about six Hollywood actors. It was only at the last minute that Nigerians started coming out of their shells to act. And as you can see, the characterization was very good. I did my best in that movie. And I thank God that it was a big box-office success in Nigeria.

In fact, this film was well acted. Rudy Walker and many others gave great performances. Could you comment on the problem of finding professional actors and how the use of nonprofessional actors affects the development of African cinema?

The biggest headache about professional acting is that neither the entertainment nor the art industry in Africa is lucrative. Although almost twenty-six universities in Nigeria have departments of theater arts, few students go into acting because there is no future for them. The film industry is not organized to ensure regular and continuous employment, and there are no good television stations.

The people in theater groups have monopolized acting. They have been in the business for a long time, so moving from the stage to film was an easy step for them. They discovered that their presentations could reach a much wider audience more efficiently on film than on stage. Furthermore, it is easier for them to carry the stage play via celluloid to the hinterlands than for the people in the villages to go to the cities to see the stage performances, which they cannot afford anyway. Stage performances used to be very popular in the Yoruba land, but film has killed the stage in Nigeria. Even the Yoruba popular theater, which was once excellent, has lowered its standards because of the impact of film.

Until recently, you were the chairman of the Nigerian Film Corporation. Before your tenure, that corporation had squandered millions of naira without producing a significant film. What did you accomplish there?

As I have said before, our people do not appreciate what is available to them. Filmmakers often go abroad seeking postproduction services when they could easily complete their films in Jos. During my tenure at the NFC, the film laboratory was established, and since then four documentaries have been produced here, including *Ruwanbagaja* by Aihaji Ramalan Nuhu, a former Kano state television producer. The last one was shot to promote the first lady's [Miriam Babangida] program Better Life for Rural Women. This film went on to win an award in China for idea and content. Also during this period, the corporation was able to loan over three and a half million naira to filmmakers. Furthermore, my film *Toriade* was processed and edited there, the sound track was laid there, and it was only sent to America for the release print to be made. Now the NFC is also sponsoring a 35mm film being made at Ahmadou Bello University called *Kulba na Barna*. The NFC has also contributed to the making of about ten documentaries for state governments, the most well-known of which is probably *Women in Development*.

Let me refer back to 1983, when you said, "As far as I am concerned, the Nigerian Film Corporation looks like another of those government parastatals established to fool the nation." Do you still subscribe to that view as ex-chairman of that corporation?

Yes, I still do. The corporation functioned as a viable entity only when I ran it. Being professionals, we were not happy with how the corporation was managed so we decided to make changes. But some people were adamantly opposed to those changes. As soon as the minister of information and culture, Toni Momoh, who supported the changes I was making, was replaced by Alex Akinyele, the board was quickly dissolved. There was no justification for doing this except for the fact that I did not give them the opportunity to embezzle the corporation's funds as they had expected me to do. And since I left, the corporation's activities have come to a standstill because there is no one there to provide effective leadership to the organization. Some of the NFC staff have put in twenty-eight years of service, and they are waiting for their pensions; productivity is not a matter of concern for them so long as their salaries are guaranteed. There was space, there was money, and as chair of the organization, I enjoyed the collaboration of other professionals (there were about three filmmakers on the board).

Furthermore, the president gave me a free hand as a professional to do what I thought was best for the corporation. He said to me, "Go and do this thing. You talk too much. Let's see you do it." So I delivered. But unfortunately, you cannot just walk up to the president every day and complain. The civil servants are afraid to talk, afraid to act, and to give constructive criticism. Every month their salary is guaranteed, so why should they make noise? The place has come to a total standstill. I think most industries should be privatized, including the NFC. The laboratory has been stagnant since I left. The lab is supposed to function, it is there to be used.

You are always at odds with film critics. Some of them have compared your films with the James Bond 007 series, pointing out that your films replicate the Hollywood formula of sex and violence. They think you have not been able to generate what might be called an African aesthetics.

When you are going to war, you don't use a slingshot, you use guns. When the British stole the mask from Africa, they shot our people. We are trying to re-create historical events, and we are living in a very violent society. Furthermore, the Nigerian film-goers are used to seeing Hollywood films, kung fu films, Italian spaghetti Westerns, and Indian melodramatic films, which are inundated with sex and violence. When it comes to the question of making an independent film, one has to treat it as a commercial venture because it is usually funded with borrowed money that has to be paid back whether you like it or not. This is a fact any filmmaker has to constantly contend with. And this is why, while you are being patriotic and nationalistic, you cannot avoid being commercially minded.

I wonder if any critic could tell me what this thing that we call African cinema really is, anyway. We certainly do not have one yet. There is not one unified film style that distinguishes African cinema. We have to create an African film style before we can talk about African cinema. At this stage, we have a cinema of diverse states.

That is exactly where African critics fit in. They are trying to look at African films and then talk with the filmmakers to jointly formulate a discourse on African aesthetics.

I would like to emphasize one last thing, that it is an achievement and a record for one African man to have single-handedly made thirteen feature films with hard-earned money. It is unfair for critics to sit in their ivory towers and run filmmakers down without considering the situation of the filmmaker. Until the critic comes down to earth from that ivory tower of his and talks to the man in the field, the man on the battlefront, he will never be able to digest African cinema. Sometimes I wonder if the critics are not envious of the filmmaker. I think the role of the critic in the development of the cinema should be to give constructive, contributive advice, instead of picking up his Biro and writing trash. That trash does not move me. I can look into that critic's face anytime and say, go to hell with your writing, I am making more films. If I die tomorrow, people will remember Chief Ugbomah as a filmmaker who made such-and-such films, as the former chairman of the NFC and secretary general of the Nigerian Film Society. Those are good achievements and I am very grateful to God. Critics should take the trouble, as you have done, to develop a dialogue with filmmakers and collaborate in the spirit of Pan-Africanism, if only for the sake of encouraging a critical thought system that would interrogate the diversity of African cinema.

With the release of your film Toriade, *you moved away from your own tradition of filmmaking.*

No! No! No! My first films were in English; only later did I start making films in Yoruba. I tried to strike a balance such that my films would appeal to both literate and illiterate audiences. Right now, I'm working on two movies: *Akoba*, a Yoruba film, and *America or Die*, an English film. I serve two audiences. I do it to survive. Luckily for me, the two audiences I am serving are paying. The English films I make sell to my diverse ethnic audience, and the Yoruba films I make sell to the Yoruba audience.

How does this affect your film style?

It kills it. It's pure murder. I'm not free to have an identity. But most of my films, like *The Rise and Fall of Dr. Oyenusi, The Death of a Black President, The Mask, Oil Doom,* and *Bulos 80,* are mainly whodunit films. They are about the problems of the society.

My film *Omiran* was one of the biggest box-office successes in Nigeria. I compare myself to Agatha Christie or Alfred Hitchcock. They are the people I try to emulate. When I shot *The Death of a Black President,* many people tried to discourage me from shooting a film about Murtala Muhammed. But I shot the film. I went through a lot of horror, but I shot the film and today it is one of the biggest successes in Africa. Now ABC-TV in America wants to buy the film. To me, this is quite an achievement.

Do you see oral tradition playing any role in the Africanization of the film language?

American movies have their own identity. British and European countries have their own identities. I think oral tradition is the only true African identity for African movies because the oral tradition is a critical element in our pattern of communication. It seems that the only identity we have now, to which we should hold tight, is the interpretation of our folklore. African film must have its own identity, and its identity is located in the oral narrative technique, just as America's lies in the violent, *Star Wars, Terminator* type.

In other words, is there a possibility for an African film language?

Yes, a very, very big one. It might sound stupid, but it is really true, the world is waiting for African cinema. Someday Africans must deliver. We must redefine an African image that is not Tarzanistic. We have not delivered. African cinema owes the world an answer.

Filmography

The Rise and Fall of Dr. Oyenusi, 1977
The Boy Is Good, 1978
The Mask, 1979
Oil Doom, 1979
Bulos 80, 1980
Vengeance of the Cult, 1982
The Death of a Black President, 1983
Apalara, 1984
Esan (Nemesis), 1985
Omiran (The demons), 1986
The Great Attempt, 1988
Toriade (Fight for the kingdom), 1989
America or Die, 1996
Aba Women Riot, 1999

PART II
VISION AND TRENDS

Flora Gomes (Guinea-Bissau)

Few people in the United States are familiar with the work of Flora Gomes, the most prominent figure in Guinea-Bissau's film industry, because none of his feature films or documentaries have been distributed in this country. Indeed, little is known in the West about either the cinema in Guinea-Bissau or the country itself. This tiny West African nation of less than a million people was under Portuguese colonial rule until 1974, when it became independent. Westerners' opportunity for knowledge of Guinea-Bissau came only during the protracted fifteen-year war of liberation against the Portuguese colonial administration, whose rule was brutal and crass. Some in the West came to know about the war from the scanty coverage given it in the news media. The United States had no vested interest in the African liberation struggles during the Cold War, when any nationalist group fighting for freedom and not bonded with the capitalist ideology was considered communist. In fact, the West supported Portugal, partly because of its status as a NATO country and partly because of U.S. interests in the region. The nationalist struggle sought to create opportunities for Africans, which had been practically nonexistent during centuries of Portuguese rule.

It was also from this struggle that the revolutionary thinker and political philosopher Amilcar Cabral emerged as an indomitable revolutionary whose writings have influenced intellectuals, politicians, and cultural producers, including Flora Gomes. Although cinema is linked to the revolutionary process through the use of documentaries as an educational and indoctrinating tool, Guinea-Bissau's cinema is still one of the least known of West Africa's cinemas. The film industry in Guinea-Bissau, which was established immediately after independence, remains a state enterprise. The government oversees the production of films in the country, but the government itself is grossly underfunded. Facing this national reality, the state could not give precedence to the cinema, especially the production of entertainment films, over the provision of necessities such as medicine for the sick.

Flora Gomes received his formal film training at the Institute of Cuban Art before returning to his country to pursue his career. It was not until 1987 that he produced his first feature, *Mortu Nega* (The one death did not want), which was supported by the state-funded film institute. This was the first fiction film produced inside the country and the second Guinea-Bissau feature film ever made, the first being *N'tturudu* (1987), directed by the exiled filmmaker Umban u'Kset. Following *Mortu Nega*, Gomes's second feature, *Udju Azul de Yonta* (The blue eyes of Yonta), was released in 1992. His latest feature film, *Po Di Sangui* (Tree of blood, 1996), is highly acclaimed. It was an official selection at the Cannes Film Festival and has been shown at various international film festivals, where it has won several awards. These films are remarkable for their creativity and sharp-witted reflections on history, culture, and society. They have received good international exposure, and through them the film history of Guinea-Bissau has been spotlighted.

Gomes's films deal with the question of identity and how to safeguard it in a country that is trying to rebuild itself after the ravages of colonial war and imperialism. His fortitude echoes the philosophical manner in which he discusses history, culture, and cinema. Sometimes very passionate, he is optimistic about the future of African cinema, but he warns that it is the Africans who must transform their future and their cinema. His eloquent and frank reflections on himself, his country, Africa, cinema and culture, and the situation of African cinema in general offer another perspective on the cinema of the diverse cultures of Africa. This interview was conducted in May 1993 at the Brooklyn Museum in New York City, following a screening of *Udju Azul de Yonta*.

How did you begin your film career?

I always say I came to filmmaking by accident. As a high school student in Cuba, I had a very good friend in school who wanted to go into filmmaking and I just decided to do the same thing. I used to play a lot of sports. I liked soccer a lot and I ran well. But after I made the choice to go into filmmaking, everything in my life changed. Very simply, that's how I came to study at the Cuban Film Institute, after which I went to Senegal to study with Paulin Soumanou Vieyra, the late Senegalese filmmaker.

How did your training in Cuba affect the way you look at cinema?

From my point of view as a filmmaker, when one goes abroad to study, what one should learn is the technique. That is what one learns in schools. It's true that the Cuban cinema is very advanced. It has a very descriptive technique, and this is where its strength lies, in its technique. That is what one must learn. Once one acquires this technique, one has to blend it, mix it with one's own personality and way of looking at life, at the world. Cubans are Cuban, so their cinema is Cuban. When I return home, to Africa, to Guinea-Bissau or elsewhere, I have to find the views that correspond to our reality. Just to take one example, let's speak of beauty. The Western concept of beauty is not the same as ours. It is up to us to find our own definition of what beauty is, because our beauty is different. It is not the same beauty as in Asia either. We have to find our own views as creators.

While watching your films, one can see some influences traceable to Cuban dialectic revolutionary film practices. Are you a revolutionary filmmaker?

I don't know if I'm really a revolutionary. *Revolutionary* is such a big word. I would rather say of myself that I am a "contester." In my films I try to bring up the most striking issues in our society. For example, in my first film, *Mortu Nega*, I tried to show how Guinea-Bissau found its way to independence.

Mortu Nega *is a landmark of African film, the first feature of Guinea-Bissau. How was it financed?*

Mortu Nega was the first fiction film shot in Guinea-Bissau. We were faced with many difficulties in making the film, which was produced entirely by the state. The main issue in *Mortu Nega* was an encounter between a people and its past. When I speak of *Mortu Nega*, I never say "my" film, I say "our" film because it was really the project of the entire population of my country.

How did you develop the theme of Mortu Nega *and what were you trying to achieve with the film?*

As I said before, I wanted to show how the people of Guinea-Bissau got their independence. Guinea-Bissau was not as fortunate as other African countries, like Senegal, the Republic of Guinea, and Mali, who gained their independence without going to war. I wanted to show that. I also wanted to show that everything people did, people such as Amilcar Cabral, who was a very great man, started to give meaning to what we were doing. As I said earlier, I do not suggest alternatives. As a "contester," I am someone who, above all, makes observations and remarks on issues. It's this message which is so important not only for Guinea-Bissau, but also for all those countries that went to war, such as Angola, Guinea-Bissau, Mozambique, Cape Verde, and Vietnam. In a very simple way, this postwar transition period is what I wanted to show—in a way as simple as the view of a child.

Mortu Nega *on one level develops as a love story. In your second film,* The Blue Eyes of Yonta, *you also use the love story to convey the powerful African day-to-day reality. Is there a correlation between love and the liberation struggle?*

I was interested in showing the part of war that does not usually get shown—the behavior and the place of the human being in war situations. The aspect of human relationships is more beautiful than what one usually shows, which is only weapons and men. My only intentions were to show the poetic aspects of the love of a woman, Diminga, who is not a militant. She was in the war because she wanted to see her husband. This issue—love—is a taboo in our society. It's the same issue I raise again in *The Blue Eyes of Yonta*—this look at the role of love, which we don't discuss openly. I wanted to show that in my second feature-length film, and also how we Africans copy from others. Think of the letter in the narrative, the content has nothing to do with our reality.

Also, there is no snow in Africa, and the girl does not have blue eyes. This is a very important issue, perhaps more important now than it has ever been—the question of what we Africans want exactly. Why, for example, did they say that blue is good? This young boy recopied a letter from a book which might be as much as a century old. I wanted to point out how, back in his subconscious, this boy might believe it from having been told that blue is better than brown. That might go back very deep in his subconscious. This is central to the concept of aesthetic. Why are black or brown eyes not considered beautiful? Why blue eyes of Yonta? Are black eyes not beautiful? Probably because we have always been told that the snow is more beautiful than the sun. I think this is where our problem lies in Africa, and we should go back to the very first steps and question what our goals of development should be, what we want, how we want to develop ourselves and our countries. These are the questions; I do not propose the alternatives.

Mortu Nega and The Blue Eyes of Yonta *bring women out of the shadows. In* Mortu Nega, *women participate in the liberation struggle and also in funeral dances, which are usually performed by men. And in* The Blue Eyes of Yonta, *women characters come out strongly as signifiers of culture and solidarity.*

First let me say that when I initially dream and think of my film subject, I don't differentiate between men and women. In my opinion, if there is a difference, one could say that women are more honest and more pure than men. This is probably because they've suffered a lot. Cabral used to say that African women went through two kinds of exploitation: that of the European colonizers and that of their husbands. This is perhaps why their look at the society is more profound. But I think that what's key to my two films are the children, because the children are the future. Since there is a very strong relationship between women and children, these two character representations are always in the forefront in my films.

In both films Cabral's image is highly invoked. In Mortu Nega *he symbolizes nationalism; in* The Blue Eyes of Yonta *his is a symbol of liberation which we see through the little boy named Amilcar. By naming this boy Amilcar, were you referring to Amilcar Cabral's leadership in the liberation of Guinea-Bissau?*

One has to say that when you speak of Guinea-Bissau, the first thing that comes to mind is the image of Amilcar Cabral. And I might add when you speak about honest men, men who have cultural and political stature in Africa, you cannot but mention Cabral. This is why in the course of the creation of this film it was hard to do anything but include Amilcar Cabral, who has done so much not only for our country but for all of Africa. Just to give you an example, most people in Guinea-Bissau have Portuguese names. After the liberation struggles, the first thing that Cabral said is that everyone should keep his or her African name. He is not against the Portuguese, but he believes we should keep our African names, that our African names are just as beautiful as the Portuguese names. An example to show how we had been treated: before the war it was impossible for girls to go to school dressed in their African *pagna*. It was impossible for them to go with braided hair; they had to have their hair straight. This is why I think Cabral has a very important place in our society.

Cabral's teaching on culture is also apparent in your film. The wedding cake reminds me of Ousmane Sembene's wedding cake in Xala*—in both cases the cake is an alien product.*

Yes, and I have to say that it's too bad that Africa has not fully realized the importance and the role of Sembene in African cinema. He has a role just as important as Cabral, Nkrumah, Lumumba, and all these men, because he was the one who had the courage to use cinema as a new medium in Africa. He said that it is possible for Africans to work in cinema. To be honest, one should say that African cinema is a synonym with Ousmane Sembene. I am not saying that he did the most beautiful African films, but I am saying he is the one who had the courage to embark on this wonderful adventure and to encourage us to join with him. When mentioning Sembene, one would mention also Souleymane Cissé as one who reflects values in the context of African cinema. Each time one speaks with them, one feels that one is truly speaking with encouraging people. I still don't know how to make films, and I have to learn with them.

There is an emotional sequence in The Blue Eyes of Yonta *where we see the children return a woman's furniture to her house from which she had been evicted. What is the film trying to say in regard to children and the changing African world? Doesn't this powerful sequence foreground children and their role in a changing African world?*

This generation is the hope, it is the future. It will mature with our way of thinking, with our dynamic, but with one more important thing, their being aware of African realities and African culture. As long as this awareness is not fully accomplished, things will not change. As in all countries of the world, our countries too, the challenges we are seeing are ones of transition, of mutation, and it takes people to understand those challenges and new realities. As long as we in Africa don't understand that black is as beautiful as blue and the sun as beautiful as the snow, we will not move forward.

Toward the end of The Blue Eyes of Yonta, *the clock stops and then everybody freezes. What happens next?*

We have to stop because we started poorly. Someone has already said that. Just like when you build a house, if you feel that something is not going right, it is better to stop or else the house will fall down. Think of the sequence in the film where the tables just roll alone. This is suffering; one would say that human beings were carrying those tables. We have to stop and start all over again because the model, the way we want to develop our country, is the dream of others. It is not the dream of us Africans who want to see our country as beautiful as France, the United States, Japan, like every other place. Ironically, never before has Africa been so dependent on the big powers, and I might even go so far as to say, not even before independence.

I have the greatest respect for men like Cabral, Nkrumah, Sekou Touré, and Lumumba, who have done extraordinary things. I respect very much what they did, but Africa has to find its own face. Africa does exist, but it is nowhere in this confrontation of nations. Last year I remember reading a book by Francis Fukuyama, *The End of History and the Last Man.* When you read what is being written on Africa you just feel ashamed. In my film I tried to show that in the look of Amilcar, in the look of the other children, Africa will one day find its place. In any African city I go to, the first thing I look at is this look of the children and that makes me believe that Africa will find its place. In this effort, African culture must play a very important role.

What do you think is the future of African cinema?

The future of African cinema cannot be very far from our own reality, the economic situation in Africa. For example, I am sure my films, *Mortu Nega* and *The Blue Eyes of Yonta,* and other African films were not shown in Nigeria, which is a very big country. If films were shown in Nigeria, Cameroon, Zimbabwe, that would bring in the money which we need to make other films. That is what Africa needs. As long as this does not happen, we will always have to turn to Europe for subsidies. We cannot make films with subsidies. There is a will of French authorities to help Africa in a way, but until when? Will they understand our vision, our way of writing cinema? Everyone has to write his or her cinema just as he or she feels it. Today we speak of African cinema, but the day may be close when we speak of the cinema of Nigeria, the cinema of Senegal, the cinema of Burkina Faso, the cinema of Guinea-Bissau, and even the cinema of South Africa. One does not refer to something such as American cinema; people say North American cinema, Latin American cinema, Mexican cinema, Argentinean cinema, Cuban cinema, Brazilian cinema, because there is a known culture and a style that is used by filmmakers in each country.

We can identify two trends of filmmaking in Africa, the one initiated by the pioneers, Ousmane Sembene et al., and the one initiated by the new breed of African filmmakers. We are beginning to see all sorts of films, good and bad. How do you situate your film practice within these cultural, political, and aesthetic trends?

When a child begins to walk, he or she has a hard time standing up. The mother or father has to stand by and hold the child. In my own case, I have my hand up, and I like it when Sembene takes me by the hand; otherwise I would fall, and if I fall, it is finished. I will have a lot of trouble standing up again. It's up to everyone else to say what they think.

Mortu Nega was shown at FESPACO. How was it received and what is your impression of FESPACO?

The reaction when *Mortu Nega* was shown in FESPACO was a total surprise. One has to remember that FESPACO is the cinematographic event in black Africa. When I finished *Mortu Nega*, I wanted to just drop everything. I never thought I would find the energy within me to make another film. When the film went to FESPACO, the response of the audience in Ouagadougou was so wonderful it just inspired me to do something else for this public that I love so much. I would add that I'm still a small filmmaker; sometimes we are forgotten. Because of that I was not able to go to FESPACO. Apparently they forgot us. First, we are a small country, and second, I do not personally consider myself a filmmaker yet. Maybe that will come. But I was told that the film was very well received over there.

Describe the achievements and failures of the Instituto Nacional de Cinema of Guinea-Bissau.

The institute in Guinea-Bissau is facing the same situation or maybe even a worse situation than similar institutes in Africa. Usually governments create those institutes, but then have problems making them work. So the activities of the National Institute are mostly limited to giving grants and scholarships for film students to go and study abroad. Very little has been done so far in production. There is an attempt to bring in some new film equipment, and maybe that will let us do something for television and other productions.

What role does television play in Guinea-Bissau?

The situation of television is the same all over Africa. We receive images from Canal France International and from Portugal because of the language issue. The programs produced locally are about visits of heads of states and conferences, but other than that we do not have the means to do more. Therefore, we African filmmakers fight against our not having television that shows African films, but rather it shows *Dallas*, Brazilian films, and soap operas. We have to fight to change this situation.

What is your next project, and what is it about?

My next project is another folly, because, as I always say, to make films in our countries, one has to be crazy. My next film is a story about nature and human beings. Twins are born who later plant two trees. One tree dies and one of the twins dies. So this will be the theme of my next film, the relationship between the surviving man and the tree of his brother who died.

How is this film going to be financed? Have you already raised the money?

Not yet. I am waiting for the response of the authorities of my country. After that, the normal way is to go to France, but I am also looking in the United States to see if I can find a production company interested in this type of thing.

Have you considered coproduction with other African countries? Burkina Faso, for instance, has given money to some filmmakers to help them make their films.

It is true that Burkina coproduces a lot of African films. I haven't looked into that, because there are so many ongoing coproductions that it's hard for me to go to this source.

Filmography

Mortu Nega (The one death did not want), 1988
Udju Azul de Yonta (The blue eyes of Yonta), 1992
Po Di Sangui (Tree of blood), 1996

Gaston Kaboré (Burkina Faso)

Gaston Kaboré is one of the best known African filmmakers. He has played a crucial role in and contributed immensely to the development of African cinema. He was educated in Burkina Faso as well as in France. After his high school education, in 1970, Kaboré enrolled at the Centre d'Etudes Supérieures d'Histoire de Ouagadougou to study history. After two years of study, he left for Paris to attend the Sorbonne, where he obtained a master's degree in history in 1972. There, he developed an interest in film—not filmmaking at this point, but, as he puts it, the "use of cinema as a means of popularizing history." He wanted to use film to extend the research on history that he was doing at that time. However, his extensive viewing of the images of Africa in the illustrated press as he examined how Africa has been portrayed in the French media marked what he describes as a "turning point" for his decision to go into film production. Thus, while he continued to use film in his historical research for his doctoral thesis, Kaboré decided also to acquire formal training in filmmaking.

In 1974, he began training at the French film school, l'Ecole Supérieure d'Etudes Cinématographiques (ESEC). After obtaining his diploma in filmmaking, the young filmmaker returned to his home country, where he was appointed director of the Centre National du Cinéma (CNC), a position he held concurrently with a teaching appointment at the Institut Africain d'Etudes Cinématographiques (INAFEC), teaching filmmaking and scriptwriting courses. It was also during this period that Kaboré launched his filmmaking career with several short documentary films before making his debut as a feature film director. This resulted in the realization of *Wend Kuuni* (God's gift, 1982), the highly acclaimed film that would catapult him to fame. Made with the help of a crew supplied by the CNC, *Wend Kuuni* made history as the first film entirely funded by the state through Burkina Faso's national film funding agency, Fonds de Promotion et d'Extension de l'Activité Cinématographique.

Today, Kaboré holds a doctorate in history and is a dynamic and highly respected intellectual, historian, filmmaker, and administrator, known for his relentless efforts to develop African film industries. A coolheaded gentleman, Kaboré is unassuming and taciturn; his eloquent pronouncements are as electrifying as they are incisive. He is a likable character in his humble way, and it is this humility that makes him a unique kind of filmmaker who is easily accessible. In my view, these are the special attributes that have enabled him to triumph as the secretary general of the Pan-African Federation of Filmmakers, a position he held from 1985 to 1997, and as a successful filmmaker whose latest release, *Bud Yam* (1997) won the grand prize at FESPACO, the Étalon de Yennega, in 1997. This interview was conducted at the Pan-African Festival of Film and Television of Ouagadougou in 1991 and 1995.

What encouraged you to work in the film medium?

I embraced filmmaking in a somewhat peculiar manner. Certainly, as many young city dwellers, I loved to go to the cinema, but actually I never once dreamed of becoming a film producer. After studying history in my country for two years, I went to Sorbonne University in Paris, where I completed my bachelor's and master's degrees. For my doctorate in history I decided to study the image of black Africa in the illustrated press in France at the end of the nineteenth century, from 1885 to 1900. I chose to work specifically on *Le petit journal illustre* and, for this reason, frequently visited the Overseas Library, which was once located at the Oudinot Street in Paris, to examine photographs and study the images that I had chosen to support my work. I think that was the turning point for going from history toward cinema.

Looking back, after my master's I wanted to use cinema as a means of popularizing history. This was basically the ultimate ambition, which, for me, paved the path toward cinema. Having decided to learn the language of images in order to use them in my discipline of study, history, I went to l'Ecole Supérieure d'Etudes Cinématographiques in Paris for two years while continuing to work on my graduate studies in history. Once I was in the film school, I realized, little by little, that I had much more of an affinity for film than I had imagined. I decided, definitively, to use the cinema to tell stories, for example, to use archaeological film to recount history. So I majored in film production and obtained my diploma. My case is not extraordinary, but this is how it happened.

What are your primary or secondary sources of influence in filmmaking?

I think, simply, that my education has influenced me the most. I use the term *education* in its most generic sense, beginning first with the education I received as a child in my family. In spite of the fact that I lived in the city, my education was profoundly informed by an ancient cultural heritage. Family education is of utmost importance, because it is the primary platform from which we see life and interpret the reality surrounding us. But in terms of cinematic influences, I must say that I was immersed in the universe of adventure films, westerns, etc. The underpinning of my "cinematic culture" consists of adventure films with many westerns, police films, etc.

Perhaps, after all, what was unique to my cinema studies—not to be mistaken as a kind of personal vindication—was that I refused to watch any of the major films that were recommended to us at school. I wanted to learn first how to speak with images before eventually learning to speak like the masters or the professionals do. That is very important. There are many films that most film students cannot even imagine not seeing but which I did not see at all. I think that was very useful to me because when I made *Wend Kuuni*, I didn't have any model of filmmaking in my head. I simply wanted to tell a story as I felt it, and as I believed it was best to attain its objective, so it could touch my audiences on the levels of their minds, bodies, and sensibilities. This is why I cannot cite a single film director who has had a conscious influence on the way I perceive cinema. Now that I've been able to make two feature-length films, I want to see important films that have marked film history, because I have the impression that I can see them without "losing myself" and my sense of doing things.

The film that catapulted you to the international limelight is Wend Kuuni. *Would you please describe your media works prior to this film?*

I made several short films that focused on diverse subjects. They are films at once documentary and journalistic. The first short film I made, *Comment stocker et préserver les grains au milieu rural* [How to stock and preserve grains in rural areas, 1977], was a film with a social purpose. Following a seminar I participated in, I wanted to make a film to promote the improvement of traditional techniques of grain conservation in countries of the Sahel region. The Sahel climate is very restricting, and it is the area where harvests are already weak and where conservation of grain is very important. After that I made a film on the sixth FESPACO. The title of this film is *Le regard sur le sixième FESPACO* [A look at the sixth FESPACO, 1979]. It was a film report on the holding of the sixth Pan-African Film Festival in Ouagadougou. Next, I made another film on a rural subject called *Utilisation des énergies nouvelles en milieu rural* [The use of new forms of energy in rural areas, 1980]. It looks at how solar energy could present itself as an alternative to the energy crisis and, most notably, how it could serve as a palliative to the problem of deforestation. If we are able to bring a form of energy as inexpensive as those derived from solar energy to farmers, it will contribute to the restoration of environmental balance. It will also allow for an improvement in hygiene and nutrition, since we are capable of drying certain seasonal foods that we eat at other times of the year when they are scarce. In total, I have made about seven short films. The last short film I have made is *Propos sur le cinéma Africain* [Discourse on African cinema, 1981]. I made it in the framework of the magazine *Communauté economique Européenne*, with the intention of bringing out, in fifteen minutes, the problems of African cinema. The film makes it clear that although

African cinema has trouble developing and that the productions are foreign in their own countries, nonetheless this cinema is eagerly awaited by Africans because it is their cinema, and they are thirsty for their own images.

With the making of Wend Kuuni, *you seem to have developed your personal style.*

I am not sure that with only one feature we can say that a director has discovered his personal style. However, I must say that in making *Wend Kuuni*, I thought a great deal about the most efficient manner to bring the story to the screen. I wrote *Wend Kuuni* first as a story that is set in an undetermined time before the colonial period. Certainly, one characteristic of the story is its timelessness, and I adapted the oral storytelling technique to the structure in order to highlight the little boy's tragic situation. I think this is what makes it more interesting to people. In a tale, there is space for poetry, there is time for reflection, for the unexpected, for dreams, and time for everyday occurrences—an everyday that can seem immutable but which is, at times, the theater of startling, unexpected events, and of convulsions that can be very swift. I think this film succeeded in certain ways in revealing altogether another possibility for telling African stories. But I think we must not rush to say that I have truly found a personal style with this film. I think I told the story in an interesting manner and this is probably why this film has received considerable international esteem. Perhaps *Wend Kuuni* has also marked a new turn, at least, in African cinema.

By 1980, African films addressed a diverse range of themes, some of which were very militant, political, historical, or cultural. Wend Kuuni *is folkloric but not debasing. How did you conceive the scenario?*

Wend Kuuni is a film that tells the story of a society still rooted in its traditions and in its profound cultural heritage, situated within its social constraints. In fact, *Wend Kuuni* is firstly the story of a little boy but with other attachments as subplots. Thus it is also the story of a friendship between two children, the small mute boy, Wend Kuuni, and the adopted sister, Pognéré, that he will have after his adoption by a peasant family. Actually, I did this film first and foremost to tell a story, and I sought the best way that my film could be understood by my people and Africans in general. I think this is also what gives it its universal appeal. In order to achieve the universal characteristics, I thought we must proceed from the particular. It is my profound conviction that it is only when one knows how to speak to the people of one's village with words that the villagers use everyday that it becomes possible to speak to people from all over the world in a language they too would understand. Hence the cinematic language chosen would be answerable to the traditional setting, and the manner in which it scrutinizes the society, to show from within the existing patterns of injustice. But the film also shows that there have always been, even in societies still anchored in tradition, forces of progress and resistance.

Wend Kuuni brings to light how each time women have refused to submit to social pressure and to custom, they have propelled history to a progressive height. The first woman, the mother of the little boy, refuses to remarry because she is convinced that her husband, who did not return from hunting, is not dead. Therefore, she wants to endure, waiting with fidelity and love for the return of her husband. The second is a young woman who was given in marriage to an impotent old man. She finally revolts because, by her estimation, she has the right to a younger husband of her choice. And the words of revelation she delivers publicly to the old man, which he considers too degrading, cause him to hang himself. This is precisely what provokes the shock that gives the young mute boy the ability to speak again upon discovering the old man's dangling body. It is from this point he tells his story, which everybody has been anxious to hear. In fact, *Wend Kuuni* is narrated in the manner of oral art. It assumes there is a restoration of an atmosphere that illustrates the lives of people committed to their environment but, with attendant controversies, is not unique to the community's space and destiny. It is not at all a film that aims to show aspects of Africa in an ethnographic manner, but truly one that utilizes all of the social, cultural, and environmental materials available to frame Wend Kuuni's story and the story of a peasant community.

Wend Kuuni *is a touching human-interest story of a simple scenario, but the narrative is composed of stories within stories, which combine to create a coherent whole.*

It's true. Many people have remarked that there is a simple narrative style in *Wend Kuuni* which is based on traditional storytelling technique, the oral tradition, and, at the same time, from the point of view of cinematic construction. For example, there is a flashback inside of a flashback. This seems to have been a rather audacious choice because it is unusual to find such a technique in conventional narrative structures. But in fact, I took many liberties in making this film because what interested me above all was to tell the story and to make it accessible to the largest number of people possible. Paradoxically, in spite of the fact that the structure is unorthodox, there is no barrier to comprehension even for the least-educated public or the most ill-informed alien of African cultures. I think the strength of *Wend Kuuni* is probably its simplicity and also the sense of truth that emerges from the characters, the sincerity that we feel at the interior of each image. For me the music played an equally large role in the film. Even though the film takes place in a traditional African setting, I decided to use symphonic music because I wanted to show that the musical themes of rural areas could be the objects of modern orchestration. In this way, I wanted to give an unusual amplitude and depth to music which some may perceive as primary. I wanted to use modern instruments, which are finally the synthesis of all instruments that have been invented in diverse parts of Africa and which were, each one of these modern instruments, perfected with Western technology.

What is an African film? Do you consider oral tradition as the quintessence of African aesthetics? What is your vision regarding the aesthetics of African cinema now that the production processes are being diversified?

As I said before, I was first influenced by my education, and this education was immersed in the global cultural heritage in which I lived. Oral storytelling is one of the dominant cultural features in my society. Certainly my manner of speaking and storytelling is thoroughly influenced by this heritage of orality. Definitely, what is important is to profoundly live one's own cultural reality. And from this point of departure, things that spring from that culture naturally nourish us. Without a doubt there is a need for research because, as Africans, we must question ourselves on the manner of expressing our cultures in film. Therefore, little by little, with the large quantity of films that Africans will be making, we will perceive a certain characteristic or tendency unique to African cinema. But this research is still waiting to be done, and also many more films must be made so that we can study the aesthetics and rhythms of African films. Personally, when I want to tell a story and make a film, I make an effort to draw as much as possible from my culture, the perception of the world unique to my society, the way people conceive of space, manage time, and live in their environment. I also want to explore their particular relationships with earth and nature, with religious aspects, but also with the affective aspects, the whole mythological universe which belongs to or has been appropriated by my society.

The use of child actors and the development of their characters are two of the things that make Wend Kuuni *so powerful. The roles they play and the rapport between the two children make the film especially gripping for the audience.*

My intention with this film was to touch the public by telling a tender story, but a story that is also harsh for the fact that the destiny of Wend Kuuni was filled with tragedy. But the friendship between the two children is incredibly touching. Certainly when people see the film they should consider the story as a whole. It is not like a cocktail mixture concocted from different ingredients. We are talking about the story of a child in conflict with a traumatic universe, of a society with its men, women, children, their customs and social organizations and whose rhythm of life can be seen also as illuminating the society's perception of the world. I think the reason this film was so well received by audiences around the world is that despite the fact that it tells with sentiment a story particular to a given society, the feeling which it captures makes them feel the story could have happened anywhere. And I believe it is this manner of impacting upon people that is most important for me in narrative construction. When I make a film, it is important that the story is deeply rooted in its own reality—the reality that nourishes itself from the force that that reality radiates. With this foundation, there are chances that the story could also touch, seduce, and question other cultures in different parts of the world.

In your next film, Zan Boko, *the style is the same as that of* Wend Kuuni *but you inter-weave different themes that are political, social, and historical. How do you exercise your thematic and stylistic discretions?*

I think that in some respects each film reflects the experiences of the individual who made it. I think *Zan Boko* translates, by means of a particular narrative style, a bit of the vision that I have of the world and the questions that I ask myself in relation to this world. It also translates my own convictions, the things in which I have faith. In telling the story of this small village, I wanted to speak a bit about the heritage of the past and of the manner in which we can use the positive values of our rural societies. I think that the prospects are good in cinema, but what I contest is all of the social manifestations of modernity. They are not necessarily more valuable than, or superior to, social manifestations in the traditional world. Clearly my films could not avoid historical, social, and political developments, because we have always lived in an environment that contains these elements. Is *Zan Boko* at once a synthesis of these elements? I am not sure we can characterize it as such. It was important for me that I showed the uneasy juxtaposition of two worlds—the traditional world still dominant in the rural milieu and the modern Africa, exemplified by the city, greed and material possessions, and political, administrative and economic powers. I wanted to show how these new values, in my opinion, are not the best in the current forms of their appropriation in the developing nations of Africa. I have the feeling that in the rural world there is much more wealth of value, even if it is a world which is considered by some as inferior today, simply because it appears to be condemned to disappear. In fact, I think that in order to construct a purposeful Africa, rather than focusing on materialism alone, we must not relent in our efforts to preserve certain aspects of traditional values that guarantee the happiness of our people while appropriating the elements of the so-called modernity forced on us.

In fact, *Zan Boko* is a social project that poses questions on the problems of urbanization and development. What I mean by that is that those who direct our countries often fail to address the profound desires or fundamental aspirations of the group that constitutes the majority of the population, that of the rural world. I think that we need to help the rural areas to develop, but all the while bearing in mind that this rural world also has riches that can be used to build contemporary Africa. I wanted to foreground those issues as well as deal with those relating to free speech. The right to speech and freedom of expression assumes a primary concern here because this film also brings to the forefront the problem of the confiscation of free speech by a minority at the fore.

The first half of the film shows different aspects of traditional culture. The images may look ethnographic but are anthropological in the African sense, the way Burkinabes live. Obviously, you chose these images to critique the conflict between new and old traditions—the rich and the poor—both of which culminate in the end of the film to highlight the clash of traditions capable of eroding societal values.

In the first part of the film, I wanted people to understand the rural world. I wanted them to see this part of the world where I live, not only through its material manifestations but also in the ways in which it sees reality, how it uses its time, and how the relationships between people are developed. One can understand that time is highly valued in this rural world, even if this value is not measured as it is in the modern world. Through the peasant world, we get the impression that we always have all of the time for ourselves. We take time to say hello to one another and to ask about the news of grandmothers, children, grandchildren, and other relatives. We take time to be silent before speaking. We take time to interest ourselves in other people. In the first part of the film I wanted to truly render the value of sociological and humanistic time. I did not want the imperatives of cinematic narrative time to force me to gloss over or to leave out important elements in the rural world I portray. That is why, for example, in the scene of the childbirth, when the elder traditional midwives realize that Tinga's wife is having difficulties giving birth to her child, one elder midwife comes out and speaks to the circle of elders, who suggest to her how to present herself. The elders then call Tinga and tell him what the elder midwife said, and then Tinga goes to see her and she repeats what she has already said to the elders and what the elders have already told Tinga. Cinematically, it is a waste of time to show these various conversations in real time, but it was important for me to do so because it was the only way to capture the reality of the cycle of communication in a society such as this.

Therefore, when we tell a story, I think it is important not to merely submit oneself to the necessities of the story. We must also know how to apply the things which we do not notice every day simply because they seem so natural and which we risk destroying simply because we did not know how to give them the necessary attention. That is what I wanted to do in the film. I wanted to show a world that has its own rhythm of life and its own values, but a world that will suddenly disappear if the city keeps growing. I wanted people to appreciate the beauty and complexity of the rural space and its physicality, for example, the land, which supports the cultural space whose affective relation with the people would disappear to the benefit of the new ways of occupying this land. This occupation only benefits the new culture—the culture of the city and the culture of modernity—that has come to be implant in it.

Zan Boko is also a film about censorship, but events portrayed in the national television sequence could also reflect media censorship in other African countries. What is the political significance of this extraordinary sequence?

Reminiscent of my earlier assertion regarding *Wend Kuuni*, in my opinion, an author's point of view most often reflects his or her own reality. *Zan Boko* is evocative of my own experience of life. But it is also evocative of the problems we face in my country and some aspects of my experience that were woven into the story, and it is true that some of these issues also have continental dimensions. The political issue the film raises concerning censorship can arise in other places throughout the rest of the world. But it is also true that the issues might not have the same connotations everywhere, and that they could be illustrated in different ways. However, in *Zan Boko* it was important for me to begin with issues that are culturally and politically specific to my local environment.

How did the story of Zan Boko *come to you?*

The story of *Zan Boko* came to me one day as I was visiting a very beautiful house owned by a rich man. When I was standing on the balcony of this house, I saw below, in the neighboring compound, a peasant home—a traditionally constructed hut. In this compound was also a sheep pen, a chicken coop, a grindstone, etc., and I asked myself how it can be possible that two houses like that coexist. The significance of these two unequal spaces is symptomatic of typical African life. I saw the existing dichotomy as images, and these two images, the rich modern house and the neighboring peasant's house, as quite distinct but analogous to modern-day contradictions in Africa. Here is the real Africa—Africa which still lives immersed in its tradition and ancestral lifestyle and the modern Africa that is rapidly changing and in the process of possibly rebuilding itself, at the expense of the former. These images gave me a first-hand emotional shock, and from this the story of *Zan Boko* developed. The story did not originate from what one would term intellectual reasoning, but rather from the visualization of the dichotomous spaces coupled with the emotional shock that I experienced in observing that particular situation. And from this emerged a crystallization of the other things I had known but had not yet found the appropriate device or mechanism to combine them to form the story which I eventually told in *Zan Boko*.

An issue raised in Zan Boko *is that of investigative journalism, where live broadcast reveals the dichotomy between the elite and peasant community. How do film and television work as instruments of evolutionary change in Burkina Faso?*

I think film and television are two important aspects of information media in Africa today. Cinema is a very important urban phenomenon, and it is a vehicle for dreams and fantasies. And in an Africa that is trying to grapple with the problems of development, African cinemas are indispensable, as foreign films which are shown in our theaters contribute to keeping African peoples in a state of subjugation. They are films which glorify the power and "superiority" of Western cultures. There is no doubt that the cinema can be used as a means of fostering social, economic, and political liberation in our own hemisphere. This means that we must make films that provide us with alternative dreams and models. That is why I have faith in the film medium contributing to social and political changes. To achieve this goal means that we must seriously consider the ways in which we make and use films. As for television, until now, it has been under state control and has been essentially used to propagate the opinion of the state, to transmit government information to the population, and to demonstrate certain points of view—governmental authority, or that of the public. I wanted to use the film to examine the effects of television because it is an area that is just beginning to be the topic of academic discourse. Actually, it would be extremely informative to examine African television programs and to analyze how local television productions in most of the countries are completely dominated by present political structures—I mean the propagandist imperatives of the powers that be.

For an individual to use this fortress of power [the state television] to express alternative views is very dangerous. However, the film constructs a superhero character, an undaunted journalist, Yabre Tounsida, who takes it upon himself to expose how television is a powerful medium of information, and how, if constructively used, it could help in bringing about societal change. When our hero goes on the air on state television with his investigative journalism to expose corrupt government practices—an alternative opinion that differs from that of the government—we see how his program is yanked off the air. This type of censorship underscores one of the determining aspects of Africa's evolution today. Basically, my film was a precursor to all that has recently happened in Africa, with the popular uprisings in many countries representative of the early stages in the growing process of democracy. However, appropriating the term *democracy* in a lesser spectacular way as it is echoed in the West, I will simply state that there have always been in Africa forces of change, and that there have always been people who have taken the risk of saying things that those in power do not wish to hear.

A recent development in African cinema is that one can now find African films on video. You are one of those who initiated this trend. What factors encourage the use of video now, and how can it contribute to the future of African cinema?

I think that evolution imposes itself on African filmmakers. It is not up to us to decide to be interested in video. Video is already making an impact in Africa; video is shown on television via satellite and it is in the process of completely changing audiovisual possibilities in Africa. We must consider those impacts. It has always been the ambition of African filmmakers to reach the public, and in order to reach the public, we must be realistic and try to utilize every medium and format available to us. In my opinion, the African filmmaker should not try to live in a world of utopia where only the use of film is sanctioned. The individual must integrate all the mutations that are taking place today in the filmic interpretation of life. I am ready to make films using the video format if I feel it is the best way to reach the public. It is another way of working, and of exploring to our advantage the possibilities of production facilities available to us. I would also like to continue using the celluloid film, but I know it is not the only means to tell stories, to reach the public, or to express myself and relate to those issues that are dear to my heart. African producers must exploit every possible means of production to bring images to our screens. That is important, and I believe our endeavors can greatly contribute to a cultural affirmation, which is necessary if Africa is to continue to exist with its own image and identities.

What is the relationship between your role as president of the Pan-African Federation of Filmmakers and your role as a filmmaker?

The two positions are not really at odds with each other. If there is any conflict between them, it has to do with time management. Obviously, the time I spend working for FEPACI is time that I cannot use to work on my own films. But I think that working for FEPACI is important as it helps to foster the aspirations of the continental organization, whose commitment is to improve the conditions under which filmmakers in Africa operate. If I can contribute to this improvement, I, too, will benefit, and I hope the work I do for FEPACI will help us make films more easily in Africa.

In the twelfth FESPACO, it seemed to me that, regarding the films showcased, quantity was emphasized over quality. Do you agree with this, and, if so, what do you think the ramifications are for the future of African cinema?

I am not sure if I agree with this analysis concerning the twelfth FESPACO, but anyway, I think quantity is also important. For me, quality can emerge from quantity. We need to produce more films because Africa consumes a lot of images. We have to confront the problem of scarcity and aim for buoyancy through not only films but also television and video. But in order for Africa to exist culturally, and to continue to project its own cultural perspective, its own ability to develop and to carry out its own development, we need to produce a tremendous quantity of African images. So, for me, quantity is not automatically a negative thing. What we need today is to produce, and through this mass of productions we may find mastery. We cannot escape this logic, even in the U.S. If American cinema is dominating the rest of the world, it is because they are producing a lot of films. The major part of these movies might not be good, but it helps to maintain the industry and to finance the blockbuster films that are produced in Hollywood. However, I must say that in this FESPACO I think we are seeing the emergence of young talents, individuals who are developing their own personalities and a particular manner of saying what seems important to them. I think we must be careful not to jump to conclusions. We may say sometimes to ourselves that the films shown at the festival are not great, but what makes a film great? Is it due to its production style and technique, or to its exterior beauty? Some will say a film is great based on the force of the message that it conveys. We need both. We need films of superior technical quality, but, above all, it is essential that through the films there are authors who speak of essential things. And I think that in these terms, the films at the twelfth FESPACO were interesting.

What are your plans for your next project?

I hope to be able to shoot three films this year, of which two will be documentaries and one will be a fiction film of about fifty-two minutes. These are projects already at hand, therefore I am not going to make any feature-length films this year. But next year I think I will be in a position to shoot a sequel to my first feature, *Wend Kuuni*. When I shot *Wend Kuuni* in 1982, I did not produce the whole original scenario, and for a long time people have asked me why I have not made the sequel. The idea of making a sequel did not interest me very much as I did not want to force myself to make *Wend Kuuni II* simply because the first film was very successful. I waited ten years to convince myself that it could be interesting to make the sequel. In fact, the sequel will not bear the same title. The title of the next film, the story of which follows *Wend Kuuni*, is *Bud Yam*.[1] That is the feature film I want to produce next.

Do you plan to use professional actors in Bud Yam*?*

Yes, I hope to raise money in Europe, France, England, Italy, maybe Germany, and, why not, the United States. So the film will be made in coproduction with money that comes from many different sources. I will use practically the same actors who played in *Wend Kuuni*, some of whom have become very good actors. We may not be able to call them professionals because they don't make a living from the money they make in films, but they have become professionals in terms of the quality of their artistic performances.

Filmography

Comment stocker et préserver les grains au milieu rural (How to stock and preserve grains in rural areas), 1977
Le regard sur le sixième FESPACO (A look at the sixth FESPACO), 1979
Utilisation des énergies nouvelles en milieu rural (The use of new forms of energy in rural areas), 1980
Propos sur le cinéma Africain (Discourse on African cinema), 1981
Wend Kuuni (God's gift), 1982
Zan Boko, 1989
Rabi, 1992
La vie en fumée (Life in smoke), 1992
Roger le fonctionnaire—Chronique d'un échec annoncé (Roger, the civil servant—chronicle of an announced failure), 1993
Bud Yam, 1997

Notes

1. *Bud Yam* premiered at the Pan-African Festival of Film and Television of Ouagadougou in 1997 and won the Étalon de Yennega, Africa's highest award for best film. For a recent interview in which Gaston Kaboré discusses the award and *Bud Yam*, see Alessandra Speciale, "Memory, Nature and Chance," *Écrans d'Afrique* (Africa screens) 19, first quarter (1997): 6-11.

Djibril Diop Mambety (Senegal)

This chapter is a special tribute to Djibril Diop Mambety, who died a few months after this interview was conducted.

They said he was a UFO. "The most paradoxical filmmaker in the history of African cinema." To some, he was "the African Dionysus," or "the prince of Colobane." Others simply called him "D.D.M."

On July 23, 1998, Djibril Diop Mambety died in the Paris hospital where he was being treated for lung cancer. Only fifty-three years old at the time of his death, Mambety was a director, actor, composer, poet, and orator, loved and admired by critics and audiences all over the world.

Mambety had studied drama in Senegal, and he worked as a stage actor at the Daniel Sorano National Theater in Dakar after graduation. But he was expelled from Sorano a short time later—undisciplined, they said—and the experience goaded him to pursue his love affair with cinema. Mambety remembered his expulsion as a kind of challenge; he refused to give up and immediately set about raising money to make films. Although he had no formal training in cinema, the twenty-four-year-old directed and produced his first film short, *Contras' City* (A city of contrasts), in 1968. Experimental and satirical, the film lampooned the freewheeling cosmopolitanism of Dakar's colonial architecture, in which, as Mambety noted, "we had a Sudanese-style cathedral, a chamber of commerce building looking like a theater, while the theater resembled a block of council flats." Mambety's next short, *Badou Boy*, was released in 1970. The film explored contemporary Senegalese society by pitting an individual against the state: a sly young hooligan, said to be modeled on Mambety himself, spends the film outmaneuvering a crass, bowlegged, overweight policeman. Although both films were box-office disasters, they were critically acclaimed—*Badou Boy* won the Silver Tanit at the 1970 Carthage Film Festival in Tunisia.

In 1973, Mambety released his masterpiece, *Touki-Bouki* (The hyena's journey), a tour de force of narrative and technical sophistication. It combined the styles of Mambety's first two films, marrying montage and narrative, challenging audiences with its unconventional collage of political and sexual images, enticing them with its story and its use of color and music. *Touki-Bouki*, Mambety's first feature-length film, was a critical smash: it won the Special Jury Award at the Moscow Film Festival and the International Critics Award at Cannes. It was unlike anything in the history of African cinema; today, film scholars around the world agree that *Touki-Bouki* is a classic. Its central themes are wealth, youth, and delusion: Mory and Anta are a fashionable young Senegalese couple on the run—from their families, their home, and their future—dreaming of Europe. The story revolves around the couple's brash and illegal attempts to get enough cash for boat tickets to Paris. But it is less the narrative than its mode of presentation that carries the burden of meaning. Mambety mixes elements of several storytelling techniques to create phantasmal images of postcolonial African society's myriad failings. His presentation invites the viewer to understand these images in dialectical terms.

Despite the film's success, Mambety did not produce another feature for almost twenty years. During this long absence, he was able to make only one film: *Parlons Grand-mére* (Let's talk, Grandmother), a short he made in 1989 while helping his friend the Burkinabe director Idrissa Ouedraogo with the filming of *Yaaba*.

In 1992, Mambety returned to the limelight with an ambitious new film, *Hyènes* (Hyenas). It was an adaption of the Swiss-German writer Friedrich Dürrenmatt's satirical play *The Visit* (1956). Mambety's authorial voice is strong and clear in *Hyènes*; as one critic observed, the uniqueness of the direction throughout the film "undoubtedly stems in part from his own magisterial sense of presence."

Hyènes was conceived as the second installment, following on *Touki-Bouki*, of a trilogy on power and insanity. The grand theme, once again, is human greed. As Mambety himself observed, the story shows how neocolonial relations in Africa are "betraying the hopes of independence for the false promises of Western materialism," and how Africans have been corrupted by that materialism. In the film, we follow Linguère Ramatou, a wealthy woman who returns from abroad to the desolate village of Colobane, her birthplace—and Mambety's as well. Many years before, she had been seduced by a young man, impregnated, and abandoned for a wealthier wife; she was then mercilessly ostracized by her neighbors. Now "as rich as the World Bank," Linguère offers lavish gifts and huge sums of money to the villagers—in exchange for the death of her onetime lover. They accept the deal, and Mambety makes it easy for us to see why. The Colobane of *Hyènes* is a sad reminder of the economic disintegration, corruption, and consumer culture that has enveloped Africa since the 1960s. "We have sold our souls too cheaply," Mambety says. "We are done for if we have traded our souls for money. That is why childhood is my last refuge." But what remains of Colobane is not the magical childhood Mambety pines for. In the last shot of *Hyènes*, a bulldozer erases the village from the face of the earth. As a California Newsreel catalog notes, a Senegalese viewer would know "what rose in its place: the real-life Colobane, . . . a notorious thieves' market on the edge of Dakar."

Hyènes confirmed Mambety's stature as one of Africa's greatest auteurs, and it seemed to herald the beginning of a new and productive phase in his career. After unleashing this pessimistic vision of humanity and society, Mambety began a trilogy of short films about "little people," whom he called "the only true, consistent, un-affected people in the world, for whom every morning brings the same question: how to preserve what is essential to themselves" (see the California Newsreel Web site at http://www.newsreel.org). *Le franc* (1994), a comedy about a poor musician who wins the lottery, exposes the havoc wrought upon the people of Senegal by France's devalu-ation of the West African franc (CFA). Mambety was editing the second film in the tril-ogy, *La petite vendeuse de soleil* (The little girl who sold the sun), at the time of his death.

A portrait of the director published in *Écrans d'Afrique* (no. 1, second quarter, 1992) describes some of his peculiarities: "His revolts, his poetry, his alcoholism, his sensitivity, his wanderings, his arrogance, and his lucidity clothe him with a halo of legend—and make him a difficult director." Mambety's dedication to his art is unassailable; he once observed:

> One has to choose between engaging in stylistic research or the mere recording of facts. I feel that a filmmaker must go beyond the recording of facts. Moreover, I believe that Africans, in particular, must reinvent cinema. It will be a difficult task because our viewing audience is used to a specific film language, but a choice has to be made: either one is very popular and one talks to people in a simple and plain manner, or else one searches for an African film language that would exclude chatter-ing and focus more on how to make use of visuals and sounds. (quoted in Françoise Pfaff, *Twenty-five Black African Filmmakers* [Westport, Conn.: Greenwood, 1988])

In other words, Mambety departs from the linear and didactic patterns of such African filmmakers as Ousmane Sembene and Souleymane Cissé in order to pursue his artistic freedom. It is this refusal to make concessions, even to the audience, that enabled Mambety to mature into a director of international stature.

With his death, Africa lost a highly talented and creative filmmaker, a rare artist of exceptional insight and perception. The legions of us who cherished Djibril Diop Mambety for his humor, vision, creativity, and devotion to African cinema—and those of us who were blessed to know him as a friend, a man of great vitality—will miss him, even as we continue to celebrate his legacy.

This interview began at the Pan-African Festival of Film and Television of Oua-gadougou in 1991 and concluded during the African Literature Association Con-ference held at Michigan State University in 1997. I would like to thank Ms. Adam Ouologuem for her assistance with the latter part of the interview.

How did you start making pictures?

I loved pictures when I was a very young boy—but pictures didn't mean cinema to me then. When I was young, I preferred acting to making pictures. So I decided to study drama, but one day in the theater, I realized that I love pictures. That was how I found myself in this thing called cinema. From time to time, I want to make a film, but I am not a filmmaker; I have never been a filmmaker.

When children ask me, "How does one make a film?" I always say that you have to have freedom to make a film, and to have freedom, you need confidence. I tell them to close their eyes, to look at the stars, and look into their hearts, and then to open their eyes and see if the film they want to make is there, in front of their eyes.

I began to make *Hyènes* when I realized I absolutely had to find one of the characters in *Touki-Bouki*, which I had made twenty years before. This is Anta, the girl who had the courage to leave Africa and cross the Atlantic alone. When I set out to find her again, I had the conviction that I was looking for a character from somewhere in my childhood. I had a vision that I already had encountered this character in a film. Ultimately, I found her in a play called *The Visit* by Friedrich Dürrenmatt. I had the freedom and confidence to marry his text with my film and make his story my own.

Many critics are amazed by how well Dürrenmatt's play has been adapted—they never imagined that anyone could do it so well. Hyènes *follows life in an African village, so it relies heavily on oral tradition, stories, and song. But there are elements of European drama and cinema as well. How did you bring all these sources together?*

Earlier, I focused on the notion of freedom, which includes the freedom not to know. That implies confidence in your ability to construct images from the bottom of your heart. When artists converge on these images, there is no longer room for ethnic peculiarities; there is only room for talent. You mustn't expect me to cut the patrimony of the mind into pieces and fragments. A film is a kind of meeting; there is giving and receiving. Now that I have made it, *Hyènes* belongs as much to the viewer as to me. You must have the freedom and confidence to understand and critique what you see.

But what are these images that rise from the bottom of your heart? What are you giving to the viewer?

I am interested in marginalized people, because I believe that they do more for the evolution of a community than the conformists. Marginalized people bring a community into contact with a wider world. The characters of *Touki-Bouki* are interesting to me because their dreams are not those of ordinary people. Anta and Mory do not dream of building castles in Africa; they dream of finding some sort of Atlantis overseas. Following their dream permitted me to follow my own dreams, and my way of escaping those dreams was to laugh at them. Mory and Anta's dreams made them feel like foreigners in their own country. So they were marginalized people, in that respect.

If we think of Draman Drameh in *Hyènes*, we find that he, too, is marginalized, although he is a well-known character in the city of Colobane; he is marginal even though he owns a market. Everyone comes in—to buy food, or to have a drink—so Draman Drameh has the key to the "tree of words." Yet he is marginal—notable, but marginal. The fact that everyone confides in him sets him apart. But this aspect of his character allows me to investigate every aspect of his society. Perhaps a marginal person can give you an accurate vision of a society because he varies from its norms. Linguère Ramatou is also marginalized, because she is exactly the same person who crossed the Atlantic to go to Europe in *Touki-Bouki*. She dared to lift up the moorings of the vessel and sail out. She is a rich foreigner. The people of Colobane feel they need her money; you could say, in the language of the World Bank, that she is a marginal person "we want to have." So Linguère Ramatou gives me a measure of my existence in relation to other things.

I noticed that Linguère Ramatou has an Asian bodyguard in Hyènes. *How does she fit into this schema?*

The point is not that she is Asian. The point is that everyone in Colobane—everyone everywhere—lives within a system of power that embraces the West, Africa, and the land of the rising sun. There is a scene where this woman comes in and reads: she reads of the vanity of life, the vanity of vengeance—that is totally universal. My goal was to make a continental film, one that crosses boundaries. To make *Hyènes* even more continental, we borrowed elephants from the Masai of Kenya, hyenas from Uganda, and people from Senegal. And to make it global, we borrowed somebody from Japan and carnival scenes from the annual Carnival of Humanity of the French Communist Party in Paris. All of these are intended to open the horizons, to make the film universal. The film depicts a human drama. My task was to identify the enemy of humankind: money, the International Monetary Fund, and the World Bank. I think my target is clear.

While *Hyènes* tells a human story to the whole world, I also wanted to pay homage to the beauty of Africa when I made the film. For me, part of that beauty is the fact that it is not very difficult to make a film in Africa. The abandoned bags of rice that the people of Colobane wear at the end of the film did not cost much; it was only the equipment for the production that was a little expensive. I have a great desire to demystify cinema—especially the financial aspect of cinema. Africa is rich in cinema, in images. Hollywood could not have made this film, no matter how much money they spent. The future belongs to images. Students, like the children I referred to earlier, are waiting to discover that making a film is a matter of love, not money.

The pioneers of African cinema often made films with an openly political, didactic purpose—one thinks of Ousmane Sembene's Xala *or Med Hondo's* Soleil O. *How do you combine education and entertainment in your own films?*

I do not refuse the word *didactic*. I follow the same principle as a story. When a story ends—or "falls into the ocean," as we say—it creates dreams. It has energy and direction. I hope that all my stories finish by presenting a lesson for society, but there is also great freedom in my way of seeing and treating things. I do the audience justice: they have the freedom to enter or not to enter into my stories. They are free to take their own path, to enter or to leave. In one word, "liberty" is what characterizes what I am doing.

Your style is radically different from those of other African filmmakers. What sets you apart?

Style is a word that I do not like. I have never pursued a single style, and the others haven't done that, either. I believe that each filmmaker goes his own way, but each person is constantly evolving, changing as he looks to the light he receives that helps him advance. So I don't like the word *style*. On the other hand, I have found that I am able to make films because each film sets me free to think about the subject I take on. When I plan a film, the ideas flow naturally from my original dream, from conception to finish.

There were certainly African films before Touki-Bouki, *but the style of your film is quite different; many people think it broke new aesthetic ground. What about the gyrating camera movements, the editing technique—the jump cuts, colliding montage, and so forth—where did they come from?*

It's the way I dream. To do that, one must have a mad belief that everything is possible—you have to be mad to the point of being irresponsible. Because I know that cinema must be reinvented, reinvented each time, and whoever ventures into cinema also has a share in its reinvention.

I will never forget the first time I heard the eerie combination of human screams and gull's cries in Touki-Bouki, *or the juxtaposition of the saxophone and the muezzin's prayer in* Le franc. *I know you were a composer before you started making films. How do you choose your music, and who do you work with?*

I do not choose the music, I choose the sound. All movement is accompanied by a sense. I like wind very much. Wind is music, just as music is wind. I try to make the image illustrate the movement. Wind, like music, is the breath of movement and life. It has to do with stimulation: from the images I do the music, from the music I do the sound. But sound is not something foreign to adorn the film. It is intrinsic to the film; it magnifies the action.

There are many symbols of death in Hyènes. *Why are the inhabitants of Colobane dressed as they are, and why do they wear wigs?*

The people of Colobane are dressed in rice bags. They are hungry; they are ready to eat Draman Drameh. They are all disguised because no one wants to carry the individual responsibility for murder. So what they have in common is cowardice. For each individual to have clean hands, everybody has to be dirty, to share in the same communal guilt. So the people of Colobane become animals. Their hair makes them buffaloes. The only thing they have that is human is greed.

So despite your insistence on freedom and immediacy, you are very deliberate, very careful in choosing costume and other forms of characterization, very careful about how you structure your films.

It seems to me that when we talk about structure, we enter into confusion. To me, structure often means premeditation. My work is not based on premeditation or planning; it is based on the instant. The instant is motivated. It arises from the necessities of discourse. Well, I do not like the word *discourse,* so perhaps I should have said the instant is forced by the necessities of movement. Movement creates its own internal dynamic, and the different effects of a film—text, music, image—arise from this dynamic; they are never separated. So costume is not an ornament, it is the reflection of a situation. In *Hyènes*, the people of Colobane would not have been able to enact a collective murder if they had each kept their individual clothing. If the mayor had dressed like a mayor, if the professor had dressed like a professor, then they would have felt individual responsibility. But the instant of murder required collective responsibility, and this required a mask. The mask is what makes it impossible for the townspeople to recognize good and bad. That is why we made them animals, because animals commit this kind of murder. For that reason, their hair is done as that of the buffalo—the laughingstock of the savanna—and the rice bags they wear symbolize their objective. Their objective is to amass as many riches as possible and to create the deadly harmony that Linguère Ramatou desires.

You've said that power and madness are recurrent themes in Hyènes, *as in your other films. What do you mean by that?*

I do not have a grand explanation of power and madness. I think that the power of madness is one thing, and the madness of power is another thing. Together, they are too heavy for human beings. That is not an explanation or an ideology. In these matters, humans are mere toys.

If humans are toys, then what about animals? Why are you obsessed with hyenas?

The hyena is an African animal—you know that. It never kills. The hyena is falsehood, a caricature of man. The hyena comes out only at night; he is afraid of daylight, like the hero of *Touki-Bouki*—he does not want to see daylight, he does not want to see himself by daylight, so he always travels at night. He is a liar, the hyena. The hyena is a permanent presence in humans, and that is why man will never be perfect. The hyena has no sense of shame, but it represents nudity, which is the shame of human beings.

After I unveiled this very pessimistic picture of human beings and society in their nakedness in *Hyènes*, I wanted to build up the image of the common people. Why should I magnify the ordinary person after this debauch of defects? The whole society of Colobane is made up of ordinary people. I do not want to remain forever pessimistic. That is why I have fished out cases where man, taken individually, can defeat money. Think of *Le franc*. The hero of the film is going crazy because of a lottery ticket, but he manages to hold on because he has the power of dreaming. In *La petite vendeuse de soleil*, all the protagonist wants is to sell her magazines, but money comes to subvert her plan. A rich man comes along, and a magazine that should cost five francs is sold for five hundred francs. Thus the rich man creates a problem, but she manages to escape this problem, because she dreams of something better. In the third part, *La tailleuse de pierre* (The stonecutter), a woman excavates pieces of basalt. She breaks them into smaller stones that can be used in construction. People who want modern buildings in their neighborhood ask her to move her workshop away. But she can conquer the ugliness and dirtiness of human beings because she is close to the truth. So *La tailleuse de pierre* shows how an individual can dream of beauty.

It's quite remarkable that you've never used the same actor twice in the twenty-five years you've been making films. You don't use professional actors at all, and yet in your films, everyone acts like a professional . . .

The professional actor does not exist. Economically, yes, but basically, no. Professional actors break the magic of the dream and the magic of cinema. I say that as a creator and manipulator of character and event. I do not want to use an actor again once we have worked together. Once we have worked together, it seems to me that the actor has already given everything, because I have already asked everything of him or her. So we leave each other in the fullness of our first meeting. When I was young, when I went to the movies, I was always angry when I saw an actor who had died in one film appearing in another film alive. That broke the magic of cinema for me. It is very important to preserve the magic of cinema. For example, at the end of *Hyènes*, if you want to know where Draman Drameh's body has gone, you risk breaking the magic. Only magic knows where his body has gone. Cinema is magic in the service of dreams.

Do you think the African film industry is capable of sustaining itself in the future?

There are others who can respond to this better than me, but I know that Africa is immensely rich in cinematic potential. It is good for the future of cinema that Africa exists. Cinema was born in Africa, because the image itself was born in Africa. The instruments, yes, are European, but the creative necessity and rationale exist in our oral tradition. As I said to the children before, in order to make a film, you must only close your eyes and see the images. Open your eyes, and the film is there. I want these children to understand that Africa is a land of images, not only because images of African masks revolutionized art throughout the world but as a result, simply and paradoxically, of oral tradition. Oral tradition is a tradition of images. What is said is stronger than what is written; the word addresses itself to the imagination, not the ear. Imagination creates the image and the image creates cinema, so we are in direct lineage as cinema's parents.

What about the silent films, before the talkies?

That doesn't change anything. Oral tradition does not just mean opening your mouth. It means evoking, creating, and writing.

Are you referring to the quality of films?

Quality, quality. Everything has to be perfect, but what does perfect mean? It means that something is well communicated. It does not mean adorned with makeup. It means clearly said. What's essential is communication.

But films that just communicate—films that aren't as good as yours—often can't be shown outside the countries where they were produced.

I am all for the quality of things—the total quality. As I said more than twenty years ago, for the educated African, Chinese, or Japanese, nothing authorizes mediocrity.

Do you see any possibilities for coproductions with other countries? You made Hyènes *with Thelma Film in Switzerland, for example.*

I don't want to talk about Europe. Let's talk about making films in Africa. Europe is not important for me. Where the money to make a film comes from doesn't matter.

In Africa, the little country of Burkina Faso has done quite a lot to develop continental film. They have built truly Pan-African facilities for education and production; and of course there is FESPACO.

I don't want to talk about Burkina Faso, either, except to point out that *burkina* means tiger and *faso* means lamb. For me, Burkina Faso is the dream of Africa's future. When I think of Burkina Faso, I see the future I dream for Africa and—why not?—for the whole world. One day, the world could all be like Burkina Faso, even if the hyenas do everything they can to prevent that.

I noticed that you are selling Hyènes *on video. Is this your way of coping with the problems of distribution and exhibition on the African continent?*

I work in my own way. We just created the notion of *films de poche* [pocket films]. We are putting a lot of African films on video, so we can distribute them to people at prices that rival the price of books. Of course, we also need more VCRs in Africa if we are to make our films truly accessible. This will revolutionize African cinema. Our premise is that our population must see our films as much as possible. We can't just dream about this. We have lost twenty years already. No miracle could just make the distribution of films in cinema houses effective overnight. So we must invent such things as the *film de poche*.

But Hollywood releases their films in the theaters before the video version.

With *films de poche*, we are trying to develop a way to distribute films in Africa. The first example is *Hyènes*, which is already a *film de poche;* there will be a whole series of these films. In a society that we call unreceptive to writing and reading, images must supplement the word. That is why selling *Hyènes* on video will make a big difference.

Your first film, Contras' City, *is an interesting film; I understand it as a critique of the social hierarchy of Dakar. What motivated you to make the film?*

The motivation? The motivation is always the picture, and for me it is always pictures from the place where you were born, the place you come from. I never dream about some other world, away from home. What I have always wanted to explore is my relationship with images, with the cinema; I want to see it, make an image of it, from the perspective of eternity. I am not a creature of eternity, though: the place I was born is umbilical. It is as if I were born into an envelope, a lake from whose waters I never emerge. Every time I make a film, the creativity comes out of that original envelope. For me, filming is remembering.

Looking at the images of Contras' City, *it is easy to understand how the film relates to you, to the society, to Africa in general, and to colonial and neocolonial encounters.*

I don't want to tell stories. I only want to create, to give pleasure. As soon as I begin to make a picture, the creativity and the images come from imagination, from somewhere, which I call accident. Otherwise it is dilettantism. If my films have a political motivation, that is not my basic preoccupation.

But the critique of architecture in Contras' City *suggests you believe that foreign intervention has amounted to an assault on African culture.*

If you have a child, you must remember that you have been a child; you cannot forget how your mother carried you on her back. And if you see that your own child is not carried as well as your mother carried you, you can react by saying, "No. No, it is not like that, that is not my mother's way. This is not my origin; it is not the way I want my baby to be carried." That's my point of view; it may relate to architecture, to today's events, to our memory, our history. If it leads to criticism, for me in any case, that criticism relates to how I imagine that my mother carried me well. I allowed myself to be amused in *Contras' City*, so as to make the viewer experience anticolonialist laughter. But anticolonialist laughter is ultimately laughter at oneself. I am not an ideologist. I can't just love and refuse to love.

Touki-Bouki is very important in this context. When I begin to dream of other places, to be obsessed by them to the point of becoming a stranger in my own country like Mory and Anta in *Touki-Bouki*, my natural instinct is to refuse the temptation. That is what has set the course of my life; I have always found it sad to be away from home.

Yet whenever I go to FESPACO, I see many films that present the norms of African culture in a harsh light. What guides your concern for tradition? Do you have any advice for ambitious young filmmakers?

I don't conduct myself with reference to other people. I am not a contrarian. So comparison with anything else stops there. Regarding my young colleagues, I have not seen many of their films. I rarely go to the cinema. Perhaps someday I will be able to explain to you why I rarely see films, even African ones. I have said to the young filmmakers, "If you want to make a film, please think thoroughly about the content of the film you would make." But I cannot compare their films to mine; I cannot talk about African cinema. I have seen fewer African films than you have.

What are your own future projects?

I will finish the third part of the trilogy about ordinary people. After that, I will make *Malaika*, the third part of the trilogy about the power of craziness. The first two were *Touki Bouki* and *Hyènes*. Then I will consult God about the state of the world.

Filmography

Contras' City (A city of contrasts), 1968
Badou Boy, 1970
Touki-Bouki (The hyena's journey), 1973
Parlons Grand-mére (Let's talk, Grandmother), 1989
Hyènes (Hyenas), 1992
Le Franc, 1994
La petite Vendeuse de soleil (The little girl who sold the sun), 1999

Ngangura Mweze (Congo)

Ngangura Mweze was born in the Democratic Republic of Congo. After graduating from high school in 1970, he obtained a degree in literature and then studied film-making at the Institut des Arts de Diffusion in Brussels for four years. As a student, between 1973 and 1976 he made two films that he says are important to him: *Tam-Tam Electronique*, in black and white, and his thesis project, *Rhythm and Blood*, in color. After receiving his diploma in directing, Mweze returned to Congo in 1976. He notes that it was, and still is, difficult to find money to make films in Congo, as in many other African countries. He accepted an appointment at the Institut National des Arts, a school of drama and music, teaching film analysis and introduction to cinema courses (not film production, as the institute is not a film school). Later, Mweze taught at the Studio Ecole de la Voix du Zaïre (SEVOZA), a training school owned by Congolese Television. He recalls, "I taught the people working at Congolese television who needed training, and I think I made a difference." While teaching, he made two short films. The first, a documentary titled *Chéri-Samba* (1980), is a portrait of a young popular painter in Kinshasa. The second film is *Kin-Kiesse ou les joies douces-amères de Kinshasa-la-belle* (Kinshasa the joyful, 1983). According to Mweze, "It is a film in which I showed how I see Kinshasa, and I chose to make it entertaining and to show the capital city by filming contrasts in the joys of the young and old, rich and poor, white and black who live there." It was coproduced by Antena 2 Television, the French Ministry of Cooperation, and Congolese Television. The films were each twenty-six minutes long.

In 1987, Mweze made his first feature film, a quasi-musical comedy titled *La vie est belle* (Life is rosy), which he codirected with the Belgian filmmaker Benoît Lamy. That year, Mweze created Soleil Films, which coproduced *La vie est belle*. In 1992, he made *Changa changa, rythmes en noirs et blanc* (Rhythm in black and white), a documentary about music and the mixing of cultures in Brussels that intricately weaves music and culture in rejuvenating ways. Following this, he directed *Le roi, la vâche et le bananier* (The king, the cow and the banana tree) in 1994, a sixty-minute documentary that has won several awards. The film is about Mweze's coming back to his roots in the kingdom of Ngweshe. In 1995 he made *Lettre à Makura: Les derniers Bruxellois*, about the people of Marolles, the oldest community in Brussels, as seen through the eyes of an African ethnographer. His most recent feature film is *Pièces d'identités*, made in 1997; in this film the collision of individual and collective identities crystallizes the problematic relations between Africa and Europe since colonization. At the time I conducted my final interview with Mweze, *Pièces d'identités* had won twenty international awards, including awards given at the Cinema Africano Festival of Milano; the International Francophone Film Festival, held in Namur, Belgium; the Southern African Film Festival, held in Harare, Zimbabwe; International Film and Video Festival of Barcelona; the International Film Festival of Amiens; the National Black Programming Consortium; and the Pan-African Festival of Film and Television of Ouagadougou, where it captured the Étalon de Yennega, the festival's grand prize.[1]

In Belgium, where Mweze lives with his family, he has established his own production company, Films-Sud, which has produced all his films since *La vie est belle*.

Could you briefly summarize the situation of the Congolese film industry?

All I can say is that my film *La vie est belle* is the first feature-length film made under professional conditions in Congo. Some feature-length films have been made in Congo, but by nonprofessionals. The first feature film ever made in Congo by a Congolese was *Le hasard n'existe pas* (There is no such thing as luck, 1977), by Madenda and Luzolo, and it was filmed in 16mm and in black and white. It was not distributed even in Congo. After that, there is another feature film, *Ngambo* (1986), made by Roger Kwami Mambu. It is an instructional film that was well distributed in schools. Of course, television directors have made many documentaries in Congo.

Does the Congolese government sponsor any film productions, and, if not, is there any effort being made now to establish a viable film industry that the Congolese and Africans could benefit from?

For all the films made in Congo, even those not produced for Congolese television, the government has helped by giving free equipment. The real problem in Congo is that we do not have an organization which centralizes film production or distribution. This leaves the responsibility with the Congolese television. The cinema has no specific organization that treats its problems.

Who controls the theaters and channels of exhibition in Congo?

They are mostly foreigners. The most well-known in Kinshasa is a man from Pakistan, Mr. Patel, who also controls the distribution of films in Congo. He distributes mainly karate films, American Rambo films, and B movies. Due to the political troubles in the country, Mr. Patel has left and a new company, CINEMAX, is managed by two young Congolese men, Sunguza Mayele and Kasuku Kotshio.

Is there anything being done now by the Congolese government or by independent filmmakers to correct this situation, such as inducing the government to finance feature films or control exhibition?

I have been an active member of the former Organisation Zaïroise des Cinéastes [Organization of Zairean Filmmakers; OZACI], and we have often been received by the Ministry of Culture, which wants to correct the situation, but so far no solution has been found. Actually, in the new regime, that association, now called Organisation Congolaise des Cinéastes [OCC], has prepared a project to create a Centre National du Cinéma, an official organization to take charge of production, exhibition, and distribution. Given the war raging in the country as we talk, I would say, let's wait and see.

Do the foreign distributors give any preference to African filmmakers? In other words, would they distribute your own films?

Are you asking me if African films are shown on the screens in Congo? That is rare.

Why is the situation like that? Why don't they show African films?

This question concerns not only the Congolese cinema but African cinema in general. There are probably two reasons: The first is that the distributors can buy foreign films cheaply, because by the time they are sold to African countries, they have already been around the world and have made the major proceeds for the producers. That is not the case for recent African films, for which the main market is Africa. African producers cannot ask for as little money as the foreigners do for their films in Africa. In my own case, distributors wanted to pay me the same cheap fee they pay those foreigners whose films have already made a lot of profit overseas. The second reason is that the African audience often considers African films less amusing and too cultural. This situation is probably due to the fact that we filmmakers can be influenced by who finances our films. Everybody knows that our films are financed in Europe. The consequence is that the filmmaker is not obliged while writing or directing his film to take into consideration the taste of the wider African audiences. For many years, African films were usually shown in free screenings in cultural centers. For example, the French Cultural Center shows many African films, because many African filmmakers sell the noncommercial rights to the Ministry of Cooperation in France, which sends those films to the cultural centers in Africa.

Some film critics and theorists of African culture consider the effect of the so-called colonial psyche or colonial mentality on the audience's perception of African cinema. They argue that Africans are used to watching American, British, and even Indian films; therefore, when they see familiar African scenes in African films, they do not take the film seriously because it shows them only what they already know, which is poverty and suffering. Do you find this to be the case?

It is difficult to say. But I am sure that when an African audience has the occasion to see movies which concern them, they always prefer those movies to foreign ones. It is important not only to make films that address Africa or African problems, but to make films that appeal to African audiences. For a long time, African filmmakers felt they had to engage in *cinéma d'auteur* [art films] style in order to offer messages to the African people. Often this did not bring Africans to these films, because they were not made to affect their emotions. For instance, someone who has problems with means of subsistence or joblessness is not going to be interested in a film depicting those situations. A foreign critic may find such a film interesting, but the man you have filmed may not be interested in seeing that kind of film after returning from a day's hard work, when he only wants an escape from his situation. African spectators are interested in finding themselves in contexts which recognize their humanity, and most of the time an African spectator cannot be fully satisfied with watching an American film depicting alien culture. For example, a woman wearing a miniskirt in New York City does not have the same significance as the image of a woman in traditional attire in an African setting. What is important now for African cinema is to bring African audiences to African films.

It seems like you are implying that early African films are too didactic, and that filmmakers should consider making commercial films that provide entertainment even when the focus is on African problems.

Yes, that is what I meant to say. Many African films, especially the early ones, were too didactic. Because of that, they did not attract enough audience. As I said earlier, I do not think that African cinema should be restricted to *cinéma d'auteur*. I am not saying that didactic films are unnecessary; rather, that many African filmmakers considered themselves impudent, thus too important and obligated to preach. In France and the United States there is *cinéma d'auteur*, but it is just a small part of a large ensemble. However, about 90 percent of African films are author films because each filmmaker wants to present himself as someone who must convey a message to the people. Actually, in 1999, I am happy to observe that the situation has drastically changed and most filmmakers now consider the "entertainment factor" important in their films.

This view seems to represent what I would call new development, and new vision for African cinema. Your position is a radical shift from the perceived notion of African cinema. You take an approach that is different from the political and expressive cinema that Ousmane Sembene and Med Hondo advocate. How do you relate your work to that of filmmakers who follow their examples and the general notion of African cinema?

I think that perceived notion developed more from the francophone cinema than, say, from the anglophone cinema—Ghanaian and Nigerian films in particular, where there exist "popular" films capable of drawing crowds to the theaters. I think that if such audience appeal had developed in francophone it would have assisted the growth of cinema. But the francophone African cinema has been for many years *cinéma assisté* [assisted cinema], funded in part by European contributors, hence the only audience for the films has been the festivals. We must speak the truth! Similarly, in those festivals, most of the critics were not Africans and so not obligated to analyze the films from an African perspective. It is sad that when a filmmaker thinks he is making a film for the African audience, in a sense, he is involuntarily giving away an important fraction of what he wanted to achieve.

I am not really obsessed with the commercial aspect of cinema, because for me the term *commercial cinema* is pejorative. I prefer the term *popular cinema* to refer to films which many Africans can go to see and feel good. *Commercial cinema* connotes certain improprieties, things like when a filmmaker has to compromise issues for the sake of making money—for example, the fusion of nudity, sex, violence, and sports cars into the story—and that is not what interests me. I am interested in making films that are constructed from popular African cultures that deal with everyday life. To clarify and to distinguish between my position and the other cinemas we were talking about, I do not feel like a teacher or a messenger of particular ideas. I am just a filmmaker, as there are carpenters and bricklayers.

What is the primary source of influence for your filmmaking?

This is a difficult question. Since I was a film student I have many times changed my conception of cinema and the kind of film I like. Years ago I thought film had to express the personal phantasms of the author. Later I began to think that film had only to show the political point of view of the author. Now, I think my perception is shifting against all that. To say who really influenced me is difficult, because the kind of films I like is always changing and evolving. Now I am most influenced by those in international cinema whose styles are closest to what I am doing. I like Charlie Chaplin and the French cinematographer Marcel Pagnol. I also like *Desperately Seeking Susan* very much and things like that. Specifically in Africa, I have much respect for Ousmane Sembene's work. He believes in what he does, and he has done much for African cinema's existence. From the first time I saw his film *Le mandat* [Mandabi, or the money order, 1968], I was really impressed.

You do not impose a particular ideology?

No. Oh no! What interests me is to present a testimony, to witness everyday life. That does not necessarily mean making a film that represents my point of view or ideology. I am not sure that an audience will get a lesson out of a film, or that a film can change things. I can be sure that when I make films people can recognize themselves as human beings. That is what I mean when I say testimony. If someone recognizes his situation in my films, it means I have given that person an occasion to see himself as in a mirror and perhaps to love some things that used to be banal in his life. You see yourself in a mirror and you judge yourself to see if you are what you really want to be.

Would you consider yourself a political filmmaker?

I tend to consider myself a political filmmaker. I am consumed by politics, but I do not see the whole of life in terms of politics. I know that politics applies to many things, but I do not think that I have to analyze the world only in terms of politics.

In the brochure advertising your film La vie est belle *when it was shown in New York City was written, "African cinema meets Hollywood-style comedy." Do you agree that your film contains aspects of Hollywood style in the comedy to which they refer?*

As you saw, *La vie est belle* is a coproduction between Belgium, Congo, and France. It was a high-quality fil n made by excellent technicians, but I do not understand the Hollywood aspect referred to by the writer. I am sure that technically, it is too poor to be a Hollywood movie. If it had been made in Hollywood, it would have included a lot of special effects. The film is not really a musical comedy in the Hollywood tradition, so I do not think that writer got it right as described.

La vie est belle *is faster paced, with faster cutting, than most African films. How do you see these specifics regarding your film style in terms of a general African film style? Were you particularly influenced by any specific kind of cinema?*

There is a mentality that maintains African films must have a slow rhythm. I do not agree with all that; I have seen many African films with a quiet feel, and to say the truth, they were annoyingly lugubrious. However, I do not believe Hollywood represents the norm, or "normal rhythm." I do think that we use rhythm as an excuse for our lacks. If we make a film with a very slow rhythm, we say it is just because it is African. About ten years ago, African films were poorly done. Now if there is an African film professionally well done from a technical aspect, people say it is not African. My film is not a musical comedy like Hollywood movies; it is a popular comedy, because the basic themes are the same as in the Congolese popular theater and music. There has been a series of popular Congolese theater on television called *Maboke* that makes everyone laugh even many years after they were made. Most of them were made in comedia del arte style. We appropriated their conventions to *La vie est belle* because the audience loves them.

This is a crucial point. Contrary to the readings of some critics, you are emphasizing that La vie est belle *cannot be a Hollywood comedy because its roots derive from the Congolese popular theater and musical traditions.*

Yes. I think people used to consider a lack of professionalism to be a part of African cinema. Almost all the time, foreign critics forget to acknowledge the origins or the cultural backgrounds of our films. That is why I emphasize that *La vie est belle* is not, and cannot be, a Hollywood film. Films can be slow if it is appropriate to the topic. If the subject needs a slow rhythm it can be good, but I do not think that all African films must be slow. African spectators are used to seeing American or French films, and they like them. So what some critics refer to specifically as "African rhythm" is ambiguous to me. I remember, one day in 1987 in Washington, D.C., during a forum at the African Film Festival, Sarah Maldoror protested against the organizers when, during the introduction of a Burkinabe film, the presenter asked the audience to be patient with the slow rhythm because it is an African film. Maldoror stated that it was unnecessary to tell the audience to be patient with an African film as if the film-makers were there [at the festival] to ask for charity.

La vie est belle *is a coproduction. What amount of work did you put into it? How did you shape the direction of the film within the confines of coproduction?*

It is a coproduction in the sense that it was financed mainly by Lamy Films and the Ministry of Culture [Belgium], Stefan Films [France], and my production company, Soleil Films [Congo]. I think coproduction is a good venture. To make a film you need a lot of money, and often that money comes from different countries. I think something not habitual is that *La vie est belle* was codirected. The codirection was imposed by the Belgian Ministry of Culture, which provided two-thirds of the 1.3-million-dollar budget. They did not want to give too much money to someone who, first of all, is not Belgian, and secondly, is a beginning filmmaker.

I presented the project to Benoît Lamy, who I had known many years ago, because he had been my teacher. He was very interested in the screenplay, and he proposed that we codirect it so we could get funding. Without that partnership, I would have had to make the film in 16mm without high-quality film and technical assistance.

What assistance did you get from the Congolese government?

We did not get money from the government, but the National Television allowed us to use everything that was available. We got lighting equipment and television personnel. People who work for Congolese television were part of the crew. They allowed us to use those people without giving anything to them.

You just mentioned that because of the money provided by the Belgians, you were required to have a Belgian codirector. Some African filmmakers do not like coproduction because the financiers impose undesirable rigid rules. How were you able to overcome that kind of control, or did it ever exist?

I think we need to distinguish between codirecting and coproduction. If it is possible for an African to coproduce with money from America, Italy, Belgium, or France, it is best that he provides the majority of the money. This will allow him to retain the power to direct without too many constraints.

Were the actors professionals?

No. For most of the actors, it was their first time in a film. As I said, Congolese cinema is not very developed. We chose the best from about 250 actors. The young woman, the musician [Papa Wemba], and the wife of the boss had never acted in films before. The man who plays the boss was a theater actor long ago, but now he works in public relations at a big company in Congo. However, many people who played extras are professional actors of the National Theater of Congo and students at the Institute of Drama. For the main characters, we had to pay attention to the appearance as well as ability to play the role, but we also wanted to protect the appeal of the film by choosing professional theater actors for the extras. So when you see a policeman in the street or the wives in the group of women, they are likely to be professional actors.

Have you made another film since La vie est belle*?*

Yes. I made four documentaries. The first after *La vie est belle* is called *Changa changa*, which talks about music and the mixing of cultures in Brussels. The second one was *Le roi, la vâche et le bananier*, which was about going back to my village and searching for my roots. The third one was *Lettre à Makura*. It is a short documentary like a video letter that I sent to a cousin who lives in the village. I explained to him how Europeans live. I made a portrait for him of the oldest community in Brussels, which is in a neighborhood called Les Maroles. It was there that I shot *Pièces d'identités* with King Manikongo, who finds himself with people that are not very rich but simple and welcoming. The last documentary I made before doing the film *Pièces d'identités* was on a boat that travels the lake Kivu. It is a poetic voyage during which I speak through the story of the boat about the history of my place of birth, Boukavu, located in the East of Congo. I had already written the script for *Pièces d'identités,* but it took me eight years to get funding. I realized that while I had reworked the script in different versions, the documentaries I made were like a preparation for the feature film. But I was not conscious of that when I was doing it.

The time spent in making the film is not wasted at all. I have already seen Pièces d'identités. *It is a wonderful film, and permit me to say that I hope it wins the grand prize of FESPACO, the Étalon de Yennega. That is my projection! What is your immediate reaction to the reception of the film here at the festival?*[2]

I have gotten some good press coverage for the film and it was well received here in Ouagadougou. The film really touched many Africans who are not necessarily intellectuals and have never been to Europe. People from all walks of life got something out of it, and each person who talked to me about the film sees his or her own story and his or her own interests in all the stories being told. Each time I see the film, depending on my frame of mind, I see a different film each time. I am sometimes more taken by the love story, or more preoccupied by the problems of racism in Europe, or with the contradictions of African traditional values. At other times, I think of the situation of Congolese citizens in Brussels. I think that the best satisfaction that I got from this film is the fact that it was well received here; some African distributors as well as some "intellectual" viewers have come to me to express their positive feelings about the film. That is enough for me.

Why did you choose to set this film in Brussels?

The city of Brussels inspired me to do *Pièces d'identités*. I live there, and I am concerned with the problems of the African Diaspora. I am an immigrant myself even if I have the good fortune of returning home from time to time. Nevertheless, I can no longer claim to live at home. This problem of immigration is of interest to me because most of the time when we speak of immigration we are concerned with the legal aspect [having the proper immigration papers] or economic and material preoccupations. We often forget that the person who has immigrated has his own identity issues to deal with. For instance, there are many Congolese of the Diaspora who have children who no longer speak their language. For the immigrant this question of identity is very important, although it is the question we often neglect the most. These are people who have changed their cultural and familial environments and find themselves in other settings. At times, even the respect that they deserve does not exist in this new setting. They are confronted with the problems of self-dignity. Because of this, I wanted to choose the character of a king, because he is the one who most embodies this sense of dignity and respect of traditional Africa and represents traditional African values. That is why the character of the king was very interesting in addressing this issue of immigration; it allows for a different perspective than just material difficulty and immigration problems dealing with having the necessary legal documents.

It looks like the film is not just for the immigrant but also for people at home in Africa who are thinking about leaving. Even the youth think about it and realize it is not easy to pack and leave. They see people who have gone and the problems they face. I think that the fact that the film is so open to such a diverse audience gives it its strength.

Already in Manikongo's voyage there is a type of initiation even though his main purpose in leaving Congo is to search for his daughter. It is an important voyage for him. Among the lessons he learns is that of disillusionment with European and Western ideals. When he returns to his palace, he is more realistic and less naive. He no longer dreams of the Europe he had admired so much. In that regard it is also a lesson for the African youth who view this film; they can realize that it is not easy for an African to live in Europe. For instance, many Africans dream about going to Europe and returning to their respective countries with big new cars and other material objects and cannot believe that there can be poverty in Europe. I wanted to tell them that the problem is more complex than that, and to make them think. They see many Congolese in Brussels having problems with the police, and in this film they see that even the king is not respected and not immune to those problems. I think that these kinds of issues might give the African youth some things to reflect upon.

The most important object in this film is the king's regalia. It was disturbing and chilling to see it in the pawnshop. If that symbol of tradition were to be lost like that, Africa would be doomed.

The symbolism that we find in the royal regalia is important. I can even say that they constitute almost a character in the film. We can identify with these royal regalia, which are highly respected and meaningful in towns and villages, as opposed to the city, where well-dressed young people, including girls in miniskirts, view them [the regalia] as mere antiquity. And in Europe we see it via the attitude of the customs officers who see the royal objects in terms of taxable import with monetary value, and the antique dealer who wants to steal them. I think that each of these cases represents a symbolic value. In Africa, it is a way of preserving valuable traditions of various kingdoms from precolonial times. But nowadays, like when the king leaves the kingdom and arrives in a foreign city, the way he is treated shows how traditional African values are no longer accorded due respect since colonization. When we talk about traditional African values we must include our own social, political, as well as religious organizations. In a country such as Congo, Christianity played a strong destructive role in making people lose their identity. When the king arrives in Europe and we see the different attitudes of the customs officers and the antique dealer, we think about the treasures of Africa that are often stolen by Europe.

In the end the objects are found; it is like a reappropriation of Africa and its own values. It is Africa after many eventful journeys that realizes that she can only be reconstructed by retrieving her lost cultural heritage. I think we have shown how important it is for tradition to keep evolving. For example, in the film, it is Mwana, the king's daughter, who as a woman and according to tradition is not supposed to touch the royal objects, who manages to return the objects to her father. We now discover that it is Manikongo's experience in Europe that forces him to reconsider the limitations of dogmatic traditional codes. In other words, he must respect tradition, but at the same time he realizes that tradition is not something static or unchangeable but evolves with time. The way Manikongo expresses himself exemplifies this need for change, but not without full consultation with the Council of the Wise [le Conseil des Sages].

What does piéces d'identités *mean? "ID" as it has been translated in English, does not seem to be an adequate title.*

I think that there are some problems trying to translate the title of the film into English. The translator basically translated it as *ID*, which means identification card, and that is not adequate. At the Los Angeles Film Festival it was titled *Identity*, and at the Acapulco Film Festival it was called *Pieces of Identity*. We are still trying to figure out the best way to translate the idea of *Pièces d'identités*. Besides, if we were to follow the exact meaning in French of the term *piéces d'identités* there would not be an "s" in the word *identités*. It is, first of all, an identification card, but it is also the pieces of identity of the many characters that are seen in the film, characters whose identities have been broken in pieces; that is also why the title is in the plural form.

Why did I choose this title? This title reflects *les sans papiers* [those without legal immigration papers], the general term used to refer to immigrants in Belgium. This is why in Europe, from its title, viewers would easily understand that such an African film made in Europe titled *Pièces d'identités* is about immigration. This part regarding the printed paper identity, *carte de séjour*, is not focused upon as much as the part regarding the general question of individual identity expressed by the characters as follows: "Who am I? I am not at home in my country of origin, with what can I be identified?" In this sense, we can see that there are many pieces of identities in the film, including that of the king irrespective of the royal regalia that followed him from his kingdom to the capital city of Kinshasa in Africa, and to Europe. There are those identities that are objects with which people are linked, like Chaka-Jo with his little medal—an insignia of sorts—that reminds him of his mother, the only object that links him to Africa. There is Mwana with her picture that reminds her of her growing up in Africa, and even Viva-Wa-Viva with all his nice clothes—without which he is nothing. These little possessions they hang on to are the means of affirming their identities.

There is also the concept of identity in general. Even the Belgian ex-colonizers in their cafés are in a way searching for their identities, which, in many ways, are linked to Africa, a certain exotic Africa—for the European, adorned with servants and maids. For them, the only thing to which they are most bound is imaginary Africa, and in some ways, they are just as lost in Europe as the Africans in Europe searching for their roots. If the film were a theater play, people would have interpreted the French word *pièce* as relating to the theater, and in that sense the *pièce* would have a double meaning—the theatrical play itself as well as the actual pieces of identities.

This concept of identity is also cultural; the characters are in search of not only a fundamental identity but a cultural identity as well.

In the film I raise essentially the idea of cultural identity. I am not talking about people with psychoanalytical problems, although the problems of cultural identity can stem from an individual conflict. However, the film does not raise this issue because it is more of a sociological than a psychological nature, based on personal problems of individuals. It is foremost a film that raises the issue of cultural identity between Europe and Africa and even of intercultural relations between the two continents. Many characters are constantly searching for their identities that hang upon the two societies. There are many African children who were brought to Europe at a very young age and who could not consider themselves Europeans and try to hold on to an Africa that they did not know. Incidentally, I think this is one of the reasons that the film was well received among the African Americans in the U.S.

To find this cultural identity must one first find a collective identity?

I would say yes. Except for some very strong individuals that can say that they are this or that and do not care about their heritage. This type of person exists, but most people find it necessary to identify with a cultural or social group. For instance, I am a Congolese from Kasai, but I also understand that we are in a world where more and more people live in a diversified social environment far from their native countries. Because people travel and intermingle with others who live far away from their homes, one wonders if the notions of origins and native languages are not becoming more problematic in terms of how to preserve the remnants of origins and languages. Maybe communication by Internet will take us to another world, and the new millennium will bring a new mode of communication so that the notion of social group will be viewed or lived differently.

Can you elaborate on the role of the characters? At first glance, many of the characters in Pièces d'identités *appear to have negative attributes. In many films, it is a common tendency to represent black male characters as crooks, swindlers, or thieves. What can you tell us about these characters, starting with Chaka-Jo. Why does he steal, for instance?*

In reference to the problems of stereotypes, I think that there is a tendency as a result of the many European feminist movements to depict the black man as the bad guy and the black woman as a saint. Actually, the general tendency is to portray the black woman as a victim of the black man. I would argue that this is a superficial way of being politically correct à la Westerner. I do not subscribe to this method of representation. I want to say first of all that the main character, Manikongo, is a black man who is totally positive in outlook. In the film, there are white men who are more or less negative or positive. It was important to avoid another Manicheism, which will be to show black men who are good and white men who are bad. I wanted to play with the complexity of positive and negative characters, men and women, black and white.

As far as Chaka-Jo is concerned, I did not want to portray him as an angel. I use as an example the history of biracial children born of European fathers before independence and black Congolese mothers who were their maids, or "little girls," as they were known, with whom they had relationships but who were not considered spouses. These children were often sent to special schools reserved for them in Congo. At the time of independence in the 1960s, these biracial children were nevertheless considered orphans and were sent to orphanages or foster families. Many of them turned out bad; some of the girls became prostitutes or stopped going to school, some of the boys became drug dealers. Even the ones who turned out decent and have legal status in Belgium are still ill at ease. I think it is such reality that allows me to portray Chaka-Jo's ordeal, what he went through in life, to reveal why he did not have the opportunity to become a stable person. But at the same time, we can see that he is not a big hustler. He is not really a negative character; he is like Robin Hood, who steals from the rich to give to the poor. That is what he does; the money he steals goes to help Manikongo, and to Mwana to help her build an infirmary in the village.

I think that the only character portrayed totally as negative is Viva-Wa-Viva, who represents a small part of the African youth that can be considered lost in Europe. It is part of the group known as *les sapeurs,* who have no other objective in life than to have nice clothes and can even commit crimes to sustain their chosen lifestyles. I honestly think that my film would have been incomplete if I neglected this well-known group from the Congolese community living at that time. I do not think that the objective was to depict the black man in a negative manner, but to show these two characters and what they represent in the African immigrant community in Europe. Although Chaka-Jo was not in the typical situation that many biracial children face, he is still a representative of many of the second generation of Africans who often live in the suburbs, are unable to find jobs, and do not know much about Africa. And although they are of European nationality, they are not really integrated in the European society; many of these young people are often ill at ease and can easily be identified as the Chaka-Jos.

If Viva-Wa-Viva's dishonesty is dictated by his survival instinct, his name is also intriguing in that it seems to convey a degree of mockery and humor.

Viva, in the popular Lingala youth's mind, refers to *le bon vivant,* the one who enjoys life. When someone says today we had "la viva," that means we had fun. Many people use *wa* to refer to "son of." In the popular culture, Viva-Wa-Viva means that he is doubly viva; all he thinks about is having fun. I think that he hustles in order to survive, but I do not think that one has to be dishonest in order to survive. There are some people who prefer not to steal by shining shoes in order to survive, but that is not Viva's lifestyle. His story is also self-explanatory because he came to Europe when he was very young; his father was a rich politician who had some political problems back home. In the film it is said that his father was hanged, and that Viva dropped out of school. This gives him a bit of an excuse, but, in fact, it is not really an excuse, it is more a way of helping us understand his character.

Mwana's character is also interesting. She was arrested on a drug-related charge. Although we are not told explicitly in the film, we know that she was Viva's girlfriend at one point. It is also not clear whether or not she knew what was in the package she was given, or if she was just set up by Viva.

At the beginning of the 1960s, during the time of independence, all the rich Congolese parents sent their kids to Belgium to study, even for primary school. Every day, during back-to-school period, there were many planes waiting to take these kids to Belgium. These planes were nicknamed "scholarly planes," and Mwana was a part of this culture. Many parents believed that their kids had to study in Belgium to get a good education. Some kids were sent as early as eight years old; Mwana was one of those kids. She was totally naive, and Viva, who had already turned bad, was her first love. He gave her a package to deliver in France. Viva capitalized on Mwana's naïveté and pushed her to make fatal mistakes. I often see these young Congolese who have gone astray in Europe but do not have the courage to tell their families about their situation—ashamed to write home for fear of destroying the image that their families expect of them. They create a wall between themselves and their families; this is the case of Mwana. She is representative of the many men and women in this situation that I personally know. I think of the problems of children from "good families" who find themselves living a life completely different from what their families thought. They are victims of Europe, victims of the idea that their parents make of Europe. Like Mwana, they remain prisoners of this ideology.

I know many Africans who are ashamed of returning home because they do not have cars, stereo, video, etc. to take to Africa. They remain in Europe, thinking that one day they will acquire these things. It is a dilemma, but they prefer to stop writing home and get lost in self-imposed exile. Mwana got herself initiated into this culture, but what I say in the film about the Belgian police blackmailing Mwana is a reality. The police manipulate the immigrants to get information about the community and it is easy to find people who will cooperate with them. Mwana is still a person with a positive attitude, but she is a victim of the image that her father had of Europe.

There are many possible ways of interpreting the end of the film. On the one hand, one can say that it ends on a very optimistic note, but on the other hand, it can be said to be somewhat unrealistic, and I am wondering if all the characters really retrieved their "pieces of identity."

Before saying whether the end is optimistic or pessimistic, let me say the film is first of all open-ended. It leads to a situation where one wonders if Chaka-Jo, who finally finds his father, is actually joining him for good. Similarly, one wonders if Mwana, who is returning to her father's kingdom in a land where she does not know the language, will not be returning to Europe, legally, in the future. Also, what is going to be the fate of chief of police, Jeffke? Jeffke knew colonial Africa so well, and even had a lover who he never really loved but proclaimed to be the only woman that he ever loved in life. With the discovery of Chaka-Jo as his son who has gone back to Africa, one wonders if Jeffke will return one day and visit with Anastasia, his son's mother, and finally have a meaningful relationship with her that is no longer a colonial relation with the little *négresse*. One wonders if the little beautiful Ludo is not going to visit Manikongo in Africa, where it is possible to imagine a European in Africa playing with Manikongo's grandchildren without thinking that he comes from a "superior" civilization to see an "inferior" civilization. The film is open-ended. For me, the coincidental side of the end of the film, where everyone finds his or her identity, is simply intriguing because I like a happy ending in cinema just as in the classical theater.

I like everything to turn out well for characters to whom we are attached. It is only a convention, but that does not mean that the problems I raise throughout the film do not exist. It is only a scenaristic convention. For me, this end also means that the most important thing is that Manikongo finds his "pieces of identity." Although he reclaims his ID, he also understands through this trip that before he returns home, many things must change. Tradition must evolve; it is not static. He understands that even if his objects were touched by a woman, it is through this woman that he found his objects, and maybe it's not the end of the world. He understands that even though his daughter did not come with a medical school diploma, his own traditional medicine cannot be relegated—even if it is assumed there were no women healers in the past. There is no reason that his daughter could not become one. He learns that things must change but nothing should be taken for granted. Unlike the colonial period, changes must be controlled by Africans, that is why in the end he proclaims a consultation with the "Council of the Wise [Conseil des Sages]." His trip also taught him various things regarding his illusions of Europe as well as his own customs.

If the characters at the end of the film leave Europe and go to Africa, it is not to say that they need to necessarily return to Africa to exist. They are not fleeing racism, they could have decided to stay and fight. It is a way of saying that we have a home and we want to develop our home. I think it is optimistic, that with all the economic problems that we have in the Third World countries, there is at times the tendency of some Third World peoples living in Europe to say, "I have enough to eat three meals a day and buy a pair of shoes, why should I return to my ancestral homeland?" It is important at this level that there be a positive message—to see people in reality thinking about how to build or rebuild their countries of origin.

Could you explain the role of music in the film?

First, I am very interested in music. In most of the documentaries I have made, and in *La vie est belle*, music plays a central role. In the case of *Pièces d'identités* we started with simple traditional music with no electrical instruments. When King Manikongo arrives in the city we used modern traditional African music. In the rest of the film there are different types of music that have specific meaning. There is a song that says: "Stay awake, wait for the morning bird, it will arrive. Stay awake." This is a song that I had written and inserted into the script. Even though the young girl no longer speaks her native language, she still knows this song. The father also sings during the scene when he is depressed. I had another song in my mind that was not in the script. I had called this song "The Mother's Song" because the mother remains the link between Mwana and her father. Other music that you often hear is when Chaka-Jo comes with his arrow to confront the racist establishments. Each time, the music is repeated. There is also music, though a little nostalgic, that is played each time the police chief thinks of Anastasia. In the film there are also times such as in the African sections of Brussels where there is modern Congolese music, and music by Papa Wemba particularly in the African nightclubs. That is to depict reality, because, normally, when one goes to the Congolese neighborhood in Brussels the first thing that strikes one's mind is the pulsating African music that makes one think of Kinshasa. For most participants of this type of social gathering it is a way of forgetting the nostalgia that they feel for the countries they left behind.

You favor the comedic style. Will this be your pattern of representation? Why is comedy important to you?

Comedy is important for me, because in my own life, I like to practice humor. I like to look at reality from a certain distance and a certain humor. Comedy allows me to say more things than I would be able to say in a serious manner and to pursue certain issues seriously. It allows me not only to have a profound view of things but also gives me the opportunity to express this frankness and not produce pretentious or mean films that will alienate viewers. By focusing on comedy, the viewer gets the impression of looking at a mirror—the mirror that allows one to look at oneself while making a conscious decision of whether to accept or refuse the film's message, even when it is didactic. Comedy has a light aspect that can reveal many things. Each in its own way, *La vie est belle* and *Pièces d'identités* weave different kinds of conventions. *La vie est belle* is what one might call a light comedy with its own characteristics. If the society is well portrayed and the sociological aspect expresses the preoccupation of the population, then the light comedy becomes that mirror I talked about before that allows people to look and laugh at themselves. When laughing at oneself I think that there is something resilient about how it reflects people's everyday behavior. In *Pièces d'identités*, I tried to move away from light comedy and to adapt a more dramatic type. In following the itinerary of the royal paraphernalia, laughter instigates a certain reflection, and the viewer is given an opportunity to think about the consequences of the king's adventure. I find that interesting because I find that people laugh with more frankness when they feel as if they are not laughing freely. There are situations when one is ashamed of laughing; but when comedy provokes reflection and introspection one is not ashamed to laugh, and that generates a stronger emotion.

I find this approach very refreshing and will stick to it. I think that *Pièces d'identités* uses mixed modes of address; overall, it is a dramatic comedy but there are also some aspects of a thriller, a romance, or a social tableau, a film that describes a society at a certain period of time. I wanted to mix these genres but I think that in order to make a film understandable to the large public, the dramatic structure must be made acceptable. As a filmmaker, my main mission is to take into account the viewer's point of view and interest. I think it is a way of respecting the audience, of stirring up emotions in them, and of making a film where they could relate no matter what the subject might be. By the same token, I would never buy a chair from a carpenter if it were not functional, because I could not comfortably sit on it.

Filmography

Chéri-Samba, 1980
Kin-Kiesse ou les joies douces-amères de Kinshasa-la-belle (Kinshasa the joyful), 1983)
La vie est belle (Life is rosy), 1987
Changa changa, rythmes en noirs et blanc (Rhythm in black and white), 1992
Le roi, la vâche et le bananier (The king, the cow and the banana tree), 1994
Lettre à Makura: Les derniers Bruxellois (Letter to Makura), 1995
Pièces d'identités, 1997

Notes

1. I wish to express my gratitude to Dr. Awam Amkpa, who helped with the second part of this interview at FESPACO. My sincere gratitude also goes to Cecile Accilien, a doctoral candidate at Tulane University whose indefatigable effort led not only to the success of the African Film Series we coordinated at Tulane University but to the conducting and translation of Mr. Mweze's interview at Tulane University in New Orleans.

2. As predicted, Pièces d'identités won the Étalon de Yennega at FESPACO in 1999. This section of the interview was conducted at the festival; the latter part took place in the same year at Tulane University during the presentation of my African Film Series.

Idrissa Ouedraogo (Burkina Faso)

From the mid-1980s to the early 1990s, the films of Idrissa Ouedraogo, more than those of any other African filmmaker, made an enormous impact internationally, in terms of both universal acceptability and commercial viability. This period saw the release of Ouedraogo's *Yam Daabo* (The choice, 1986), *Yaaba* (1989), *Tilaï* (1990), *A Karim na Sala* (1991), *Samba Traoré* (1992), and *Le cri du coeur* (The heart's cry, 1994).

Idrissa Ouedraogo was born in 1954 in Banfora, Burkina Faso, and was educated at the Institut Africain des Etudes Cinématographiques of Ouagadougou (African Institute of Film Studies in Ouagadougou). While studying at this institution, he directed his first short, *Poko*, which received the grand prize for best short film at the 1981 Pan-African Festival of Film and Television of Ouagadougou. After graduation, he worked with the state's office of film production, directing several short documentaries. Interested in furthering his education in film studies, he lived briefly in Kiev in the former Soviet Union before proceeding to study at the IDHEC, the French Film School, from which he graduated in 1985. He also obtained a diploma in film studies from the Sorbonne.

The release of *Yaaba* firmly established Ouedraogo as a prolific director with the enviable status of dean of the "new wave" in African film. Filmmakers who are part of this new wave are considered as belonging to what is generally termed the "second generation" of African filmmakers. They are credited with initiating what is believed to be a new trend in African cinema exemplified by the belief that if African films are to be competitive and profitable, there must be a reorientation of all factors of production. Ouedraogo vigorously pursued this idea, deliberately eschewing the traditional films of protest initiated by the pioneers and opting instead for narrative forms in which the humanistic and the universal coalesce into a pleasing aesthetic formula

151

that in turn translates into acceptability and commercial viability. I have noted elsewhere that in terms of universal acceptability and commercial viability, *Yaaba* is
exceptional if not unprecedented in the history of sub-Saharan African film production. It is one of the few African films that have been widely received in international
commercial screenings with good box-office returns. Critically acclaimed at Cannes,
it has been well received by audiences in Africa, Europe, Asia, and the United States.
Tilaï, like *Yaaba,* premiered to receptive audiences, winning coveted awards both at
Cannes and at FESPACO.

During the FESPACO premiere of his controversial *Kini et Adams* (1997), Ouedraogo stunned his audience, who had hoped to see another ethnographic vérité-
induced narrative, with structure, style, and aesthetics markedly different from all his
earlier films. In all respects, *Kini et Adams* is an ambitious project; the film was
shot in South Africa after the demise of apartheid, and the international composition
of the cast and crew seem to suggest the possibility of an intrastate and interstate
coproduction. According to Ouedraogo, the new style is an important strategy, rep-
resenting "the great work of my cinematographic career with an alternative vision
and curiosity, a new voice." However, for his detractors, it is this new voice that has
earned him the nickname of "French director." In this interview, begun at the 1995
FESPACO and concluded at the 1997 FESPACO, Ouedraogo speaks about the new
vision and new voice he has developed in relation to the problems of African film and
the quest for survivability.

*You have established yourself as one of the world's best-known directors. How have
you developed from* Poko *to* Kini et Adams, *a period spanning over ten years of labor
and success?*

I started making films with *Poko*, a film that got the short film prize in 1981 at
FESPACO. I made a lot of short films, but I was looking for my voice. I also wanted
to make a film that my audience could enjoy aesthetically as well as for the contents.
This is not easy to do, because African filmmakers do not have abundant resources.
I was looking for this voice for a long time. *Kini et Adams* is, I think, the great work
of my cinematic career, with an alternative vision and curiosity for the world. At the
same time, it was a discovery of new characters and actors and new kinds of production that will allow me to go a lot further with my next films. It is true that I took
more than ten years to find this voice. The other films I made before are good, but I
want my future film styles to look like this [*Kini et Adams*]. I tried with *Le cri du coeur*,
but I didn't succeed. *Kini et Adams* is really the second breath for me.

Politically, Poko *hit hard. But in regard to* Yaaba, Tilaï, *and* A Karim na Sala, *you were
accused of being apolitical because you dealt with human-interest stories. After you left
for France to direct some films, some critics say that you became a French director.
How do you deal with these criticisms?*

When someone does things, those that do nothing are never criticized. If you do nothing, you do not get criticism. When I do things, there are people who like me and people who don't. I do not say that what I do is perfect, but I think people must be more tolerant. *Poko* was a period of youth, but also of intelligence because I was thinking that the cinema has a social and educational character. That is why I made *Poko*. But 85 percent of the population, the people who live in villages, do not have theaters for films. They don't have lights and electricity, so our films don't reach them. That means that the films that Africans make, even if they say they are for Africans, they aren't. In each of our countries, 85 percent of the population does not see our films. It is not for them that we make films. They are elitist films, made only for the cities, because only the cities have the means to watch them. I said to myself that films of social and educational purposes are good, but in the cities, people are used to seeing other films, such as American, French, and Indian fiction films. The African is also a curious being who can laugh and cry. That too is political. It just depends on level and degree, that one sees politics.

When I am invited to Cannes, all of Africa is proud, whether it be *Yaaba* or *Tilaï* that is shown. Politically, the African is proud. I think politics is bigger than that. There is also political action. In that case, one stops making films and joins political parties. Militant cinema is fine, but cinema that shows Africa in another form is also militant because it permits Africa and others to see that there is laughing and crying here. Cinema is universal, so I am not ashamed or afraid of the manner in which I approach filmmaking. My audience is proud too. They say so when they see my films. I think one has to respond more to the inspirations by which we live.

And your "special" relationship with the French?

Sometimes when you make films, even people who don't like you are obliged to love you. I have many personalities. Sometimes I am kind, but sometimes I talk too much. But I do not think I am really made to do films. I was made to speak. I choose to make films, but maybe I will stop and only speak about cinema. But what is my point of view of African cinema and our relationships with France and Europe? In regard to GATT [the General Agreement on Tariffs and Trade] and AMI [Accords multilater-aux sur l'investissement, or Multilateral Agreements on Investment, an agreement sponsored by the OECD (Organization for Economic Co-operation and Develop-ment)] I wonder where Africa falls. I think I will fight for a percentage of African films in Europe and North America because it is not fair that we be excluded from all these pieces of the cake. That is politics, but making films is love.

That's an important point—Africa's relationship with Europe, America, the rest of the world, and other factors in modern development such as the Internet and new tech-nologies and how they affect African cinema.

I agree with the point Ramadan Suleman made [at the African Film Festival in New York] when, while acknowledging that the new technologies will benefit African cinema, he also asked, "How can they be made accessible to people in Africa?" This points to other important issues. The perception people have of Africa is of a country, but it is a combination of big countries and lots of smaller ones that make up the continent, with about 90 percent of the population living in rural areas with no electricity or movie theaters. That tells me that 90 percent of the population has other priorities. Health is a major problem. AIDS is rampant, and there are problems in education as well as problems of hunger and thirst. Today, almost all of West Africa is suffering from drought. That tells me that cinema and audiovisual media are luxuries. Looking at the larger social problems around us in Africa, even the cost of putting a film on video is a luxury. If the fundamental problem is that of the market and distribution, how can the markets of small countries of about eight to nine million people sustain a national film industry?

The continent was colonized by the French, English, and Portuguese, so we speak different languages. So we do not have a market right now. Today, this lack of a market makes countries like the United States work with countries like South Africa to be able to better broadcast throughout Africa. All of Europe will do the same. The problem, which I think is the point of the discussion, is that some people in Africa decided to make cinema their profession. They are looking for television and cinema markets. This means that they will have to work with other people. Now, what can these other people bring to filmmakers so that their films can be seen in France, in the United States, and on television no matter what the format? Out of the films that I have seen in New York over the last couple of years, how many of them have been shown on U.S. television? That is the real problem. How can this new technology enable people who have chosen this "luxury" profession to survive? How can this technology allow their product to eventually get to these markets, creating an economic market such that little by little we can create a huge market in Africa? We must not forget that cinema in Africa is only thirty years old and that there are language barriers, that the countries are not "the United States of Africa"; regulations and fiscal codes do not apply collectively.

This is why when we discuss cooperation with African Americans they must realize that they are blessed with American technology. The point is, how can African cinema and television practitioners work with the black community in the United States? That may be the right response to our problems. The technique is like driving a car which may be accessible to anybody. The problem is not technical accessibility; we have doctors and engineers, so technology is accessible. The true problem is that the continent has not been able to create its own market. If we take the problem of GATT and AMI, do you see Africa in any of these transactions? We do not exist because we do not have a market. Now if those who speak of these new technologies are able to create television and have the material means to broadcast African films throughout the world then, cinema will grow in all of these aspects.

*Cinema and luxury . . . is African cinema approaching a dead end, given the economic
and social problems you just mentioned?*

When I say that cinema and video are luxuries in Africa, I am aware that every
people has its own culture and that their cultural products must first work in their
own culture. The Egyptians do not need anyone else for their cinema to exist. They
have the population and the means for their own production. Indians as well. Americans as well. Africans have the simplest way to speak about their respective cultures,
which is the story, popular theater, and, more so today, radio. Film and video are very
expensive today in relation to the buying power of the population and the cost of
production. But it is not because of that that we don't want to make films. We do want
to exist in our countries, but in our cities only few people have access to our films.
That is why we go overseas.

Because of our colonial past, and all we were deprived of, the young in Africa
identify themselves with African artists and athletes; anyone who makes a name outside in the world looks like a hero to them. That is why we continue to make films
and suffer because we know we can't live on making films today. Everyone who makes
films today knows that the market is outside of Africa because our local market is
not organized. People do not have the money to patronize the cinema. The price of
production is so high that the price of the ticket is too expensive. You can see that we
have big problems. We must not think that filmmakers do not think of doing things
for Africa. I just said that the easiest way to accomplish a profitable goal is to establish more theaters and television stations. If filmmakers choose to remain in the business it is because we think that one day all these suggestions will be implemented.
That hope continues to drive our impulse to make films.

*Do you still believe, as you once stated in an interview, that films made in Africa with
only Africans in mind cannot generate enough revenue to defray production costs?*

The production of films in Africa cannot generate money, because the true market is
in the villages, the countryside, and the people who live there have no access to
African films. In order to tap into that market, films must be made to correspond to
the people's financial capacity to pay for tickets. They do not have the means to pay
the thousand CFA [about fifty cents] we ask for the films we show. So we must make
cheaper, popular films, even on video, so that our film industry can prosper. The
problem of distribution for me is a problem of reorganizing the potential industry.
India does not have a problem. The United States does not have a problem, nor does
Egypt or Brazil. Our problem is compounded because some countries are so small that
astronomical production costs do not benefit our filmmakers, and I think we must
find some ways of reducing the cost of making films. For that to happen, we have to
train people so that the salaries can correspond to the local salary range. If our films
are too expensive for the local economy, then they are not meant to serve the people
they were created for. To make them profitable, we need other markets. We must

perhaps develop, country by country—like cinema verité, like New Wave cinema—a certain number of reflections that can lead countries to take on their problems of production and distribution.

I do not think we can look at the problems on a continental scale; we must consider each country separately. Each country can learn from the experiences of those countries that have film policies, and when all states have their own policies, then relations of coproduction can be born. Each country needs its own cinema legislation. African cinema is like a castle without a foundation. That is the truth. If I have to bring over a cameraman from the United States or Europe to film in Africa, I have to pay for their fares, including local transportation, food, and accommodation, and that is very expensive. But if I had a trained cameraman here, in Burkina Faso, that would cost an amount consistent with the local salary market. Similarly, if we had a laboratory in Burkina Faso or reliable postproduction facilities in other African countries, that would reduce costs. Our production costs are inflated because we do not have local cinema industries. The films we make—even if we claim they are aimed at the people of our country—cannot be seen by 80 percent of the population. We need to ask how our people can experience the full potential of our films, or is cinema actually a luxury that can be avoided by Africans? There are many other questions to be asked. Is not video becoming more accessible now? Would that create the possibility of a true industry? What about 16mm? Why don't we make 16mm films? Why make a film in Cinemascope?

It is my duty also to say that with the difficulties I have encountered, if I had it all to do over, I would not do the same things. When I see the very popular Burkinabe film *Kaïta*, which is fantastic and done with very few resources, I realize that we must accept making films like that—films that people like, even if they are not distributed in Europe. However, when we aim at distributing our films in Europe and having them selected for prestigious festivals, it takes a certain budget, labor expertise, and maneuvering to reach that goal. But African cinema needs diversity. Filmmakers should have the freedom to do what they want to do. There is no theory, no dogmatic formula, and there is not a single African cinema; there must be African cinemas.

What can we call your film style? You have moved away from ethnographic vérité to a more commercially oriented or, as some put it, conventional avant-garde structure in your new film, Kini et Adams.

I think a man is born, grows, and dies. His film is like a life. If you make four or five films, it is difficult to make more. I was very lucky to have a second birth, to be able to give new things to the people. You can look at it that way. My end in the old way of thinking was *Tilaï*. This new film is what I was looking for; a new style.

Why was Kini et Adams *set in Southern Africa?*

It was set in Zimbabwe and stars top South African actors, Vusi Kunene [Kini] and David Mohloki [Adams]. The actor Vusi Kunene is the head of Market Theater in Johannesburg. He used to live in the United States. He is also in a new film by Michael Douglas. This move toward South Africa comes from a desire to discover this country that is going through enormous changes and moving away from apartheid.

Did you ever think of doing this movie in Burkina Faso, or did you always think to do it in Zimbabwe or in English?

I made this choice because I was thinking about new experiences, and I knew that because of the apartheid system, South Africans developed their fight of liberation through theater and songs. I believe they have a lot more experience in those areas than people from West Africa, who didn't live through that kind of struggle for liberation. I think South Africa is a new country that will give a lot to Africa with regard to music and theater and, therefore, to actors in cinema. They have roughly the same level of living as we do, and it costs less compared to our means of production. That means we can discover an African cinema that is more developed not only in terms of directors but also of actors. I am sure that South Africa will give actors of a good quality to all of Africa. It was a great experience making the film there, and I believe other African filmmakers will aspire to a collective endeavor that would involve the people of South Africa. Africa is divided into linguistic zones; the English-speaking areas are highly populated, and we must aspire to make use of what is available. There is a proverb in Burkina Faso that says when you sleep on someone's mattress, if that person takes away the mattress, you end up on the floor. Therefore, my preoccupation was to explore the markets in the Southern Hemisphere.

What were some of the daily problems of working in a second language, and how did you resolve them?

There are two things. Filmmaking is a collective effort—a group of people working together to achieve a goal. There must, of course, be someone in charge. If there is no boss, everything collapses because everyone assumes power. So I do not eat with my technicians. I eat with the actors. They can't take the power. They become friends. Since the script was in English, I asked them if something went well. They would say, well, no, he should do such and such. Since I understand a little English and can sense whether it is right or not, it was done on a daily basis with spontaneity. There were not many problems except that I could not insult them because I don't speak English well enough [said jokingly]. But it was a very good experience for me. We talked about many things, and they taught me many things. But I think it will be the last movie I make in English.

How did you approach the casting?

I didn't know the cast very well. I went to South Africa to prepare for the shoot. As I said before, Ramadan Suleman had used Vusi Kunene in his films, so when I arrived I was introduced to him. I saw quite a few other actors, but they were not good. As we were about to leave, Adams [David Mohloki] arrived. When I saw him, I said, "This guy looks really naive." We didn't go through casting, because I felt that he could do the job. He looked so pure and attractive. In real life he is what he is in the film. I also thought Kini an ideal character because he had a different perception of things. Adams was an actual person, whereas Kini was a performance. For this particular film these characters were a good match.

You have used comedy before in your films, but in Kini et Adams *there is a lot of comedy.*

One of my friends told me that in cinema there are two big themes, love and sorrow. I tried to put together loving and crying. Am I a good student or not?

The theme I notice throughout your film is that of work and the worker. It's there that I find your own politics.

It's true that there is this passage from the peasant class to the working class. This brutal change creates all the problems with these people on the level of friendship. I think my films are engaged. You are right; there is that in them. But other people have other analyses. Perhaps for them, only a militant film is a political film. But a political film can speak of many other things.

In Kini et Adams *you were no longer confined to oral narrative patterns or indigenous cultural forms.*

That is because I traveled for such a long time that I learned a new culture that is not only oral.

But there is a lot of orality in the jokes.

But I think that every people and country has riddles. That is universal. I tried to be individualistic.

And to enjoy your new freedom to express yourself?

Yes, I am free because I have nothing to prove. I am not afraid of what people expect of me. I know that if I can no longer make films, I will be able to do something else. I am very free. Many people in African cinema cannot do anything else if they relinquished filmmaking. That is why it is very important that cinema take its real place in Africa. The real filmmakers should express themselves.

Given what you have just said, is African cinema in a crisis?

No. Not a crisis, but a maturity. We are going through new phases and it is good. If you want to leap forward, criticism is important. We must take the opportunities that arise through this spirit of soul-searching.

You seem to have succeeded where other African filmmakers have not. Kini et Adams *is an expensive film.*

Oh, there are other films much more expensive than *Kini et Adams,* which was only 1.5 million U.S. dollars. That is not expensive at all, even by African standards. When people see the film, they automatically assume it is expensive, but the contrary is the case. There are no stars in the film.

In your films, landscape is an asset. Is that why you used Cinemascope for Kini et Adams?

No, I used it for all of my films. I like pictures.

Filmography

Poko, 1981
Les écuelles, 1983
Issa et le Tisserand (Issa the weaver), 1985
Yam Daabo (The choice), 1986
Yaaba, 1989
Tilaï, 1990
A Karim na Sala, 1991
Samba Traoré, 1992
Le cri du coeur (The heart's cry), 1994
Afrique, mon Afrique (Africa, my Africa), 1995
Kini et Adams, 1997

Brendan Shehu (Nigeria)

Born a Muslim in Northern Nigeria, Brendan Shehu is one of the oldest pioneers of African cinema and has played a vital role in the development of Nigerian cinema. He has served the Nigerian film industry as a filmmaker, bureaucrat, and administrator. Although Nigerian films are not well-known internationally, Nigeria produces more films than any other African country, with filmmakers catering specifically to the local population. Nigeria also has an enormous cinematic infrastructure, an ultramodern film studio, color laboratories, and sound facilities, which, according to Shehu, are well equipped to handle film production from "concept to finish."

Shehu launched his film career as far back as 1966 after completing his film and television studies in London. Following this, he worked for the Northern Nigeria Broadcasting Corporation as a producer, director, and editor of a weekly documentary program. In 1976, he was called upon to set up a film unit for the Northern Nigerian government, which was situated in Kaduna. Over a period of nine years, he produced more than thirty public enlightenment documentary films, focusing on agriculture, health, drug addiction, and so on. In 1985, Shehu was appointed general manager of the Nigerian Film Corporation, a controversial government parastatal that, he says, "only existed on paper" at the time he assumed office, but that he transformed into Africa's most modern superstructure for filmmaking, grossly underutilized to this day. According to Shehu, "It will be easier for [African] filmmakers to produce films in Nigeria without having to travel abroad to do postproduction work." But why is the NFC's capacity for postproduction ignored by African filmmakers, most of whom do their postproduction work in Paris and other Europeans capitals? In his effort to appeal to African filmmakers to utilize the facilities in Nigeria, Shehu maintains that "African filmmakers have no need to go overseas since [the NFC's] rates are competitive." So far, the only significant feature film made at the NFC studios is Shehu's first feature, *Kulba na Barna* (1992), which won an award in Italy. Since its inception, the corporation has thrived only on the production of government documentaries focusing on the general development of the country; one of these is *Better Life*, which won an international award in North Korea.

This interview highlights aspects of Nigerian cinema not previously documented. Shehu offers a provocative assessment of the two cinemas in Nigeria—the Yoruba tradition of filmed theater along with other independent practices and the Nigerian/ francophone relationship with FESPACO. In contradistinction to the views expressed by Chief Ugbomah, the former managing director of NFC, also featured in this volume, Shehu offers his own account of the operations of the NFC—for example, how the NFC commissioned a pioneer laboratory and sound dubbing studio, the first of its kind in West Africa if not the whole of Africa, and why it has taken so long to complete. Other current issues of the Nigerian film industry discussed include the enactment of a film policy for Nigeria, the establishment of a long-awaited film archive, the video revolution, the proliferation of foreign television broadcasts via satellite, and the effects of foreign television on the film industry.

This interview was conducted at the Nigerian Film Corporation's headquarters in Jos in July 1995.

You are a bureaucrat, administrator, and filmmaker. How do you combine these roles in the running of the Nigerian Film Corporation?

Essentially I think I am a filmmaker. I happened to find myself doing an administrative job. But the experience I have acquired over the years in filmmaking assisted me in running the NFC.

Before you became a full-time administrator, you were already a well-known Nigerian filmmaker. When did you launch your filmmaking career?

I started as far back as 1966 after completing my film and television studies in London. I joined the broadcasting company of Northern Nigeria in about 1965, but soon realized that I was doing more television production, even though I was trying to jealously guard my own interest in filmmaking. I didn't think that it wasn't professionally conducive to work in both television and film production. However, I concentrated more on film because that has been my background. I started off editing films. During that period we had an expatriate film director who after about a year or two departed and left a big void in the organization. I felt that this opportunity would allow me to try my hand at virtually every aspect of filmmaking. I was forced to prove my worth, and my skills were enhanced on the job. For a long period of time I was responsible for producing, directing, and editing a weekly documentary program. I received further encouragement in 1968, when one of our affiliates, the Staff Development Center, asked me to make *Office Security*, a 16mm training documentary film. *Office Security* is a training film for staff development. I was provided with all the necessary materials I needed to direct and edit the film. To my surprise, it was very successful. The producer was the expatriate director of the Staff Development Center, but I got all the ideas and packaged it into a film.

Although the film gave me a lot of encouragement and exposure, what made me consolidate my career as a filmmaker was when, in 1976, the Kaduna government invited me to set up their film unit. I was offered other opportunities to learn and sharpen my skills. For a period of nine years, I produced over thirty documentary films purely for public enlightenment. These films were shown in rural areas by mobile cinema vans, and copies were sold to other northern states that did not have film units. The documentaries we made were educational films covering topics such as public enlightenment on agriculture, health, and drug addiction. In 1985, I was appointed the general manager of the Nigerian Film Corporation. It was there that I faced the greatest challenge of all because at the time of my appointment the NFC existed only on paper. We had to start from scratch, building to where we are today, establishing the modern facilities we have.

Were the documentary films you made during these years preserved?

Yes, we still have some of the documentaries in print, the master negatives, and sound tracks. We have set up a national film archive where the films are preserved. Some of the copies are worn out due to overuse. But I made video copies of the films for myself.

You are one of the pioneers who worked with the Federal Film Unit and in the Nigerian Television Authority [NTA], which now relies exclusively on video production. Does this mean the death of the film medium?

Film is not dead, but we are going through a very difficult period. In view of the economic and political climate in this country, it has been very difficult to produce films. But over the years the government has shown interest in the industry and has given us financial support. For example, the color laboratory has finally been completed. The idea of creating a lab started as far back as the early 1970s, but it never materialized until the plan was resuscitated in 1988. It took a long time to convince the government to build a laboratory, but with the facilities we have now, the lab, the dubbing studio, etc., it will be easier for filmmakers to produce films in Nigeria without having to travel abroad to do postproduction work. We are considering how these facilities can be effectively utilized to assist filmmakers. Providing them with the facilities is one thing, but maintaining adequate funding for running it is another. For this reason we are proposing the government establish a film development fund for filmmakers to produce films.

How would you describe your first feature film, Kulba na Barna?

It was my first attempt to direct a fictional feature-length film. As you might have noticed, the structure of the film is inundated with documentary style. If I were to make the film today, I probably would have taken a different approach. It was not easy for me to make the film while also doing my official duties. At times I would be called from location to attend meetings in Lagos or Abuja, and therefore some scenes had to be handled by the assistant director. It was a difficult task trying to convince the government to fund feature-length fictional films. In one instance, the NFC managed to get limited funding, and to supplement we had to embark on coproduction with Ahmadou Bello university. The university also encountered a lot of difficulties getting funds. It was a big risk because we started filming without knowing if we were going to raise the necessary funds to complete the film. We were doing production piece by piece, which is not an efficient way to make a film. It was an anguishing and expensive experience for me, but I am looking forward to another production which I hope to begin soon.

How was Kulba na Barna *conceived, and who is your intended audience? The fiction/documentary synthesis rendered* Kulba na Barna*'s message extremely powerful, but what were you trying to achieve with the moralistic tone?*

My target audience is young women; what was depicted in the film is an everyday occurrence. You find that the affluent people in this society are greedy and want to seduce young women while at the same time protecting their own daughters. When a rich man says, "I love you," it does not really mean he is in love. It may mean that he wants something from you. I hope the film sends a message to young women. Our intention was to make this point clear to the youth; however, not everyone welcomed this message. When it was launched in Kano, some critics were unhappy that after the young man was jilted by the young lady [the main actress], he marries an illiterate woman. Critics questioned if I was implying that illiterate women are better wives than college-educated ones. That is not true, for we did not mean to show educated women as morally bankrupt. The important issue is how to compel young women to take their studies seriously, to remind them that they do not have to depend on a rich man for anything. The film was adapted from a book written in Hausa for secondary schools in northern Nigeria. We had to modify the scenario slightly to reflect the way we live. I tried to integrate cultural aspects of our life, such as marriage customs and dietary habits, into the film's structure. Also, our national characteristics were infused into the structure through the use of Hausa, Igbo, and Yoruba characters. From this perspective, the story is no longer specific to Hausa or the Muslim Alhaji—it cuts across ethnic boundaries.

You present a positive message on the question of illiteracy. It amazes me how the issue was resolved in the film. Our hero marries a woman who did not go to school, but later on we see him tutoring her at home. It is like saying we are all equal, and one should marry for love, not for status.

It depends on the way you look at it. You have your own views and see it as a positive message. Others view it differently. My critics thought I was trying to show that educated women are not good enough and that if you want to have a happy marriage you should marry an uneducated woman. That is not the idea. It just happened that he met that woman and tried to bring her up to his standard. In the film, we learn through the dialogue that he had no problem with his first fiancée acquiring a university-level education. He is not biased against education, hence his interest in supporting his wife in her endeavor to get an education.

In Kulba na Barna, *as in other African films, love stories or love situations are depicted cautiously. Although physical intimacy is not actually shown, it is suggested in the film. How do culture and tradition influence the way you depict societal issues?*

It is true that we handled the love scenes in a very subtle way. We did not want to copy the Western way of expressing love. Although the love scenes were mild, there are some people who are unhappy with such portrayals because the film is set in northern Nigeria, which is predominantly Islamic. But in the South, where Western influences are stronger than Muslim influences, it is possible to show mild physical contact, like hugging and kissing. That does not mean that northern Nigerians do not kiss and hug, they just do it in the privacy of their own homes. During filming we ran into trouble when we wanted the actor to dance with the actress. He refused to dance with her because of his religious beliefs. In another scene in which the actress was wearing a long nightgown, he refused to remove his robe. He was worried that people would misinterpret the scene. Most African filmmakers face these types of problems, whether they be cultural or political. In terms of cultural specificity, an African filmmaker is forced to exercise enormous restraint and practice self-censorship, which is quite different from the experience of Western or American filmmakers. In the West, it is not unusual to see actors and actresses kiss on-screen. Even married actors and actresses kiss other actors and actresses on-screen. This is not accepted in the Islamic north. In Africa, we are very concerned about respect for the people, their culture, and religion. Considering that there are religious fanatics around, one has to be extremely careful about what is presented onscreen. Otherwise, you may end up losing your film. However, there are exceptions. If your target audience is outside the country, then it is possible to show the African way of making love, if it even exists, which white people would be very curious to see. It may be the same Western way that you see in their films and about which you read in books. I am only saying that kissing and hugging are done openly in the West but are done secretly in our own part of the country. That is the dilemma we must contend with as filmmakers constrained by strict cultural and religious codes.

I think it was well handled. Turning to a related topic, what would you say about the ethnographic film view of Africa, in which in almost all cases naked people and huts are treated as objects of fascination?

In content, *Kulba na Barna* is different from Western films which, arguably, corrupt youngsters. Those Western films are often inundated with outrageous, vulgar love-making scenes. The Westerner may not view these films as offensive, but in Africa, we try as much as possible to prevent decadent aspects of Western culture from polluting our culture. This does not mean that we don't have any negative aspects of our own culture, we just try to accentuate the positive ones. Unfortunately, there are some African films that have copied Euro-American decadence just to entice Western audiences. In the same vein, we do not have to emphasize the exotic either. For instance, when we showed our films in Europe, some people in the audience who have never been to Africa were surprised to know there are paved roads, Mercedes-Benzes, and mansions just like in their own communities. They were shocked because of the misconception that Africans live in the jungle. African films should be able to present both negative and positive aspects of African life in order to present a realistic view of Africa. They should also show how the continent is developing in spite of all the cultural and political forces that impede our progress.

So far, we have considered African films as a single entity, undermining the dichotomy that exists between anglophone and francophone film practices.

Definitely. Francophone films have received more exposure than anglophone films. The francophone produce films to suit their audience, and that is why the filmmakers can easily find the financial support from the French government and various French funding organizations. In anglophone countries, filmmakers try as much as possible not to pander to foreign interests. Comparing Ghanaian films to Nigerian films, we find similarities in presentation of style or technique, meaning there is a deliberate attempt to select images that represent "real life." I hope that with more exposure, the Western world and other advanced countries will be able to appreciate films from anglophone countries. Moreover, we should challenge African filmmakers to be mindful of what they produce. When I participated in the 1993 FESPACO, some films from Burkina Faso, I cannot remember their titles, were set in the slums and bushes, showcasing the poverty that exists there. However, the decent ways of living in that part of Africa were not depicted. Why should images of misery dominate our screens?

There is another point that this topic of so-called jungle film relates to, that is, the notion of a positive view of the society. If you look at Heritage ... Africa, *for instance, a positive critique is made of the negative aspects of Africa's development. It enables one to understand history and culture in relation to the outside world. What is your position about this notion of "positiveness" in African film?*

I am not advocating the presentation of only the positive aspects of our society on-screen. Of course, when you show the negative aspects you can also show resistance and opposition to it, and how we have developed over the years. I saw the film *Heritage ... Africa* and I saw the way it is handled. It is history; it is true. We are in a new era, changes which alter traditional ways do occur. So I do not see anything wrong with that, but to close your eyes to the positive and concentrate only on negative things because the filmmaker wants to entice the audience or get financial support from the Western world is wrong. I do not think it is good for our children, and we should not condone such images.

Do you envisage a homogeneous African film language?

I think it is difficult. It has been a big problem. Take Nigeria, for instance; it has been very difficult for filmmakers to come together on a common platform. Before we start thinking of an African film language, we must aspire to improve our techniques, develop more interaction between filmmakers, understand existing problems and how to solve them.

I think it is still possible to Africanize the film language.

Yes, of course it is possible. In my films, actors spoke their native dialect. If we had done it in English, no matter how educated they are, they would not speak as fluently or act as naturally. I have always advocated the use of indigenous language in our films, just as the Indians do. Many people do not speak or understand Indian languages, but their films are internationally appreciated because of specific cultural codes they deploy. They produce more films than Hollywood, so I do not see why we cannot Africanize film structures with African cultural codes inherent in language, music, dance—the oral storytelling tradition. As long as there is dialogue, voice-overs, or subtitles, the audience will understand the film. If the camera is well used, even without subtitles, it is possible to understand a film. If we can overcome the preliminary problems, eventually we will be able to develop an African-oriented film language. The main thing we need is unity, because at the film festivals we attend it becomes obvious how different the anglophone and the francophone countries are, politically, ideologically, and culturally. I do not know when we can come together as one. For example, the Pan-African Federation of Filmmakers is dominated by the French-speaking countries. In fact, the Nigerian delegation to the recent FESPACO left the last meeting early because nothing was being accomplished from the anglophone perspective. We found that all issues addressed the francophone perspective. The only triumph for the anglophone filmmakers came as a result of Ghanaian Kwaw Ansah's *Heritage ... Africa,* the internationally acclaimed feature winning the grand prize, the Étalon de Yennega. The officials think that this type of mistreatment is right because they have financial backing from France and her international allied organizations. The question is, when will changes occur? I mean genuine change geared to Pan-African transformation.

Lots of people agree that the French dominance of FESPACO is a problem. Has the matter been addressed at the FEPACI level?

The key positions of FESPACO are held by representatives of French-speaking countries in Africa. In fact, the president, the secretary general, and the zonal directors want FEPACI and FESPACO to remain permanently francophone. We do not agree on certain issues. For example, francophone filmmakers insist that films shown at the festival must be subtitled in French. Simply put, anything that is not approved by their colonial masters is not to be allowed. Questions asked in the francophone circles include, if FESPACO is supposed to be Pan-African, why would the francophone organizers insist that all films be subtitled in French and yet no adequate English translation is provided during meetings? How can this problem be resolved, or what should the anglophone filmmakers do? I do not think the Harare Film Festival of Zimbabwe is the answer. I still think the Pan-African spirit should prevail through speaking from one perspective in regard to the development of African cinema.

Are there any plans for interstate cooperation agreements to boost production and exhibition in the anglophone regions?

In most African countries, film is not considered a priority in comparison to other sectors of the economy. But if various governments, particularly those of anglophone countries, show more interest in the film industry at the initial stage of development it will be easier for the filmmakers to interact in a productive way. But right now, filmmakers are left to struggle on their own. For instance, if the government provides facilities, it should support it with laws that will make interstate distribution of African films more equitable. Ghana should be able to distribute a certain number of Nigerian films, and Nigeria should be able to distribute an agreed number of Ghanaian films. Even with this arrangement it is still difficult, because the issue of Ghanaian filmmakers getting back their money from screenings in Nigeria has not been resolved. If people hawk their films like Nigerian filmmakers, or those from any other anglophone or francophone regions, then they escape paying the government taxes needed to increase the production of African films. But if distribution and exhibition channels are regulated as a policy of the two governments, filmmakers can show their films and pay appropriate taxes as stipulated by the laws. Most African filmmakers cannot show their films in Nigeria because of high entertainment taxes. For instance, in Kano you pay at least 45 percent entertainment tax to the government before the profit made from the film is shared with the owner of the theater where the film is being screened. This is not healthy for the industry; I cannot see filmmakers from other African countries coming to show films in Nigeria if the exhibition tax laws are not relaxed.

Who made this tax policy?

Our own constitution is based on the federal system, where the states can make their own laws. Regarding the cinema, states can establish their own censorship boards. They can set their own figures for entertainment tax. State governments are always looking for revenue. The Kano state tax rate is the highest; in other states it ranges from 10 percent to 25 percent. The last time we showed *Kulba na Barna* in Kano we made over one hundred thousand naira in one night, but we ended up retaining only about twenty thousand naira, which did not even cover the cost of transportation and accommodations for the staff that went to Kano to screen the film.

Does this rule apply in all cases?

The rules apply to any film that is shown in legal cinema houses. You have to pay the taxes. That is why most of our filmmakers hawk their films; they want to minimize paying high taxes. They hawk their films anywhere space is available for screening; usually filmmakers have to bribe law enforcers to be able to use spaces as makeshift theaters. In normal circumstances, films are not distributed/exhibited in this manner. This lack of effective coordination also affects the artistic quality of our films. The ideal situation is to have a distributor to deal with exhibition problems, taxation, etc. while the filmmaker plans for the making of new films. In this way, the distributor and the filmmaker work together to ensure compensation for services rendered. If the process works well, the profit accrued can help to offset the filmmaker's loan. However, no such system exists in our country. It is unfortunate that distribution and exhibition are controlled almost entirely by foreigners. They determine which African film to show, good or bad. However, they are more interested in showing cheap Indian and Chinese films and American B movies.

What happened to the indigenization policy enacted in the 1970s by the Nigerian government?

The Indians and Lebanese, who own most of the cinema houses in this country and in other West African countries, connive with unscrupulous Nigerians to thwart the laws. In many instances they have used the argument that films made locally are not yet "acceptable" to our audiences. This is one way of killing their industry. They do it because they make more money showing Indian, Chinese, and American films. This is a perennial problem affecting the African film industries. The problem could be eliminated if the government enforced policies that would enhance the growth of local film industries.

There cannot be a thriving film industry if there are no distribution/exhibition channels. What is your office doing to stop high taxation and exhibition problems in Nigeria?

The Nigerian government created the Council of Information, whereby federal and state commissioners of information meet periodically with officials of the NFC. On several occasions, we called for uniform taxation at a reduced rate that will benefit the industry. We are suggesting that if the government wants to retain the entertainment tax, there should be a waiver for a period of two to five years—a tax-free break for

Nigerian filmmakers to recoup production costs. The government is adamant about this issue, but we will continue to fight for a reduction of the entertainment tax. In addition, the cinema houses are dying because they do not have enough films to show. The distributors are caught in a bind because only a few Chinese and Indian films are in circulation. The Nigerian film policy stipulates that some days of the week be set aside exclusively for the screening of Nigerian and African films; however, if the law is enforced, right now there aren't enough African films in existence. And again, we have not fully addressed the challenge posed by video technology and video "films." Because of the scarcity of films, it is common practice for the theaters to show videos. You would be surprised that they even show obscene films. They advertise them in newspapers and exhibit posters in public, but nobody challenges them.

The government says it is trying to set up a censorship board; I hope they do it quickly to control the recklessness. Also, cinemas are under concurrent lists, and we have not been able to ascertain which cinema houses are meant for film or for video. The governments are only interested in how to make money; they do not care whether the format is video or film. They are only interested in enhanced revenue through the entertainment taxes. We are also pushing for some of the collected taxes to be deposited in the Film Development Fund that we are about to set up, which would be utilized for production. As of now, cinema houses have been getting big box-office returns from the films they distributed over the years, but none of the profits have been invested in production.

In the Nigerian film practice there are two traditions of filmmaking: the Yoruba tradition of filmed theater, that is, the transfer of theatrical plays to film, and the imitation of dominant practices. It seems to me that the theater tradition, which is extremely uncinematic, is ironically the one most popular with the public.

Nigeria produces more films than any other African country, but internationally our films are not recognized because of poor exposure and poor craftsmanship. It is true that we have two groups of filmmakers. In regard to the group that transfers their theatrical plays to film, technically their films are not very good, and that is why they cannot be shown outside of Nigeria. But they have their audience, specifically the Yoruba. That is the advantage. However, the popularity of the genre is gradually dying because they have maintained the same style of production over the years. It will only be a matter of time before they completely lose their audience. Now, more educated filmmakers are coming out and are making films that aren't just theatrical plays translated to celluloid. Furthermore, the popular dramatists and actors who created this genre and made it so captivating are dying off. Our hope lies in the younger generation of artists like Ladi Ladebo. He has his own style of production and his work has been well received. I have also met a few others whose styles are quite different from what the other group produce. Since the young, educated filmmakers can produce good scripts, it will also be easier for them to raise money to make films. That is why the NFC is interested in going into coproduction with them. It may be not through financial assistance, but by providing some other services, such as the use of the NFC facilities. These are the areas we are going to look into and see how we can assist good filmmakers who can produce films that are marketable both in and outside this country.

Are you saying that at this point in time there is nothing we can classify as Nigerian cinema?

I will put it this way: we are still in the developmental stage. It took the government a long time to really show an interest in the film industry. With this new direction, I think things will improve within the next few years. All we need is to create that awareness and support for the growth of the industry. We must continue to work hard to steer the industry in the right direction. It is a slow process.

The Nigerian Film Corporation recently commissioned a pioneer color film processing laboratory and sound dubbing studio, the first of its kind in West Africa. Why has it taken so long to reach this stage?

It is the problem of not being able to convince the government of the importance of cinema in national development. Film is not a priority in comparison to agriculture or health, and the proliferation of television has dampened government interest in the film industry. When the powers that be see themselves on television, they think that is no different from film. They do not know that filmmaking is a complex art that demands expertise and energy. For example, when we shoot a film, we have to wait for days for it to be processed, but for television, it is possible to preview it instantly. However, that official perception is changing, which is why the government, over the years, has provided funds for the lab and dubbing studios. It has not been easy; in fact, that is why I praise General Babangida's administration. His regime understood the power of film in national development and invested heavily in the NFC. I have always emphasized this point because of the lukewarm attitude of preceding governments, who instead of investing in the NFC would rather pump money into state FM radio and television stations. We had a situation where various states created their own television stations at the same time that the federal government was also expanding its television stations.

Regarding the NFC, some of the films made from 1988 to date were processed here. In fact, some of the equipment that was bought as early as 1982 was discarded for lack of maintenance. Bad leadership was also a factor. People have their own priorities and interests. My priority as soon as I was made the managing director of the NFC was to fight for the provision of infrastructure for the industry. I believed that with this kind of assistance we could take off. That is exactly what we did, but unfortunately it took a long time to convince the government to come to our aid. From 1985 to 1988 we were helpless until the government gave us a green light. In fact, we had to convince the Council of Ministers to support the NFC and its agenda. Surprisingly, they sanctioned it; however, they warned us that if we failed, then it would mean the end of the film industry and aid in the advancement of the television industry. We took it as a challenge and devoted all of our time and energy to the formation of the industry. Today we can all smile. We have set it up, but we still encounter a lot of problems. Setting up a project is one thing, making it function is another. We are doing everything in our power to produce a functioning industry.

Will the provision of this super-infrastructure for postproduction services force Nigerian filmmakers to stop going abroad for postproduction?

Yes, I think so. If the difficulty in acquiring foreign exchange continues, it will force filmmakers to utilize the various facilities available at the NFC. In fact, during the official opening of the lab, the minister of information made it clear that there will be no foreign exchange approval for completing films overseas, because the NFC is well equipped for production, from concept to finish. The basic facilities are here, we have the crew to handle all aspects of production—camera work, processing, editing, sound mixing, etc. So why do we have to go overseas? Hollywood did not start overnight. They had to crawl before they walked. I am sure that the more films we produce, the better quality our films will be. In order to provide adequate services and training of our staff, we hired a foreign technician to temporarily run the lab. He has been here for a year, and his contract has been renewed for another year.

Describe the state-of-the-art postproduction equipment available at the NFC so that African filmmakers will know exactly why they should come and utilize the facilities.

In terms of filming, we have sound technicians, directors, a number of cameras (both 16mm and 35mm), Nagra recorders for sync sound, sophisticated lighting equipment, and microphones. We also have the facilities for processing both 16mm and 35mm films, editing facilities, ultramodern sound transfer equipment from one-quarter inch to either 16mm or 35mm magnetic sound track for editing. We have a dubbing studio where we can mix sound to produce a master sound track along with having the optical sound recording facility, where the sound is recorded photographically. From there, the master optical sound is taken to the lab for final printing. We can also do negative cutting. These are the facilities we have here. We are making arrangements to have new film stock readily available and to have that in bulk so we can sell to film-makers in this country, since foreign exchange prevents their importation.

It seems to me that the government has been able to lay the foundation on which a viable film industry can thrive. The question is, how can Nigerian and African film-makers be convinced to come and utilize NFC's equipment in order to generate funds for sustainable growth of more grandiose and elaborate projects?

We want to mount a publicity campaign. The lab, the dubbing studio, and all the facilities we have will be run purely on a commercial basis, and that is why we have mapped out a strategy for running the corporation. First of all, we must be convinced that we can satisfy the needs of people outside of this country before making our facilities available to them. We have used my own feature film, *Kulba na Barna*, and Eddie Ugbomah's *Tori Ade* as a test, as both were processed and edited here. If we are able to get one more feature film and maybe one or two more documentary films, we intend to go around to African countries and show them what can be done at the NFC.

We maintain that African filmmakers have no need to go overseas. Our own rates are competitive. We do not expect to make a profit in the first few years, but we want to at least be able to meet our expenses. So these are the things we are trying to do. Once we get started, I think we will be self-sufficient. We believe that with the facilities we have, the NFC should be able to sustain itself. We are now a commercial entity. Maybe that is why the corporation had to change from having a general manager to a managing director. This will amuse you: the corporation has been elevated to category "E"—the same standing as other Nigerian government corporations. So it is left for us to work very hard so that we can determine our salaries and our future, just like the Nigerian National Petroleum Corporation [NNPC] and other giant parastatals.

Have you launched any publicity campaigns to promote the activities of the NFC? If you made a short documentary of the facilities you have here and show it at FESPACO, you may be able to find filmmakers interested in using your facilities. This film could also be taken to other film festivals to convince filmmakers that the NFC has sophisticated equipment waiting to be used.

I think that is part of our plan. In fact, we took one video to Burkina Faso last year, but we want to develop it a little bit further. Now we are making a ten- to fifteen-minute 16mm film version for FESPACO to show that the NFC has facilities to make films from concept to finish. Yes, it would be nice to go around to African countries to promote the use of the facilities available at the NFC.

Why was the Nigerian Film Corporation headquarters moved from Lagos to Jos?

Well, I want to ease your mind. It was not political decision. A lot of people have read meaning into it and politicized the movement to Jos. Jos is an ideal place for the film industry. As you might have noticed, it has the same topography as Hollywood. The decision to move to Jos started as far back as 1982, during the tenure of the first directors. The decision was made when Bayo Oduneye was the chairman of the corporation. The people commissioned to look into this matter traveled to Lagos, Abuja, and Jos, and they found Jos suitable because of its topography. The centrality of Jos and the semitemperate tropical climate make it ideal. It was later on that we discovered that the water in Lagos is not conducive for film processing, because it contains a lot of impurities. It would mean refining the water, making it more expensive to process films. But when we used the water from Jos we found it very suitable. You do not need to clean the water before using it for processing. These are the factors that influenced the decision to move to Jos.

You state elsewhere that the Plateau state government has been immensely helpful by providing land. Has work started on the building of the film industry complex?

Work has not started yet. Ideally, what we have here, the lab and dubbing studio, should have been in the industrial complex. But because of funds we had to construct the lab in the building which was donated to us by the Plateau state government. We restructured the building so that the lab is downstairs and the offices of the technical staff are on the top floor. All we did was build the administrative block and the dubbing studio. The land for the main complex is still not developed, but it is about 169 hectares in a beautiful area of Jos near a lake. In the building plan are provisions for a film institute and a training school for the film industry. We hope to work so that the corporation, in partnership with the private sector, will be able to accomplish its task. We want the NFC to be cost-effective, the primary objective being to have the cost of filmmaking here less expensive than in Europe.

What you have told me and what I have seen in the corporation so far is very encouraging, but I am very concerned with the technical side of it. The sophisticated equipment demands expert handling. I hope this is not going to be another white elephant?

Having the facility is one thing and running it is another. So far, we have been able to recruit competent technicians. Because it is too expensive to send our technicians overseas for training, we are arranging for technicians from Australia to come and organize training workshops for our technicians for up to six weeks. Funds permitting, this workshop will be retained on a yearly basis. We are very particular about the maintenance of our upgraded equipment. Therefore we want to finalize cooperation agreements with Australia for the supply of new equipment. Also, another brand of equipment is coming from the United States. We must be capable of basic maintenance so as to keep the industry running effectively. I assure you that as long as I am here we will try to maintain a high standard in this organization.

Since its inception, the NFC has been plagued with controversies. Critics charge that the NFC has squandered too much money without making any significant films. Since the NFC has been reorganized and there is no longer a politically appointed chairman but rather a chief executive in charge, is the NFC now in a position to account for its actions and expenditures?

It is true that until I took charge, the Nigerian Film Corporation did not live up to its expectations. It took us about three years to convince the government that the NFC had a real purpose. Budgetary allocations in the past were so small that it barely paid the staff's salaries. There was also some mismanagement, but I am not here to open old wounds. We are now working to move the industry forward and to provide adequate services with the little resources we get from the government. I do not even listen to what people say anymore. Until they came for the opening ceremony, a lot of the critics did not believe that we have the facilities for film production, and that they are being utilized. They thought that the money given to us was squandered, but all of our work attests to our goal of pushing the industry ahead. We do not believe in blowing our trumpets, but these days I am learning to be more outspoken. Our accomplishments depend on teamwork and leadership, and we have been able to get the right staff working together in pursuit of the goals of the NFC. Let me note that we employ people regardless of their state or ethnic backgrounds, provided they are good.

What are the significant achievements of the Nigerian Film Corporation?

We have produced a number of documentaries, particularly for the government, which has financed some of our projects, and we have produced documentaries focusing on the general development of the country. We have made about eight or nine of these films for the government. One of them, *Better Life*, won an international award in North Korea. Recently we made *Kulba na Barna*, which is the first feature film from the Nigerian Film Corporation. It has been shown in a number of countries, winning an award in Italy. In 1995, we received funds to make two documentary films, and we are studying scripts from private filmmakers so that we can go into coproduction with them. We may not have adequate financing, but our services can be considered as an investment that will increase the number of films produced in this country.

Why can't the NFC redirect its focus to fictional feature-length films instead of making only documentaries?

The problem is funding. I do not think that the total allocation for film production is more than three million naira for the whole year. Out of that, we produced two government documentaries. What do you have left? Our plan is to initiate dialogue with private filmmakers to coproduce with them. Though we are not in a position to make any financial contribution right now, once we come up with good scripts, we hope to find common terms on which we could work together in a way that would be beneficial to both the filmmakers and the NFC. Under this proposal, we hope to be able to produce at least three feature films this year. I am already working on my second feature film, which will be made entirely with the facilities available at NFC.

Can the NFC succeed without curbing the menace of foreign films?

We can, but we cannot live in isolation. Inasmuch as we want to show our films, we should be able to show other foreign films in this country. But we have to be very selective. We should not have a situation where foreign films are more acceptable than our own. We addressed that issue in the new Nigeria film policy. We should be able to know which films are acceptable to our aspirations—films that project a positive aspect of our culture. Obscene or violent films are the sort of films that we do not want, because they are detrimental to our youth's growth and development. In essence, there should be some kind of control in order to maintain our culture and integrity.

What kind of partnership exists between the NFC and the Nigerian Television Authority?

At the present time there is no partnership, but we are not ruling out any future collaboration with the NTA. However, we do not want to make the same mistake that the Ghana Film Corporation made by going into video. We would rather preserve the negatives and the sound tracks of the films we produce so that we can later make prints out of them, and if there is demand for them, transfer the films to video. Then comes the question of the national archive. We have acquired films about this country which need to be preserved. In the process of doing that, we have just acquired a viewing machine. Right now we are viewing the films, categorizing them and identifying their running times. As soon as that is completed, we will compile and present a package of available programs. Many of them contain important national and African issues which the NTA will be interested in.

What is your view on the proliferation of foreign television channels via satellite in Nigeria?

Cable TV is not only morally damaging to the youth, it is killing the growth of the film industry in Nigeria. Today, in most homes, particularly those of the affluent members of society, Nigerian television programs and films are not watched. The children more or less watch foreign programs. We are getting very disturbed, and I do not know why the government allows that to happen when it is killing our own television programs. In the next few years, nobody will watch NTA programs unless there is a change of policy and control. The future is bleak. I think the best person to answer that question would be the minister of information.

You have a close connection with the minister; have you discussed the problem with him? We admire foreign ideas, but in the United States, for example, it is difficult to find where to buy shortwave radios, whereas AM/FM radios are widely available and provide local news whose content may be said to be ideological. How is it possible that Africans blindly appropriate foreign ideology and foreign culture and make it our own?

These are policy statements; I do not want to commit myself. These are issues for the honorable minister to address. However, that policy was already in place before the present minister, and it has caused a big controversy. I remember one of the ministers, Tony Momoh, who vehemently argued against it. It is sad that as early as 10:00 A.M. some channels are already showing obscene films. Imagine the effect of such images on our children.

Last night in my hotel room, I saw a music video featuring the popular rap star Shabba Ranks. It was disgusting to see the kind of close-up shots of women's crotches being displayed in a provocative manner, with people doing, if I may say, nasty things. I had just finished watching your film in which you very discreetly depicted what might be considered indecent exposure or obscenity. That presented a telling contrast to Shabba Ranks's video and other MTV shows that can be viewed right here in our country.

That shows a double standard. The government says one thing, but what you see is another thing. There is a limit to what we can say as civil servants. You cannot come out openly to criticize a high-ranking government official. That is the dilemma we find ourselves in.

A new national film policy has just been enacted. What is the NFC's stated role, what is the purpose of this policy, and how is this different from past policies?

The Nigerian Film Corporation is supposed to be the central body that coordinates the activities of the film industry in Nigeria. In the past, efforts have been made to legislate communication policy, cultural policy, and the cinematographic act. In general terms, all of these areas do not strictly deal with the film business. So we decided there should be specific policies for filmmaking in this country, and that is why we had a workshop to which we invited filmmakers. We brainstormed and came up with specific policies for the film industry. We looked at the impact of the policies on the content of films to be produced. We were interested in formulating certain guidelines that would regulate the portrayal of both the negative and positive aspects of our life. Films, for instance, should unite this country, not destroy it. We need films that will portray this country positively to the outside world. The participants of the conference were unanimous regarding the content to pursue in film production. They felt that the NFC should play a vital role in the implementation of policies to enhance the infrastructure of the film industry and to assist in its growth. Thus we emphasized the improvement and maintenance of the lab, the dubbing studio, and other production facilities. We also looked at the training aspect and recommended that there should be a film institute to handle training and research in the film industry. That is a specific policy. Then we have a policy on the administration of the film industry— what role administrators should play. We also discussed the role of the national film archive and the part the NFC should play. We eventually proposed that the archive should operate as a separate entity. It could also be merged with the film institute for research purposes. We looked at the distribution system and found that there was no structure at all at this point in time.

In fact, in that workshop, it was difficult to agree on the structure of the distribution network. However, we thought that the Film Corporation should handle film distribution along with the private sector. We proposed in the film policy that the government should set up a film development fund for financing films similar to the one commercial banks established for other sectors of the economy, such as agriculture. As it is now, it is difficult for filmmakers to get loans from any of the commercial banks to finance production.

There was a fund established by the government a few years ago, but, reportedly, it was abused by some filmmakers.

Yes, before my administration, our predecessors lent money to private filmmakers. When we came in, we examined the assets and liabilities of the corporation and discovered that several filmmakers still owed the NFC money. We have written to the defaulters, and up to now they have refused to pay off their loans. It is because of this problem that we are refusing to offer anybody the use of facilities on credit. One of our obligations is to assist filmmakers, but at the same time, we are making it clear that the Film Corporation is not going to be run as a charitable organization. The NFC cannot be Father Christmas to every Nigerian filmmaker.

The film policy is extremely interesting, but what of its implementation? It is very good on paper, but somebody has to enforce it.

We are aware of the problem of implementation, and at the launching of the film policy, the minister of information addressed this topic. It is true that in this society we often have good ideas, but when it comes to implementing them, we run into difficulties. That is why we have taken the initiative to rigorously pursue the NFC's agenda, but we also know that it will be impossible to do it alone. We have invited filmmakers to work out a strategy on how to implement the policies.

The NFC has also set up the long-awaited national film archive, as you mentioned. What kind of archival materials are stored there, and who is utilizing the facilities?

We have just retrieved our negatives and sound tracks of films made about Nigeria dating back to the early 1950s. These are documentary films that were produced during the colonial period and the various regional governments after independence. They cover all aspects of our life and culture. They belonged to the various states of the federation, and they were almost destroyed because the states did not have places to store them. During the process of retrieval, the NFC discovered that a number of states defaulted on loans provided by companies to have them made. The lending companies gave the NFC an ultimatum to pay back the loans or the films would be destroyed. The Film Corporation made a plea to the members of the National Council of Information, explaining the importance of the negatives and why they should be preserved. In the end, the NFC was allowed to use some of the money allocated to its budget to pay all debts owed to the companies. That is how we finally acquired the negatives. We hope that scholars will find them useful in their research. With the proposed partnership between the NFC and the Nigerian Television Authority, we may be able to present some programs and television series from the negatives. Furthermore, the archive will be especially invaluable to filmmakers and researchers.

Will this archive hold the works of independent filmmakers?

Yes, we have spoken to the filmmakers. So far, only one person has sent in his film. He was around when the archive was commissioned, but other filmmakers are still very skeptical about the archive's intentions. Our movement to Jos has created ill feelings among Nigerian filmmakers. It has been so politicized that they cannot understand why the NFC was not set up in Lagos, since the bulk of the filmmakers come from or live in the Lagos metropolis. I am sure there will be a change of heart, and eventually they will bring in some of their films and increase the number of locally produced films in the archive.

How much money has been spent so far in this corporation?

It is difficult to tell you off the top of my head exactly how much we have spent. As I said earlier on, some of the equipment and some of the processing plants were bought as far back as 1982, and up to now we do not have the exact figures of how much was paid for them. That is why we have not been able to calculate the total costs. Under my administration, the government has spent a substantial amount, between eleven and twelve million naira, on the lab and dubbing studio. This also includes renovation of the building structures housing the lab. The records show exactly how much was spent.

Filmography

Office Security, 1968
Kulba na Barna, 1992

Cheick Oumar Sissoko (Mali)

Cheick Oumar Sissoko who won the Étalon de Yennega at the 1995 FESPACO with his film *Guimba the Tyrant* (1995), has, with the release of *La genèse*, (The genesis, 1999), solidified the indelible mark he has left on the minds of critics and spectators, who unanimously applaud the unparalleled artistic quality of his films. The elaborate settings and costumes that adorn Sissoko's films exemplify the filmmaker's persistent search for creative autonomy. They not only emphasize Africa's rich cultural heritage, they illuminate its significance and application to the enrichment of African film aesthetics.

Since the release of *Finzan* (A dance for the heroes) in 1990, Sissoko has become one of the most prominent and acclaimed filmmakers of the African continent. Moreover, apart from the intense subject matter he fearlessly depicts in his films, which has brought him much public attention, this filmmaker's humility and amiability distinguish him from some of his counterparts. He holds degrees in higher education from both the Ecole des Hautes Etudes-Sciences in Paris and the Louis Lumière Film school. Upon returning to Mali, Sissoko worked as a film director at the Centre National de Productions Cinématographiques (CNPC), an organization he headed from 1991 to 1997. He now owns his own production company, Kora Films.

Sissoko prides himself on being a politically committed filmmaker who uses his films to engage social issues. His works combine a search for individualized forms of representation with a desire to provoke discourse on important social issues: the plight of children in *Nyamanton* (Garbage boys, 1986), resistance to tradition, the oppression of women and their emancipation in *Finzan*, democracy and power in *Guimba*, and the universality of human conflicts and reconciliation in *La genèse*. With *Guimba* and *La genèse*, Sissoko's superlative competence as a filmmaker is affirmed. These films

181

show him to be a master craftsman who uses both continuous research and an artistic vision of issues to offer an irresistible articulation of African experiences. Although the subject of *La genèse* is universal, Sissoko Africanizes the story through a deliberate exploitation of his native cultural heritage. He built an imposing set of stone dwellings and huts in Hombory, about three hundred kilometers away from Bamako, the capital of Mali, to re-create the architectural setting of the story. This search for authenticity reflects Sissoko's belief in the necessity "for African filmmakers to move more and more toward expression—artistic expressions that exist in our societies and which have always conformed to their cultures." *La genèse* was selected to appear in the "Un certain regard" section at the Cannes Film Festival in 1999, and it won first prize at the tenth Festival Cinema Africano in Milan in March 2000.

In this interview, Sissoko lays the foundation for an indigenous aesthetic paradigm, stressing his abandonment of the classical narrative forms he studied at the university, his debt to the African oral narrative traditions as a springboard, and his commitment to activist filmmaking. The interview was conducted at FESPACO in both 1993 and 1995, and in New York City in 1995.

Would you please tell me about your background and how your career as a filmmaker began?

I was in France, where I studied mathematics, and I was very active in the movements of African students for the mobilization and consciousness-raising of African populations. These issues truly confronted us collectively and individually. Often I asked myself, "How can I make my contribution?" And realizing all the possibilities that literature, radio, and mass media could offer, I came to the conclusion that cinema must be the best way for me to express myself in a continent lacking democratic liberty, in an alienated continent where people generally don't know their rights or duties. Thus cinema, with its images and national languages, could allow me to express myself, to communicate with African peoples and to make my contribution. I wanted to depict members of the societies as they actually are in images that retraced their daily lives, the problems and realities of their societies. This is the reason why I chose cinema. The objective of my new vocation was to figure out what it was I was to achieve. I studied history and sociology and obtained a D.E.A. [diplómé d'etudes approfondies]—a diploma of advanced studies in African history and sociology from the Ecole des Hautes Etudes en Sciences Sociales.

Before Nyamanton, *which other films did you make?*

I made an eight-minute film in 1982 on the condition of schools in Mali to show the institutional decay and the lack of infrastructure for education. And then in 1982 or 1983, I made a video film on rural audio libraries. It is a project of the United Nations Development Program, sponsored by UNESCO and Mali, about the use of audiocassettes to lead the rural populations to listen to new technology and then to record their own knowledge so that they could experience an exchange of communication. In 1985, I made *Scheresse et exode rurale* (Drought and rural exodus) at the time of the severe drought in the Sahel region. One could also call this film the "tragedy of the man of the land," because it showed the dilemmas of the rural people, who, faced with this natural calamity, were forced to migrate to major cities only to find another tragedy—unemployment.

It was really Nyamanton *that catapulted you to the limelight. It deals with a human-interest story, with concern for humanity and for children. What inspired the making of* Nyamanton*?*

Nyamanton is a film that imposed itself on me and I became interested in the issues due to my commitment to film as the medium of expressing the realities of our societies. It shows all that constitutes the roadblocks for progress in our country. In October 1978, when I was on school vacation in Mali, I saw several children carrying benches on their heads, and several minutes later a little girl carrying a platter with oranges on her head. That sight struck me, and I took photos, which I have kept. Three years later, I went back to Bamako and I lived in a neighborhood where I saw the same phenomenon. I proceeded to make inquiries about those issues, which permitted me to create a working scenario, because I thought that the situation was truly scandalous. The situations people live are intolerable, especially in countries aspiring to progressive transformation. The future of a country is based on its children. They must be healthy in both body and mind. And that is why right after the making of *Scheresse et exode rurale,* I developed the script of *Nyamanton,* on the basis of this research. The research focused on real people and their problems and their answers to my questions. It illuminated their concerns regarding the indifference of the authorities concerning the deficiencies in education and health matters. For me the awareness we offered the society through the film is an obligation, and I believe that the goal was attained.

The language used by the boys in Nyamanton *is quite shocking. Do the swearing and cursing truly represent the situation in Mali with regard to the street kids?*

As you may know, in African countries right now, life is so difficult that children live more and more in the streets. Nowadays, children are forced to live like adults and no longer lead the lives of children. Additionally, they have the same behavior as adults. And this life generates frequent violence. And the expression of this violence is often in the form of arguments with extensive swearing.

The family unit is completely decentered by the incapacity of the family heads to respond to the needs of children. Furthermore, family leaders who provide for the children are forced to leave home every day very early in the morning in search for means to provide for daily meals. They have very little contact with their children; they are compelled to provide not only their daily meals but also school requirements and health and medical needs. Therefore, the child who lives in the street becomes delinquent.

This phenomenon is multiplying in the major cities in Africa. And sadly, today the problem is spreading to the villages. Consequently, children are acting outrageously in the streets. It is exactly like the situation in New York City. Several years ago this situation was less extreme, but today, children's education comes from anyone they find in the streets who could influence them. But the city streets can no longer respond to the needs of that type of education. Sadly, children behave poorly by swearing because adults aren't able to respond to their demands. That's the reality.

African cinema seeks to reveal; it looks at the whole society, seeking to draw people's attention to what is going on around them. And while filmmakers understand that one single film cannot change the whole world, they also understand that they are trying to make people see the reality. How has the government reacted to the issues you raised in Nyamanton *concerning the problems of children? Was your goal accomplished?*

As far as shocking people, yes, we did it with *Nyamanton.* First, at its release, people were thrilled and considered it their film. It is the film which to the present holds the record of entrances and total receipts of any Malian or foreign film shown in Mali. This is because everyone can identify with the issues it depicted. People recognized the deteriorated condition they lived in, realizing the grave consequences. For example, during a meeting with the state leader at the time, women took *Nyamanton* to heart. They expressed that they no longer wanted to live under the situation portrayed in the film and that appropriate measures must be taken. Also, the people no longer wanted to see their children continue carrying their own benches on their heads to schools. But unfortunately, even today, children continue to carry their benches on their heads.

The consciousness-raising was significant. But at the time, illusions existed concerning our reality in relation to how power was wielded. This power wasn't oriented toward the amelioration of the living conditions of the population. But it was especially important that the people themselves took charge of the problems and compelled the authorities to reconsider the problem of education in Mali. I am convinced, for my own part, that today, even during the trial of Moussa Traoré, the former head of state, the film *Nyamanton* is an issue. The film is remembered for how it explained the frustration that forced young people of Mali into the streets to challenge the status quo. And the people were forced to mobilize themselves while taking into account the stance of *Nyamanton,* which carried important weight in the consciousness-raising and in the mobilization of the society.

Similar dilemmas exist in the African metropolises. Has this film been distributed all over Africa, or are there any problems with distribution and exhibition?

Yes, this film faces similar problems as those suffered by all other African films in regard to distribution and exhibition. We were able to show it in Burkina Faso, Côte d'Ivoire, Senegal, and it is scheduled to go to Guinea next month. It has been shown at conferences in countries like Central Africa Republic, Benin, and, I believe, Gabon. I took it to a film festival in Kenya in 1986, where the organizers wanted to acquire the film free of charge in order to show it. They insisted on having the copy that I took to the festival and I was not able to leave it for them. The film has been shown in France and has been purchased in Italy. Other television companies have purchased the film, but it has not been seen very often in Africa. I sincerely regret that because I made this film to raise awareness of the problems of education on the entire continent. My philosophy is to use every film that I make to address specific problems of the continent.

Nyamanton should be taken to various African cities. However, to be able to distribute this film, or any other francophone films in English-speaking African countries, you have to face the enormous task of dubbing to English.

This problem of dubbing was discussed yesterday at FESPACO by film directors from several African countries. We must install a structure of dubbing in Africa in order to be able, for example, in the case of Nigeria, to dub in Yoruba, Hausa, and Ibo; other countries could do the same by dubbing in their major languages. In the West African region, we can use coproduction to solve the problem. For example, one country could take charge of establishing a dubbing studio for systematic dubbing into our languages. Otherwise, there will be no solution. For me, I regret that *Nyamanton* wasn't dubbed because even if the film is shown with English subtitles, in Lagos or in Kano, people will watch it but they will not experience its full effect, because the dialogues are important. I think the solution is to decentralize cinema in Africa. We should make it happen by creating film schools, for example, in Accra, which has a film studio. There is a laboratory already in Nigeria; we should also establish dubbing studios in Côte d'Ivoire, Guinea, or Mali, so that each time a film is produced, it can be dubbed in the major national languages.

Through Nyamanton, it is evident that the Koteba theater was one of your primary influences. How has it influenced your cinematic aesthetics?

Koteba uses satire to expose the problems of the village, and therefore of society. My film uses the same technique as a tool for illustrating societal problems. It is a way of enlightening the public. For me, any problem as important as it is must be expressed as a performance to the society. However, it must be a performance that leads people to absorb the messages through humor and drama. Drama and humor are interwoven in the narrative structure. This is important to me because I do not want my audience to forget the dramatic side of the equation. In fact, it is in *Finzan* that I first experimented with the actors in this combination. Bala, the protagonist, was an actor in Koteba theater. I think that it's necessary for filmmakers to move more and more toward expression—artistic expressions that exist in our societies and which have always conformed to their cultures. In fact, that is why I now write my scenarios in the form of oral tradition. I am abandoning the classical forms that I studied at the university because I have come to the conclusion that oral tradition allows for a better treatment of the problems. Because of my cultural heritage, I feel that it is important for me to utilize our cultural modes of expression; that is how life has been expressed before, and it is important that we continue to improve upon this method of telling our stories. In any case, we should strive to adopt its positive aspects.

You mentioned the importance of satire and comedy—and it is true that it worked very well in Nyamanton *to convey the sociopolitical messages. Similarly, every African film-maker emphasizes the importance of oral tradition in African film language. How is your own use of oral tradition different from that of other African filmmakers?*

When one sees my films, one distinguishes between the two stories which are not far separated from each other. Traditionalists have two roles—they are, simultaneously, authors and storytellers. As storytellers, the traditionalists start with the first story, which they narrate to their audiences. And when the traditionalists are authors, they place themselves in the story itself even if the story took place over a time span of several centuries. They claim to have personally witnessed the actions in the story. And then to reinforce the first story, they introduce a parallel story which is relevant to the first story. When one watches *Nyamanton,* there is the story of her children, which is the documentary part that I created. This is the viewpoint of the author himself, candidly integrated in the fashion of documentary realism. In this segment, the child and his father wander around the city market to observe the daily events of the society. Here there is no rearrangement of the reality, no fiction; it is a documentary. And it is the storyteller who is present that narrates the past. And it is the filmmaker who ensures that even the fictional film deployed in the narrative is not false either. And there is a second story that comes to reinforce the first story. I had to find a way to unite the two stories concerning the pregnant woman and her relationship with the second woman. It is therefore evident that the oral art technique was quite effective in illustrating the hardships of pregnant women and children in society.

Oral tradition features prominently in *Finzan's* narrative construction. In this film, the first story concerns the first woman, Nayuma, who is to be married, against her wish, to the younger brother of her deceased husband. In rebellion to this situation, Nayuma flees to the city. It is important to note that there are two versions of this film—the short and the longer version for Africa, which contains more documentary sequences. In the long version, one sees the woman upon her arrival at the market. She arrives in the city, having fled the village and having passed the roadblocks on her route. Crossing the city where the women are working, the audience views her as insane prior to her arrival at her brother-in-law's house. Clearly, she is the new element introduced into the narrative, and she is shown in the process of moving forward with her life. And the second story concerns the young girl, Fili, and her experience of the practice of excision [female circumcision]. This is to illustrate that women are truly oppressed. Just as in *Nyamanton*, the story concludes with the first characters. I apply this technique to show how oral tradition enables her to narrate her story. One uses one thing to reinforce another and another to show that it is possible to learn by looking at how an event has been introduced—in the fashion of candid documentary technique. I like to experiment with these modes of expression, which is why I have been attacked by critics who claim that I introduce too many elements in my films. Some critics have suggested that I should have simply limited myself to the problem of Nayuma and, that, certainly should have been sufficient.

The story within a story, the multiple-story structure that Finzan *uses, makes it a complicated film. However, the message is direct, but also controversial.*

I chose cinema because of its relation to politics. So each time I make a film, I try to accomplish my objective. With *Finzan* it was clearly the problem of the oppression of women and the necessity for their emancipation. But there is also the essential question of legal rights and liberty for a nation, and for a continent. In the context of Mali, the main character chosen is Bala. This is not by accident; the president himself was called Moussa. But all the Moussas around the world, at least in Africa, could be called Bala. It was a question of showing through this man, Bala, and through this woman, Nayuma, who we see bound up, that Bala represents power, oppression, and leadership in this country [Mali]. And the binding and delivering of this woman, with her feet and wrists tied up, symbolizes the treatment of individuals in our societies by the retrograde forces. So, with regard to Nayuma, her mistreatment splits the people, and this is not surprising because if you know this period of Malian history you will understand well that aspect of society. To try to bring people around to this point of view, there are relatively delicate situations which must be addressed. For example, in the film, the scene when the children fall and Bala releases his gun represents many statements about the political system and the attainment of power in Mali. When Bala is asked to pick up his gun, it is because it is his symbol of power. I was attempting to show the cultural belief that weapons give power to a few people who rule Mali. At the same time, when the village leader contradicts himself in the presence of his wives, he is reminded about his previous stance concerning the issue of excision. In response, he says, "You mean that I have become the mole and you the porcupine?" In another story, it is often stated that "the mole digs a hole which the porcupine occupies." It's a proverb! And the women respond, "No, you are not the mole at all, because if there is someone who works, it is us. Whether it rains or the wind blows, it is we who are working. All the time, all the time, all the time. And when it comes to making decisions this will never be us either. It is you. Consequently, if there is a mole, it is certainly not you." And the porcupine in Bambara is also called Bala. In a country like Mali, if someone is the porcupine, it is to say he is the chief of state. If someone is the mole, it is the people. It is the people who work—who produce material goods. Furthermore, these hardworking citizens do not participate in making decisions pertaining to their lives, no matter what the issues are. Thus absence of democratic liberty permeates the system.

At the same time, there is a call for unity in this film to show that in a country where there is no democratic liberty—where the populations, especially rural, are submitted to extortion by the state—they could mobilize to stage opposition against the tyrannical administration. This was to show that when the populations are united they could succeed at whatever they try to do. But disunity exists among the rank and file of the village women. Those are the elements which are difficult to grasp if you do not know the situation in Mali. But as far as the problem of excision and the village, I think that it is satire that leads people to understand more truly the nature of those problems. The controversy is really in the ignorance of Malian problems. Why would I make such a film? I think I have been able to explain this, but there are certain points like this that do not permit one to situate the film in time, especially in the situation in Mali. Clearly, there are some misunderstandings regarding the animals featured in this film. I wanted to tie their symbolisms to the image or place of Malian women. I wanted to foreground the maternal feelings that exist in women toward their children, such as the pains of women and the attention that women pay to their children.

What is the parallel between the characters of Nayuma and Fili? A strong link of sociocultural importance is evident. For example, Nayuma loses her husband and tradition is going to force her to marry Bala. Additionally, Fili does not go by the traditional excision, which is also another kind of sociocultural problem that the film addresses. Could you relate these two parallel structures to the overall message of the film?

At first there are two people, Nayuma and Fili, who come from different backgrounds. Nayuma comes from a rural setting and Fili comes from an urban environment. Consequently, they have completely contrasting experiences and behaviors. Nayuma considers the inheritance of tradition as an essential element in society, and her refusal to abide by those traditions is not categorical. She prefers to use familial structures to try to resolve her problem. Cognizant of the fact that Fili comes from an urban setting, familial structures do not interest her at all. There is only one thing that interests her—herself. She takes charge of herself. This represents a larger democratic tradition of taking charge of one's person. In the city, this democratic tradition is more significant than in the village. Thus one sees two completely different paths of action. The action of Nayuma that emanates from a situation born from a strong presence of traditional education in villages and the use of familial structures as an empowering institution leads her to take charge of what she desires. Fili also takes charge, using the tradition of democratic life—the increased degree of feminine voice and freedom in the cities. On the question of excision, she is firm and resolute. She says, "My body is mine. I feel good that way. I will not be excised." This contrasts with Nayuma, whom we first see in her village, and then entering into the large city to understand and learn the realities of life. Before the drama concludes, Nayuma ends up adopting the same attitude as Fili. Hence the influence by Fili on Nayuma is evident near the end of the film, due to the shock experienced by the forced excision of Fili. She leaves vehemently opposed to what has occurred. She becomes withdrawn from society and continues to exist in her own world.

Would you call Finzan *a film about excision?*

No, no, not at all. The main theme could be called "liberty"—the right to assume control over one's life. It's truly a film about the tragedy of women. It follows my method of reflecting on the society as in my other films: *Scheresse et exode rurale*, about the tragedy of the man on the earth; *Nyamanton*, about the tragedy of the African child.

All my films so far have depicted tragic situations experienced by certain social classes in our populations, situations that completely block progress in our societies. The film does not address just excision. Excision was used to illustrate the lack of liberty for women and men, and in the entire continent. Consequently, we cannot state that the theme is excision.

Sissoko, this is exactly the point. Finzan *is very popular in the United States, specifically in classrooms. It is used in women's studies, cultural studies, African studies, and viewed as an ethnographic film. But the dominant discourse of the film always centers on the theme of excision, and yet the sequences of excision are only thirteen minutes long. However, it is the most powerful part of the film—it is what people talk about the most, and it is the area that people misinterpret the most. The character of Nayuma was very well developed. We understand why she should be given the liberty to make a choice, because a woman is supposed to be able to choose somebody she loves, not somebody that tradition says she must marry. But in Fili, the problem that arises all the time is that we do not know the cultural reasons why excision is practiced in Bambara. The viewer knows that this practice occurs in the culture, but the audience is not given the opportunity to debate the cultural ramifications, even if one disagrees with the practice. Western analysts have analyzed this aspect of African culture as cruel genital mutilation, calling it barbaric. And some people have argued that you did not develop the character of Fili the way you developed the character of Nayuma, so that the film could force viewers to debate the issue of excision. Consequently, some people do have problems with this excision sequence, which is why this film is often celebrated as a film about excision.*

The reasons are less important than the consequences. Furthermore, it is the consequences that we had to show, to demonstrate the inutility of excision and the grave consequences for the health of women and even the health of children to come. In truth, if I did not give it adequate information it is because even the people who practice excision are themselves unaware of the reasons why they practice the ritual. There is a justification in any case, which is given in the film. It states, "You will be a woman. You will go to the excisioner. In fifteen days, Fili, you will be a woman." And Fili answers, "I am already a woman." That is the reasoning the excisioner applies. A second reason evoked by the village leader is that ever since ancient times, when this practice began, it has been one of the foundations of our society. The big problem is that in reality, people do not even know the origin of excision. The excisioner in the film is the excisioner of the village. I asked her why she performs excision on women and she said that it is traditionally in her family because she is a woman of a certain caste—she is from a family of blacksmiths. Her mother did it, and she does it now. I asked her why she did it; she says, "Because it must be done, and every girl must pass through that in order to become a woman." But I talked with her about the cosmological elements that explain excision. She did not know anything about it. That came from the research that I did that should have probably been elaborated, but was not incorporated into the film because that would not have been productive.

The film is educating people about the consequences of excision, something the people themselves were unaware of. And even better, today, people practice excision a few days after the birth of a baby. This means an excision is no longer used as an initiation into womanhood.

African filmmakers and cultural critics alike have dealt with a number of issues concerning culture and have suggested that no culture is static. It has also been suggested that certain cultures should be either changed or developed to embrace modern times. Isn't it important to look at why Africans continue to maintain certain traditions?

In Bambara cosmology, in the beginning of the creation of the universe there were four elements: wind, water, earth, and iron. The earth was represented by an old bald woman, Musokoronin Kunje. In fact, they speak of her in the film. In the film, a woman says, "That is the fault of the old bald woman." She is referring to the creation of the universe, when the old bald woman had sexual relations with a tree—or the *balanzan* in Bambara. This is a characteristic tree in the Bambara land. It becomes green when the others lose their branches and it has leaves only during the dry season, while the others have leaves during the rainy season. They explain that this tree does not want to bear leaves during the rainy season to prohibit men from resting under its shade, because it is also the season of labor. It is the period of work. The *balanzan* started having sexual relations with girls. The old bald woman started going insane with rage because of her sexual relations with the *balanzan*. Consequently, she started to plant terror in the world, to injure young boys and girls. And from this time on, the Bambara land decided to circumcise the boys and excise the girls. That is why they have this attribute that the old bald lady brought them.

There were also two other explanations which take the form of initiation. In all societies, initiation cycles exist. And when young girls are nubile, before going into marriage, they must submit to excision. During the big ceremony marking the initiation, they are interned for several weeks, during which they receive an education from matrons. These matrons are women who will explain the human body to them as well as its role; the dangers and pleasures of sexuality, the life of women, how to be a woman, how to carry oneself, and one's role in society. This form of initiation is of capital importance and is preceded by the excision. Men also receive the same internment, in addition to being circumcised. During this internment, they receive an education from a teacher who delivers them knowledge. Additionally, they must pass difficult tests. The tests show bravery and courage. Among the Bambara, boys are initiated into *komo*, an ancient tradition where the quest for knowledge is paramount. Thus it is the learning of the knowledge of life that is necessary to enable them to enter into the cycle of adult life. One is considered that way until the age of forty-nine. The same applies to women: the internment and excision are for moving them beyond the adolescent life stage.

This is the explanation that is given, in any case. But there are many people who also attribute this belief system to the Islamic doctrine. However, in various conferences I have attended, I have witnessed the acerbity with which the practice is denounced in worse terms than the purported barbarism of the ritual. I always intervene to state that the film does not speak of the practice in only that tone. I think that Europeans and Americans really should remember that there are aspects of their cultures in the Middle Ages and beyond that are reprehensible. Even in these modern times, there are many European/American phenomenal sociocultural abnormalities that we ourselves (Africans) truly consider to be barbaric. When I explain to my mother that in Europe and America people rape children, that makes her cry. She does not understand how children can be frequently raped in civilized societies. We consider that the epitome of barbaric behavior. And for the people who deliberately attack excision as the practice of barbaric cultures, they do it as a means of asserting their own cultural superiority at the expense of African traditions. That is why I have formed the habit of speaking up quickly when this issue arises to remind the audience that in occidental societies there are forms of barbarity that are much, much more enormous than excision.

In terms of aesthetics, the opening sequence of Finzan *is marvelous. I like the two goats on the leash, and I liked the framing of the houses. However, in African films such originality is usually misconstrued. What Africans may consider to be a real-life situation, Western critics may interpret as ethnographic. How do you address this problem? Would you be offended, for instance, if somebody described* Finzan *as an ethnographic film? What is your own notion of African reality and ethnographic reality?*

But that makes me smile. That is because, very simply, some people think that everything one shows about Africa is the product of specific studies, even though that part of the film is meant to show not only the beauty of places but also the stature of man and woman, and their space and environment. And so what can I say? I would state that Western ethnographic vision of Africa reflects how they have painted our reality. They cannot see our continent except through a microscope, which is why their African reality is most often superficial and different from our own construction of African reality.

The scene, that beautiful sequence in the bush where we see the lion three times. The way it was shot, I loved it. It was well composed, but I have a problem with that sequence. What statement were you trying to make, and why did Nayuma use oil to rub her body?

At a certain point Nayuma tries to see the dust in the direction of the wind. Because the lion senses her prey with her nostrils, the lion moves toward her. So if she puts oil on her body, the lion cannot smell the human odor. So that is why she takes the dust and sees the direction of the wind because she has noticed the lion's presence. The lion roars, so she knows about where it is located. Since she is in the direction of the wind, she puts oil on her body so that the lion will not be able to smell her.

How did you film that sequence, especially that lion sequence?

Stock shots. You know there are filmmakers who film animals. They keep animal shots in their archives which they sell. I bought the stock shots in Paris. In doing this, one must remember to be careful in choosing which stock shot to use because it is important to watch for color balance, lighting, and the shot/countershot in relation to the juxtaposition of the other images.

How has your life changed since your film Guimba *won the Étalon de Yennega, thus bringing you recognition as a major African filmmaker?*

My life has not changed. This prize recognizes a group effort, because a team of people contributed to the making of *Guimba*.

Who was involved in this collective effort?

It was a group effort on the part of the technical team and myself, who worked for one year to complete this film. I need to mention my assistants, among them the costume designer, the set designer, the actors, both men and women, and the European director of photography who came to Ouagadougou for the shooting. As a group we gauged and monitored the importance of our work. This cooperation also reinforced the ideas we had on African cinema.

How much of a role did African technicians play in the production and postproduction?

The help of my African technicians and assistants was invaluable in the production and postproduction of this movie. In this respect I need to add that in my view this is a necessity if we wish to develop African cinema. In the movie's end credits, one can observe that the majority of technicians are Africans. The film's producer, my direct assistants, the executive producer who is in Paris, and the person responsible for post-production are all Africans. The editing was the work of a Tunisian and a Burkinabe in Burkina Faso. On the production side there were people from Mali, Burkina Faso, and also two Frenchmen. So my concept of cinematographic production does involve the use of technical teams composed for the most part of Africans. I personally believe that this will help compose and consolidate the technical base of African cinema.

What is your view regarding the establishment of a viable film industry in Africa with coproductions and interstate cooperation?

This is an important question, and it deals with what I call my concept of cinema. I have dealt at length with this issue in the February issue of the magazine *Écrans d'Afrique*. I think that the constitution of an autonomous and financially viable African cinema requires not only an audience, but also an expansion of cooperative efforts between state-owned production companies and privately held ones. My own production company, Kora Films, coproduced *Guimba* with the Centre National de Production Cinématographique du Mali, and the Direction de la Production Ciné-matographique du Burkina Faso [the national film production companies of Mali and Burkina Faso]. It will be the same coproduction team for my next film. In my view, such links are necessary to the development of the African film industry.

With the release of Guimba *you proved once again that political and social situations, as well as issues of power and democracy in a changing Africa, continue to influence your narrative. Is there any relationship between this film and the situation in Mali?*

Yes, but the film is also relevant to the situation in Africa in general. There are two aspects to the situation on the continent today: one is the result of our historical her-itage; the other can be attributed to the events which recently shook the continent and confirmed the people's will to reject dictatorship and support democracy. I am mostly intent on exposing both the great wealth of our continent and the major problems facing it. It is at this level that this film is political.

What is the origin of the story of the film?

The story of *Guimba* is the product of my imagination. It is inspired by the wealth of our oral tradition and storytelling techniques. Those fables and legends are an inte-gral part of the formative years of my youth.

The film is replete with animal symbolism: hyenas, vultures, and others. Could you comment on your own use of allegory in the narrative and explain the importance of allegory to the film's structure?

In the oral tradition, narration through allegorical means is very often expressed through symbols. They are expressive means of developing our power of imagination, but, for the most part, these tools are used to convey powerful images and representations.

Oral tradition is the quintessential basis of African cinema. As an African, I did not have any problem understanding the film, but non-Africans might find it confusing.

This is an important issue. It is necessary for African audiences to like this movie, understand it, and wish to see it again and again. But the question is, should we make African films which are faithful to the realities of our societies or films for a foreign audience? I believe that the answer to this question is that we should make films faithful to our societies, because if we have things to tell the world it is only on the basis of a dialogue between the artist and his audience that this can occur. My film, like all African films, opens the door to audiences for understanding our history through our cinema. Obviously, some aspects will seem odd or not readily comprehensible, but the door to dreaming and discovery is open to those who wish to enter it. Too often, and to our detriment, Africans put too much effort into understanding Europe and America. Europe and America, on the other hand, do not make the effort to reciprocate. For instance, when it comes to understanding Japanese movies, this question does not come up. Japanese films engender the same problems, but because Japan is well developed economically there does not seem to be any discussion about understanding their films. The viewer of Japanese movies is willing to expend the energies required to discover and understand the messages they convey. I think that when this criticism is made, one needs to respond that some effort needs to be expended by America and Europe to understand and learn about Africa, its histories, and its cultures.

The characters in Guimba *are not fully developed in the traditional Western narrative style, where one person's actions are followed throughout a film. Is this a rebellion against Western narrative style, or is it indebted to the oral tradition to which you referred earlier?*

Guimba is the product of my reflection on the question of how to make a film using our oral narrative tradition as the springboard. So with this script it was not a question of rebellion against representative patterns of the West, but rather an attempt at a different kind of cinematographic expression. The script was written in the traditional oral style and not in the classical style because I think that the narrative structures found in our fables and tales are well adapted to telling our stories. I should mention in passing that using classical forms would have created problems with my producers as well. At the same time, the means of expression we possess, such as the Koteba theater tradition of Mali, predisposes us to certain writing styles. The representations of those forms are often ways of punctuating the narrative in the oral traditional fashion. This is something I am working on, because it is one way we can say something to the world in our own way with our own knowledge and know-how.

I can see from the film how the wealth of possibilities in African narrative structures makes it possible to use one love story both to pay homage to African women and to make a political statement. Do you think this duality downplays the political aspect of the film, which, nonetheless, is capable of provoking censorship?

At this time period there is no censorship problem in Mali. I meant to make a political film, and I considered the representation of women as a crucial part of that political process. It is not just a matter of paying homage to women but also of treating the question of their emancipation. Also, an essential aspect of Malian narrative structure is to include all components of society. The narrator often interrupts the narrative continuum to insert another element adjunct to the story before going back to the central theme. This is part of my experimentation with scriptwriting.

You talk about the viewer discovering and understanding Africa. What is the impact of culture on your narrative style and your films?

African culture is one of the richest hitherto unappreciated. It has been despised by colonialists, ignored by the rest of the world, and marginalized by today's African powers. I find it necessary to point this out because these references to our culture instill an attachment to our rich cultural heritage and will eventually shape African cultural and political developments in a harmonious way. In my film, stressing culture means constructing positive images of Africa in a universe of images which are mostly ones of affliction. I intend to remedy this absence.

It is interesting to see African architecture in this film, such as the grandiose palace, as well as the elaborately rich and colorful costumes. Where was this movie made?

This movie was shot in Djenné, which is listed in UNESCO's world patrimony of cities. It is several centuries old and had a university in the sixteenth century. Djenné is also called "Timbuktu's twin sister."

One rarely sees an emphasis put on costumes in African films, other than the recent film Hyènes, *but your film reminds us that Africa has a rich costume tradition. How much was invested in these costumes?*

These costumes were made for the film and are the property of Kora Film Productions (or Kora Films). We engaged the help of Kandjoura Coulibaly, who has done research in different kinds of clothing. He designed and created fabrics as well as the necklaces, which were very important in the film. The overall cost is hard to estimate, but is about sixty thousand U.S. dollars. That figure does not include about 70 percent of the necklaces, which belong to the designer.

The cast comprises mainly nonprofessional actors as well as some actors who have appeared in other films. What is your view regarding the use of professional actors in African films?

This is also an important question. I think it is our responsibility to train professional actors to sustain cinematic expression on our continent. A professional actor devotes his creativity and his intelligence to the role. We must all work to this end as creators, cinema critics, teachers, and theoreticians of cinema.

The acting in Guimba *is good, and the film is pleasant to watch. Did you have any problems with directing the actors?*

We have to face the fact that one of our [African filmmakers'] weaknesses lies in directing the actors. A film relies heavily on casting. If I am not confident in the quality of the casting choice, I work with the chosen actor to prepare him or her for the role. I even take it as far as to indicate before we start shooting which corporal expressions are appropriate. I am very strict when it comes to this matter.

In Guimba, *Coulibaly is tied with a rope, and in* Finzan, *Nayuma is tied. Another touching event is when a man almost kills himself by violently hitting his head on a wall. Why is violence important in your films?*

The violence is representative of the oppression under which our people live. A woman is tied up in *Finzan*, and in *Guimba* the abuse of power by a tyrant is expressed by tying up one of the characters. Being tied up represents the loss of all freedoms. It shows the suppression of individual abilities to function when all fundamental human rights are taken away.

Power actually corrupts, and Guimba at times speaks in tongues.

Those clips are only there to show how popular imagery expresses itself in supernatural powers and is used to scare off people from transgressing the rules of the society. In the film, it is used to add a touch of the "fantastic," but mostly it is there to suggest the power of Guimba.

Were you influenced by Souleymane Cissé in regard to the invocation of the supernatural?

No. I was influenced by our common traditional heritage. Cissé and I are not from the same ethnic group, but we are from the same society. Growing up, we were educated in the same system, although I might even say that I am closer to traditional mores because I am Malinke and grew up among hunters and others. But we were both influenced by the same culture.

In the film, men and women played a collective role, but children are absent. The people win in the end, but does the humiliation of Guimba suggest the notion of egalitarian society or African progressivism?

This film meant to reflect on a crucial time in the history of the continent when the era of the tyrants is slowly ending and democracy beginning. The film introduces issues dealing with the relevance of the human spiritual and cultural heritage to the goal of a developed African continent and the avoidance of the pitfalls that have ensnared us in the past. What we mostly need is the strengthening of the democratic process which started in the nineties, so that, without drifting into utopia, the reality of the participation of people in the management of the countries materializes. We need to stop the politics of marginalization and heavy-handed government planning and work to mobilize our countries in the pure democratic tradition, and in the form of traditional African societies. I believe in the democratization of our societies.

The establishment you attack also provided partial funding for this film. Did this cause any consternation?

I am not attacking the Malian government; rather, I am standing up against dictatorial forms of governments in Africa. The Malian government did not fund the film. The help I received from them was in the form of access to equipment.

Have you found a distributor for your film in the West as well as in Africa?

There is no established distribution network in Africa. I am currently setting up such a network for West Africa, but my aim is to dub the movie in the major African languages. A company wants the movie dubbed in Zulu, so I will go to South Africa for that. I am looking into the possibility of doing the same for Swahili, Hausa, Yoruba, Ibo, and Fulani. I want to try this experiment, just as I am experimenting with showing this film in major U.S. cities with large black populations. Yes, I am talking with distributors in Africa, France, and the United States, but my interest is not so much in the financial aspect, but rather in the exposure the film can generate.

In African cinema one of the problems is that filmmakers make good films but Africans do not see them or even know they exist. When will it be possible to show Malian, Senegalese, Nigerian, or Ghanaian films in cities across Africa? Part of the solution to this problem involves money, but where will the money come from?

Yes, dubbing is very expensive. Fortunately, the South Africans I am working with have a very reasonable fee structure, and I will attempt to raise the money for dubbing little by little. Somebody has to take the initiative when it comes to dubbing. It is the only solution to turn African cinema into a financially autonomous and viable industry. We cannot leave the arena open for only films from the West. Africa needs to see its own images. So, I am going to try it. The South African organization and I will share the expenses. I have established a financial system, but I do not know if it will succeed. If the film is sold to European television, I will have some of the money I need.

I see a progressive film industry coming from the video sector. Have you thought about dubbing on video and protecting the images from illegal duplication?

Video is a solution, but I do not know of a way to prevent unauthorized copying. Since you say the technology exists, then that is certainly the best solution today. I know that my films *Finzan* and *Nyamanton* have been widely copied and distributed. In fact, the many video stores that exist in all African countries make their biggest profit from pirated copies of films, and it is done in front of everybody. The pirated versions are not hidden. My concept of cinema is dependent on viewership and accessibility to our films. Therefore, I support whatever means it takes to reach for that goal, and I will certainly look into the new possibilities.

Where is the future of African cinema?

African cinema needs to be funded and supported at different levels, starting with the technicians, distributors, actors, and audiences. The movie industry needs to be at the scale of the continent. Cinematic laboratories exist in Algeria, South Africa, Zimbabwe, Nigeria, Morocco, Tunisia—we do not need to build more. What we are sorely in need of are postproduction facilities. There needs to be one such facility for each of the five main regions of Africa. I have used the postproduction facility, Cinafrique, in Ouagadougou for six years. The equipment needs maintenance, but the Burkina Faso government is finally doing just that for tomorrow's African cinema. There is the National Film and Television Institute of Ghana, and there is a television production school in Kenya. But no African country can sponsor a film industry on its own; it is not possible. All those schools and centers need help. As to the distribution aspect, there existed the Consortium Inter-Africain de Distribution Cinématographique, also known under its acronym, CIDC, but it failed. It failed because it was run by civil servants. We need one such company but in private hands, and whose mission would be to create distribution channels and movie theaters. The postproduction facilities could also be used for dubbing our movies in the main African languages. To conclude, I will say that we need to ensure the artistic and financial autonomy of our cinema, because the sources of European financing will eventually dry up. We need to prepare ourselves for that day.

The director of the Nigerian Film Corporation told me that they have ultramodern facilities to make films from beginning to end, but the problem, as he related it to me, was in getting francophone filmmakers to come to Nigeria to do postproduction work.

My answer would be that he has not worked hard enough to promote his facilities and bring people to Nigeria. The first time I heard of such facilities was at the last FESPACO. I was not aware of it before. I made *Finzan* in Ouagadougou, but had I known I could make it in Nigeria under better conditions, I perhaps would have utilized the facilities. I inquired about Zimbabwe at one time, but it was too far.

What is your view about African film style and aesthetics? Where are they heading?

We filmmakers are researching the question of aesthetics. We are trailblazers in that regard. We have an enormous burden to found an African cinema both in terms of the given economic, commercial, and technical parameters and in terms of style and aesthetics. I personally work on narration based on oral tradition as an aesthetic form, and my next film, *La genèse,* will emphasize that concept. Other filmmakers may have a different focus. I also believe that it is for critics and theoreticians of cinema to promote that aesthetic style and to define the aesthetic foundation of the African filmmaker's work. Filmmakers often do not have the opportunity to theorize as do the critics.

Filmography

Scheresse et exode rurale (Drought and rural exodus), 1985
Nyamanton (Garbage boys), 1986
Finzan (A dance for the heroes), 1990
Guimba the Tyrant, 1995
La genèse (The genesis, 1999)

King Ampaw (Ghana)

Of all the filmmakers featured in this volume, King Ampaw is one of those who spoke most freely with me. He never shied away from contentious issues affecting the development of African cinema. The amazing thing is that King, as he is popularly called, is always open to criticism and even welcomes it as the only way to reach the heart of a matter. For this reason, it is interesting how we agreed to disagree or disagreed to agree on some pertinent issues.

After graduating from Accra Technical Institute in 1960, King went to Germany for higher education; there he obtained a diploma in directing and production. From 1961 to 1972, he trained in filmmaking at several institutions of higher learning, including the Academy of Film in Potsdam, Germany; the Academy of Television and Film, Munich University, Germany; and the Academy of Music and Performing Arts, Vienna, Austria. It was in Germany that King made his first film, *They Call It Love*, a thesis film, which depicted the life in Germany of an American GI who had refused to return home after his service because of the racial discrimination in the United States.

On returning to Ghana, from 1976 to 1983 King worked as a film director at the Ghana Broadcasting Corporation, eventually rising to the level of senior film director. Because GBC-TV was not producing films, he was forced to produce newsreels, short documentaries, or whatever else he was instructed to do—this led him to quit his position and pursue independent filmmaking. His first feature, *Kukurantumi: The Road to Accra,* was made in 1983 and is a coproduction between Reinery Film Production of West Germany and King's production company, Afromovies Limited. It is one of the few anglophone African films that has been widely distributed and well received by international audiences. Following the success of *Kukurantumi*, King directed his next film, *Nana Akoto* (1985), also known to the Ghanaian audience as *Juju*, teaming up once again with Reinery. *Nana Akoto* was filmed in Accra, Tema, Koforidua, and Oyoko, with a combined West German and Ghanaian crew and an all-Ghanaian cast.

King's production strategy hinges upon coproduction as the quintessence of African cinema. Surprisingly, despite funding difficulties in the production of his own films and the fact that other filmmakers lament the lack of government funding, King advocates government noninterference with film funding. Cautioning all filmmakers, King categorically declares that "African film producers should once and for all learn that we should take our minds off of governments trying to fund and produce films on a commercial basis. We should try to find different avenues of funding our own films." Similarly, on the question of aesthetics his position is antithetical to that of most African filmmakers. He is of the opinion that because there is only one universal film language, there can be no specific African film language; rather, there is only a "camera language."

When King is not directing his own films, he is either coproducing or acting in other films. He appeared with Klaus Kinski in *Cobra Verde* (1987), directed by Werner Herzog, and starred in *African Timber* (1989–91).

This interview was conducted in Ghana in 1994 and 1995.

How would you describe your relationship with movies?

I received a scholarship to go to Germany to study engineering. When I got to Germany I was interested in what the Germans call fine or light mechanics, which specializes in watchmaking. I began my practical training in a factory where still photographic cameras were produced. However, my experience with still cameras forced me to change my mind about studying engineering. I became interested in the capabilities of the photographic camera. So I went to another factory where they manufactured Super-8 cameras. I became interested in Super-8 cameras, the stories one can produce with them, and the images they capture. I decided that I wanted to learn how to work with cameras. I applied to go to a film school and was accepted.

What is your first film, and what is it about?

The first film I made was a sixty-minute film. I made this film as a thesis for my studies. The title is *They Call It Love*. It is about a black American GI serving in Germany, who, after serving, decided not go back to America because of racial discrimination back home. Fortunately, he was a singer and he started to make music for a living. His difficulties in making friends with German ladies is what motivated me to make *They Call It Love*. I wanted to show the ladies' relationships with him. They did not really love him, but they found him interesting as a singer.

Is this film still in circulation?

This film is still at the university in Germany. It has never been in circulation.

What other films did you make after this?

As you know, *Kukurantumi: The Road to Accra* was my second film. After my studies I returned to Ghana; I worked with the Ghana Broadcasting Corporation Television [GBC-TV]. I thought I could come home and produce films for television, but in Ghana I found that the system was quite different. GBC-TV was not producing films, so I produced newsreels, short documentaries, or whatever came. I found it so boring that I resigned after four years. I began to write the script for *Kukurantumi.* I went back to Germany when the script was completed, because I have a foundation there. Germany is the only place where I have friends, and know people, including television producers. With a script in my hand I went through all of my contacts. Luckily I found a German television company that gave me the funding to make the film here in Ghana for German television.

Did you receive any funding or technical help from Ghana?

Since I was still working with GBC-TV, I knew I could use their production facilities. Because I was producing the film for German television, they gave me their television crew, consisting of a cameraman, a sound man, and a production assistant who came down to Ghana. This was the main team. All other assistants came from the Ghana Film Industry Corporation.

Were you able to do any postproduction work in Ghana?

No, I did all of the postproduction in Germany, including editing.

Postproduction is another consistent problem for African filmmakers. What is it like doing postproduction outside of your own country?

It may sound funny, but Germany is like my home country. That is the place where I studied and began my career. It was not a problem to finish the film in Germany. I was happy that I could work in a place I was familiar with.

Other African filmmakers may not be as lucky as you.

Other African film producers must also have learned their film production somewhere so they could do their postproduction in any country. If they learned in Africa, they could also edit in Africa.

Discuss the success of Kukurantumi. *Have you shown this film in other African countries?*

To my surprise, everywhere I showed the film *Kukurantumi,* it was very successful. People only commented that the film was good. I wanted to meet people who would say the film is not good, but I never met one, whether in Europe or in Ghana. I sent this film to FESPACO in 1985, where it became the first African film in the history of the FESPACO festival to receive the Film Critics Award. Since then, *Kukurantumi* has been shown in South Africa, Canada, San Francisco, Berkeley, and anywhere I am invited to show it. Regarding showing the film in other African countries, I haven't been able to take the film to Nigeria, for example. As soon as I completed *Kukurantumi* I was eager to produce my second film, *Juju*. I decided that if I had to take *Kukurantumi* under my arm to Nigeria and try to make money, then I would not have time to sit down and write another film. So I never promoted the film, and no distributor came to acquire it. In Africa, for any independent filmmaker to exhibit his film means personally taking it around to other countries in order to be able to collect cover charges, otherwise you do not get any money. Because I was unable to follow the film around, it has remained under my bed.

Kukurantumi *depicts the people's way of life and the actual circumstances relating to society. The signs on the lorry, "No condition is permanent," or "God's time is the best," make me remember my own Nigerian environment and culture. When I was growing up, the transportation vehicles (lorries and taxis) had similar identifications and messages.*

When I came back from Europe, I discovered that the lorries, like Addey's in the film, which were very popular for transportation in those days, were gradually disappearing from our roads. Today one rarely sees them. I thought that before they vanish someone must somehow document their social and cultural significance. This concern was pertinent to relating the story with the driver, his lorry and culture. Another factor was to portray city and village life. In order to do this, one needs to emphasize the mobility between the city and the village. This driver who shuttles from the city to the village and from the village to the city is a familiar icon. He is easily recognized. That is why I built the whole story around this driver.

You tried to allude to the problem of prostitution. Are there any sociopolitical implications?

I had to deal with a young girl; that is, maybe, why I was forced to allude to prostitution. I just wanted to tell the youth that there are no job opportunities for them in the big cities. So any youth who leaves the village hoping to find a better life in the city should learn from the experiences of Emi and her friends, who had to do anything to survive.

But prostitution is also one of the problems of the city. You portray the city in Kukurantumi *as any other city, replete with frustrations, crime, lawlessness, and so forth. All those things are in the film and are traps for the youngsters who may not be prepared to deal with such situations. These issues are also very intense and challenging for an actor or actress.*

The main actor, Addey, is a professional stage actor. So is the young lady, Emi. She was at that time working with the drama group at the University of Legon. I am the first Ghanaian filmmaker to bring their talents in front of a movie camera. I had to spend some time to train them, to teach them how to act for the camera, which is unlike how they acted on stage. Because they are talented people, it was easy to direct them. It was fun working with them; that is why we achieved some professionalism in the acting. In terms of directing, although *Kukurantumi* was my first feature film, I did not have that sense of amateurism. When I was studying in Munich, I worked in one of the biggest film studios in Europe, the Film Atelier. I gained a great deal of practical experience working with Germany's creative producers and directors. My German student friends and I capitalized on this great opportunity. We loved going to the studio and working with people. When I shot my first feature, I did not feel like a beginner.

In the film the actors were not delivering their lines as fluently as they would in their indigenous language. Would you be willing to use indigenous African languages in your next film, if for nothing else than to have an impact on your African audience?

If you want to reach your widest audience, in Ghana, for example, the best language to use is English. In Ghana alone we have eighteen different languages, not dialects. Even though we are used to these differences in languages, when one goes to school, the English language becomes the common language for Ghanaian people. We in Ghana, like in many African countries, speak the English language as the lingua franca. You are right, the impact of gestures and facial expressions is greater when speaking in one's mother tongue. But I think in modern Africa, and in Ghana specifically, filming in English does not make much difference, because when we meet our friends on the roads, we speak English. Unfortunately, we are used to this colonial language.

Some specific issues are best expressed with one's mother tongue. Would it not be appropriate to use the mother tongue and if need be subtitle the sequence?

Personally, I hate subtitling. You lose something somewhere. What can you gain by making a film in a local dialect or national language, then have it subtitled to accommodate a foreign viewership? My colleague in Nigeria, Eddie Ugbomah, has utilized such strategies to communicate in local languages. I have seen some of these films, and they appeal to their audience. It is true that the actors were more comfortable using their mother language than English. Filmmakers in Ghana have also used this style. Whether it will become a trend, no one can really say. I am giving this interview in English, so I feel it is a common experience for Africans. If one uses English to make films in anglophone Africa, it does not really make a lot of difference as long as it is properly handled.

In the present decade, the Ghana film industry is experiencing challenges posed by technological revolutions in video. The Ghana Film Industry Corporation (GFIC) has turned to video, and the Nation Film and Television Institute (NAFTI) emphasizes video. Is film dying in Ghana?

I think film is dying almost everywhere in the world. You can even start with Hollywood. If large institutions like Metro-Goldwyn-Mayer are selling their Hollywood studios for video production or television production, then it is an indication that film is dying. Unfortunately, film is dying in a country like Ghana because film production has always been a problem to all Third World countries, especially sub-Saharan African countries. The revolution in video in Ghana is promoted by young people trained in film schools who are eager to make films. However, these young people cannot afford the high costs of celluloid filmmaking, so they are forced to go into video production. Also, it is easier for individuals who lack celluloid filmmaking skills to go into video production. The productions are set in the African environment. For example, stories are about contemporary Ghanaians. For this reason people accept these videos whether the technique is good or bad. Saying that the GFIC has embraced video simply means that video films now dominate the GFIC theaters. That is a boom for video producers who want to show their productions in the GFIC theaters, because it is an opportunity to make money.

Video producers seem to be getting patronage, but is anyone questioning the quality of those films?

Of course they are technically bad, because some of the producers are not equipped with broadcast-quality cameras and the expertise to produce films. But the people who go to see films these days do not care about technical quality anyway. All they care about is how the films depict Ghanaians' life problems. They appreciate this local stuff. It entertains them, and it is as simple as that.

What is the impact of foreign films on Ghanaian film culture?

Foreign films are shown in Ghana, but in most cases the films arrive in Ghana through piracy. Videocassettes from around the world are brought to this country freely. These videos are shown everywhere, without regard to copyright laws. Recently a copyright administration was introduced into Ghana, but who enforces these laws if a theater is showing alien films to a paying audience? Nobody! There are no official representatives to protect such films (except the videos) shown in Ghana. Foreign films have always run alongside the videos produced in this country.

Do any African films get shown on a regular basis in Ghanaian theaters?

We have come back to the old problem again. It is really unfortunate that African films, those produced in Nigeria, Burkina Faso, Mali, Senegal, etc., are not distributed

in African countries. African filmmakers have been appealing for an effective distribution cartel. We have not been able to have a large number of our brothers and sisters
see our films. My dear friend, it may surprise you when I say I have not seen any
Nigerian films shown in Ghana, neither have I seen any films from Burkina Faso
being shown here, nor have any of Ousmane Sembene's films been shown here. Why?
It is obvious that the Lebanese have monopolized the film theaters and they have no
interest in showing African films. It is a pity that African films are not in circulation
here. For more than twenty years, at African film festivals in Ouagadougou, Tunis,
Accra, and Lagos, African filmmakers have spent countless hours talking about the
distribution problem, but up until now we have achieved nothing. I do not know
when this problem will cease. We must work together and try to create a common distribution cartel. I think the filmmaker should not have to take charge of distribution.

*Ghana's situation is very sad, because the government could have protected the GFIC
to maintain its mission to protect indigenous productions.*

Ghana is not the only country having problems with indigenous film production.
African governments have nothing to do with film industry, period. I do not understand why African filmmakers would want the government to provide the money for
making films. Governments should not interfere with film production. They can
make government newsreels, they can make their documentaries or whatever, but I
do not know any government that has anything to do with commercial film production. Although the Russian government spent a lot of money in the 1920s during the
Eisenstein time to make movies, that was a different case which should not apply to
the African situation. Let us go back to Hollywood. Hollywood studios are in the
hands of private people. I am not an American, but I do not think the government
has any interest in these big Hollywood production companies except to collect their
taxes. African film producers should once and for all learn that we should take our
minds off of governments trying to fund and produce films on a commercial basis.
We should try to find different avenues of funding our own films.

*If governments are unable to provide the necessary funding, wouldn't it be beneficial
to enact laws that would protect film business? Given the economic problems in Africa
today, it is almost impossible for individuals to generate funds to make films. Do you
think this is a problem that independent filmmakers can tackle on their own?*

Here again, I do not think that any government should get involved in the business
of film distribution. In Ghana, for instance, the government does not own any of the
film theaters or cinema houses. All the cinema houses are private enterprises, in the
hands of private individuals, the majority of whom are aliens. It is time that we begin
to ask our own African entrepreneurs, institutions, and organizations to devote part of
their resources and investments to culture and entertainment. By doing so, they will
help to produce more films in Africa. I still maintain that it must not be the business

of the government. Rather than producing films, African governments should provide hospitals for the people.

Is it possible to develop an African film culture?

The film or video culture is not an African culture because film as a medium is foreign itself. If you are asking about how I see film as a mass medium in Africa, I understand it to be the construction of film with our African language, African stories, and African mentality.

The media may be foreign, but we are witnessing what critics are calling cultural colonialism because of the proliferation of cable channels—CNN, MTV, BBC, et al. transmitted via satellite to African countries.

I think we have to be more specific. To me CNN is a news medium. Bringing news from around the world has got nothing to do with any culture. I do not see any problems with that. We are happy to hear what is happening in and around the world through CNN. Other than that, we have no way of witnessing visually what is happening throughout the world.

The news you are talking about is never neutral. It is ideological. It originates from a non-African point of view and that means that Africans should be enlightened to understand the media's cultural, political, and economic hegemony. Consider CNN during commercial breaks: they advertise foreign products and give viewers foreign telephone numbers in Chicago, London, Paris, etc., rather than in Lagos or Accra.

I get your point. However, to be informed, I am happier to know something from somebody else's point of view than not know anything at all. If we insist on knowing about what is happening in the world through the African perspective, then I think it is time for Africans to get their news agencies functioning to expedite the dissemination of African news through a central African news agency. Why can't Africa also try to have a central news station to broadcast to its people and the world just as CNN is doing? Why should we sit down here and watch products which are sold in New York, Chicago, or London advertised on CNN in Accra? My answer is if I produced cocoa and I want to sell it in New York, and if I am capable of paying to have my product advertised on CNN in New York, I would think that CNN would not say no.

In other words, in your own terms, because Africa has not got the facilities to set up a cable network, it is all right for Africans to receive foreign broadcasts without questioning the ideology behind the dissemination of such information. Don't you think it makes sense to argue for some kind of control? The reason is not to advocate a news blackout, but rather to be concerned about uncontrolled ideology and what it does to the people; it could be opium in the rawest sense.

You asked why we should keep on watching foreign news and foreign programs and digest them without questioning their perspective. My answer to your suggestion is, ask Africa to make their own.

Since we are discussing foreign influences, let us turn to the topic of coproduction. Do you see it as the quintessence of African film production, that would save African film practice from stagnating? Also, how do you maintain the Africanness of the cinematic images under foreign pressure?

You have seen my film. Although the film was financed by Germany, I do not think anybody can tell me there was any German influence in the whole film. It is only African countries who have a different idea about coproduction. Even America produces with Germany; Germany produces with France; France produces with Italy; Italy, France, and Germany join together and make coproductions, mostly because of financial restraints and because of interest in the story. They all coproduce with organizations within specific cultures—whether you are French, German, or Italian, it is still the European culture we are talking about. So the producers can come easily to agree on topics and coproduction tactics germane to their interests and needs. Whenever it comes to coproduction between an African country and a European country, then it is subjected to all sorts of scrutiny. Whose interests will it serve? All I can tell you is that it depends on the topic, on the story you are handling. If the story is an authentic African story, then I do not see why there should be any fears about cultural differences, coproduction interferences, or difficulties. But when the story deals with black-and-white issues, then problems begin to manifest. Before two cultures agree on coproducing a film, they must have a point of general interest. If this general interest is not there, then I do not see how the production can be carried out. Lastly, film production as you are talking about has become a financial blandishment, which is to say, money problems have forced us to go into coproduction. At times it is only when you go into coproduction that your story or your film can be marketed in other countries. If you do not explore other channels, your production remains at home—just as all African films have been remaining at home—in closets. If an American comes and tries to produce a film with you in Nigeria, he would also like to show the film in America. That is one point of view. So I am also free to seek coproduction advantages.

About Juju *and* Nana Akoto, *why do you have two titles for one film? I know that one is for television and the other is for theatrical release. Would you also talk about the story in this film?*

The film deals with Nana Akoto, the chief of a village. He has a lot of influence primarily because of his powerful adviser, a *jujuman* [a native doctor]. The chief has implicit confidence in his adviser and often implements the *jujuman*'s suggestions. After shooting the film, I told the German television authorities that the film's story line emphasizes chieftains, so I would like the film to have the title *Nana Akoto*, the chief's name, for the foreign audience. I blew up the film from 16mm to 35mm for theatrical release. This chieftaincy situation that I showed in the film is nothing new to Ghanaians, but the *juju* aspect, or the *jujuman's* influence on this chief is new. I decided to call it *Juju*.

How was this film financed?

Again it was financed by the same German television station from Hamburg which financed *Kukurantumi*. Since *Kukurantumi* was so loved and so successful, they agreed to provide funds for the production of the second film.

I read that the success of Kukurantumi *propelled the GFIC to think about giving you support for the making of* Juju. *What kind of support did you receive?*

I received support from the GFIC when I was shooting *Juju*. I told the authorities that this film is another film which can be shown in cinema houses. I suggested forming an agreement with my German television producers stating that the GFIC would offer its supporting crew free of charge in exchange for the raw cash it did not have. Then when the film is finished, the Germans should give GFIC the rights to show the film in Ghanaian theaters for at least four or five years.

Did the GFIC help to promote and distribute the film?

They had the rights to promote and distribute the film only in Ghana. When the film premiered in Ghana, I was in Germany. I heard it was a great success and that the GFIC had screened the only copy available to them so many times that it is now totally disintegrated. The television copy was shown about two years ago.

Did the film make any money, and who has the rights to the film?

I did not lose any money because I never put in my own money. I have not received any money either. The minute the film is finished it is finished. I am paid for the work I do and that is all. I had a deal with my sponsors, the German television station, that they got only the rights for the television screening. I hold the world rights to screen the film anywhere I choose.

It seems to me that you are not pushing enough to show your films in African countries. Why can't you go to the National Theater in Lagos, Nigeria, for example, and say to the authorities, "Here are my films, I want you to have a retrospective of King Ampaw"?

You are quite right. I would have to move my ass and fly on a plane to negotiate for it. However, I never have time, because after each film I am always working on another film. I have always believed that promotion, distribution, and exhibition must be the responsibility of another person. It is difficult to function as the filmmaker and the marketing person at the same time.

That is the exact opposite of how the African film industry operates: the filmmakers make the film from concept to finish. They are their projectionists and their accountants, because there is no organized system of doing things the way it is supposed to be done.

You are quite right, and that should not be. That is why, for an example, my friend, Kwaw Ansah, has made only two films in the last ten years. When he completed the first one, he had to become the marketing expert, accountant, all roles.

Your films interweave a number of themes that are social, political, historical, economic, and cultural. What is your view regarding the inseparability of film from politics?

I always try to entertain, that is my priority. Let the political part be for others, and I will never do political films, because I do not know how to make them. Political issues are never the main theme in my films. It is just conversation—like two friends in a conversation. They talk about family affairs, they talk about disco, about everything. These issues may be connected with politics, but it is mostly dialogue. I try to entertain. I do not go into politics.

Do you have problems with political films?

I do not think I could make a good political film, because I do not have a desire to make one. It would be too brutal. I am an entertainer. I am a storyteller. I try to tell stories to people after they have eaten and before they go to bed. I do not emphasize politics in my stories.

But that does not mean that you are apolitical.

Who is apolitical? You cannot live in a society where politics is part of the society and not be political. What I am saying is that there is sports, politics, entertainment, and religion. I have chosen entertainment over politics because I do not regard political films as instrumental to understanding African problems. If you take a political topic and you want to translate it to film images, then you run the risk of not being free to fully express yourself. You are not free in the sense that you are toeing a specific line. I want to be able to express myself. I do not know if I have been able to explain myself well to you. You choose sides when you make a political film. There is no hero in *Kukurantumi.* It is a story which I show to the public for them to see how things are. I did not tell them, "You should go this way."

But you did address political issues in Kukurantumi.

Yes. What came to be politics in *Kukurantumi* is coincidence. When I was shooting the film, the so-called Ghana revolution happened. It was not planned. I am not like Fela Anikulapo-Kuti, or the other African revolutionaries. Fela equates music with politics. Concerning the works I have done, I think I am a realist. I try to deal with what is happening to the human around his environment socially. I am more interested in the social aspects of the human stories rather than the political aspects of it.

Ousmane Sembene is also a realist, and his films are extremely political. How do you compare your work with the work of Ousmane Sembene?

We are two different people. Ousmane was a good writer even before he started making films. He is first evaluated on the power of his writing and secondly on the sociopolitical aspects of his films. I base my strength on my power to explain social events critically and realistically. This is evident in my second film.

You are saying that social criticism and politics are not interwoven, but in Nana Akoto *you tried to deal with that problem. Remember the conflict between the king and the son when the latter wanted to bring new ideas? You had to intervene through your narrative structure to show the changing politics or the changing order of the time. You made a strong criticism of the system, and you say it is not politics. How do you explain that?*

I do not see this criticism of the system as politics. I do not see it as the central issue governing the film. Chieftaincy is culture as well as a traditional institution. I do not think that has much to do with politics. It is a cultural thing. I deal with the cultural aspect of the chieftaincy: the dos and the don'ts, the aged and the young, the differences between the aged and the young in social environmental situations, the misunderstandings between the institution and the collective, which is not a power struggle. It is the respect for elders in the traditional sense that I tried to convey to the audience.

Do you envisage African cinema as playing any role in Africa's cultural development?

The example of Ghana that we are talking about has shown that Africans want to see films which analyze their own culture, which deal with their environment. In that case, African filmmakers must be encouraged to write stories, to portray the true African environment. That can make a great impact. The only problem is that African critics are not sympathetic with African filmmakers and the films they produce. For example, I have been criticized in one of the Ghanaian dailies for using German technicians in making my films. I have also been accused of parading Ghanaian miseries in my films. You have seen *Kukurantumi*, can you point out the Ghana miseries that the critic is referring to? Do they want me to write stories that only glorify Ghanaian people? We have to learn to make our own constructive criticism and to accept the portrayal of the good and bad things about our society. I do not think that Africans should overreact to seeing their environment portrayed as it is.

I have not seen you at the Pan-African Festival of Film and Television of Ouagadougou, where you are supposed to be attending FEPACI meetings. Are you in regular contact with other African filmmakers?

I do not like to go to festivals without my own work. If I have a new film to show, I enjoy attending FESPACO. I do not have much contact with other African film-makers because we only attend FEPACI meetings during FESPACO, which is held every other year.

It has been a long time since you made Kukurantumi *and* Juju. *How do you make a living when you are not making films?*

I am working on another feature-length film, and in between, I make short documen-taries for German television and Transtale. Transtale is a German film institution which sends films to Africa. I have done a lot of work for this organization, which has produced numerous international stories. It is a nonprofit organization like the British Council. They always come up with good ideas for these documentaries: how an African child learns how to dance, the role of a grandmother in an African house. They are mostly fifteen to twenty minutes long, and I make about four a year.

You acted in Cobra Verde, *a film with which many people were not happy regarding how Africans were depicted.*

It was the only time I acted. It was not one of the best films of my friend Werner Herzog. The film deals with slave trade, and whenever any references to slavery are made people react to it negatively.

But Haile Gerima just made a film called Sankofa *which strongly indicts slave trade and has been very successful.*

To me, there was nothing Herzog did wrong in *Cobra Verde*. It is a film about the abolition of slave trade and how African chiefs organized themselves to fight slave trade. It is a film about women, the Amazons, who rose against whites who had come to buy slaves. It is a true story, a sensitive one.

If you were commissioned to make such a film, would you have done it differently?

According to my knowledge of history, I would have done it the same way. The prob-lem is that whenever you show Africans using bows and arrows, the critics castigate you. They think Africans would rather be depicted using machine guns and rockets than bows and arrows.

Almost every African filmmaker claims indebtedness to oral tradition in narrative structures. Do you see the oral tradition as developing an African film culture or film aesthetics?

It is clear that in the African cultural heritage there are dos and don'ts. In the African tradition, if you go to a house, you enter the house, get a seat, sit down, and are offered water before you are even asked the purpose of your visit. Unlike in Europe, when you visit a house and you just start asking your questions. That is the dramaturgy and aesthetics I am talking about, the way we act and do things. Maybe what you are trying to hint at is the pace of the story in African films. In African films, too much time passes before the point of the story is revealed.

In light of these differences and changes we have discussed, do you think there is a need for an African film language?

As far as film is concerned, there is no need for a European film language, so there is no need for an African film language. There is only one film language. If you tell me that there can be an African cinematography in the storytelling, I will agree with you. But you cannot tell me there is a specific language for an African film. I will never agree with that. What I am trying to say is that there is only one universal film language. We know our close-ups, our medium shots, and our long shots. It is these shots that we put together to construct the film language. There is no African film language! There is only one film language, and that is the camera language!

Filmography

Kukurantumi: The Road to Accra, 1983
Nana Akoto/Juju, 1985
Cobra Verde, (coproduced with Werner Herzog), 1987
African Timber (coproducer), 1989–91

Jean-Pierre Bekolo (Cameroon)

Since coming into the African cinema scene in the 1980s, Jean-Pierre Bekolo has established himself as one of the youngest African filmmakers to combine imagination, innovation, and courage in his meditations on the contradictions of African film. In this interview, conducted in New York City during the 1998 African Film Festival, he provides one of the most candid and provocative assessments of African cinema in this volume. His responses to my questions also exemplify the earnestness and defiance that characterize all of his films.

Bekolo trained in France as a television film editor at the National Audiovisual Institute (INA) from 1988 to 1989. Upon returning home, he worked for Cameroon Radio and Television (CRTV), where he also experimented with filmmaking. His short films include *Boyo* (1988), *Un pauvre blanc* (1989), and *Mohawk People* (1990); he has also directed music videos for Les Têtes brûlées and Manu Dibango.

Bekolo believes that imagination is the key to the future of African cinema. He asserts that the time has come to reassess the old traditions of filmmaking, the language of cinema, and African representational patterns in general. He acknowledges the diversity and quantity of African films, but wonders "if there is [enough] cinema in them." For African cinema to transcend its present predicament, Bekolo believes, there is a need for an urgent intervention on the part of "the younger generation" of filmmakers, who, as he puts it, must "eliminate all the dinosaurs and make sure there is no *Jurassic Park II*." In metaphorical terms, he urges his counterparts to refrain from all the dogmatic binds that stifle innovation, to question the language so as to pave the way for the emergence of progressive and sustainable autonomous art forms. This philosophy shows in his first feature-length film, *Quartier Mozart* (1992), a work of unparalleled imagination and stylistic and aesthetic virtuosity unknown in African cinema since the release of Djibril Diop Mambety's *Touki-Bouki* in 1973.

Bekolo was only twenty-six years old when he made *Quartier Mozart*. This film, which won the Prix Afrique du Creation award at Cannes, and which the jury called "audacious," electrified the film world when it was released in 1992. Widely seen as a film that has established a new trend in African cinema, *Quartier Mozart* has been compared to other breakthrough films of young directors, such as Spike Lee's *She's Gotta Have It* and Jim Jarmusch's *Stranger Than Paradise*. Its editing technique has been compared to music videos for its jarring, syncopated, eruptive tone. Many observers have noted this young filmmaker's subversive inclinations—his ability to subvert Western and traditional African cinematic codes to articulate a new film language that does not wholly absorb, as he puts it, "the formula and content of Western cinemas." In *Quartier Mozart*, humor and caustic satire are cleverly juxtaposed with sexual politics in the celebration of urban youth culture—laying bare all colonial, postcolonial, and cultural contradictions.

Bekolo's second feature film, *Aristotle's Plot* (1996), is another landmark of African cinema. It was commissioned by the British Film Institute for its series of films commemorating one hundred years of cinema. Like *Quartier Mozart, Aristotle's Plot* continues Bekolo's intrepid experimentation with conventions. Instead of replicating the conventions of the traditional documentary, Bekolo develops an alternative and autonomous mode of inquiry. In this vein, the film's structure repostulates notions of both dominant cinematic codes and indigenous aesthetics. This hybrid is indicative of Bekolo's relentless quest for alternative ways of seeing movies and negotiating the complexities of making and marketing competitive African films.

You once said to me that you do not care for African cinema. Could you clarify this statement?

I think it is very difficult to be both an ethnologist and the specimen studied. That is what I would say. The word *care*—what does it mean? You have to be specific about the idea of caring. What drives me and interests me in making films is not African cinema, but Africa itself and other films in the world. I am not a scholar of African films. I am teaching now, but I am teaching films, not African films, because I do not know anything about that. I also think that very interesting things are happening in African cinema and with African filmmakers such as Djibril Mambety, whom I find extremely creative. I made a film about him because I admire him so much. The film is called *Grandmother's Grammar* [1996]. I am interested in people and in some works, but not in African cinema as such.

How can you separate African cinema from the notion of the cinema? Are you referring to the work initiated by the pioneers? They were concerned about this notion of African cinema and how to redefine Africa. They wanted to teach the outside world as well as Africans with the images they constructed.

I think there is a real problem. First, when you make films, you have to define for yourself what is the cinema. Another thing which you have to define as an individual from Africa is, What is Africa? Those two questions are very clear in my new film, *Aristotle's Plot*. What is the cinema? I am not the first to ask that question. André Bazin asked it. It may be seen as a way to teach people things. I remember, when I was teaching for UNESCO in Zimbabwe, I had fourteen students from the region. I started by asking every one of them to summarize a film they would like to make. Most of the ideas were about issues such as child abuse, corruption, etc. I asked them which films they would like to see or had seen recently. They said *Four Weddings and a Funeral* and other popular American movies of the time. Then I asked them if they would see an African film if it were showing. Obviously, it was clear that they would not. Why then do we make films if our people would not go to see them? Most of them felt that most African films are like tools for teaching, and that is why I started having problems with that definition. Film is a medium of expression and an art form. Being a filmmaker is like being a priest. But the priest has to go to a ten-year school/college, if not more, to be able to communicate his doctrine. I do not know if African filmmakers can use the film medium to teach in that sense, or if they have the right background. I think it is wrong for us to teach, even if we feel we have learned something. Film could be a good medium for a type of education that is very different from teaching. I do not pretend to be a teacher. I do not know how to do that very well.

I think I prefer to work on the expression level because film is an art form, a tool for self-expression. In that end, I have not seen a place like Africa, where I can say in general that people have energy for that kind of expression. The way Africans talk is very creative. I believe the idea of teaching with films came from the West, and we integrated it into our own system as with many other inventions we have appropriated. As I was saying in the conference panel earlier on, we went in there [abroad—East or West] to take the container and we ended up getting the content. When I was making *Aristotle's Plot*, which is about one hundred years of the cinema, I realized that Western codes of aesthetics are very different from ours. For example, a beautiful woman in the West is not what a beautiful woman is in Africa. So also, a story considered good in the West may be seen as boring back home in Africa. Similarly, some people may see linearity as not good aesthetically. These kinds of contradictions are numerous. As far as African films are concerned, they have never, except with Djibril Mambety's films, where narrative styles have been integrated, addressed those issues. Anyway, I am not interested in those issues. I do not think they serve Africa.

Our filmmakers have been very good students of the West. I would say that somebody like Ousmane Sembene, even if his films are wonderful, is still a good aristocratic disciple, which means, for me, that he has been doing (considering his time) "the right thing." I still have a problem with that. I believe that he absorbed the formula more easily, and the formula, for me, is the problem. It is what I believe Africa is suffering from—the Western formula and the content that we are appropriating.

But the pioneers, all the early African filmmakers, like Ousmane Sembene, worked under extreme hardships to open up the way for other filmmakers.

I would like to talk about Ousmane Sembene's contribution. Most of his films are good, but they deal with tragic situations in Africa, things we can't get out of. The old mentality in *Xala* is an example. Even if the films are very interesting and good, my work focuses more on the other aspect, which is that tragedy is pushed on Africa. This is how the pattern works: if I or anyone else makes a film about something bad in Africa today we will be supported and we will recuperate our investment. You take any problem as an example, as when Joseph Conrad said, in speaking of the "Dark Continent," that most of the time we are dealing with our own darkness. Take a problem happening in New York, bring that problem to the African environment, try to raise the money, and you will find people who will provide it to you to make the film. Tragedy is sort of manufactured. That is why when there is tragedy in Africa it will be broadcast on television and nothing else. People consume such images and absorb those issues and, for me, that is actually what is keeping us down in a way. I believe that Africa is everything but tragic.

Consider Aristotle, the author of the most beautiful aesthetic art form for storytelling. He wrote how-to books which are extremely poetic, but I would argue there is no African perspective. Cheik Anta Diop has commented on these issues. When we talk about Africa, sometimes we are confused—everything reverberates with memories of the Egyptian theater. Egyptian theater was made tragic by the Greeks, like the stories of Isis and Dionysus. Now we go to the West to study, but what do we go to study exactly? Cheik Anta Diop is the one we should emulate when we go to study in the West. Many people study everything. I remember when I left Cameroon to study in Paris, my parents told me to study everything the French offered, but not to forget that the real thing is here, in Cameroon. I will never forget that. But I believe that in terms of filmmaking, we just reproduce whatever we have been doing. This means that people in African cinema are, in my own opinion, working hard to destroy Africa.

I can understand the perspective you are coming from. But look at this from another perspective. In the pioneering phase, African cinema had a mission. That mission was to use the cinema to rewrite African history, which has been badly distorted. Thus there was an attack on colonialism, neocolonialism, and imperialism. Some of those filmmakers could have made blue movies to become rich, but they didn't do that. They wanted to use the cinema to teach people, African and non-African, about African reality. Don't you think that you are being impatient or dismissive of African cinema?

I really do not, to be honest with you. I never actually talk about African cinema, but people always ask me about it. That is what I don't understand. When they meet Spielberg, they don't ask about American cinema. You ask a question, and I just say what I know. I don't know about African cinema. I never studied it, and it's not my field. My film *Aristotle's Plot* has the answer to your questions. I have been asked political questions. I am not a politician and have never studied anything in that field, which is very clear. I have studied filmmaking and storytelling, from Hollywood to Aristotle. This is my field of interest, not making statements about politics. I do not put anyone down, even Ousmane Sembene. I cannot put down any African film-maker in general. I am just trying to analyze the situation in relation to storytelling. I hate talking about the problems of distribution and about politics. In the African circle, we never talk about aesthetics, and that is what made me enter this business of filmmaking.

I was coming to that, too, but if you talk about politics, your film Aristotle's Plot *could be read as political. Political issues are there, but you have chosen to tell these stories in a different form, which is very interesting. There is what we might call a quasi-democratization of aesthetics. You seem to be a bridge between the pioneers and the new breed of African filmmakers now aspiring to push African cinema to a new progressive level.*

It is not just African cinema, it is Africa. I don't know much about the pioneers. I took Sembene and I analyzed his films and came up with a certain idea. I would say I am concerned about Africa. I am really passionate about Africa. Any time a discussion of Africa comes up, I say yes, I can analyze Africa. That informs my film structure and that is what I talk about because I have an idea of Africa. But I also try to question that idea by asking, "Why discuss only Africa and Africans and not integrate African American issues and all the problems blacks all over the world are subjected to?" That is why I really wanted to go back to the essence. You can talk about racism, but there is something more underneath it that is really the bigger problem. It is that thing that impacts upon everything we do that I am trying to reflect on. That thing is exactly what compels the rap singer to disrespect the rule of law when he puts his fingers on the gramophone machine and stops the record from playing normally as he manipulates it to create a different kind of rhythm—at the risk of breaking it and losing his money. Ordinarily, that is an attitude deriving from not respecting dogmatic rules, but in the process, this artist creates an entirely new art form and aesthetics, and a new market too. That may be the thing that makes us be in the field together, but we never talk about those issues. That may also be the same thing that makes people fight us. I feel like I am part of that thing; I can't define it very well, that essence, but that very thing is what I want to address.

Racism is just one small consequence of it. It is that same thing that made Africans who were brought to the U.S. as slaves survive in this harsh place. Maybe we have something, but they tried to prevent us from retaining the thing which is essential, and which human beings as a whole need. That is responsible for the imbalance and confusion in the world today. I would say that intuitively. When I talk about the plot, I am trying to look for things that do not make sense around us. These things that do not make sense are still very much around us, and we never question them or get the answers. Nevertheless, we still try to bring Hollywood to Africa. I am not interested in that. I am going into deeper things. I feel I have a problem with something and that thing is what I am trying to define.

Could that problem be the problematic concept of African filmmaking/filmmakers? I know some filmmakers do not feel comfortable when you call them African filmmakers.

It is true, but that is a shame! I remember at Cannes some filmmakers said, "*Je suis un cinéaste tout court* [I am a filmmaker, period]." I am sorry, *tout court* is not a country. And wherever these filmmakers are from, I think they are shying away from the content by trying to change the name, and these are the people who would be proud if they won the Academy Award instead of the Étalon de Yennega. Being African is never the problem, but it is the content—what they do in their films. They are ashamed of what they do in a way, and they think changing their identities is the answer. It is not a problem for me being called an African. Call me what you want. I am more concerned about the work I do, the essential things which I still have not been able to define completely; I am just trying to define it.

Would that be what separates or sets the line of demarcation in your own work from other African filmmakers?

I do not know, because when I came to filmmaking, it was by accident, and I didn't know many African filmmakers. I found a field of concern, a tool, a meaning, and I have been trying to play with all that. I discovered I was in a circle of people and some of those people were interesting. For example, I worked with Djibril Mambety and made a film about him. But I found that I was not interested in many African filmmakers, and did not gain anything from them.

Why?

Just because they are Africans is not enough. I am not interested in every American or every Frenchman either.

Could this be because of the way you perceive cinema and cinematic aesthetics and the way the other filmmakers perceive the cinema?

Yes, I would say I am opposed to them ideologically, because film is about ideology. Unless you do not understand it well, you put together some beliefs and create a new world. Just to give you an example: I was a member of a jury at a film festival. I saw fifty films in ten days. I started realizing that I was feeling this abstract thing. It was what is wrong with humans. It was not about Africans. It was what is wrong with humans. In China they have this problem, in Japan another, in Russia another, in India or France, etc. Then I could see it like a dance. They were doing a painful dance around a sort of monument. This monument is what makes them suffer, but they themselves are responsible for building it in the first place. The films are about those dances. This monument has a system of values, morals, and ethics, but this system is also making the inhabitants suffer. Everything relates to that kind of bizarre circumstance. That is how I came to realize that what I do as a filmmaker is important. Until then, I did not believe that being a filmmaker was important or interesting. Then I realized I was going back to the essence of who we are as humans, what kind of animals we are. That was when I read a book, *Moses and Monotheism*, by Freud, where he shows how Moses established a value system similar to what we have today and that Moses was an Egyptian and a Jew. Then I started to understand how we are trapped in a system of belief and values, and why we are suffering, because there is a conflict.

Nietzsche also expands on that in *The Birth of Tragedy*, where he shows how these viruses were put on humans and became guilt and suffering. But when I go back home to Cameroon, people never ask me anything, they just tell me stories. Most of the time I find myself crying, being really moved by the stories in general. I will leave the country with those stories indelibly etched in my memory. Then I realize that the stories are actually the essence of the human being. They know how to manipulate you. Nevertheless, it is clear that when people tell you stories about their experiences, you do not leave without thinking about their total relevance. They are stories about people you know—mother, father, brothers, sisters, cousins, and others. I understand the weight of these stories. They carry a big ideological charge, even religious, in the African ways and values. This is why when I am here, in the U.S., I feel like I have to go back home. I carry those feelings around with me. I guess that is what shapes humans, in a way. My way of seeing films has really changed based on that experience. I started understanding that it is not just political or religious, but at the very beginning of all these things.

Then what is your own vision of African cinema? We see people in the field doing different things, including yourself.

Yes, that is the discussion I just had before. I believe that now I have my perception of what cinema is—not African, but the cinema. I feel as if there is no cinema. I know that is really hard to say, but there is no cinema according to my own definition of the cinema. I am not putting anyone's work down, but I am just saying, having clearly examined what cinema is, I feel that there is no cinema. There are African films, but I do not know if there is cinema in it. Echoing what I just talked about before, one of my problems with African films is that French people write many of the films. The pen and paper and the writings used in putting down the ideology—not necessarily the heavy stuff, but the basic script—are not even written by Africans. The questions are: What are all these works and what are we doing?

That is what I meant when I asked you how you see yourself in relation to other African filmmakers.

People always criticize African films as too slow because of the editing, for example. Most of the editors who work on these films are French women. Editing for me is a heartbeat, a pulse, the rhythm. What can a French woman tell me about the beat, the pulse, or the rhythm of my film? It is a problem, and you can see why I feel there is no African cinema. Our people are making films, and they should be honest about defining what their films are. Maybe I have a big idea about Africa, and am idealistic like Diop, Sankara, and others, but I do not think theirs are African films. Senghor talks a lot about freedom for Africans. Editing is about freedom, so I think Africans should be the best editors of their own films. Actually that is what film-making is all about.

Is this situation the result of the problems of funding, postproduction, and how the funding organization may also exert influences to shape a film's content?

I really believe that money has nothing to do with the problem. The British funded the reggae exponent Jamaica's Bob Marley when he was doing his music. But he knew his music well enough to shape it the way he wanted. When you are in control of the medium, your art form, and you have a vision, money cannot be the determining factor in style and content. When money shapes you, it means that you do not have anything to offer on your own.

There are also some African filmmakers such as Med Hondo, who refused to surrender his script to Hollywood and who said he would make Hollywood's version of his script but that his version will retain the authentic history according to his vision of Africa.

And let me tell you that while I was doing *Aristotle's Plot*, I wanted clips from Ousmane Sembene's films. He wrote to me to say that not one piece of his movie would ever be cut off. But in closing his letter he wrote, "*La lutte continue* [the struggle continues]." Souleymane Cissé also said he would never give me a clip of his film. To make a long story short, I believe that it makes no sense to make such strong statements, or to adopt such an uncompromising stance. So also, Med Hondo should not have been so emphatic because of the circumstances sorrounding his last movie, *Lumière noire*, made in 1995. There are many things I could be saying about this film-maker [Hondo] who makes money in Paris dubbing Eddie Murphy films into French to contradict his assertions, which are ideologically problematic. I am only telling the truth and do not intend to put anyone down, but I believe that in the process of func-tioning as a filmmaker that we should cultivate some measure of integrity.

We all have different stories to tell about our own experiences.

I believe you should stop working with these people. It doesn't help Africa. In Africa you are always old or young and upcoming. All these questions you have asked me I have answered in *Aristotle's Plot*. You are always either young or the father, but you never mature as an African artist in general, which is very symbolic. Djibril Mambety got an award in Cannes at the age of twenty-four, and the next time he went to Cannes he was almost fifty. Young and old, but never mature—this is the problem, and this is why Ousmane Sembene and Souleymane Cissé are worshiped, because they are old African filmmakers. And this is an idea of the West—that we never mature. How many African writers have been seen as young and upcoming, but afterward, what happens? There's a big hole! I believe that Ousmane Sembene is doing great work, but I believe he was too much into being the Western model of a good student—speaking French better than the French, making films better than the French. I am very suspicious about the West, but not paranoid. When they can define you in their ways and in their own terms, then you very quickly become an icon.

You have stressed imagination as the key to breaking out of aesthetic gridlock.

One of the things I like is that people who oppress other people try to reduce their imagination to reality. They try to prove that the truth is beautiful and have the ethic meet the aesthetic. For me that is wrong and it is a tool to keep people down. To make a film, even in a black American community, it has to be true to life. The theme has to be a social problem, always referring to reality. Why? Imagination is the essence; maybe that is the thing I could not define. I think that is what made the slaves survive here in the U.S. as they were working hard and singing the blues while being oppressed. Maybe that is what the white people are fighting us for. Maybe that is what they are jealous about. I do not need to follow their aesthetic formula. Formula is for those who do not have any imagination, and we don't need it. That is what I have a problem with.

Without this imagination, do you think African cinema will gain the industry status it hopes to attain?

But there is no cinema without imagination. What have we created? You have documentaries and all that ethnographic or anthropological stuff, and recently, *Rouch in Reverse* and all what not. I mention this film because we are here at New York University, where we are conducting this interview. Have you seen this film? In your mind, Jean Rouch and the filmmaker, who reversed each other? It is a joke. We talk around those issues, but we have to deal with them and move ahead. I am saying it again that imagination is the key.

We make strategies up to a certain point, and we feel like we have achieved something. Sometimes it works but we should be ready, know how, to get what we want. We are thinking about getting out and taking on the world, and being more offensive, and that could be the goal. I was saying to someone to think about stock, where they will promise you a 20 percent return or 10 percent return a year, and you are happy with it. But when I think about myself ten years ago in Cameroon, when I was struggling, and compare it with my status now, I think the growth is more than

1,000 percent. Take someone like Spike Lee, for example. If you compare him at the very beginning with today, it is 100,000 percent growth. I believe people can do that. It is almost a miracle. I believe working on that kind of growth in a sustaining way is more profitable and dynamic than any business out there. The strength, whatever the motivation, is in the potential. This potential is endless. We should be more ambitious. That's what I believe in and that is the purpose of the film *Aristotle's Plot.*

I feel that we have come to the West to learn the wrong things. We are not supposed to be learning the content as in *Aristotle's Plot.* Why do we have to follow those rules? In a way, what we need is technology, but we also have to know how to subvert the technology, and that is what I see as the main challenge. But the first time we come here to the U.S., we see beautiful landscapes and architecture and then we see New York and we forget our purpose for being here. It is amazing how people quickly forget to focus on what is actually essential. They do many things, like getting married or whatever. I wish they would just learn and take home the essential, everything. People like Cheik Anta Diop are good models. I would argue that he was one of the few who consistently knew exactly the essential things he wanted to take home. He took the analytical and the tools and transformed them into scientific means for discovery. But now, people are not confident enough to embark upon such challenges.

Is it because people do not have faith in their cultures, in themselves, and could that be responsible for all the failures?

Film is first an ethnic thing, and you can see that even for Spike Lee and Woody Allen, it is not just a matter of making films. Coppola's film *The Godfather* is ethnic and it is an ethnological film, which means to say that he was using the film's structure to tell stories not only about humans, but about a group of humans. He was not just trying to make a cocktail out of the ordinary. The story needed to be rooted in something tangible, and that is why the more specific you are, the more universal you are. You tell people, this is something I know about, even if it is about a group of people you never heard of before.

Do you think African cinema is not doing this? Is that part of the problem?

Absolutely. Throughout the Diaspora, black cinema is not doing this. Take the film practice in Africa as an example; does not the word *ethnic* there assume a different connotation? Is it not because our filmmakers go to the villages and shoot all their people bare-breasted? I will ask you a question about the film *Yaaba* by Idrissa Ouedraogo, because you are from Nigeria, and an African. Have you ever seen an old lady being buried with only two kids and a fool present where she is being buried? Where have you seen that kind of thing practiced in Africa?

Surely the filmmaker has the right to imagine.

What I am saying is that the imagination there is actually too narrow. When such a film is shown in the West, all the white critics talk about how everyone is great, and how great the film is. In their own country they do not do that, considering how critical of other people's work their critics and audiences are. That is how people progress—through constructive criticism. In Ouagadougou there used to be no previews of films before they were entered for competition at FESPACO. Any film, good or bad, so long as an African made it, was entered for screening. We live in a competitive world. Not everybody can be good. I think criticism should come from inside, otherwise it may not have the intended effect of changing for good the way we operate. At least I would feel proud to be an African filmmaker if there were constructive criticism from an African perspective. But if there is no criticism, and everybody is nice as they all are in Western eyes, then we have a problem. That attitude does not make us progress. But also, is it constructive or destructive criticism?

I keep going back to music because that is the place in African American culture where this has played itself out. The musicians, even if they are in competition, have a respect for each other. They will quote other musicians in order to begin their own pieces. They then manipulate, change, and alter rhythms until it becomes something else. This person either answers it or gives up. But they do it in a spirit of admiration and challenge.

I am glad you said that because if I go back to the history of African cinema and the work of the pioneers, one can see they laid the platform. It is on this platform that someone like you stands to initiate some new trends and discourses. I see the emergence of new creative minds as a good initiative for African cinema.

When we refer to the jazz musicians, it is because they have set standards for themselves. Right now in African cinema, who is setting the standards? We have to set the standards ourselves. We do not have to wait for outsiders to come in and tell us what our standards should be. We must develop our own perspectives and critical attitude.

Talking about imagination—imagination is very ideological. I remember it was Jane Campion who said that people who oppress others try to make people believe that those whom they control have no imagination. That is one of the obvious things—always reducing African people's imagination to reality. The main difference between Africans and the West is imagination. How can you believe in witchcraft? It relies on your imagination. In the environment in which I grew up, the imagination was really the essence of life. People grew up without television. People would tell stories, and the truth didn't matter. The idea of being a liar or not was not an issue, they just took you there, where their story was. Here people have to validate everything. If it's true, they enjoy it; if it's not true, they don't enjoy it, I would say that imagination is shocking to the West when you talk about Africa in general. That is why Africa, for them, is really a movie by itself—just the way it is naturally perceived.

The worst thing is that African filmmakers play the game, but they are not even aware of that idea, of the suppression of the imagination. That is why yesterday [at a New York African Film Festival forum], when people were talking about technology and saying that people are too poor in Africa to think about those things, it was mainly because they have been convinced that only reality matters, that Africa is poor. But how do you create hope? How do you transform reality into something else? How did African slaves in America free themselves in their minds? It was by imagination, and that is what created jazz music. That is the key. Even Einstein said that imagination is better than knowledge. It is just not there yet in African cinema.

Are you referring to creativity?

No, I am talking about imagination. What makes European writers or artists important is the level of imagination they display in their works. That is one of the key elements. However, I do not like how the Europeans apply their standards to us.

I remember asking you some time ago if you ever see or work with any other African filmmakers in Paris. You said no, which means that information and resources are not being shared. Also the spirit of collaboration, growth, and development is not occurring either. You cannot be your own island and develop and grow.

We know clearly what the resources are—for example, the French Ministry of Cooperation. Obviously, we are all in competition for the same resources. It is clear, I think, that we do not share the same ideas. I feel I do not share the same ideas as many of the other filmmakers. I know those I share ideas with. I would say we talk about issues, but at the same time, we are frustrated. There is a system, even within our filmmakers' circle, because some are very close to the power, or the funding agencies, so there is a lot of politics going on. The whole problem is that when we get together, we talk, and the next thing you see is that your dossier is not considered, or has disappeared. So we become suspicious of each other. I would say that I always work in the opposite direction. I start films and then look for money afterward. I do not want to simply stick together by any means. I mentioned the idea of the "godfather," and I really believe that is a system that works—dealing with somebody who can get things for you and wants something back in return. We live in a world where we have a lot of interests. Sometimes somebody will just come up and say, "I am going to help you just as a brother," but it is so difficult to get things done that you wonder why this sort of thing is happening. I always want to know the reason. There is nothing wrong with giving help and expecting some kind of help in return in one way or the other.

I think about this idea of brotherhood or sisterhood—that we black people should all stick together—especially in a place like Paris, where there is no network of Africans in general. Then there is the feeling that you should not hang out with black people in France. All the Cameroonians are happy to say they do not have any

Cameroonians behind them. I say they are silly. I think there is too much hypocrisy. We know the system we are dealing with; the only thing missing is this idea of a godfather.

There is nothing like African cinema, but we do have African films that reflect the plurality of cultures in the African continent. So there is no single entity called African cinema. But as time goes on, we will be comfortable talking about Ghanaian cinema, Cameroonian cinema, and so forth. That is understandable. We should move away from that narrow confine where Africa is seen as a country instead of a continent composed of fifty-five or so nations.

It is more than just the distinction of countries. African cinema was almost invented in foreign lands, such that now we have to bring it over to Africa, which could be an interesting concept. We should know, however, the limits of what we are talking about here.

And that is . . .

When we talk about future ideas, to quote one character in my last film, *Aristotle's Plot*, "we don't know where we are coming from; how do we know where we are going?" When I said "we," what do I mean—we filmmakers, or we Africans? I bought "how-to" books on how to write screenplays. In the beginning of one of those books, the author quoted Aristotle as saying that a good story should inspire pity and fear. I had a problem with that. I realized another thing, which is that all the questions about film bring you back to reality. Somebody said that the truth is beautiful and that aesthetics meet ethics. This is applicable to African films, but to talk about the idea of film aesthetics, is that what makes a film good? When I went to France to study, my intention was to concentrate more on technology than content. I started as an editor in television to study the technology. But I ended up getting both the technology and the content—which is bad. I think that when you examine the credits of African films today you will find that few African technicians worked on them. When I was making *Aristotle's Plot*, my question was, What is film—the content or the container? Although the container can have some content, I felt that the content should be invented in Africa.

Learning both created a big problem for me. I felt that when I go to Aristotle, which is the bedrock of European storytelling, something is there. I did not research this idea that a good story is supposed to inspire pity and fear. I am from Cameroon, and I think humor and satire are basic elements of culture. As I was reading *The Poetics*, I realized that something was missing—comedy. That is why I became paranoid, as the title *Aristotle's Plot* seems to indicate. So, the "plot" is not just the plot in storytelling, but also the subplot. To go back to the container, and thinking back to the rap music discussion we had earlier, I remember one thing I always asked myself: What made the rap musician use his fingers to manipulate the record player in such a way that he created a new rhythm with it? What inspired that first kid—the inventor—to manipulate the record's normal pattern of play the way he did? He started to do all this stuff on the machine, and that is where you see the container and the content meet. I think he did that to become the future. I keep coming to the point that there is no African cinema. It is an invention, a myth. We are trying to make a myth become a reality. We do not even question that.

How would you like to be introduced to the reader?

I am a film director originally from Cameroon. When thinking about what I was going to talk about today, I found a book by somebody I like. He wrote, "To abdicate from the belief that the two validating wonders of modern existence are the love and invention of the future tense." I felt like the "invention of the future tense" would be something I was interested in and would talk about. I am interested less in the future than the invention process. My African and technical background, because I started as a video editor for Cameroon television, brought me in a way to make films and question the language I was using. My first feature film was *Quartier Mozart*, followed by *Aristotle's Plot*, which is a film I was commissioned to do by the British Film Institute for the celebration of one hundred years of cinema. It is in a series with people such as Martin Scorsese, Bertolucci, and more. In two months I will complete a film called *Have You Seen Franklin Roosevelt?* which was shot in Memphis, Tennessee. What brought me here [to the United States] is that right now I am working at Virginia Tech on a project which is a cross between different media of information and different art forms, which are leading to a new language with the use of new technologies.

You have also tried out working in the other areas of the film business.

It is true that I tried to distribute my film in Cameroon and it did not work, so I came to the conclusion that this was not my business. The experience I had in Cameroon was that I had a film, I went down there, and I tried to make a deal with a theater owned by a Cameroonian but run by a Frenchman. This Frenchman told me, as we were in a plane going to Cameroon, that he had bought sixty American films for the year, which means that even if he were to show one every week, he still wouldn't use them all. According to him, he bought them in a package for about two thousand dollars per film. Then he said, "If I show your film, then I would have to split the money with you, which is a loss for me. You don't have Schwarzenegger in the movie or Van Damme, so I don't see why I would show your film." Finally what happened is that he did not show my film.

I had to go to public places like the Palais de Congrès, where conferences are often held, to show the film to the public. At this conference center, only one person, a lady, could run the projector. But when I wanted her to run the projector, we discovered the projector needed to be repaired. She started to fix this Chinese projector in Cameroon, but obviously she had no parts available. However, we started to advertise the film, because we didn't have a choice. Christmas was approaching, and yet we did not know if we were going to be able to have any screenings. We advertised as well as we could. Like the French, we put posters on cars and drove around, everywhere. As days went by, the date for the officials of the censorship commission to see the film was also approaching. The day before they came, we picked up the projectionist at her home to help with the screening. She was our main hope, but when we got to the theater, although the film was available, to our surprise there was no sound. The censorship board watched the film without sound, but they said it was fine and gave it an approval. We had a few more days before the film opened and still the sound was not available. Luckily, two days before the film opened, the sound came. That is how we premiered the film in Cameroon.

I also wanted to show the film on television and decided to see the general manager at the television station where I had worked before, inquiring about the possibility of screening my film. He said, "This is your film but it is not a television film, so we can't help you." Because I knew former colleagues who work on TV, I was invited one day and we talked about the film. We had posters all over the city and the suburbs and also went on the air, on radio and television. *Quartier Mozart* was everywhere, making people wonder what it was all about. A company that sells condoms helped us with advertising, but it became a problem, because people thought our film was about AIDS. At the end of the process, I lost a lot of money. I went back to Paris very tired, and during that time I reexamined my role as an exhibitor and concluded that it was not going to be my business.

That is exactly the reason why I asked how we have prepared to counteract the effects of hegemony. What I am thinking about is, here is J.-P. Bekolo, he made a masterpiece called Aristotle's Plot; *the question is, why isn't this film being distributed the way it should have been?*

Go to an African festival and they will tell you about distribution problems. I feel a lot of people are already talking about those things and I think it is wrong for me to engage this issue. There are problems, but I prefer to focus on the issues that have more meaning for me. I like to *do* things. That is where my interest is. I don't really want to think about distribution now. People have too much respect for the market. I do not. Maybe that is my problem. Something should stand next to the market. The market cannot be the only ideological outlet. The market doesn't respect humans. It has been hurting humans all over the world. The market can give you more tools for less money, but the damage the market is doing is awful. The slave business and colonialism were market driven. It's like using a knife that killed my ancestors to eat. You have to be careful. There is a need for a strategic ideology about how we deal with the market, and what for.

How does the content of the film reflect how a film is promoted or not promoted?

I don't want to think about promoting. My main concern is about making the films first. I do not even know how to approach this market. I feel uncomfortable with just being out there and talking about marketing and distribution. I was talking before about the long-term goal. If you aim to jump one meter, you might jump 0.8, but if you aim to jump three meters, you may jump two meters. But a film may be more appropriate for an alternative marketing strategy. The idea of alternative structures sounds good, but once you succeed where do you go? Most of the time you are lost, because you did not plan for it. You did not anticipate it. It is not an accident if these people are planning a hundred years ahead.

Would you speak about your points of engagement with Hollywood after making Aristotle's Plot?

Aristotle's Plot was more of a reflection on myself, on Africa, and on African cinema in general. It is a film I needed to do in order to grow and move ahead. It set up very clearly what is needed. I would say that Hollywood is just a place and that there is a specific industry there with standards. I believe we cannot talk about the cinema without first understanding Hollywood. We must also see what kind of relation we will have with that kind of environment. Making quick judgments is not enough. We need to go deeper. If Hollywood really oppresses us, what do we do? We have to get rid of the problem in a way, or at least deal with it, but we can't just forget it. It is very important to find a way to either respond to it, destroy it, or live with it, but in my own case, to have a clear relationship with those matters. One must understand Hollywood's influence even if it is not in film, but just about people. You have to understand Hollywood and develop an attitude about it. That is the point.

How has Aristotle's Plot *been received so far? It is a good film, but yesterday you did hint that because of the content and its critical aspects that its reception may be ambiguous.*

I always have strong reactions. Either people are very excited or they are really angry, which is the same reaction actually, because it shows the message is getting across. I am interested in having an impact. It does not matter how. I do not want to make a film that is neutral, so in that sense I am quite happy with it.

To what extent has this film been distributed?

On television, it has been shown on Channel 4 and Canal Plus, and we have some other stuff happening but I am not nervous about it at all. I didn't do it for distribution. It was a commissioned film, and the purpose of the film is very clear in my head.

It was to have been this tool that could help to change the way we perceive things. I didn't make a consumer's product. I am happy it's out there.

The way you weave autobiographical stuff into the narrative is interesting because you can define the cinema from your own perspective. I find that structure reminiscent of your first feature, Quartier Mozart, *where you had to deal with urban life to make a collage of popular culture.*

I would agree that *Aristotle's Plot* is autobiographical; even *Quartier Mozart* is autobiographical. But I did not just want it to look like a personal film. The only thing I have is myself first, and the only things I can trust are my feelings and my opinions. I always try to be subjective in that sense. In my opinion, there is no such thing as objectivity. Bringing everything back to me was to be sincere. I believe that when people watch the movie they can see the sincerity between the cuts. In that sense I believe in the medium and the power of the medium.

This power of the medium doesn't have to come through the linear narrative style. Quartier Mozart *and, to some extent,* Aristotle's Plot *are sort of disruptive and syncopated. The editing style is jarring, but they make their points.*

I am not interested in just taking a film and copying it. I do not want to make a simple film I would get bored with. I always try to express something new, and I feel as if I always start with nothing—no formula or anything. I always question myself and test all the feelings I have, all my sensitivities and opinions about the issue I want to deal with. Sometimes I even integrate some things I do not agree with. When I work, I try to forget everything I learned before.

Is this the style that you want to apply to your future films?

That is what I am saying. Each film has to help me discover filmmaking. Each film should give a definition of film. Otherwise I do not learn anything and I do not feel interested. It is like an adventure, and my definition of film is changing. I want to crystallize it in every film, and it cannot be the same. You are supposed to have as many definitions of film as you have films out there, but it's not true. You have a formula and you apply the formula with that one definition of film. I know what I do not like right away, so I can say, "I don't want this or I don't want that." Once I have made clear what I do not like and have what I might like, then I start playing with that idea. What I like is what I am, and what I think is good. It is easy then to start working. Because we are dealing with how so many people will feel, if I do not feel it myself, then I know nobody else will feel it. When I watch other people's films and I see what I do not like, that might make me conclude that I would never make a film like that. I try to have opinions about things, about life.

I believe more and more that what everybody has said about film is wrong, so I am trying them all out. Some feel that to make a good film you need a good story. I feel that is wrong and you could make a film without a story at all and it would be a very good film. Story-driven films are made to please the industry, which means they have something for which the industry can appreciate the value, invest in, and get a good financial return. Film is pictures and sounds, and you can do a lot with pictures and sounds that would be interesting to many people.

That is right, and that is why the way you integrate sound editing into the picture makes people look at, say, Quartier Mozart *and ask what this film is about. One of my students told me, "I don't know what it is about but I enjoyed it."*

I had this experience with music. Growing up in Cameroon, I would listen to some American music without understanding anything about it. The only thing I know is that I love this music. This means that we have something within ourselves. We tend to forget we are animals with imagination. We have another part of ourselves, other than just the logical one. The West tries to reduce our humanity to a primary level with simple emotions. When you define a human well enough, then you can produce things or bring out things that will affect people, outside of the fashion of the formulaic or logical way that has been set up.

Tell me about the characters in your films. Do you favor the use of professional actors?

My goal is to get things across, and I would say I work a lot with nonprofessional actors, but we always have a three-week practice session. The principle of the three-week session is mainly first to know who they are, because I believe that any actor can be a wonderful actor. I try first to see who they are, because with films you don't have to perform very much, you just have to learn how to be; sometimes just being is enough. I try to see who they are—their faces, their looks, their attitude, and I try to build the base on which they can relate to the visual character I have in my head. I have the kind of line I want for the ideological aspects and principles of the character I want to create. To be the character in that respect—the physical looks, the attitude, and the movements or the way they present themselves—is very important. For the cast, I make open calls for professional or nonprofessional actors.

In other words, it depends on the story ...

And the people whom I am trying to portray and the group I am trying to put together. It's a way to re-create a world. You can take some specific faces, not because they are good, but because those faces work in this film because you see that the world is also made up of those faces. It is not just about the skin color; it could be about various details that tell us about our humanity.

In your vision of African cinema, where does the Pan-African Festival of Film and Television of Ouagadougou fit in?

FESPACO is an institution. It is a very conservative institution that is dragging along all the things we need to get rid of to move on. It is dragging colonialism; it is dragging all the weight Africa has to get rid of. Even if we can admire all the work people do around the institution, this institution is still too old for Africa, the new millennium, and for whatever we have to do. Definitely, the festival has become a giant dinosaur, but it is not just a dinosaur in terms of the festival itself, but also in terms of the people in charge. It is not just a matter of creating a generational war. No. That is not the point. The problem may be because many African filmmakers are rooted in this tradition of respecting the elders, some of whom I really respect and like; but at the same time you cannot respect an elder who is keeping you down or preventing you from moving with the times. You cannot respect a corrupt father who is selling your future. That is why I would say that the younger generation has to eliminate all the dinosaurs and make sure there is no *Jurassic Park II*.

FESPACO still remains a place to showcase African and black films. If you say do away with FESPACO, we know there are flaws, but it has also achieved many things. Where else do we go? What are you advocating?

When you think, you have to analyze. But if you are just analyzing according to the practical aspect, somehow, I feel like you may be reducing everything, and the analysis may not be accurate. I would say that first we have to decide what we want. We don't know what we want. We need to know what we need to do, and I don't see those elements very clearly. We are just sustaining something because it is there. What are we trying to build? For example, our African American friend here, Keisha, was complaining about the fact that she would never go back to FESPACO because it is an institution she believes should be open to African American films. African Americans currently participate as members of the Diaspora, but who is the Diaspora? All those Africans living in France and all over Europe—they wanted to be able to participate. They feel they have been marginalized. They wanted to have a place in Africa where African Americans can meet with Africans and show their films. This cannot be a priority for FESPACO because it is French funded, and that is not the kind of move the organizers would want to make because the French might be put off. It is as if we do not even know what we are doing anymore. Speaking this way is to be sincere, and it is a way for me to make people think.

Consider Jean-Marie Teno's comment to you a moment ago when he said, "You make a living out of African cinema and yet you criticize it?" I thought that was narrow-minded because of his refusal to engage the issue we were discussing. Because he does not want to think, he does not want others to think. Now he wants to put us in the survival mode. For a filmmaker like Teno to utter such a statement, that you criticize African cinema and yet make a living off of it, misses the point and is really absurd. It is ridiculous in the sense that all the great humans who made the world advance had to be critical and were also criticized by others. The idea of limiting your choices to your brain and your belly is very stupid. That is the difference between human beings and animals. When people go around the world saying all the wrong things in the name of Africa because they are hungry, it is really a shame. I am angry because of the tone and manner in which he said it. The irony is that he said it very sincerely: "You make a living out of African cinema and yet you criticize it?" But when you told him that you wrote a favorable article about his film *Afrique, je te plumerai,* he was very happy and gave you his address to send it to him in Paris. This is the type of self-centeredness and hypocrisy I spoke against earlier. Teno totally forgot that what we are doing is talking about how things could improve for the benefit of our continent.

Even as developed as the Western world is, people are still critical of their system, because development is not static.

But criticism has made art grow and flourish all over the world. I would say that is why I would never agree with the kind of thoughts that would make me part of African cinema. Ours is not only resistance, but some people who try to keep us in survival mode have hijacked the culture. What then are the differences between these types of Africans and the ones starving in the continent? I think it is better to be hungry than to not maintain the principle one believes in. I think Karl Marx spent his life hungry. We just keep reducing everything to the level of the ability to find something to feed the stomach—and that is why we remain enslaved by the system. In this case, the authorities are afraid of someone who, out of principle, does not want to eat if eating what is offered to that individual means humiliation and subjugation.

You talk about self-dependency. How does this apply to film funding?

So far I have made films before I actually got the funding. I believe that first you do what you want to do and then involve people who want to be part of it. I do not shape what I am doing according to the funding, which is the case of many African filmmakers. They shape what they are going to do according to who is going to give them money. They sacrifice the content and ideology just to be able to function, and the price is too high. Selling out just to pay some bills? The price is too high. I do not want to position myself with that way of thinking and doing things.

Should African governments subsidize African films?

I would say it is better in a way to deal with corrupt African governments than to deal with the French. At least we are dealing with people at the same level and can thus discuss real issues. But what are you going to say to the French about the content? I do not talk to people in Cameroon about content. They may not like the content of the film I may be proposing, but it is possible that they would give me the money to make it. I prefer to have that kind of relationship, because we know that this corrupt government has to deal with France, so why go to France thinking the French government is not corrupt?

You have reaffirmed the concerns of Aristotle's Plot, *and the position you take regarding the cinema in general is very challenging, if not persuasive. Is there one last thought on this film and on the nature of the cinema in Africa?*

I do not have any more to say, but I'll just tell you how the film was made. I went to Zimbabwe and had an open call for actors, and then we had three weeks of rehearsals. The idea was to involve them in the making of the film. We started on improvisations that we recorded. Then we edited that and brought it back to them. It was a way to get the best performance. At some points I didn't say anything. I would just ask them to comment on African films. I think it is important to know their views because at certain points they even made fun of me, but it did not bother me. There are three elements in this film for me that are critical: the policeman, the filmmaker, and the gangster—the gangster because I think the African audience watch most gangster films in Africa. The youths are very keen about watching films. Maybe this is true with mainstream films only, but I can say that about films in general because the range of films shown in Africa is so wide. It is wider than here in America, with the films we get from India, Hong Kong, Italy, etc. I think it is very important to consider the audience, if the only way to talk to the audience in Africa is to make them aware of something.

One example I like is that of language. Let us take Cameroon as an example. The way people speak on the street is very different from when someone takes a microphone on the radio or television and starts to talk. It is like a play. People play a character to be able to speak to other people, but as soon as the mike is off, they go back to being themselves. Sometimes, it seems to me, that when people set out to make a film or play, they cannot avoid applying the same principles as in the West. They want to prove to the Western audience that we have traditions, countries, and cities like theirs. I do not find this freedom in the choice of subject. I do not have anything against films set in the villages or educational films. I am concerned about the lack of freedom in deciding how our stories should be told. There should be some defining factors; for example, why am I making a film on this or that subject? Is it a story that needs to be told? Making a film is already a message for me. When I talk about style, it is not just style, but the whole choice of making a film on certain terms. In a way I am happy that people are discussing these issues. I think *Aristotle's Plot* says enough, and I really do not need to talk more.

Filmography

Boyo, 1988
Un pauvre blanc (A poor white man), 1989
Mohawk People, 1990
Quartier Mozart, 1992
Aristotle's Plot, 1996
Grandmother's Grammar, 1996

Salem Mekuria (Ethiopia)

Salem Mekuria is an associate professor of art at Wellesley College in Massachusetts and an independent film producer, writer, and director from Ethiopia, based in Boston. For a number of years, she worked with *Nova*, the Public Broadcasting Service's premier science documentary series, and with numerous international film productions focusing on issues concerning African women and development. She is the recipient of numerous awards and fellowships, including the Rockefeller Foundation's Intercultural Media Fellowship in 1995; the Lila Wallace–Reader's Digest International Artists Residency Fellowship in 1993; a fellowship at the Bunting Institute of Radcliffe College, Harvard University, 1990–92; and the Massachusetts Artists Foundation Award in 1991.

In 1988, Mekuria directed *Our Place in the Sun*, a video portrait of the black community on Martha's Vineyard. Broadcast on WGBH, Boston's PBS station, in February 1988, it was nominated for an Emmy. This was followed by *As I Remember It: A Portrait of Dorothy West* (1991), a documentary about the veteran Harlem Renaissance writer, which was broadcast on WGBH in September 1991. That film won the Corporation for Public Broadcasting's Gold Award for local programming as well as first place in the nonfiction category in the Black Filmmakers Hall of Fame, and was also nominated for an Emmy.

Mekuria released *Sidet: Forced Exile* in 1991. This documentary film tells the life stories of three Ethiopian/Eritrean refugee women driven by the ravages of war and destruction from their homelands to the Um Gulga settlement camp in Sudan. This film, which was funded by the United Nations Development Program for Women and the John D. and Catherine T. MacArthur Foundation, and produced in association with and broadcast by Channel 4 TV in England and WDR in Germany, was filmed on location in the Sudan. In this remarkable film, which demonstrates Mekuria's meticulous attention to detail, the women narrate crucial moments of their experiences of life in exile, how they manage to cope with their children, and their frustration at not being able to communicate with relatives from whom they are separated. It is this film that solidifies Mekuria's status as one of the most prolific initiators of the African documentary film genre. Through a masterful integration of cinematic and cultural codes, the film's structure articulates an aesthetic form that is not only unique to African feminist discourse but shows the medium's potential for the reclamation of black female subjectivity.

Mekuria is also writer, producer, and director of *Ye Wonz Maibel* (Deluge, 1997), a one-hour personal essay on history, conflict, loss, and reconciliation. Told through a first-person narrative, the film explores the momentous events that took place in Ethiopia between 1974 and 1991. The film is critically acclaimed and, like *Sidet*, has been widely shown internationally in major cities, including Amsterdam, Frankfurt, Geneva, New Delhi, Sao Paolo, Tokyo, Toronto, Zurich, Johannesburg, Ouagadougou, Minsk (Belarus), New York, Los Angeles, Oakland, and Boston. It has also won numerous awards and took first place in the National Black Programming Consortium's Prized Pieces '97.

I would like to thank Robert Lane Clark and Kathryn Lauten for assisting me in conducting this interview on April 7, 1996, during Mekuria's visit to the University of Michigan to participate in the film and video series "Screening Social Change," organized by Clark.

In some of the scenes from Deluge, *you used drawings to depict certain events rather than re-creating the event or using newsreel footage of the event. Was that deliberate? Because at the beginning of the film I noticed your love of art, especially when you talked about King Solomon of Ethiopia.*

I chose to use visual depictions of massacres and executions in two places. The first one was of the massacre of the former government officials. The drawings were taken from murals on the walls of the memorial that was built in their honor. Because the families of the dead officials basically designed the memorial, I felt that using the murals in my film was appropriate, because that was how the families wanted the massacre to be represented. Also, footage of the event, which I doubt exists, was not available to me. The second place that I used visual depictions was of a massacre at a local theater. I had an eyewitness of the massacre to recall the event and show what the survivor remembered. I have nothing against reenactments, but I had limited funds and I felt that the paintings more effectively communicated the high emotions of the event because that painting was done from the heart.

You applied silence and then later ambient sound, and I felt that was one way of transmitting across the emotional impact to the viewers. One thing that makes the film captivating is the use of composition, silence, and sound to draw the audience into the narrative structure.

At times I was so emotionally drained that there was nothing more I could say. In fact, there was nothing more anybody could say and silence actually said it better. Also, at times I felt that people needed time to regroup and that any additional sound would just be clutter. Also, at times I couldn't think of any sounds that wouldn't seem out of place. Sometimes the only appropriate thing to do was pause. I didn't set out to provide silence as a reprieve—the moment just called for it. I would like to use silence more to carry the weight of whatever people have been exposed to right before that.

Isn't silence a traditional weapon of African women? We can also see from the film that silence helps to create African feminist aesthetics.

The original working title of *Deluge* was *Silence Is Not Golden*. I don't believe in silent struggle because it doesn't work for me. Perhaps it works for others. Silence in films is fine if it accentuates a point or functions as a transition between two irreconcilable spaces. Silence can make a point when used effectively, but I don't want to philosophize the use of silence in struggles because it is not my way.

Your film powerfully expresses what you called "irreconcilable differences." It is amazing to see how politics and social problems tear families apart. How did Ethiopia come to the point where brothers and sisters don't trust each other? Is there a way to remedy this, and what is the present situation?

Part of the reason I embarked on this project was to understand why what happened did happen. There are many reasons, but there aren't any answers. There are some generalizations one can make. One of the reasons is that as young people we had idealistic visions that weren't necessarily rooted in our culture and history. We tried to impose on ourselves the values and cultures of people we did not know much about. We didn't examine these ideals enough to see if they would work in our own societies. I have no doubt that Ethiopians involved in various movements genuinely believed that they could make things better, but we started from the wrong side of the equation. Before we knew what was wrong and understood what we were going to change, we had already brought about that change. Of course, eventually these things take on a life of their own. There was a vacuum. We had no design except on paper. Those who knew what they wanted to do with it, the military, immediately filled that vacuum. This is just a sweeping generalization, because there are many being omitted. My focus is not to analyze who was doing what and when, but more to show the differences we created ourselves. At the beginning of the student movement, everybody's focus was that change was necessary, that the emperor had to go and that the desirable replacement was a socialist system. Then when it looked possible, we had to decide how to accomplish it and that became our new focus. It was deciding how the socialist system was going to be created that led to the destruction that took place. This was easily exploited by the military. So it is difficult to say why, because you have to examine all the conditions—the famine, economic downturn, 1973 oil price increases, and so forth. There was a confluence of events and, although we had been talking about change, setting up a socialist system and getting rid of the emperor, we certainly were not ready to take over at that time. Things happened so quickly that everyone was taken by surprise and searching for the quickest road to socialism. That quickly paved the way for military dictatorship.

The rest of the world, Africa, and the Western news media had the impression that the former ruler, Mengistu Haile Mariam, was a Marxist, although they say he was not. In the film we see the overturning of the statue, for instance; it was about allying with the Eastern bloc, but for some reason, not about Western mediation in the conflict. Was there nothing like that at all?

During the emperor's rule, Ethiopia was a client state of the United States. After the fall of the emperor, all of the outward signs showed that Ethiopia had converted to communism; few material conditions suggested this, so it was based on rhetoric. As you see in the film, communism was really fashionable at that time; however, the change happened mainly because of all the other events and because of the agitation by intellectuals and students. Their agenda was to set up a socialist system. The military's agenda was to take the rhetoric from the intellectuals and socialist groups and make it their own to gain acceptability while clearly establishing a military dictatorship. The military usurped every program that the students and intellectuals had drawn up to convert Ethiopia into a socialist state and used them to mollify the people and to make new alliances with the Eastern bloc; there was no historical affiliation of the military with socialism. Mengistu was a minor military official during the emperor's rule. He was just one of the lucky ones who rose to the top. He had no socialist education except for what he received from the intellectuals who allied with him in order to attack the opposition and other student groups. So it was more appearance and charisma rather than a seriously studied Marxist program. As for what happened in the switch from the West to East in 1977, Somalia invaded Ethiopia and at the same time President Jimmy Carter used Ethiopia's abuses of human rights as an excuse to deny Ethiopia military assistance. The Soviet Union immediately seized this opportunity, dropped their client state, Somalia, and allied with Ethiopia. It all happened within a matter of days. Meanwhile, the United States in turn supported Somalia and therefore, the West lost any influence it could have had. The Soviet Union sent weapons and men and Cuba also sent troops to fight against Somalia, and the invasion was repelled.

The film wields tremendous information, but what I found really interesting is how you wove the personal and autobiographical into the narrative structure. For instance, it is emotionally devastating to see how communication was cut off between you and your brother.

So far I have only been talking about the events from the Ethiopian perspective. In doing all of the research and in wanting to cover a lot of ground because so little is known here, so many details have been left out, I was really overwhelmed. If I had done it the way I wanted to, the film would have been way too long because I am not a historian. I wouldn't have known which details to leave out because everything was so important to creating a true account. I wasn't even there when all this occurred. I am not an expert, a politician, or even a journalist, so obtaining access to historical documents, even for me, was not possible. So I asked myself why I was doing this story in the first place. Then I remembered that my brother had died, at least I assume he is dead because he has been missing since 1978. My best friend was killed, along with many other close friends and relatives. So I decided to use them to tell the story because this is a human story. This happened to real people and families. Fortunately, we were intellectually close. My brother and I corresponded a great deal up until the time he decided it was no longer fruitful. So I decided to approach the narrative that way, to use my brother and my friend as guides and to include my own naïveté, misconceptions, and disregard of several issues at the time. I included my own confusion because I think many people were just as confused, and that a few were reacting to the situation without fully understanding it. In that situation, I had to confront painful issues such as what happened between me and my brother, my brother and my best friend, and where my sister fit into everything. That's why when I went back through all of the letters my brother wrote me, and I had actually forgotten that he had cut off communication with me, or at least political talks, I felt that it symbolized what was going on in Ethiopia at that time. Things had reached such a level of hysteria that even the closest of people—a brother and a sister—could not continue political discussions. To me that still symbolizes our potential future. Unless we say, "Let's stop and talk about this," nothing is ever going to change.

As I was watching the film I thought about other families who must have gone through similar ordeals. Although it is a very personal story, it also represents what happened collectively. Were you influenced by your knowledge of pioneering African films while making your film—as opposed to traditional documentary methods of representation? Your film seems to focus more on the collective struggle, which I think is more powerful.

Two films that have influenced the way I chose to tell my story: David Achkar's *Allah Tantou* and Raoul Peck's *Lumumba: The Death of a Prophet*. Those two films were released around the time that I was deciding how to approach *Deluge* and they were very instructive in showing that personal stories have a place in political films. It is legitimate to tell one's own story from one's own perspective. Other non-African films were helpful in my conceptualization of how to do this story, such as *Before the Rain*, a story about Macedonia; *The Inner Circle*, the story about Stalin and the defection that takes place around a mad leader; and *Burnt by the Sun*. I was influenced by all of these films. I was searching for structure, and these were around and they were very helpful.

Until recently, and I am glad you mentioned Raoul Peck's film and the others, the documentary film was not emphasized in the African film industry. Why did you choose this format?

One simple answer is that I was trained to make documentaries for six years while working on *Nova*, a science documentary series on PBS. I also like the documentary form, the evolutionary roads it is taking, and where I am going with it. In fact, I was trained in one of the most traditional and well-known documentary production centers, WGBH. The documentary format is evolving a much looser and less formulaic, more personal and self-reflexive style. I will continue to do documentaries, but I also hope to go into drama, fiction, and other styles. However, I will have to learn those styles as I go, without a training center like I had for the documentary filmmaking. I am willing to do it and not afraid. I don't understand why documentary is not practiced as much as fiction. I guess it has to do with the political situation in most of Africa. If the film is perceived as real, then people will get into trouble, but in fiction you can go further without worrying about censorship.

In Deluge, *your brother talks about the two of you returning home after your education. When we first came here, to the United States, nobody thought of staying a day longer than necessary after graduation. We were all anxious to go home. In* Sidet *we see Abeba and her son emigrating to Australia. To me this poses a serious problem, for it makes me think about lost Africans; we are faced with two situations in which one has to participate in the struggle and at the same time go wherever one is asked to go, even if that means living in permanent exile. The little boy was two years old when he was exiled to Australia. After becoming an adult, is he to be considered an Australian black, an Aborigine, or an Ethiopian? How do we reconcile these problems?*

Well, that is the postcolonial condition. Wherever you are, you carry what you were with you and proceed with who you will be. We are all in transition. I am sure Abeba's son is in transition, and depending on what happens in his future he will turn more to Australian Aborigine ways or remain an Ethiopian, and that is something one cannot will. As far as my brother was concerned, he went home because he was connected to a particular historical struggle of which he felt he could not become a distant observer. He clearly analyzed his situation and made a conscious decision to go back. People such as myself had already accepted life as it was lived, and I was also in graduate school, so I chose not to go back. I am alive and he is not. I ask myself, if I had gone back would I have met the same fate? Nobody can say. That is a question many others face as well. A lot of people have gone back since, but there is no guarantee that the same thing will not happen all over again. Going back does not mean going back to being the same Ethiopians we were before. No, we have had different experiences and we are changed people. We return to Ethiopia with different expectations. There are so many complex questions and no answers, and I don't know what is what or who is who anymore. My brother always told me that I was an Ethiopian and that I should never forget that. I haven't forgotten that I am Ethiopian, but I am not the same Ethiopian that I was when I left home. When I go back I don't expect to find the old me there, and I don't expect to find things the same as when I left. So who are we? I am not lost; I am just displaced.

Hamid Naficy of Iran talks about exile discourse. He says people want to run away from the problems they are facing at home, but that the problems tend to loom larger than ever in exile. The problems don't go away, they haunt one forever. That is the position many African immigrants find themselves in today. It is a painful situation.

Nothing in life is easy. When I first came to America to go to school, I planned to be here at the most four years. However, at the end of four years I was married, so I stayed. You don't necessarily plan to be exiled. I am in exile by choice; I haven't been forced. My sister was forced. Many people had no choice, but I did, although now I am not sure how I would define my choice. I could go back, but what does going back mean? I do visit, but the reasons people voluntarily remain in exile are complex, and I don't know if I'll ever be able to say what they are. I know a few of them, but that is not the complete story.

Abeba's experience with her children is extremely disturbing. How did you manage to capture that oral and spiritual reunion between her and her other son in Ethiopia, where you played back the message from the little boy? Also, how did you manage to get the inspirational song he sang for her?

Some documentary filmmaking is serendipitous, such as her interview at the United Nations high commissioner for refugees office. That was not planned. The scene where she is listening to her son's tape was staged. I visited her family in Addis Ababa, and they had made a tape of messages from various family members, including her son. They asked me to take the tape back to her. When I took the tape to her, I told her that I wanted to film her listening to the tape, but that if she wanted to listen to it in private first then that was what we would do. She told me that if I wanted to film her listening to the tape then she would wait until I was ready to film before she listened to it. That was a gift from her in a way, because that was her first time listening to it.

You must have great determination as a black African woman to make films in the United States. What are the pros and cons?

As an African woman in exile, an alien in the United States, trying to make a film about issues in Africa, that not many people are interested in funding, is how I would describe my condition. I guess I am in a more privileged position than African women living in Africa, who have not made as many films as I have. It's a double-edged sword. On one hand I am privileged to be able to make the films I want to make as an independent, but to make them under conditions of deprivation. It is time-consuming to make my films: I don't pay myself, so I have to work night and day. But I feel that the positives outweigh the negatives. I was able to remain in the town where I have worked for many years and was able to become a part of a film community that is very supportive in terms of access to free equipment, free labor or deferred labor, and critical analysis of my work. They are a diverse group of people, both ethnically and nationally. All of those things make up for the problems that I deal with. I do get some money, which helps, although it takes a long time. Channel 4 in England has been the backbone of my films. They helped me after I had received a hundred rejections while working on *Sidet*. They legitimized the film. They were also involved from the beginning of *Deluge*, when nobody would have even looked at my film. I don't know what is going to happen in the future, but they have been extremely generous. The MacArthur Foundation supported me for *Sidet* and the Rockefeller Foundation supported *Deluge;* hopefully, now that people have seen my work money will be more forthcoming. It is a burden to be an African woman in exile making films independently. It can be lonely and discouraging when I don't get the responses I expect. On the other hand, because of my uniqueness, I tend to receive the money set aside for those marginal people.

Sidet was the film that first brought you to my attention, but what other films did you make before Sidet?

When I left WGBH in 1987, I made a half-hour documentary for WGBH on the [black] history of Martha's Vineyard, a small resort island off the coast of Massachusetts. That started my career as an independent filmmaker. It was short, but it showed I was able to begin and finish a project. The next project was a biography of Dorothy West, a black Harlem Renaissance poet who lives on Martha's Vineyard. I was intrigued even though I was not familiar with her work because she was a part of one of the most stellar art movements in this country and nobody knew about her. The video portrait was sixty minutes long and it showed the breadth of my commitment to the documentary tradition. It was broadcast on WGBH and simultaneously distributed by Women Make Movies. It was a difficult project to get funding for, and simultaneously I started research for *Sidet*. I ended up finishing both projects at the same time. I used money allotted for *Sidet* to finish the Dorothy West project.

You work primarily with video. Do you plan to use 16mm film?

Sidet was a 16mm film. I use video because it is less expensive than film. Otherwise, what takes four to five years now would take closer to ten years. I would love to work on film; I enjoyed working with it on *Sidet*, but I don't have a print of it. I had to transfer everything to video from the negatives after it was finished.

It is interesting to hear you tell of African stories from your female perspective. Because of the emphasis on women in your films, I refer to Sidet *as a feminist film, or, shall I say, feminist-oriented film.* Deluge *also has a feminist aspect. Are you a feminist?*

I am a filmmaker who deals with issues that have feminist perspectives. Yes, I am a feminist, but I am not sure that I am making feminist films. I am not even sure what that means, but I do deal with issues that are overwhelmingly women centered and display female perspectives. They also display African perspectives because I am an African.

That is very important; is there a dichotomy between African and Western feminism?

No, there is more than one feminism. Western feminism deals with Western issues, and I am not sure that there is an African feminism, but there are many feminisms. It is important to me to focus on issues of importance to women. I believe that is feminism and I don't have to use any canons to describe our condition. My preoccupation is to see feminine political, social, psychological, and personal issues explored in depth.

Sidet *moves away from generalization toward intense individual family problems, which also reflect the collective endeavor we talked about. How did you decide to focus on the families you chose in* Sidet?

There were three families in *Sidet*. There was absolutely nothing scientific about how I chose the women I profiled. During my research I met many women and talked with them and planned to focus on a few personal stories rather than refugees in general. I had hoped to use about four women, but when I went back with the filming crew these were the only ones who were available and willing to be filmed. They ended up being rather representative of the whole refugee experience, but the selection process was not systematic at all. The situation in the Sudan was difficult and they were really clamping down on the refugees. What little information I received I had to take advantage of quickly and get out before they closed the doors on me. The shooting ration was low and I was fortunate to have excellent camera- and soundmen. The footage was very good.

Were all of the members of your crew from the United States?

Yes, they were all Americans. I was the only African.

Sidet shows how women struggle to create a living in exile and the extreme conditions under which they live, but the story was told as if you lived in the refugee camps yourself. Your film contains details that were quite different from Ethiopian news on television networks.

I am not sure that I meant to suggest that I spent a great deal of time in the refugee camps, but I did spend more time there than any news organization. I had an advantage because those women opened up to me. They had never received the amount of attention I was giving them. Also, I was an Ethiopian who could understand their language as opposed to an American journalist who would have had to use a translator. I was also very explicit in expressing what I wanted to show so I took both from what we saw and what they told us we should see. I actually felt very strange in those camps, but whenever I was with the women I forgot what was going on outside. I shared meals with them and developed a relationship with them that was probably evident in the film.

Toward the end of Sidet, the last woman you talked with and her children were talking about their career plans. Have you heard from them and where are they now?

I was in contact with Terhas for a couple of years. They were in need of a lot of help and they weren't getting it. Then Eritrea became independent and I thought they would return. The last I heard, which was about a year ago, three years after Eritrea's independence, they still hadn't returned. I lost touch but my understanding is that they may still be in the Sudan. Things are really bad in the Sudan, particularly for Eritreans and Ethiopians. I am not sure what is going on with them now. It's hard— to build a string of relationships while making these films and after a while they die off. I hope in this case that I will rediscover them one of these days.

Similarly, in Deluge, we learn about a complicated story from an insider. You must be traumatized by the Western images of famine that don't provide the basis for understanding of a society torn by political turmoil.

My desire to make a film about the situation from 1973 to 1991 was motivated by what confronted me in the popular media here, in addition to my personal reasons. I realized I had a lot of work cut out for me—to give a historical context for Ethiopia in general, to show that it wasn't just a bunch of crazy Africans going around shooting at each other, that there were real conditions that created the situation. Then I had to introduce the characters in the story and their relationship to me and to introduce the economic material, and political conditions. All this had to be done in a short period of time so that I would have time to explore the story to my satisfaction and to the satisfaction of my primary audience—Ethiopians and Africans at home and in the Diaspora. It was a major undertaking to condense all of this information into an hour and eight minutes. To me it had to be done that way or not at all, otherwise there would be no reason to do it. I can't say that I was traumatized by the images I saw in the seventies and eighties, because I knew better. But I was angered and frustrated by the news media's constant fascination with negativities. At the same time, I could not educate the entire American population, so I guess this approach was a response to that.

For instance, you see a lot of water in the film. Ethiopia is not a desert, but that is the image many people have because of the frequency of drought and famine. The famine is a reality, but not the whole nation starves. There are fifty million people in Ethiopia, and at any one time perhaps six million are under threat and maybe two to three thousand people are actually starving. That is not to minimize the gravity of the suffering and the starvation. It should not have happened, especially in this day and age. I simply wanted to underline the perceptions created by the reporting during that time. People used to ask me if my parents were okay, which shows tremendous lack of knowledge about the history of Ethiopia and its people. So *Deluge* is a response to all of these things in addition to being my quest for answers.

Religious icons are strong in Deluge. *In the beginning you show the story of King Solomon and how it signified a common faith. Later, the society became so divided that it was impossible to trust one another. Could you elaborate on this point?*

I wasn't trying to emphasize the common religious background as much as I was trying to put myself in the historical context I grew up in. Mythology is very strong in our culture, and part of our mythology was that our first emperor was the progeny of the Queen of Sheba and King Solomon. The other mythology is that Ethiopia is a Christian "island" in a Muslim sea. That was what I was told as I was growing up, and that is another mythology which the facts don't support. Of course, I didn't know that as a child, and much of my historical knowledge was based on these mythologies. I mentioned later that we didn't know much more than the cursory lore or oral histories of Ethiopia. We were never educated about our own history. These very strong icons and mythologies colored what little we knew. I am not discounting the importance of these mythologies and icons; they are organizing principles for many communities, but they can also be used negatively. I can't go into this issue in any detail. When you are a multiethnic country, certain mythologies seem to predominate over the mythologies of other groups. It reflects the dominant ideology of any particular power. So I felt it was important to come clean about those mythologies as well. I am a product of them. When we were in the student movement we felt those things were not important and we could just throw them away. Our new mythology was socialism, but that mythology didn't originate in our culture. We threw out my father's mythology. He never had a chance to keep or, at least, look at these mythologies with knowledge and put them where they belong and then create new mythologies from experience.

Isn't that what colonialism did to us, so that we had to accept everything we were told without questioning?

Yes, that is why I gave it as much space as I did in the film. We need to look at these things because we are all products of them whether we acknowledge it or not. As long as we refuse to look at them critically and analytically, then they will continue to create all kinds of conflicts for us.

Let us deal with some of the cultural motifs in the film. There are repeated images of people in mourning, and they are dressed in white. In some African countries and in the West, black is the color of mourning. I think that many Westerners may not understand this.

It actually depends. Ethiopia is a culturally diverse nation. We have sixty languages, as many or more ethnic groups, and each ethnic group has its own customs and rituals. I am an Asmaran, one of the larger ethnic groups, and in my culture, people wear black. It's also a class issue. In the past, people used to dye white cloth black and cut off their hair, or they would wear a black dress and they would tie their *netela*, which is a large shawl, in a way that would indicate that they were in mourning. In the rural areas where they may not have black dye or the resources to buy clothes for mourning, they wear white, but they wear it in a different way. Normally, one wears the *netela* so that it falls down like a cover. When you are in mourning, the embroidered edge, which is usually black, will be pulled up and the other end will be tied around the waist. If you see any woman dressed like that, then she is in mourning. If you see a woman in mourning today she will be completely in black.

I saw you at the 1993 FESPACO and wondered if you gained any insight concerning the treatment of African issues. More specifically, where do the priorities lie and what is hoped to be achieved with African films?

The 1993 FESPACO was where I saw Raoul Peck's *Lumumba,* and that was very inspiring. I am inspired by many African films. There are so many ways that African films can be experienced. My all-time favorite African film is *Finzan,* which I consider a feminist film. I do get a lot of inspiration from them, but I don't think that African cinema as a movement and African cinema as an art have to mean the same thing. I think that there should be enough room to accommodate African cinema as an art so that people can deal with issues that aren't economic or political. As far as using African cinema as a political, social, or economic tool, I think we should focus less on the 35mm format and more on 16mm, so that we can make more films. More women need to become involved in filmmaking, because their stories are not being told. Also, young people need to be encouraged to engage in this form. Furthermore, critical studies of these films need to be more rigorous and films analyzed within the context of their production, etc. If I am going to grow as a filmmaker, then I need to hear from the scholars and from the critics. I am self-motivated and I can do what I have to, but there is a serious role for scholars and critics in this movement.

Filmography

Our Place in the Sun, 1988
As I Remember It: A Portrait of Dorothy West, 1991
Sidet: Forced Exile, 1991
Ye Wonz Maibel (Deluge), 1997

Haile Gerima (Ethiopia)

Haile Gerima is one of the best-known African filmmakers and one of the world's most creative directors. He is also probably the most radical of African filmmakers, comparable only to Ousmane Sembene of Senegal and Med Hondo of Mauritania.

Gerima was brought up in a Christian family; his father was an orthodox priest, a teacher, a historian, and a playwright. His mother taught home economics in a vocational school. While growing up, he performed frequently as a member of the itinerant theater troupe his father directed, which staged shows across the country. He was thus exposed to his father's daring and provocative ways of directing and composing music for his plays. His mother and grandmother were great storytellers, and listening to them, he acquired mastery of the legends and tales of the Ethiopian oral tradition, which was later to become the quintessence of his cinematic narrative style. This mix of parental tutelage provided Gerima with fertile ground for training and development.

However, his initiation into cinema came when he began working part-time as a ticket boy at a local movie theater. The movies he saw were foreign films of the Tarzan melodrama type and Westerns, and he vividly recollects how he and his friends of the same age group would side with the cowboys as they massacred the Indians. This was a very important development. The young man discovered the hegemonic foreign values these movies propagate while at same time these films forced him to question his own traditions—to look down on them, as it were—but also helped him to develop a deep apprehension for aspects of both traditions.

After finishing high school, Gerima went to Addis Ababa, where he studied drama. He left Ethiopia in 1967 for Chicago, where he enrolled at the Goodman School of Drama to study acting. It was there that he experienced a deep sense of estrangement and sociocultural alienation. The issues that made him uncomfortable included having to take classes to change his accent—if he was to become a "perfect" actor—and the problem of coping with growing racism in the United States. The only way he was able to deal with the political and social oppression facing him was by studying the writings of black militants of the 1960s and by identifying with African American communities; this, he says, helped him to regain his sanity and identity.

In search of a more tolerant atmosphere, in 1969 Gerima moved to the University of California, Los Angeles, to continue with the study of drama, only to find himself discontented with playing subservient roles. It was in 1970 that he discovered the motion picture as a powerful means of communication and expression and concluded that, unlike an actor in the theater, a filmmaker is more able to control whatever he or she does. The 1960s and early 1970s marked the pinnacle of awareness of revolutionary struggles for liberation all over the world. At UCLA, Gerima became acquainted with the works of Frantz Fanon, W. E. B. Du Bois, Amilcar Cabral, and Che Guevara, as well as with the emerging Third World cinema from Africa, South America, and Central America, whose structures, replete with Marxist dialectics, were channeled toward liberation. It is not surprising that in this orientation a new revolutionary thinker was emerging; Gerima's first film, *Hour Glass* (1971), made in Super-8, is audacious in its experimentation with form and content as well as the exploitation of artistic, technical, and political possibilities of the film medium. This was followed by *Child of Resistance* (1972) and *Harvest: 3,000 Years* (1974), a provocative and highly creative film shot in Ahmaric, the main Ethiopian language, at a time when the military junta was consolidating power after the overthrow of Emperor Haile Selassie. Other features made by Gerima include *Bush Mama* (1976) and *Wilmington 10–USA 10,000* (1979) a two-hour documentary on political prisoners in the United States. For this documentary, and partly in recognition of his other filmmaking endeavors, Gerima received two awards in 1979—the Freedom Journalist Award and the John Simon Guggenheim Memorial Foundation Fellowship to continue his research for future projects. He made *Ashes and Embers*, a film about a black Vietnam War veteran, in 1981, and in 1985 he made *After Winter: Sterling Brown*, a documentary that celebrates the black poet, essayist, and literary critic (the latter was funded by Howard University, where Gerima is currently a professor of film).

All of Gerima's features mentioned above, except for *Harvest: 3,000 Years*, focus on the African American experience, raising the issue of whether this filmmaker should be considered an African filmmaker or an African American filmmaker. Although both crowns could fittingly be bestowed on him, when I asked him to comment on this question of wearing two labels, his answer exemplified the typical Hailean style—he responded with a compelling and up-to-date assessment of black cinema and Diasporan connections.

Gerima's most ambitious project to date is *Sankofa*, made in 1993. This film, shot on three continents, is a compelling indictment of slavery from a Pan-Africanist perspective. In terms of innovation, marketing strategies, process of realization, and unprecedented success, *Sankofa's* record-breaking adventure has undoubtedly changed world film history. An enterprising warrior and a longtime ardent advocate of economic self-reliance, Gerima, who might as well be the Diasporan filmmaker, now heads (with his wife, Sirikiana Aina) the Sankofa Organization in Washington, D.C., which distributes African Diaspora movies on film and video and organizes film and cultural symposia and exchanges. This organization has been able to prove that black films, if well coordinated, are capable of building a profitable movie industry that does not need the backing of Hollywood and its conglomerates to survive.

Gerima granted this interview in 1997; it took place in the tranquil basement of his Washington, D.C., home, where his editing studio is located.

I would like to use this opportunity to tell you that I appreciate everything you have done for the development of African cinema and world cinema. When I was in England studying film, my intention was to become a well-known Nigerian filmmaker, but I discovered that I could not make films because of lack of money. So I understand what you are doing and the challenges of working as an independent filmmaker. You have done something that I could not do myself. How did you become interested in cinema? Could you talk about growing up and your family influences and all the things that helped you discover this wonderful medium called cinema?

I would say I had two introductions to film. In advance I have to tell you my background. My father's playwriting and directing has influenced me since I was a child. I began to do plays at an early age in high school. But that is more of an indirect influence. What I have grown to recognize as the strongest is my father's influence as a storyteller. In terms of cinema, my experience is more that of a victim of its effective imperialist venture. Cinema came to my town as an imperialist cultural manifestation that trampled over everything local. My introduction to film was more as a subjugated African amongst others than as an active participant in any of the branches of film business. So my early introduction to cinema was overpowering. I cannot call it an influence because, although I was a colonial spectator of this culture, it never encouraged me to grow up and make my own movies. Then, Africans were not encouraged to learn how to make films, for filmmaking was considered an elitist art too sophisticated for Africans. Cinema was an alien force which, I would say, made me inactive. The more I watched films, the more I withdrew from the influence of my father and that powerful local narrative style I grew up with. I became a totally colonized fixture, a disfigured obscene zombie that you can see all over Africa, where we act and imitate movies which displace our indigenous cultural heritage. Colonialism and the alien movies I watched were not positive influences that said to me, "You can make films." It was when I got to the United States to pursue theater education, which is the initial storytelling medium that I inherited from my father, family, and community, that I accidentally stumbled into filmmaking. Even when I had the opportunity to grab the camera, I did not have a mentor, until African Americans embraced and sanctioned me. When I made my early films, I was more like a migrant worker. I did not consider myself a legitimate filmmaker because it was not my tradition. I did not inherit that tradition as I had with the theater. Given the way film trickled into my life, if it had not been for the African American community, I would not have been encouraged to make films. If I had not been sanctioned by them, and made to believe that I too could make films, and if the audience had not responded in a very emotional way to my early work, I would not have pursued filmmaking.

After you made Harvest: 3,000 Years, *your other feature films focused on the African American experience. Some people see you as an African filmmaker, Ethiopian filmmaker, African American filmmaker, or, with the release of* Sankofa, *a Diasporic filmmaker. Do these labels, in light of what you mentioned about your relationship with the African American community, bother you?*

I am not an African American filmmaker. An African American filmmaker is of African descent born in the U.S. and has experienced an African American historical reality. I came to the U.S. a fully grown-up person from Ethiopia. It would be dishonest to delegitimate the historical experience of African Americans by claiming that label. The African American culture helped me to defy that colonial position and link up with my father's resistance tradition. This kind of encounter works for many people in different ways. If African American culture had not liberated me from my bondage to the colonial position, then Hollywood cinema, the Peace Corps, and all the American influences would have made me a grotesque imitation of America. Having come to America, I am indebted to the fact that African Americans made me respect myself and link up with my history of resistance. I think I began to appreciate the work of my father when I was embroiled in this culture trying to define who I am. African Americans embraced me and, in fact, made me be self-confident and realize that not only white people can claim the right to make movies. However, it would not be correct to call me an African American, because all I know of their heritage is what they taught me.

I am impressed to see that your Sankofa Organization, where you live and work, is situated right in the heart of the black community. Prominent black people, including intellectuals and businessmen, often live apart from black neighborhoods. I think they have a lot to learn from you.

For me, this is the struggle. When we made *Sankofa*, we were in a basement. We now own this modest building and some infrastructure. I have always dreamt of having a production company in the middle of the community. I wanted the community to be able to familiarize itself with our facilities and our work, and to be able to see from my perspective that cinema production and consumption should not be an abstract concept developed in a remote corner of some luxury hotel room. When you bring the community along with you and help them understand the struggle and the process of film making, you bring them along to the threshold. Failure to do so means being exiled from one's community, and when you lose your community you lose a strong base. Your community will never understand you; but if you want your film to be accountable to the community, then that community has to be part of your daily struggle. This does not mean dismissing the multiracial audience which is there to round up the figures. But to always beg for funds to produce films and not cultivate the basis for your product consumption is counterproductive. Out of this concern, I also have an office in Ethiopia and have been struggling to distribute my films there for the past five years. I have been fighting the bureaucracy there, attempting to put into effect the distribution experiments I have carried out in the U.S. It is very much connected to filmmaking.

It is unfortunate that the intelligentsia is so disconnected from the community and, therefore, lacks the power to affect that community. This is very disturbing, especially in consideration of the African American or Diaspora experience, of the way plantation masters and the slave system worked. You cannot announce the liberation of black people from the plantation owner's radio station and be heard. Even if you are telling the truth, you will be a suspect in the community.

How serious is the impact of the culture of poverty in Africa and the mortgaging of the continent's economies to the World Bank and International Monetary Fund on film production, content, and style? Some critics have charged that French filmmakers do not frequent Africa anymore to make ethnographic films because that is the focus of most francophone films funded by French agencies.

The reason is that financial aid is not usually awarded fair-mindedly. With its neo-colonial ramifications for Africa, financial assistance has found ways to implant itself in the chamber of the creative womb. Very few filmmakers admit that they do not give birth to any new ideas for a movie in a vacuum. They consider the source of the money first and operate in a creative way on the dictations of those resources for their work. It is clear that long ago, the Europeans, especially the French, understood that they did not have to physically police their colonial interests. Once they created classes of people, once they shaped the intelligentsia in their educational and cultural institutions, then they were able to make the intelligentsia respond to a predetermined colonial ideology. Filmmakers postpone the films they want to make by always addressing the issue of prominence; for example, "The French gave so-and-so movie an award and so my film has to be about the same topic." It is really that African filmmakers, due to the historical circumstances of domination and subjugation, are raped and impregnated just to make a movie. In Senegal, South Africa, Burkina Faso, and Ethiopia, every incident from customs and immigration at the airport to your hotel and home, wherever we go, is material that triggers a great many film topics; but how many of us would pursue them? As long as we incorporate colonial interests, white characters or white ideas, and exotic things about Africa into our stories, we get money to finance our movies. Even in the financing of the movie, you do not need to have white people make the judgment as to which film is to be funded. You can have a panel of neocolonized Africans that still serve the purpose of the colonizer.

I challenge the uninformed to examine the works of Med Hondo and Ousmane Sembene and compare them with the present state of affairs, where we are being bombarded with "jungle" movies. I remember a very important, well-placed Frenchman who once said to me that the first film of African cinema for him was *Visages de femmes* [Faces of women, 1985], by Désiré Ecaré, because "for the first time you people are showing us how you fuck." That is what he said! Then I said to him, "Why are you obsessed about how we fuck?" "Because," he said, "this is the first time African cinema is born for me." This means that *Black Girl* [1963], *Borom Sarret* [1966], *Soleil O* [1969], and *Peasant Letter* [1974] did not exist on his map because there was no sex or nudity in them. They were all marginal until he saw us "fuck" in *Faces of Women.* I am saying it the way he said it because it dramatizes Europe's abnormal interests and perceptions of Africa in contradistinction to our own interests.

This means to me that until African filmmakers battle the idea of national cinema policy, of production, distribution, and exhibition, individual and collective efforts will continue to be stifled. It is not enough to make a movie, but also to own a movie is part of the struggle. You do not make your face for white people to own, otherwise you remain in the plantation and slavery systems, even though you appear to be free. If I make a film about my mother, my children are going to be the inheritors of that intellectual property. I would not want Europe to own it. The new breed of filmmakers has weeded out the ideological vision that the early African filmmakers injected into the practice, which was intended to be used as a springboard toward liberation cinema. All of those contributions are now ridiculed and discouraged by the Europeans, especially the French, who are hell-bent on marginalizing all the anticolonial filmmakers of the early sixties and seventies.

What you just said about African cinema is very interesting, especially regarding the antagonistic posturings of the younger generation of African filmmakers, who seem to have forgotten that without the pioneers they would not have had any base on which to launch their careers.

They would not even have fantasized about filmmaking. The situation is pathetic, but colonialist forces encourage it. If you have noticed, people like Sembene and Med Hondo do not compromise their attack on colonialism. They always identify primitive colonialism and neocolonialism as the principal forces in the displacement of the intelligentsia itself. Even though the French, for example, used to honor these pioneer filmmakers, the filmmakers insisted on continuing the attack on colonialism and neocolonialism. The colonizers then gave up on them and began to cultivate younger filmmakers so as to displace the pioneers and make them what I term "nonexistent." The French can only tolerate one or maybe two anticolonial films from an African filmmaker; if you go against this policy, you have to be punished by being made nonexistent. They transform all the young filmmakers into mercenaries to attack every aspect of your work. In so doing, they try to make the pioneer filmmakers nonexistent in the consciousness of the society. This is a technique of sophisticated colonialism. They deny moviemakers the press, refuse to show their films, and do not properly recognize them. Not that it always matters, because I do not think that Sembene gives a damn about being honored by France. I remember Sembene once saying to, I think, a French person, "France for me is a whore. She is not my mother. I fuck her like a whore." The point I am making here is that you have very intransigent anticolonial filmmakers who are also the products of history. Like Amilcar Cabral, Samora Machel, and Kwame Nkrumah on the political diagram, Sembene and Med Hondo are the political fathers of Africa's liberation movement in cinema. To overthrow the idea of Pan-Africanism, you also have to go around and overthrow Pan-Africanist visionaries and cultural activists.

The younger generation is often given grants, which, in turn, force them to be hostile. I remember in Holland there was a fight because a younger filmmaker attacked Sembene. It is not by putting down Sembene that I become a filmmaker. It is by understanding how he showed me the possibilities of filmmaking with African characters as a legitimate venture. It is sacred ground for me. It does not mean that I worship him as the perfect human filmmaker. No. I just know that he is the person who opened the tracks and closed the holes in my consciousness and made Africans speaking their own languages exist legitimately in movies. We owe the pioneers a great deal. Disrespecting the elders at this point is tragic and, for me, unacceptable. I was born in Ethiopia and grew up respecting others. It goes back to a tragic and, I would say, cannibalistic generational contradiction interjected by colonialism, which does not want to hear its history, which is a history of absolute enslavement of the continent of Africa. This is the continuing exploitation of Africa. If the younger filmmakers were smart, instead of attacking and discrediting the pioneers they would join the anticolonial filmmakers in order to exorcize the evil of colonialism and build a better society.

A lot of the anticolonial films made by Africans are not in circulation as much as some of the new films sponsored by the French. However, critics are quick to point out that although some of these new films have dealt with specific aspects of African culture, they have been assembled in ways that negate intelligence and crucial societal meanings. Africa is a continent of fifty-four or fifty-five countries with thousands of cultures. Yet these haphazardly assembled images, distributed all over, are used to study African cultures in generalized terms. Are the filmmakers not perpetuating the colonial syndrome themselves?

In the U.S., California Newsreel is not in distribution in order to advance African cinema or African culture. It is a distribution arrangement financed by the Rockefeller

Foundation to preempt the challenge of normal distribution. America and Europe have total domination over distribution in Africa. It is ironic, because in their countries we have no right to make normal films because we do not come from the Greco-Roman/Anglo cultural base of cinematic expression. The problem starts in Africa, where we do not have a distribution policy or right in our own countries. There are no legitimate institutions that take our films to be distributed tricontinentally like normal films. What you have here in the United States is a false distribution arrangement whereby African films can be checked out of libraries for free and watched. To whose benefit? I do believe that African culture in film should not be made to satisfy only the exotic curiosity of the developed countries. We are not exotic fixtures. Our cultures have values. Our intellectual property has value. We need to unleash institutions to defend and restore those traditions. California Newsreel is a token organization that presents African cinema for free. Most of the filmmakers are exploited. They are not rewarded with standard distribution payment. You have to first look at it from that perspective and then go beyond and examine the types of films the organization acquires for distribution, because I think Europe and America, especially Europe, interfere in production processes. They selectively decide on the kind of movies that are to be made.

Furthermore, how then can it be said that African filmmakers are organized when the filmmakers have become attention seekers? They are not contemplating their goals, nor configuring the rights to defend our work as normal cinema. There is no reason why Americans should say to me, "I want to show your film to introduce your work to Americans." I do not want anyone to introduce my work to Americans. Africa has been introduced to America from the day we came into contact with Europe, but it was for free. All the resources I have and all the resources Africa has are free for them, and everything Europe and America offer I have to pay for. This unequal transaction in the cultural, economic, and political spheres is devastating. This is where neocolonialism will not allow us any influence on our own destiny. So California Newsreel is an exploiter of African cinema. They are welfare workers pushing to make African cinema a welfare cultural diet to be given free of charge to Americans.

Actually, you have redefined the history of cinema, especially with this question of distribution. Do you think you have proven that alternative marketing or distribution methods can be put to the black filmmaker's advantage? Do you think this will work to rectify the situation in Africa? Could this method have worked for a nonhistorical film that is not about slavery like Sankofa? *Could it have received the support* Sankofa *has received from the black community?*

If people tracked my history from early times, they would see that my interest has always been to cultivate the community and be accountable to them. I am the kind of filmmaker who says, "I do not have to politically advance your theory Mr. African president or African intelligentsia or black people, but to make the movie I want to make. I have the right to make movies, even if it does not live up to your expectations. The fact that I am tangling with the memory of our people should not be your responsibility." When it comes to people of African descent, we do not realize, however critical the manifestation of culture is, that our survival depends on it. You do not get empowered just because you have money or real estate. You are also empowered when you are culturally restored to your human essence, when you look at the world from your own vantage point. To recall Walter Rodney, Africa has been derailed from its historical track since we came in contact with Europe. No civilization is to emanate from our deeds without restoring our derailed identity. We have to reconstruct the memory and use it as a forward movement. Even when they are bitterly critical in their representation of society, the producers of culture are still very important for the survival of generations and for the transmission of information. People of African descent from here to Africa who have money are feudal. They do not understand the implications of culture in their economic endeavors. They feel it is simply a matter of amassing money or material possessions. Likewise, we import exhibitory instruments to show Europe to our children and we raise them by having them watch *Sesame Street*, a product of an alien culture. This makes them lose our heritage. Here is an important factor of displacement, and nobody seems to care.

Having said that, if you look pragmatically at, for example, Ousmane Sembene or Ola Balogun films, they have audiences all over the Black Diaspora because, like me, Brazilians, Jamaicans, South Africans, blacks in Europe, and so forth are hungry for their images. To normalize ourselves, we want to see our own images, but distribution and institutional infrastructures are not in place to make those images of reality available. We have a major market that is unrealized by the intelligentsia, such as the African MBAs who do not understand the power of investments. African descendants all over the Diaspora need not work for Sony, Columbia Pictures, and Metro-Goldwyn-Mayer. They can start their own companies to tap the unexplored market of black people. This is what we proved with *Sankofa*. There are Brazilians who came to take the film to Brazil. Ghanaians were equally hungry for *Sankofa*, as were African Americans. Ordinary community people in Washington, D.C., black people—not rich black people but ordinary black people—put us on the map. They enabled me to make prints and to rent a theater, and they launched me into the universal realization of black cultural need. The appetite of black people is what we discovered in our marketing experiment. This did not only start with *Sankofa*. When I started *Child of Resistance, Bush Mama, Harvest*—when you look at all my films—the predominant money source that came for them, all the way to *Ashes and Embers*, was money recuperated by and through the films. I have always wanted my films to make money to be used to make another movie. In principle, that is also why I teach; I do not want to spend the money my films make on family maintenance, even though teaching takes too much of my filmmaking time. This is to say that the seed money invested in *Sankofa* came from my other films.

How did I make my earlier films? I did gardening and washed dishes to finance them. I have gotten several grants, but they were not decisive in the making of the movies. I always wanted to free myself from grant begging to move toward recycling personal resources. I try to make all my films have a built-in obligation to perpetrate the making of more films. With *Sankofa* we are closer to that realization.

Dependency, on the other hand, basically impacts on the artists and the common people who consume commodities manufactured outside of the community or from businesses transacted in a lopsided way. It is normal, for example, for a Pole to own an African painting, but for all African paintings to be owned by Europeans is surreal. If you look at the African American experience, all their music, their creative and intellectual property, is owned, patented, and copyrighted by white people. That is not normal. When all the music of your culture is owned by somebody else, that says you are a slave, a cotton picker, a daily laborer. But to me, what is normal is to own your own culture. Black kids are born into a mortgaged culture, and the cycle will never be broken until they realize they have to break out of dependency. But to have independence purely as an idea owned and copyrighted by European descendants perpetuates that unequal relationship in which we have found ourselves since we came into contact with Europe. It takes us back to the fifteenth century, when Europeans defined the rules of the game.

They still define the rules to this very day. Take, for example, FESPACO, which stands to be taken over by France.

FESPACO has always been a francophone affair. I spoke to President Thomas Sankara in front of Sembene and a lot of people, and complained that FESPACO, though a Pan-African concept, is too French. I called it a francophone film festival, because it fails to recognize the ideas and philosophy of Pan-Africanism. It only recognizes the linguistic configurations of the French colonial orbit. In so doing, it is a cultural manifestation in Africa by Africans slanted toward France. FESPACO would die if France did not give it money or recognize it for one day. I told Sankara when he was worrying that the Senegalese would try to move FESPACO to Dakar, that if it goes, it is because francophone domination killed it. And that, furthermore, it risks killing itself because the francophone cultural alliance with France would expedite its death.

I was on a jury once at FESPACO in 1983 with a Frenchman whose name I cannot remember, and he bragged about how he started FESPACO. The point is that even though its origin is alien, I think African filmmakers have tried and failed to control and liberate it from the francophone curse. In the process however, the neocolonial bureaucratic sector won, and they have since succeeded in making it a mediocre imitation of Cannes in the middle of the desert. For me FESPACO has lost its purpose. As I see it, to liberate FESPACO is the most impossible task.

When was the last time you went to FESPACO?

I have not been there since 1987. I never went after Captain Sankara was assassinated.

You have criticized Hollywood and some black films for, as you put it, "defocusing our mental consciousness." You have also noted that Hollywood backs young blacks to make films that do not raise consciousness. Is this not comparable with most francophone films funded by the French, which are criticized for lack of imagination?

Oh yes. In fact, the metaphor for how I look at Africa and Europe is how we operate here in the United States. America is the place to study the workings of race, to examine how it continues to maintain its powerful position and how it manipulates the black community. In the case of young filmmakers, it is Hollywood that decides who they are. You see the same thing happening in francophone Africa, where desperate young people who never contemplated the complex nature of Africa with any sincerity are manipulated. They come out of a fantasy and fall into the hands and bosoms of colonial power structures that give them money, not because of their credentials, but for what they can do in the service of colonialism. There are, as well, local colonial situations in the United States in operation to disenfranchise militant filmmakers. They use this mechanism to sponsor desperate filmmakers and make them operate as neocolonial mercenaries. Elderly white men in Hollywood who control the industry select the new breed of filmmakers and dictate to them the content of the films they should make. In these films we find the disfiguring images of a film culture that reduces the struggle of African Americans to a caricature. It serves a purpose in the larger struggle for Hollywood, an industry that claims to be liberal, but which has a bad history in terms of race and how they represent African descendants and Native Americans. The use of desperate young filmmakers to subvert genuine struggles also serves to absolve their guilty consciences.

I am not here saying that there are no desperate white filmmakers out there, but if you look at the range of white films that are made yearly, they represent a particular pattern of filmmaking. They may not be masterpieces of expression, but they mirror a specific ideology. In black cinema, by and large, we are subjected to viewing black life as if it were the most irredeemable "hood" movie. There is no variety and there are no choices for comparison in terms of how the experiences of black people are depicted. In fact, the full spectrum of human life in black communities has never been a concern for Hollywood films. To maintain this hegemonic tradition, the older black filmmakers who make socially relevant films must be displaced through the use of young people who do not care if they are paid so long as they have the opportunity to make a film.

I am not surprised about what you just said because I talked with a young African filmmaker recently in New York City about distribution. I asked how his two films acquired by California Newsreel were doing. He said that he tried his hand at distribution, and that the difficulties he encountered made him decide that he cannot be part of the distribution mechanism. He made it clear he did not care how his films are distributed and who distributes them. I did not quite understand why he would say he does not care if his films made money or not.

This is one of the problems of African filmmakers. Our problem is that we want the limelight but do not want to confront the difficult issues. For example, I am the wrong person to be in the film distribution business, but I am stubborn also. I just do not agree with making a film like *Sankofa* and giving it to a white distributor. It does not look right in terms of the intent and content of that film. I believe African filmmakers and African communities must work together to invent and create distribution cartels. We must struggle to do it because if you do not master distribution tactics, you will kill your own film, which I have done on many occasions. But I prefer killing my own films to enslaving them just to have them shown. A lot of African filmmakers need to grow out of their exhibitionist mode, out of being fixtures at festivals. We are the bums of film festivals. Most often we look bad. Sembene once said that we are beyond airplane tickets, free hotels, and food. Our films have to mean more than food and hotel rooms. We have to have normal distribution and exposure. African filmmakers have to realize that there is a major, more concrete, prouder way of making films. We do not have to look like the bums and beggars of the town.

How many white people in Hollywood hide from black filmmakers? When their presence is announced the reaction is usually "Here they come again asking for money; hide." How many of us are raped and sexually exploited to make our movies? A lot of African filmmakers are sexually abused. That should be their story. They would tell it best, and it would say a lot about what is happening to African cinema.

As a way to rectify these aberrancies, do you have the intention of distributing some "good" African films? Why are Heritage . . . Africa *and* Sarraounia *not distributed in the United States?*

We have *Sarraounia,* but the problem with where we are is that we are trying to take more films into video distribution. We need capital, but banks are hostile toward us by and large, even though we proved with *Sankofa* the ability of our vision to turn adversity into financial success. Although a lot of filmmakers want us to take their films, we do not have the finances to produce prints and videos for distribution. We have *Sarraounia,* and since Med Hondo films are like my films in content, we need to make video transfers and manufacture jackets to put them out in distribution. We are now trying out pay television, and as a limited experiment, we aired *Sarraounia* and *Sankofa* in Baltimore. Actually, our biggest thing here in the Sankofa Organization is video distribution. With the resources from *Sankofa,* I was able to put most of my films into video. Blockbuster said they did not have the clientele for our films, so we contacted African American bookstores across the country to create our own "Blockbuster," our own distribution outlet. Always, when they say no to equal exchange, we start our own. That has been my policy. When Hollywood and the conglomerates say no to distribution, we distribute the films ourselves. Now we have a big distribution plan. We distribute through the Internet, and African American bookstores serve as outlets for our videos, and, eventually we will have films like *Sarraounia* in our store/showroom here in Washington, D.C. The goal is to perpetuate the distribution technique that we learned from *Sankofa*. However, our ability is always arrested by the absence of capital—a resource that is readily available to many white people.

Are you thinking of applying for funds from the Rockefeller or Ford Foundation?

No, we told them when they initially came to us that we were not interested in presenting African cinema free to Americans. We do not want to be conduits to that culture of valuelessness. All the time, space and products in the United States are quantified as material reality. All human beings' time in this capitalist society is transacted within the terms of capital and finance. African filmmakers do not need free distribution but that which is profoundly built on the idea of returning revenue to African filmmakers in order to enable them to make second, third, and more films. That is how Hollywood subsists. They make their own movies by assigning a value to their films. For us to go through so much for our films and then have them in a very flimsy way available to Americans to check out from libraries for free is wrong. But a lot of our filmmakers are desperate, and the problems should also be understood from that perspective. You have to realize also that if the French produced your movie and you did not attach any monetary value to it, you can give it to California Newsreel for ten thousand dollars and be satisfied. But that does not make you an independent filmmaker.

Exactly! That is why Haile Gerima, Med Hondo, and Kwaw Ansah are exemplary. Ansah, for example, refused to give away Heritage . . . Africa *for free.*

He is right. That is what I admire about Kwaw Ansah. He tries to get value back. A lot of people try to besmirch his name. I believe his position is 100 percent correct. Med is 100 percent correct. People have to have value. You cannot throw our culture around and make us look like disgraced homeless filmmakers.

You consider Sankofa *to be "a turning point and amalgamation of everything you have done to date."*

In aesthetic terms; I am talking about the language, where I have always felt, again stubbornly, that it is not enough to make films, but that you also have to defend your accent as a filmmaker. Filmmaking is not "monkey see, monkey do." It is about recognizing a technology and then harnessing the power of that technology to accommodate and effectively transmit one's identity, culture, and language. I know from the panels that I have been on that many African filmmakers and critics think that the content is what determines African cinema. I disagree with that. I think we must advance beyond that, because content and theme are universal. We will not invent a new theme in the world. All human beings, thematically, are one people, but the problem is how to fit a theme to a particular cultural identity and psychological makeup. What makes it challenging is the power of the medium. Once this power is recognized, then it is possible to move to reinforce it with our own accents. I feel it is not the actual dialogue, but our thought system that is critical.

Images are formed and they are particular and cultural. These images have to find their ways into our cinema. Our metaphors and paradigms come out of these images to begin with; they come out of a thought system that uniquely reflects our diverse cultural identities that originate in Africa. All the different parts of Africa have their thought systems and value systems. There are images that juxtapose and empower these value systems in the form of metaphor, allegory, and symbolism. We must reinforce them. We cannot say, "If African cinema is to speak like Europeans, if it is going to be like a French cinema, let the French make the film." They have the technology, but let us not bother them. For me, what makes it challenging is the fact that a Frenchman will never make the movies that I make. How my accent registers in the commentary I make about hunger, love, and so forth will be totally different.

If I make a movie it is because I also want to empower my voice. Our historic task, therefore, is to invent our own cinema. In fact, we do not need to invent African cinema, since it has existed for thirty-five to forty years. All we have to do is to contribute our share, irrespective of how imperfect it may be. I do not think, given the confusion in African film practice, that there will automatically be what might be termed a pure African cinema. There will be experiments and explorations, but we have the right and a historic responsibility to design and forge our cinematic language or languages.

But can there be an African film language? What criteria define your own film language?

When we make a film from our village vantage point, and if it is honest, though aesthetically set in my village, its honest expression will enable it to have a home, say, in Nigeria. If I am dishonest in my village, then my story has no place in the world. But if we honestly and particularly express ourselves as from the village we come from, then our narrative, thematically, can be embellished with an automatic universality. Our accent starts to mushroom on the basis of this affinity. Both in my dreams and fantasies, I know I have a closer logical affinity in my image making to most parts of Africa. Most of our cultural foundations come from a common basis. Our languages arise out of some common paradigms and logic. Mozambicans have seen *Harvest: 3,000 Years* and have had no problems with it. I believe that if we have the right to make films as we should, there will be an automatic universal understanding of those products. But if we try to address the world with this false notion of having to make films like Hollywood and Paris, it will go nowhere and prove nothing. That is a critical issue. I cannot see an African cinema without a particular African cinematic language emerging also.

In the exploration of African film language, would it be possible to consider patterns of indigenous storytelling, such as the techniques of the oral tradition, and how they could be used to subvert the conventions of dominant cinema?

When you are miseducated or schizophrenically existing as half French, half black, or half Burkinabe or half Senegalese, you must first exorcize those evil spirits. The dishonesty about African cinema is that the filmmakers, from North to South, do not turn the camera on themselves. They always make a film about something else. We are good at looking at the dirt of other people, the dirt of a community, such as how polygamous and fundamentalist Africa is. We seem to make movies for other people—to preach to convert—and that has created filmmakers that are like arrogant landlords sitting on the pinnacle of their power. Some of them pose as if they are judges and magistrates, above the cause, above the issue. They criticize the world, but they are the sexist ones; they talk about racism, but they crave white women—they crave them not because they love them as people but because they crave whiteness. Because African filmmakers abnormally crave white women, I think that most of them should be in the insane asylum. If their love was in the normal mode of knowing and loving a person, race would be irrelevant. But we have not even made movies about our obsession with whiteness; we accept this illness as normal, and continue to point our big magnifying lenses on African societies, on polygamy, excision/circumcision, bureaucracy, feudalism, and militarism. Rarely do we turn the camera toward our own contradictions. For me, to expose others' contradictions and not work on your own contradictions as an artist stops one from reaching the moment of exorcism, healing, and, thus, transformation.

Colonialism, for example, is not fully understood by the filmmakers because they have never examined their own neocolonial situations and obsessive compulsions. Maybe it does not matter, since Africans rarely see their films anyway. They are shown in Paris for the French or for the interracial groups somewhere in Holland. But this is not how to mobilize black societies and get necessary feedback from them. Basically, what you have now is a cinema that has forgotten its agenda and the processes we must undergo in order to be healed. Rarely do people know this, but for me, most of the films I have made have a lot to do with liberating me first, before anyone else. When I made *Sankofa*, I never thought people would line up to see it. I did not even care if they lined up or not. All I did was to make the film and satisfy my own appetite for specific subject matter, because I see myself in the contradictions. I might dress it up in an era or in some characters, but I am in there. As long as the process of filmmaking helps to free me, I am fine with it, even if it does not help anyone else.

So if we do not know ourselves, how do we know the riches and heritage of our parents and our ancestors? One of the disfiguring aspects of colonialism is that the minute it grabs you, it begins to "body snatch" you and put its tentacles all over your brain. When this happens, the first few people you look down on are those who look like you. You begin to see that your friends are beneath you. Anybody who crosses your path is beneath you. You even succumb to the idea that your parents are bare-foot, backward people, but I will tell you that my father in his bare feet was more civilized than many Americans I now know. He was literally the Shakespeare of my village. He wrote epic plays. But when American colonialism grabbed me, the first person that was dwarfed was my father. I began to disrespect him and thought his writings were beneath those of Europe and Shakespeare. I was quick to accept Shakespeare, Doris Day, and John Wayne rather than my father.

Similarly, I hated my grandmother's folkloric tales that she used to tell me around the fire. They looked uncivilized and backward, and instead I preferred the John Wayne character that kills numerous Indians. I identified with the white world; I was hijacked by European and American culture. How could I have respected the oral tradition of my people when they are backward and uncivilized? That is what the literary masters told me. The texts subliminally whispered into my ears that my people are backward and uncivilized. How then could I have tapped into the aesthetics of oral tradition? I did not have the wisdom or the natural generational transaction right. When an African is intercepted by European culture, he is being, literally, mentally hijacked. I am not trying to romanticize the transactional relationships of generations. There is always the old denying the young, the young denouncing the old, but it is in the process of transactional contradictions that we invent and are influenced by our logic, our thought processes, and our stories.

If you are an African filmmaker hijacked by Europe, you no longer have any respect for oral tradition, no time to study the speech patterns of our people anymore, and you forget their thought systems. Filmmakers are forced to look down upon the traditions they come from; they are supposed to study Orson Welles, Truffaut, Godard, Fellini, Shakespeare, and Molière. If you turn down this manner of assimilation, you are made to feel inferior, even if there is no ideological, cultural, and aesthetic connection with those people you are expected to imitate. You are respected only when you have been completely assimilated. Now silence drops, but there were violent ruptures in our communities when colonialism grabbed African children. To fix and solder the fiber of this disconnected umbilical cord, which has direct implications for culture, echoes a different kind of rebirth, which is needed for one to begin to tap into the aesthetics of oral tradition, metaphors, and symbolisms. How many African filmmakers study the masks of Africa today? Eisenstein studied and utilized Japanese masks to empower his own cinematic identity. How many filmmakers know the artistic patterns of the continent of Africa? How many of us know Cameroonian art? How many Cameroon filmmakers think they have a responsibility to study the psychological logic of color in African cinema? What do we mean by red? What is the implication of green? What are the rituals that directly implicate cinematic ideas? We are too busy studying European and American cinemas. When Africans do not go to see our movies, we blame them for not understanding them. I think that Africans are saying, "Look, if you are going to make stupid awkward movies like white people, then we prefer to see white films." But the moment Africans recognize their true selves in a movie, no matter how aesthetically imperfect that film may be, they are happy to embrace it. That is what happened with *Sankofa*.

In your films, you are always concerned with foregrounding African and black subject positions and with addressing the issues of oppression, resistance, and self-affirmation. Why do themes of struggle and liberation dominate your films?

There are many angles to this commitment, but I am trying to make people realize that I am not doing missionary work of any type. I have my own interest, and that is to cultivate a society where children of all ages, classes, and races have the right to express themselves. In a society such as ours they have no hopes. I have an automatic affinity—just on the basis of my own oppression as a filmmaker—with people who are economically or politically disadvantaged and do not have the power to interpret history and to ascertain their own humanity on this planet. In my capacity as a professor and filmmaker, to compare myself with people who need bread and shelter might sound obscene, but somehow I have rationalized my needs, my exclusion, as the cause of my perpetual gravitation toward marginalized peoples. On many levels, it is my own personal interest as a filmmaker, and my position in history, to advocate rights and equality. The fact, though, is that I am excluded from the power structure because I am not white

Your position echoes the philosophies expounded by Third Cinema exponents of the 1960s and 1970s. You made Harvest: 3,000 Years *during that time. Do you still subscribe to the idea that film structure should be combative and used as a political weapon à la Third Cinema ideology?*

I was in film school at the time when the African, South, Central, and Latin American cinemas as well as Cuban cinema were emerging. I was certainly affected, because they did represent, with all their imperfections, the rage that comes out of being oppressed and marginalized. I had a great affinity toward Latin American, Cuban, and African cinema. At the same time, Third Cinema found itself in the universities, actually in a state of siege, abducted and held hostage for academic exercise, its meaning and purpose quickly compromised. But the way I understood it, Third Cinema was to be placed at the advantage of the struggling oppressed peoples; it was to be an activist cinema, and also a cinema of indigenous, dramaturgical origins. It was trying to forge and transform itself into a viable cinematic culture. However, in the 1980s and 1990s it became an exotic paradigm infrequently recalled in limited university curricula. And so also its historic mission to activate the audience and forge a new cinematic language became defused.

In fact, Third Cinema did change film history. Some of us cannot teach film history without recalling Third Cinema. But now, it seems like nobody cares about it anymore. Also referring to African film practice, now people are rebelling against all that the pioneers initiated. What is the direction of African cinema? Is African cinema at the crossroads?

Lazy people have not thought of Third Cinema as a good cinema because it did not digest well with noninnovative cinema. Mediocre cinema found itself in a dominant position and decreed that the ultimate purpose of cinema should be entertainment. They took the struggle of a people and brought it into the establishment, and the establishment as we know it is a neocolonial establishment. Colonialism did not allow our own establishments such as Pan-Africanism and the Organization of African Unity to be institutionalized, in part because they originate from African intellectual thought. Europe always discouraged this self-reliant mode of thinking and promoted instead African imitation of Western ways. Hence on the cultural level it becomes apparent that most of the people that we parade as filmmakers, including the intelligentsia, like to go the easy way because they have embraced miseducation and imitation, the ways white people do their things. This is why I refer to their films as "imitation cinema," and that is killing African cinema. Innovative cinema demands imagination and new relationships, not only because we want to be different, but also because we want to liberate ourselves from the conditions in which we find ourselves. A built-in aspect of Third Cinema is the realization of the need to create new human relationships based on criteria other than exploitation.

If we make a film based on a love story, for example, the purpose of such a story in Third Cinema is not primarily to entertain people, but to change our deformed relationship with love, desire, and lust. Filmmakers who found these principles too challenging opted for the easier way—to awkwardly imitate Hollywood cinema and pretend to be filmmakers. In innovative cinema, we are expected to be governed by the past and the complications of the present; and to forge the vision of the future, producers of culture are supposed to create new relationships between generations of people and men and women of all ethnic divisions. When you look at the ethnic problem of Africa itself, where does it point beyond the workings of neocolonialism? It puts the contradictions right at the doorstep of the incarcerated or castrated intelligentsia. So the failure of Africans, for example, to prevent the genocide in Rwanda and the other atrocities in many African countries, including Liberia, is a direct result of the bankruptcy of the African intelligentsia.

With the question of film appreciation, I think one of the good things that Third Cinema did was to initiate a new brand of criticism and theory that takes into consideration the cultural and political specificities of the producing nations. Do you think African critics have a role, in the same way that African or black audiences have a role, together with the filmmaker in developing a viable African cinema?

Not when African critics are, for example, clones of the Eurocentric traditional order of criticism, because a new relationship does not only point the finger at objects of change, but also at the self who also should be in the process of individual transformation.

We have to make changes in this society because it is very hostile toward our humanity. If that is the case, and is the reason why we make movies outside of the mainstream, then we cannot imitate the establishment and claim to be transformers and arbiters of change. If the critic is in the Eurocentric tradition—i.e., a commentator upon the cultural product for the sake of just commenting—he is simply spurious. But if the critic engages in an activist role, then that individual is participating in the struggle as a warrior and not as an academic politician or pseudoscholar who exploits black political movements for personal gain and the limelight via newspapers and television. If we are unable to construct a cinema and cultivate new relationships, then all of us have to commit suicide for accepting tainted credentials, titles and honors bestowed on us as a result of the miseducation programs we have been subjected to for years. My appeal to them is to join in the struggle with clear consciences, for the society you are about to change belongs to you and not to the establishment that you sometimes allude to as yours. I think that this is the only way that the activist critic will contribute to advancing our goals, not only as a mediator between the activist filmmaker and the audience, but as an activist and progressive participant in a new cinematic order, including ideology and language.

I think we are beginning to see light in African film criticism, because a lot of the "mainstream" critics are now attacking some of the Africanist critics for proposing what is termed an "African-centered criticism."

Now, that is a power struggle. Those critics are in a very precarious position. Cinematic movements invented the African critics. Sometimes they forget that cinema created them and that they did not create the cinema. African filmmakers, the diligent die-hard filmmakers, created the base for African film criticism. It is not like in Europe, where a mutual procreation took place. For a long time after African cinema came into the picture, most of the critics were Africanists of European extraction, such as those in *Le Monde* in France and all the way to *Cineaste* in the United States. They were the "Columbus-discovered" African cinema group. Then came Africans in the image of Teshome Gabriel and others, who confiscated criticism from white people. That is the power struggle. They used our political struggle as a slogan to intimidate and relegate white critics from African cinema. Then, finally, the reality sets in: because African critics have never made a fundamental link with the African audience and African filmmakers, because they remained in university fortresses, they did not think the day would come when white Africanists would threaten their positions. While we cannot assess the effects on African cinema, the truth is that the white establishment is bent on hijacking African film discourse, and that means that jobs are at stake. This is a serious issue whose impact people try to conceal. Sometimes we exploit the struggle for personal uses, forgetting the larger consequences.

It is a chic thing to have African cinema. I have lectured all over this country and in Europe and concluded that to them African cinema is an exotic dish that exists as a side order and not the entrée. Even for that, Africans and African descendants are being displaced by whites, because they have more power to publish what they want to publish. These Africans and African descendants work in universities as nomads, like I do at Howard University, because we have never put in a cent for the establishment of an institution. But whites understand the situation differently. With the Diasporan Africans making their African sentiment a primary point of struggle, whites are beginning to make an inroad to take over this market with white-established trust funds and endowments; they use whiteness as power to preempt African descendants. In England, the British Film Institute recently closed down a whole Black Diaspora media division and terminated the appointment of June Givanni. When blacks enjoy a period of acceptance, they do not know that they are nurturing white cadres. This is historically the situation African intellectuals have always faced. They have always nurtured white cadres to take over their own jobs.

Yes, we know those problems exist and it is not getting any better.

But you see it is Africans debating with stronger adversaries who control the overpowering white establishment. When I went to film school at UCLA, the nonwhites were the only ones who had no bank accounts, no tradition, no legacy, no inheritance, no trust funds. Even the stupidest white kid who had the illusion of being a good filmmaker had more economic power to back up his aspiration than any of the nonwhites. The point I am making here is that it was predestined for African intellectuals in black film criticism to be armchair critics relegated to the universities, and that only brings their destruction. They have always come into these universities through the struggle of the black community, people who relentlessly argued for diversity and expansion of the curricula. Once they are put into those positions because of the community's pressure, then the establishment uses this person's presence as a window dressing and as an opportunity to alienate the people who made it possible to implement tokens of diversification. In the process, we find ourselves isolated from the people who brought us to power. To make it worse, it puts us in the precarious position of needing to train the white people who will eventually displace us. This is the cycle of power struggle amongst the upper mobile black intelligentsia and white power structures. It is very well-known here and it is now becoming a big issue in South Africa.

Black South Africans are now realizing that white liberals did not mean that they would sacrifice their jobs for the liberation of black people. They just meant that blacks could be free but not for them to come after their jobs. With the arrival of black filmmakers, white South African filmmakers now feel threatened and intimidated. Whites want to continue running the show in distribution, film and television broadcasting, and to continue making reductionist films like Doris Day speaking Zulu for the natives. Before the crushing of apartheid, whites never thought that blacks would one day come asking for the position of general manager. They never suspected there would be the kind of changes taking place in that country now, and now they are talking about reverse racism. They are talking about affirmative action, which they never allowed to exist during the apartheid era. The whites subjugated blacks and denied them education and now complain about black incompetence. I am trying to bring this whole ideological discussion to the full attention of the black film critic. If the black film critic is in activism with the rest of us, then that individual should not be commenting only on the finished products but should be equally concerned about why we Africans do not have the finances, technology, and a cultural/cinema policy. The film critic should also be concerned with why we have reactionary governments and all the other obstacles that keep us from being productive.

That's right. That is why I am doing this book—to give opportunity to twenty African filmmakers to discuss the varied problems in the African film industry.

For me, that is the key, otherwise the system, the contradictions we face are very oppressive. Regarding problems of production, distribution, exhibition, etc., we do not really need commentators. We need activist participants in the reproduction and in guaranteeing some sense of continuity for our cultural expressions.

Let's discuss film structure. Your films exhibit sophisticated structures with complex stories. How do you approach researching your films?

I would think my films are imperfectly structured because of the problem of dealing with the medium's complexity. An African filmmaker or a nonwhite filmmaker who does not inherit the legacy of filmmaking from his or her community has two responsibilities. One is identifying, understanding, and streamlining the technology of cinema to submit to our culture. That means that I have a concrete culture and that I have to know how to subvert the conventions of the dominant cinema in order to respond to the needs of my culture. With historical circumstances of this kind, the homework of a person like me is to understand the intricacies of the medium. That means understanding the history of this medium and the different experiences it has gone through in different parts of the world. It is especially important for me to understand that cinema is not a neutral medium, nor is it a universal medium. It is a highly particularized medium with an ability to introduce false universalities. I am referring to the industry that I am immediately confronted with, the Hollywood industry and the formula it unleashed, where people no longer know how scriptwriting came to be and how it has been formalized and the origins of this formalization over the years. We would want to know how it developed from the European theater and the role European theater played as it came in contact with the cinema. All of this is important information for an African or nonwhite filmmaker because understanding the history of the industry, the technology, and the way it has been used in Eurocentric forms is key. To study the technology, there are scientific features—the optics, the light, the measurements of lights, etc., but the application of these technical and scientific principles have cultural, ideological, and identity-determining implications. It is important that we understand how Americans and Europeans utilized this weapon to advance their culture and indoctrinate other people.

The other issue that is important for me is my own culture, where I come from in Ethiopia, and the kind of plays my father, my teachers, and I used to write and perform. Above and beyond my grandmother and the stories she told around the fire, all of these are important studies for me as a filmmaker. On one hand, cinema is a new technology, one hundred years old—still new in comparison with art and theater; but at the same time, cinematic storytelling is informed by technological devices. Storytelling is not new; it is an old convention. All societies have always told stories, but how my people told their stories is important for me. All of this homework culminates in how I practice cinema when the opportunity affords it. The structure of film is important to me, for I believe that our cultural nuances are not limited to the shooting of the film. When we shoot, the way the characters relate and especially how the script is organized, and all the other necessary things we do, are important to us, because we never submit to any formula. Formula for Hollywood is a crucial buzzword for monopoly and also a strategy for exploitation. They opted for an easy way that exemplifies the three-act play, for instance. It is Aristotelian, it is neotraditional to their theatrical legacy.

In the African context, we tell stories in interesting ways, which reflect our system of thought and values. The way we make metaphoric judgments and value fixations comes out of those traditions. The ways we use our voices, our movements, our actions, the physical nuances we detect to unravel guilt, shame, love, and hate are all important codes. When they are woven into the script and subsequently into the shooting you are halfway done, but it does not die there. How you structure a story to reflect these concerns poses another challenge. I think it is the wrong way to start when an African filmmaker or any nonwhite filmmaker says, "Film is told this way, therefore I tell my story like this." We should always be saying to ourselves, "How am I going to tell my story in the most comfortable way to me?" because every time one tells a story, if it is comfortable to the individual, then he or she is closer to telling the story. The judgments of white professors at white universities trying to change your way of telling stories is bad teaching. They should recognize your culture first, and then show you the techniques and filmmaking procedure. But because we do go to Paris, Russia, and America to study film, they teach us as if we all belong to the same culture. From the earliest we have to battle to sustain our ways of telling our stories while we are on a mission to learn how to use the medium.

Is this not the reason why, for instance, people like Ousmane Sembene, Med Hondo, and you, even though your narrative structures differ from each other's, all claim that your styles are indebted to the oral tradition? And that refers specifically to those cultural codes and backgrounds that you just referenced. Can oral tradition now be considered the quintessence of African cinema?

I have a problem with the concept because I inherited both oral and written traditions. In Africa, there are places where the written language is as developed as the oral literature. They both echo in my head. How they come out, I do not want to claim. This is part of the problem with African filmmakers that I do not identify with. I do not think we should claim the success of our experiment in cinema or the success of our narrative. The community should tell us we are getting closer to the perfect journey. Imperfect or not, I know that in my film, my accent is strong and always insists that I survive. It is an imperfect trickling of our identity, which is visible, I think. But I can see in many African films, among those that could be classified as innovative cinema, that the filmmakers are genuinely trying to do something. I see in them the African accent exemplifying what I call the "original temperament of a village," whether it is oral or written. I see the African logic taking a frontal position in the narrative structure of many of the films.

I have also seen many films which their directors claimed to be original but which are more French than African. I have seen many francophone films that are basically French in their psyche, where even their worldview is French. These films are, however, interpreted as African because the events are staged in African huts, jungles, and deserts, with black people in them. We have to challenge ourselves to go beyond that kind of image construction. I will not even attempt to analyze my films. I will leave that to society, or to a critic who has the audacity to go and study my father's work and come back at me to find out who the hell I am, and where my narrative style originates. I am trying to link up with something that is echoing in my head. It is an echo and does not have a material name yet, but I know I am at more peace with myself than many restless African filmmakers even though I have made only a few films. I have always made it a priority that what is echoing in my head has a firsthand influence in how I structure a film. I notice the glimpses of things trying to come out in my work. They imperfectly make entries here and there, but not necessarily in absolute terms. I would not speak absolutely.

Another problem with African cinema is that of casting. How do you select your actors?

If the professional actor is traditional, in the terms we used when we talked about the critic, I like to use them. But if the professional actor is starstruck, Hollywood influenced with the mystique of what stars are supposed to look like, I have no patience for that. I prefer noncontaminated original community people. Many actors would like to do parts with me; however, the state of mind of the person must be relevant to my work. If they believe they are stars, they are the last people in my movies, because that is an insane asylum case, not an art case. In filmmaking one needs sober, awakened normal human beings, not crazy people, because before an African filmmaker begins his film he has already inherited crazy circumstances with the lack of finances and infrastructures. I prefer nonactors to Eurocentricized contaminated actors. But at the same time, I would use professional actors who have integrity in their work and who are more concerned about acting than the glamour and limelight. I know how to take nonactors and train them in the process to act for me in the parts. I do not know what they do beyond their working for me, but I remember that during the making of *Bush Mama* I experimented with the use of both professional and nonprofessional actors. In *Harvest*, I mixed a few professional actors with many nonprofessionals, peasants who did not even know acting, but who I had to take through some communications in order for them to understand what was already there in them.

More important than the question of professional or nonprofessional actors is that directors need to know which of the actors are closer to the kinds of characters they have invented. Then, the big question is, are they willing to commit themselves to the project, to work with me in a professional manner and to be capable of illuminating the roles assigned to the characters? I also have to be very careful not to generalize in terms of nonprofessionals. I have had problems with known actors on different takes. For example, some known actors cannot give you many takes. Filmmaking demands that ability because many things can go wrong beyond the performance, and that means reenacting the scene for as long as it takes to get it right. There are actors who cannot repeat the performance they gave you a second ago. There are actors who can give you the performance they gave you earlier and even transform it onto another level, either beneath or above it. When we look for actors, we have to compare our ability with their own acting abilities; the convergence of these two talents, if properly explored, can forge a unique creativity even beyond one's expectations. Not everything is preprogrammed, which means we find ways to balance the equation. Does the director know how to make that happen?

Sankofa is more episodic than sequential. You use a lot of flashbacks to tell different stories, and those stories are wonderful moments that remind me of growing up, being baptized, and being confirmed a Catholic. The church sequence makes me reflect on that past and think of the role of Catholicism and Christianity in colonization.

It is not only *Sankofa*. *Sankofa* was, as you said earlier, a turning point for me. It is where I succeeded to some extent better and to some extent not better than in *Child of Resistance, Bush Mama, Harvest,* and *Ashes and Embers*. I always wanted my narrative to be invisible. I did not want it to stand simplistically on this episodic stance that you observed, which I think corresponds to life. Everything we do today is episodic.

In terms of the episodic point, that was how my father's plays used to be. His stories were episodic. My grandmother also told her stories in that manner. They link up sometimes over a period of one year. In the evenings, around the fire, we were told all the small narratives in episodic form and it took a full year before the master narrative was linked up with the other stories.

After my grandmother died, I recollected a story she was telling me about a king that was overthrown. She told me the story in episodic form about the king that Emperor Haile Selassie overthrew to come to power. I did not realize the full details then, for the narrative did not gel until she died. As a piece of primarily fragmented information, some episodes are like puzzles in that they are finally resolved over a period of time. There are many unexplored textures in Africa's narrative styles that could manifest within us as something to look out for as we try to tell the story that is echoing in the chambers of our minds. I think we sometimes censor those sensibilities and echo chambers, keeping them from talking to us and making us more receptive to our roles as arbiters of change.

One can see how you fuse or juxtapose documentary with fictional elements. Could you tell me something about these documentary and fictional syntheses that permeate your narrative structure?

I am always interested in making my films look like a documentary. Most filmmakers want their films to be believed as if they are real. One thing that distinguishes cinema from the theater is that in the theater, the event is understood as a play. The cinema comes at you and makes you doubt whether the image is real or not. Cinema, from its origins, has always reproduced images that appear to be real even though they are illusion. Unlike theater, which is itself mesmerizing, cinema conveys the idea of believability; how to captivate people is the key. When I work as I do, juxtaposing documentary and fiction, I learn how to insert reality, to consider how it can look real in film without depicting the actual reality, because reality is not always dramatic. When you dramatize reality, is it still possible to maintain the true identity or the appearance of realness of that event? I think, especially as an African, that because I believe in the cinema as something that represents the real, I want to utilize it as a legitimate tool for capturing African reality.

What is this new thesis you are proposing that you call triangular cinema? I have read one of your articles where you talk about Dinknesh versus Lucy. It could be described as activist in tone, highly polemical, and unabashedly political.

It is not enough to be just a filmmaker and especially a traditional filmmaker. It is not enough to be a critic and especially a traditional film critic. It is not enough to be a traditional passive audience. This is the triangle. The filmmaker from an isolated booth cannot invent cinematic language. Similarly, the critic from his or her computer cannot create African cinema. The audience, when it is looking at Western cinema every day, does not invent the African cinema. We are all hungry for our images. We have a common cultural bond. That is what I felt and still do feel, and it is in fact what *Sankofa* is all about. Actually, from a nonaesthetic but pragmatic distribution approach, *Sankofa* brought those realities to the forefront. When we showed *Sankofa* across the country, first the community was involved in the distribution of the film. Second, every night, every show, for forty minutes, we made a contract to have a discussion between the film people and the audience. This happened in thirty-five cities and in some cases in seven places simultaneously. For four months, we took turns going to Baltimore to talk to the audience about distribution, cultural exploitation, and racism, as well as Hollywood hostility toward African and African American cinemas. I am writing a book now about this whole experience. We have piles of people writing to us and communicating with us through the Internet. *Sankofa* is still being debated on the Internet left and right. The audience discusses the role they played in distribution, for example; and they photocopied pamphlets and mobilized to form the *Sankofa* family. The filmmaker also has to be present always in the community discussion in order to learn and advance his or her own aesthetics.

Cinematic language will not be invented or forged in coffeehouses in New York with a few critics and film buffs. The audience missing it and not getting it, getting it and not missing it are critical ways of learning how to develop and transform our cinematic language. So the triangular cinema is the idea to make all of us activists. If I am not a member of the traditional Hollywood arrogant cinema, but a filmmaker that is capable of leafleting the audience, talking to them and going door to door to bring them out to their study groups to discuss issues, that will make me happy. It is not enough to make movies. It is not enough to comment on movies. It is not enough to just see a movie. We do not want the audience to just see our films and go home. We want them to have a referential comprehension of what they just saw. This mutually activated coexistence is critical in order to have a truly independent cinematic movement.

I noticed that Sankofa *was coproduced with Ghana and Burkina Faso. What are the possibilities and problems of coproductions with European countries and African countries?*

Let me tell you, by the way, that in FESPACO 1985, my wife and I organized a symposium in Ouagadougou on the concept of a Pan-African cinematic approach in order to relieve the pressure on us and our own shortcomings. We invited all the filmmakers. We brought representatives from the United States, and the African Diaspora from Europe, and created a panel discussion. Our idea was that if Africans can tricontinentally develop a coexistence concept whereby if you have a camera and you are a Burkinabe, and I have sound equipment and am Ethiopian, and Dakar has postproduction facility, then we could collaborate with these resources to enable a filmmaker to make a movie. A lot of African Americans who know the technology could work as camerapeople for our work in Nigeria and so forth. But nobody jumped on that proposal. After the panel it all died. But my wife and I went ahead, and *Sankofa* is an "imperfect" experiment of that idea. We felt that we had to put resources together.

Burkina Faso had camera, lights, and crew, Ghana had lights and crew, and from here we put together a Pan-African concept of coproduction. This arrangement may not be a perfect romantic union, but when it is articulated and understood better by all parties it is still the most visionary self-reliant approach to filmmaking in Africa. One of the most successful things about *Sankofa,* with all of its shortcomings, is the fact that we did it in the Pan-African spirit, borrowing the ideas of the late President

Kwame Nkrumah and all the other Pan-Africanists. In fact, when the cast came together, this amazing Pan-African union took place. The crew from Burkina worked with the crew from Ghana and Puerto Rico, and everything exploded with passion.

That is really interesting.

It was very tiring and took years to mobilize bureaucrats in Africa. There were big problems, left and right, but in the end we succeeded. When they opened the film in Ghana, you could not even see the end of the lines. Ghana's government made a lot of money with the print we donated to them, and Burkina Faso is trying to organize its own distribution. Because they supported our effort, when we gave them the print we told them to exploit it and make any amount of money they wanted. This is the success story of this coproduction experiment. I have a presale arrangement with Germany and England. Nobody owns *Sankofa*. Nobody owns my movies. This presale arrangement gave them only the broadcast right, which has already expired. I have the theatrical right. Our distribution company, Mypheduh Films, has every right to distribution because I do not believe in partnerships whereby my films are owned by outside organizations that are hostile to my people.

Filmography

Hour Glass, 1971
Child of Resistance, 1972
Harvest: 3,000 Years, 1974
Bush Mama, 1976
Wilmington 10–USA 10,000, 1979
Ashes and Embers, 1981
After Winter: Sterling Brown, 1985
Sankofa, 1993
Adwa, 2000

Ramadan Suleman (South Africa)

The demise of apartheid in South Africa raised hopes for the emergence of black filmmakers. Under the white minority's repressive rule, blacks who wanted to study film or art were excluded from attending educational institutions reserved for whites only, and, economically, such education was out of reach for them unless they received support from foreign funding. As independence paved the way for artists, intellectuals, and other political exiles to return home, the emergence of a young filmmaker, Ramadan Suleman, and the international impact of his first feature, *Fools* (1997), rekindled this optimism.

In 1981, Ramadan Suleman completed a three-year drama diploma at the Center for Research and Training in African Theater. He was actively involved in the alternative theater movement in the 1980s as an actor and was one of the founding members of the Dhlomo Theater in Johannesburg, the first black theater in South Africa. After the theater's closure by the apartheid authorities, he left South Africa to study filmmaking in Paris. During this period he experimented with a Super-8 camera, and in 1985 he made two short documentary films, *Secuba* and *Arouna*, each twenty minutes long. In 1986 he had a great opportunity, as he puts it, to assist the veteran Mauritanian filmmaker Med Hondo in the making of *Sarraounia*, as trainee editor and also as assistant director of the award-winning film *Yeelen*, by the Malian director Souleymane Cissé.

From 1987 to 1990, Suleman was enrolled at the London International Film School, majoring in directing and scriptwriting. His short film *The Devil's Children* (1990), based on the short story *The Park* by James Mathews, won him several prizes, including awards at Fifrec '90, and the Prix Bicentenaire; at the 1990 Chicago International Film Festival, he was awarded a certificate of merit. After his graduation, he returned to France, and in 1991–92 he worked as technical director at Theater de la Main D'or in Paris. Determined to continue filmmaking, he could not resist the opportunity to become assistant director of *Lumière noire*, a film by Med Hondo.

Suleman directed his first feature, *Fools*, in 1997. This film, which Suleman also cowrote with Bhekizizwe Peterson, is the first postapartheid feature film by a black South African to hit international film festivals and to win the Silver Leopard at the Locarno International Film Festival, Switzerland. In the following interview, which was conducted in New York City in 1998, this promising young director, a dynamic and soft-spoken man, articulates with utmost insight the political, social, cultural, and economic issues affecting the newly formed South African film industry—some issues never before confronted since the dawn of the new era initiated by that icon of liberation, President Nelson Mandela.

As one of the latest African filmmakers in the limelight, how would you react to the phrase filmmaking in Africa*?*

The situations in which African filmmakers make their films are no different from the futile manner in which their governments are run. In other words, a president in Africa might have twenty-five ministers working with him in the government, but they are mere figureheads. It is the president himself who is the minister of justice, the minister of defense, the prime minister, minister of finance, everything. The president runs the government as if he is a village chief. The African filmmaker tends to work in the same manner. He might have a crew of people who are working with him on a movie set, but at the end of the day, he is the producer, director, scriptwriter, and distributor, as well as the person who handles set design and wardrobe. He does everything! I have also observed that even the technicians and actors look upon him as God or village chief. He makes decisions all the time without realizing that a bad decision could be fatal.

Why is this so? Why this hegemonic control?

It is because of the African tradition in which the elder or someone who has made it in the family is always looked at with awe and respect. You cannot contradict him nor question his deeds. It is taboo in African culture, as we all know, to ask elders questions. If your own brother is crazy, you do not go against him, because he is the elder of the house. We have seen African presidents think insanely, while others have gone mad. But you do not say to a president that he needs to go to the hospital, insane asylum, or that he is sick. The African filmmaker tends to make mistakes while he is filming, but the people around him will not dare open their mouths because he is the priest, the chief, the president, the supreme filmmaker that knows everything.

Filmmaking for me, from my experience and what I have seen and read, is a collective process where you have ideas and you transfer those ideas to people. The others help in making those dreams of yours come true. It has to be collective. You have to listen to others. I work from the premise that nobody knows everything. That is the dynamic of cinema, and that is the dynamic of our world. Unfortunately, African filmmakers have not been able to democratize the production process.

Don't you think that one of the problems is due to the nonindustrial nature of African cinema by which the filmmaker, who suffers for a long time to raise money, may also want to ensure that production goes the way he intended it?

I agree. But again we need to delegate and trust other people. I do agree that the five years taken to raise funds and to write that script, to make that project come true, are important to the filmmaker. At the same time, he cannot make all decisions himself, simply because in one corner of his left brain he is thinking of the financial considerations and in the right brain he is thinking of the artistic/aesthetic problems. Therefore, something fails along the way. The problem is that we do not delegate. We need to learn to delegate and trust our fellow African brothers, friends, or people that work with us. It is the only way we can maintain leadership and achieve success. We tend to work in the mafia way, where it is always a family affair. I think some filmmakers are afraid to work with the very few or quasi-professional actors in Africa simply because they do not want to be challenged. They resist actors who ask questions, and who have suggestions to make. This is one of the problems of African cinema.

In addition, the manner in which funding is allocated, by which nobody who has received funds is answerable to anybody, because the money is guilt money from the French, is also destroying African cinema. There is no producer or executive who says to the filmmaker, "I am giving you four million French francs and I want returns." It is aid money and, therefore, no accountability is required.

Did the French Ministry of Cooperation not assign overseers to control the funds dedicated to African filmmakers?

It is a difficult process in which one section in the French Ministry of Cooperation manages the affairs of African filmmakers who have submitted scripts to them for consideration. As long as those scripts conform to the French ethnographic perception of Africa, then they will be funded. But if these scripts challenge certain ethics and morals, or question French politics, then the filmmakers may receive no funds. Hence, over the years, we have been seeing certain trends among ethnographic films funded by the French. The French no longer make ethnographic films in Africa. They use the services of the people they call *cinéastes sur le terrain* [filmmakers in the field] who can do it for them. French filmmakers no longer pry into African exotica since they have trained Africans to make ethnographic films for their titillation.

Are you disturbed by the kind of African films selected for festivals and distributed in Europe and North America?

It is disturbing how the pattern has evolved over the years. What I find amazing is that the films of Ousmane Sembene and Med Hondo are no longer distributed as much as the films made by people with a certain political understanding of their surrounding, culture, history, and country. What you now have are films that reinforce a Western ethnographic vision of Africa, in a word, underdevelopment. I consider some of these films disturbing since some of them have now become objects of Western fascination. Their clichés remind me of the clichés of the western [movie]. We know the ingredients that make a western spectacular: a street with a saloon, the dance hall girls and a lonesome cowboy in the saloon, the scenery in the background with an Indian standing up on the mountains with his buffaloes. In African cinema today there are also stock ingredients: there are always three women passing by carrying baskets filled with maize, wheat, or barley. Then the actor will pass them carrying his gourd filled with drinking water and dressed in his traditional outfit, sometimes loincloth, tattered or dirty, with the sun in the background. You will always see a group of elders sitting under a thatched hut or baobab tree, and our young girls and older women will appear topless or half naked. The latest trend now is to feature dwarfs, what the French call *les sorcières*, the witches. Finally, the setting is always in the village. Upon release, the French would call that poetry.

Actually, a friend of mine has described the kind of films you described as "calabash" movies. He laments that when he wants to teach African cinema here in the United States, he does not find circulating films suitable, for the reason that too many of them wallow in the bushes glorifying exoticism. How do you feel about the tendency to misconstrue these images as representative of the general situation in Africa?

There is the tendency that when Europeans or the outside world speaks of Africa, it is never perceived as a continent with fifty-five countries and a diversity of peoples and cultures. I think it is the only continent where more than one thousand languages and dialects are spoken. As you pointed out to me earlier, in Nigeria alone there are nine official languages and more than two hundred dialects. And South Africa already has eleven official languages and many other dialects.

The proliferation of exotic movies is a result of too few films being made, because of financial problems and because of our governments' inability to place culture at the forefront of the fight against illiteracy and domination. The English-speaking African countries, I think, are in a different position simply because the British do not and cannot at the moment impose themselves or their will upon their former African colonies. They do not have the resources like the French to control filmmaking and film aesthetics in Africa. However, the anglophone countries also prioritize the sociopolitical nature of films. They talk about issues that affect societies, which show the urgency of change. Filmmakers working in that direction do exist in West Africa, but are in the minority, scattered here and there. However, it is the other group, the majority, that make the calabash, pastoral, or village poetic films that we see around the world. I think it is a question of defining priorities.

Again I have the feeling that it is lack of democratization of production that is affecting innovation. In other words, some filmmakers are scared to confront the urban political and economic situation of their countries because they fear being sanctioned. Hence they opt for the easy way out by making apolitical films. This also applies to Kenya and Nigeria. Love or romance melodrama films dominate the Nigerian screen. It is very rare to come across a Nigerian film that looks critically at Nigerian society from any political standpoint. The films of Ghana, Nigeria, and Kenya always deal with love and romance, like Kwaw Ansah's *Love Brewed in the African Pot.* I suppose also, although I may be wrong, that the filmmakers are heavily influenced by the Indian romance melodrama films which are extremely popular in those countries. I remember seeing a Nigerian movie made by Ola Balogun where there was a young couple in a forest and suddenly a snake appears. It is reminiscent of Indian films where suddenly a cobra appears.

But let us not forget Kwaw Ansah's masterpiece, Heritage . . . Africa, *which is a wonderful and extremely political film that is highly entertaining as well. Nigeria's Eddie Ugbomah has made more than thirteen features, and some of them deal with Nigerian crises. We see a genuine concern for using film as a political weapon. Unfortunately, those films are not distributed in the United States and in Europe, like the francophone films.*

Again, that is the sad aspect of our continent. It is a dilemma for which we all need to find some kind of solution or compromise. On the one hand, it is easy to criticize the British, French, or the U.S. for monopolizing our screens, but we need to find a common ground for distributing African films on the continent among our respective countries. African filmmakers need to use the latest technologies, like cable, to overcome the continuing problems of distribution and exhibition. If we were equipped with a cable network system, South Africa could beam their programs to Nigeria, and Nigeria could beam theirs to South Africa. We need to explore the possibilities of the latest technologies instead of viewing them as a threat. We need to look carefully into all these areas that might resolve those problems in the future.

While cable is a progressive element in this direction, cable television and satellite television can also be detrimental to the development of African cinema. MNET in South Africa, at least as far as I know, promotes foreign films at the expense of African films. People who have money to buy cable television no longer tune into the local programs or news.

You are right, but for me there are two issues to be concerned with. We now have a different system of colonization in Africa, which is invisible—the satellites are millions of kilometers above us. You cannot touch them, you cannot even see them with the naked eye, and you cannot shoot them down. I believe that we need to find some other ways to fight or accommodate them—to our advantage. I do not think we can win by adopting a defensive posture. The world is moving much too fast for all of us.

I think we need to find ways to be partners in what is now called media globalization. We recently witnessed a new sign: the American president Bill Clinton showed interest in Africa, even though he visited "selected" countries. The second concern, though, is the one I fear most, which is that if we choose the defensive, ten years from now we will not participate in global trends and changes or make any kind of visible input. African governments have the power to say to MNET, "If you beam programs into our countries, then we require a percentage of African films to be shown on your network." On the other hand, it does suit the African president if American films dominate our screens because the people will remain complacent. Information media move so fast that by the time we try to understand what cable television, video, the Internet, and digitization are all about, it will be too late.

We are still emphasizing the celluloid film in terms of our filmmaking, and it is only Ghana and Nigeria that are now producing films on video. I often hear my colleagues say things like "I am a filmmaker. I only make movies on film stock." This is a myopic way of synthesizing the reality. Even Hollywood is greatly exploring the potentials of producing on digital equipment by editing on video and transferring it onto film. In the years to come, there may not be film stock. Are we going to scream to Kodak to supply us their remaining old film stock when the rest of the world goes digital? All I am saying is, do we sit back and complain, or do we find ways of evolving with the mechanisms that are overtaking us?

MNET has its headquarters in South Africa, but who owns it?

MNET is owned by white South Africans of the Broederbond Afrikaner business lobby, and is 99.9 percent white. MNET, in my opinion, does not participate at the moment in the changes that South Africa is undergoing. You see it on their screen, and the claim that they have spent one, two, or five million rands on local productions is preposterous. They need to do twenty times more than what they are doing now.

How has MNET been supporting the production of African films?

Supporting one or two films is no support. It is like the French supporting five features a year in the whole of Africa. It does not help, because one film made each year in Burkina Faso, Mali, Senegal, Cameroon, and Côte d'Ivoire does not change anything. The films come and disappear; the people forget about them easily, and this is because of the sporadic nature of production, which does not add up to making an impact. This situation forces people to look more toward American and other foreign films, and when they become addicted they will not want to see African films even when they are available. It is from this perspective that MNET, producing just a couple films, is a nonstart.

Interesting, because yesterday, at the New York African Film Festival forum, we were talking about the use of professional actors from the African Diaspora in African films.

The use of professional actors is good, but given the paucity of African films, do you think that a star system is the answer?

I come from a country where theater is high powered, as is also true in Nigeria, Ghana, and other African countries, like Egypt, Algeria, and Tunisia. My feeling is that the use of African American and African actors in the U.S., as discussed yesterday at the New York Film Festival forum, in our films is a problem. We need to ask ourselves when we make a movie in English, whether it is to appeal to Americans as a compromise. If we are to make our films in our national languages using Zulu, Xhosa, Swahili, Wolof, or Bambara, then the issue of African Americans or nonnatives may be a problem. Again, there are no rules for me. Rules depend on individual projects. You might have a movie shot all in Wolof or Zulu that might have a scene requiring an English-speaking person with accent. That could be a role for an African American—if the director is in dire need of one. It depends on individual projects. I think what is most important at this time is whatever improvements can be made in our production process, be it in acting, costume, technical aspects, and so forth. But it is also important for us to consider creating our local heroes.

I do not see why we cannot do what the British are doing at the moment. There is an emerging British cinema featuring British actors who are not international stars. A case in point is a movie like *Naked*. There is a whole list that includes *The Full Monty* and the type of films Ken Loach and Mike Leach are making. Consider a film like *Trainspotting*, which is a Scottish movie, which has done very well but does not make use of internationally recognized stars. But these are British, Scottish, or Irish actors who act very well. It is on that basis that the British films are breaking box-office records. We can learn from these experiences.

The British are also having problems with American films conquering their market, so the African situation is not unique. The only way individual countries can resolve the problems is to make films that are authentic to their cultures and to their realities. The British do not rely on the use of American stars but find alternative ways to propel their film industry. British cinema now appears to have been revived after its fourteen years of struggle against the Thatcher government. In our own situation, I believe that using South African actors means putting a touch of professionalism into our films. However, I do not think we should create barriers, and as I said earlier on, filmmaking is a collective endeavor. African Americans or any other people can come and work in South Africa and contribute to the enhancement of the South African film industry. I am open to that, but it depends on what terms.

Yes, that is right. It seems to me that your argument supports the fact that to think about the use of famous African American stars is not the question now, but rather, that there is the possibility of internationalizing the expertise of lesser-known African stars. If you look at how African productions are funded, they are low-budget films. They do not have the money to pay big stars. The big money may come if they are able to coordinate all these factors we are talking about and make films that appeal to the larger audience. Now, each country has its own stars, but these players are not known across the continent. So I come back to the same point I was making, that there must be enough films made to make it possible to use a wide variety of actors and actresses and create a viable cinema in Africa.

I think also that we should not undermine television. Consider the South African public television for instance, which is the richest public television in Africa, but does not do business with other African countries. It will enhance business if Nigerian television could consider buying Malian films, Senegalese films, Kenyan films, South African films for Nigerian popular consumption, for example. If we can crisscross our films for television in Africa, that is good for the economy. It all depends on the willingness of our governments and our television stations to initiate this plan. Everybody is complaining about there being no money. Is it not a problem that African filmmakers all want to make films for the screen and none for television? I think it is a problem because we all target the big screen, and yet we do not seem to have control of the screen. As a compromise, I often ask myself, why not consider producing for television, since television is accessible to more people than the big screen? Is it a problem with us that filmmakers do not want to move with the times or technology? Are we afraid of technology? Why do we insist on showing our films only in the theaters? Are we not contradicting ourselves?

How many African countries can afford to pay African filmmakers a reasonable amount of money to show their films on TV when the filmmakers know that showing a film on TV makes it prone to piracy? How many African governments are willing to compensate the filmmakers adequately for taking that kind of risk?

You have raised the issue of copyright, which I agree is a problem. It is, maybe, only South Africa, Zimbabwe, and the other southern African countries and Ghana that can control about 60 percent of the copyright issues. The rest of Africa, including Nigeria, does not enforce copyright laws. All I am saying is: How can we explore the potentials of television to change perceptions? An examination of individual countries will prove that we all started the other way around; in other words, we began with filmmaking, which is extremely costly, and neglected the more affordable video and television. I think it is time for us to begin to reexamine our priorities in relation to the economic and general situations in Africa.

The reason now that people do not go to the theaters is that they are watching television, and in most cases they watch foreign programs. In Nigeria, for instance, the government allowed private television stations to exist, but the people who had the money to establish them did not have any local programs ready when they started to operate. Why can't they commission their own programs to promote creativity, originality, authenticity, culture, and history? Why make Europe or America the source of information and entertainment?

Well, everybody talks about American films being cheap to acquire in the Third World. The Americans churn out hundreds of films per year, like the Indians. Like American films, Indian films are affordable as well. Is it time for us to consider less expensive projects and equipment as a way of working ourselves up—not from the top down but from the bottom up? Why do we still come to America to complain about African cinema when we as individual filmmakers are not reconsidering our methods of working on our own continent?

Television could offer the remedy sought, but we all know it is not easy, because the bureaucrats in charge of the television stations are shortsighted. Maybe hope lies at the moment in South Africa, where the newly established Independent Broadcasting Authority is trying to propose a quota system in which local programs will occupy 30 to 40 percent of the programming time. I think it is the right beginning; it is only when we are able to see our products on television that we can begin to envisage industrial status. But on many occasions, in Africa in general, we are faced with individuals who run television and who are not business or politically oriented, and who do not have vision. The whole of Africa, including South Africa, lacks a vision in terms of what to do to change society. For me, these are the fundamental problems that we are faced with.

I agree that it is a continental affair, but we talk about all these issues and problems but do not really address the question of how to initiate some kind of changes that would enable the creation of industries that would be competitive like other nations.

As I said, the problem that we have, as you mentioned, is competitiveness, be it in the quality of our films or the economy. I put an emphasis on television because the cinema cannot exist without television. It has happened, and is still happening in Europe. The two complement each other, and they cannot be isolated. There is nothing we can do about that. For me, we need to try to find ways to integrate both. As I said earlier, in South Africa there is hope because the mechanism has been focused in that direction. It is an interesting beginning when an independent body is taking the initiative. The next stage, in my opinion, is to help safeguard the existence of this body so it can guarantee the future existence of our cultural productions on television.

In terms of South Africa, the ball is now in the courts of the filmmakers. I urge them to stop complaining and to lobby for continued progress and for the opportunity to go out there and produce. Go out there and produce as well as create the culture necessary for promoting outlets for low-budget, quality films as well as for blockbuster films. Young American, French, and British filmmakers are able to make low-budget, quality films with interesting stories. The challenge is to use the available infrastructure and aggressively pursue the goal of having sufficient films for local consumption. We cannot sit back and expect governments and television stations to allocate huge budgets for our productions. I do not want to be part of the type of culture of dependence operating in francophone Africa, where filmmakers depend on France and the European Union. I want to see a situation where we find ways to make cheap films. When I say cheap, I don't mean mediocre films. I mean low-budget films that we can use to build an industry. At this point in history, the filmmakers have to create the industry, not the industry creating the filmmakers.

Talking about film industry, what is the present situation in South Africa after apartheid?

We are undergoing an interesting yet confusing period at this point. It is interesting in the sense that South Africans are beginning to see the government confront the issue of cinema, television, and media in general. The authorities are putting in place legislation in this regard, but I think that it depends on the filmmakers to make the legislation work. What is legislated cannot remain static, for it is bound to be updated to reflect changes. This for me is where hope lies, because such has not happened in any other part of Africa. The next stage is to build the industry. The government is already allocating some funds to do this. We are now undergoing a second budget allocation of about ten million rands. It depends on how this fund is managed. It should not be managed as if it is an aid package where everybody gets a share of, say, two thousand rands, but the fund should be distributed according to merit, to the filmmakers whose scripts are promising and innovative.

Looking at the whole issue of funding from another perspective, I am also afraid of the danger of filmmakers becoming dependent on our government for funds. I am more concerned with what you said earlier about being competitive. In other words, the government must be there to get us off the ground, to help the young filmmaker who has just completed training or college education and wants to make his or her first film. Once that filmmaker has gotten that initial help, he must not be part of the dependency syndrome. We must now create the mechanism whereby the film-maker is part of an industry that raises money through businesses or corporations— all channeled toward attaining the status of an economically viable industry. I am very wary, and I am saying this very carefully, that people including myself, should not be dependent on the government to make our second and future films. The government has helped me to make my first film. The next stage is for me to take that first film around the world, and say, "This is what I can do. Here are my credentials." We need to educate potential South African or African businesspeople to understand that there is money to be made from the entertainment industry. We must convince them that film production is a long-term investment. Parallel to the industrialization of African cinema, we need to create a culture of business that understands the potentials of filmmaking. At the moment there is confusion because everybody is trying to find his or her niche, but I think it is just a question of time. Let me reemphasize that it also depends on filmmakers to fight hard to address the issue of distribution.

Talking about the success of this industry, how about the problem posed by foreign films? Foreign films have indoctrinated South African audiences, like the audiences in other African countries. Do you think the audiences indoctrinated by foreign films will patronize the indigenous films to create economically viable local film industries?

I am once again optimistic with regard to South Africa. It depends on what kind of strategies and mechanisms are in place. South Africa has a population of about forty million people, out of which about 80 percent are illiterate. We are right now at an advantage because of the demise of apartheid and the rapid industrialization taking place in South Africa. The government at the moment, through its housing projects, is working on industrialization. In other words, electricity, telephone, cable, satellites, and water are now in supply even in the remote areas of the country, and the educational system is also being restructured. These are progressive signals. With regard to the domination of foreign cultures in our country at this stage, our societies are already impregnated with those influences. I do not believe presently that they could be eradicated. We do not have the economic muscle to fight that. They are there to stay with us as long as technological channels of communication are left open. What we need to do as South Africans is to find alternative mechanisms for dealing with the monopolies without going to the extremes. The elite who control the channels of communication are comfortable at the moment with the one million or so white cinemagoers in the country while the potential black South African audience is neglected. However, as black filmmakers, we need to develop alternative methods of winning over those potential audiences who are neglected. I am not saying that they should be forced to go and see our films. With the given structure of South Africa, you cannot expect people to travel long distances in taxis to watch films in the theaters. People simply do not have the economic means; rather, we should be thinking about the possibility of transporting 35mm prints with portable 35mm projectors or even video and taking this material to the hinterland, to schools and communities.

Historically we all know that Africans or Third World people have the tendency, if they like something, to see it two or three times. For example, you know that in Nigeria when they love a film they will see it ten times and buy the video copy to watch it sixty more times until even the color disappears. We have even experienced in movie houses that the audience knows movie dialogues by heart. They memorize; they even tend to talk to the screen characters! This is why I believe that using 35mm prints and video copies and going into schools and showing the films to students with accompanying materials about the film, the actors, and the story would build our audiences. It is a lot of work, but we need to plan for five years from now. Those students who are sixteen and seventeen are the audience of tomorrow. We need to go to them instead of waiting for them to come to us. Our task should be to speak to them.

We need to find ways of speaking to our people, making them aware of what our culture is and how they need to look at themselves on the screen rather than copy the American perception of motion picture images. They need to understand and learn to look at their subtleties on the screen. When they understand our concerns, I believe that the majority of the students will eventually explore African films and be happy to pay one or two dollars to watch them.

You are speaking from a black South African perspective. South Africa is a multiracial, multiethnic country. What are other filmmakers doing, such as the Indians, whites, and women?

South African democracy is only three and a half years old. Every one of us is trying to understand and discover each other. Many South Africans were scattered all over the globe before the 1994 elections. Some of us were in the U.S., France, England, and so forth. Now they are gradually returning home, and are beginning to understand who is doing what and where. Each of us has his or her own domain. Like the men, women are working in television or learning how to do programs. A culture is beginning to emerge, but there is confusion because people are learning and trying to define their future, language, and culture. So the coming together and understanding of the people takes time, because we all come from different backgrounds. A South African film culture will begin to see light, maybe, in the next three years, if our people are producing more films. When this happens, then we will begin to realize that positive things are emerging out of an organized struggle, and we will begin to understand that which is emerging. It is like a child being born. Everyone looks at the child; they try to understand the child and how it is developing.

What inspired the making of Fools*?*

Fools arose out of a certain political/cinematographic confusion in the mid- to late eighties, when I was studying filmmaking at the London International Film School. I remember a friend of mine, a close colleague, Bhekizizwe Peterson, the cowriter of *Fools*—when we were in London, we talked about the unhappiness of South Africans regarding quite a few films that had been made about apartheid. Many South Africans felt that foreigners had no right to make films about South Africa, and that South African people should do it. Others felt that only South Africans were eligible to portray apartheid accurately because they underwent the historic struggle against oppression. These are tricky issues that I do not think I can fully address. On the other hand, why deny an artist the right to do a piece of work about another country? For me, art is art, but you also have art for social and political reasons. I remember an experience with some friends in London. We watched a movie, *Cry Freedom*, by Richard Attenborough, that revolved around the life of Donald Woods, who was a friend of Steve Biko. People, however, were expecting on the screen only the life of Biko. I understand it was more the strength of Steve Biko that captured the movie; however, the way apartheid affected the white man touched the Western audiences more than did a black person who was massacred by the white agents of a white repressive regime. It occurred to me then that this confusion was not to be prolonged, for it was up to South Africans to begin to tell their stories. Nobody is denying them that opportunity, but they must struggle like everybody else to find ways of telling their stories.

I had read Njabulo Ndebele's book *Fools*, published in the early eighties, and I had found the book quite revolutionary for its period. It was at the height of the struggle in South Africa against apartheid, and he was very critical of the black situation within the apartheid structure. I found it very interesting that a writer would dare write such a critical view. He was criticized, even by black academics, for having dared to criticize the victims of apartheid. I decided with Bhekizizwe, my collaborator, to adapt this story so as to give a black perspective on what makes black people tick. How have black people survived apartheid and how have they been involved in this continuous struggle, in their silence, in their anger, without throwing stones all the time? We resorted to adapting this book. The interesting thing about the movie and the book is that they raise several issues and questions about black people at that time. Even today there is the whole issue of women's involvement in South African culture, history, and politics. I liked the book, but I tried to go a step further in the film to try to make South Africans reflect, especially at this democratic period, on their relationships with women. I looked at my relationship with my mother, my aunts, my sisters, and how we treat each other in South Africa and at this whole patriarchal tradition of the man being the head of the family. I think the days are over where the man decides everything. A woman in a family situation should be considered an equal partner. A man cannot do it alone. The strength and the force of that relationship in a family are based on how the couple goes about building that family. I felt those issues were very important in South Africa and should be addressed in the film.

It also resurrects for me the whole question of how, today, South African politicians tell us that we live in a rainbow nation. It is fine to import a fancy African American slogan, which I learned was invented by the honorable Reverend Jesse Jackson, but when I walk into Soweto, I still see poverty; I walk around the city and it is full of misery, and I feel the contradiction inherent in the so-called rainbow nation that the politicians have failed to see. I recently did a movie magazine about football [soccer], and I went to an area called Phola Park. There, poverty hits people hard and it stinks—and yet the politicians tell us that we are a rainbow nation? It is painful that it is that easy for them to run away with slogans and not to deal with poverty. For me, *Fools* is some kind of warning to the politicians not to look for easy answers to society's problems. The amount of damage done to our people by apartheid is immense. We must look for practical long-term ways of resolving those issues instead of only saying we are a rainbow nation, which could be misread to mean that in South Africa, blacks and whites are on equal terms.

Black people have a history, which is to say that they need to come to grips with themselves first before coming to grips with white people. That is the issue at hand. Consider the African Americans in the United States, they do not speak among

themselves, hence they are disorganized and voiceless. They make up about 13 percent of the U.S. population and yet are caught in the slow process of making their
voices heard. The South African population is forty million now, less than the African
Americans. African Americans are still struggling with the realities of being black
in America. In the same vein, I think South African citizens must be practical and
accept the task of helping politicians understand that the damage done by apartheid
is immeasurable. We are a dehumanized people and need to move quickly to regain
our humanity. *Fools* was inspired by all of these issues.

*In working with the novel, how much did you change the story line to reflect your own
ideology and to reflect the current situation in South Africa?*

There is the whole issue in the book where Njabulo talks about rape, but he does
not deal with rape as the larger issue in the book. He deals more with the relationship
and dilemma between the two characters Zani and Zamani. We had a problem in
adapting this part of the book because the issue of rape is very important and needed
to be addressed fully. How can you let a teacher who has committed rape continue to
teach? It is a big issue, and a dilemma for society. You cannot let criminals continue
to teach our children morals; the society or the community is not confronting the
problems of immorality. And how can the rapist be the moralist? Njabulo's examination of the issue in the novel was somehow surrealistic and narrated in a dreamlike
manner. The book itself is wonderful literature, but we offered a different perspective
by defining rape as a terrible crime.

There is this scene, for example, where a young girl has an abortion. It is not in
the book, but we felt we could go a step further. So we created this scene, and we put
our characters into a dilemma to show how women can be in conflict, and when the
struggle is over, how they are capable of regrouping and resolving those issues. In
the earliest stages of the film we saw the conflict between women develop, but later,
Zani's sister, Busi, who was against Nosipho, is the first one to ask for the teacher's
wife, who is a midwife, to come and help with the abortion. Being a woman, and
seeing another woman in need, Nosipho does not hesitate to assist. She helps Mimi,
who was raped by her husband (the teacher, Zamani), abort the fetus. We extended
the issue of rape further in terms of the characters, including the teacher's wife. What
does rape mean to her, and can she live with this criminal again? These are the fundamental issues that we looked at in these relationships.

Another interesting moment is at the end of the film. We had dilemmas within
ourselves about the end, especially with regard to the coming of the white man. Do
we let the teacher laugh off the pain, or does he defend himself and kill the white
man? The logical way to kill him would have been with a hail of stones. We remembered South Africa as a violent place; our struggle was violent, and we were all fond
of throwing stones. Njabulo wrote about this so beautifully, which made it a challenge
for us to show someone laughing off pain and using that pain and laughter to destroy

his enemy. It is something very powerful. In the previous drafts, we were moved by the energy driving the character to want to kill. We reflected upon all the ramifications of such a sequence and rejected it. If he were to kill the white man, it would obviously have reflected the popular zeal of South Africans during the apartheid era, seizing the opportunity to take that kind of revenge they always wanted. However, Zamani is able to withstand the pain inflicted on him with a horse whip by the white man—a pain which is symbolic of the 350 years of suffering black South Africans have endured. This image, rather than killing off the white man, we thought, presents a more powerful argument—letting him live and, hopefully, regret his deeds. It is basically saying to South Africans that throwing stones or using a gun is not the only way left for us to deal with our current problems. We wanted to state that there could always be alternatives.

Is not this ending the reason that some people see the film as not powerful enough? As you said, people would have liked to see the white devil killed. But I also read a statement by a white South African critic who in one sentence dismissed the film, probably because he thought the film reopened old wounds and incited violence. How do you respond to that kind of criticism?

I am not surprised, but to adopt that perspective shows naïveté and a lack of understanding of history. In which era is this critic living? No film in my opinion has ever created a revolution. No people anywhere in the world have entered a movie house, come out after the film ended, and created a revolution, or started shooting everything in sight. We should not lie to ourselves. What we try to achieve with films as filmmakers is not to give people answers but rather to raise questions and let people themselves deal with them. Initiating a discourse and letting people discuss the issues is all we intend. People should not be deprived of reflecting upon their histories and the issues affecting them. You cannot easily change a people just through discussions; even out of the million, you create dialogue among a hundred people or among couples. For me it is fantastic when, especially in South Africa, people are able to dialogue among themselves. It is great when black people go to the movie theater and on their way home discuss the film they saw in relation to the issues affecting their day-to-day lives. That for me is the revolution, not necessarily the actual killing of tyrants.

Tell me about the character development in the film. And could you talk about the use of professional and nonprofessional actors in your films and other films in South Africa, as well as plans for the part professional actors could play?

There are professional actors in South Africa. I always feel that it is important and challenging for us to use professional actors simply because as far as I am concerned, a film script is just a guideline. It is incomplete without the contributions of actors. The beauty and advantage of professional actors, for me, is how they are able to bring life into the dialogue we created. They go out and research their roles and the history of the character they are to play. But what I find more interesting, and challenging to professional actors, is the use of nonprofessional actors, which is also a challenge to me because it is not easy directing nonprofessional actors. But a nonprofessional actor can challenge a professional actor because the nonprofessional actor has no discipline in terms of how to do things and in terms of limits. A professional tends to be disciplined and guided in terms of how to deliver a monologue or dialogue. When the two are brought together, the nonprofessional, in naïveté, can challenge the disciplined actor as to where the limits are.

The polished dialogue perhaps contradicts the people's real ways of living. While nonprofessionals may act normally just by acting as themselves, professionals may have the tendency to go two or three steps beyond normal. The differences and challenges between the two are interesting to play with. The tendency of the nonprofessional, as Haile Gerima once said of his experiences with *Harvest: 3,000 Years*, is that nonprofessional actors tend to repeat themselves. There is a certain manner in which they do things that we in our professionalism tend to forget. We tend to forget because of the insistence on following the script. For example, my father would warn me, "Hey, don't do that." But he said it differently all the time. However, the tone detects the saturation point, and when the last "Don't do that" comes in, you know that is the limit. That, for me, is the acting that we no longer observe.

Is this not also associated with the oral tradition?

It is, exactly. But again, because of industrialization and modernization oral traditional cultures are dying. We no longer sit with our grandfathers and listen to their stories. They live in the villages, which we do not have the time to visit; hence we have lost the great traditional heritage of oral storytelling. For me, that knowledge is vital because it nurtures. At times it is important to go back to the village and interact with people. The same effect could be achieved if we would sometimes forgo our own means of transportation and take a public transport to the cities to observe people on the trains and buses, to see how they move and speak. It could also nourish our works! So it is important that I always keep in contact with the masses rather than writing scripts in a vacuum or on my little laptop, thinking that is how it works for every other person.

Unlike Cry Freedom, Fools *deals with apartheid in a different way, and another well-known film that portrays apartheid partially from an African perspective is* Mapantsula *[directed by Oliver Schmitz, 1988]. How do you situate your work relative to these two films?*

Mapantsula is an interesting film in that it looks at certain issues from within the South African environment—criminality, for instance. The director, I believe, wanted to impose his understanding of what blacks do. Hence there are two things to be considered revolving around those issues. The first is the criminal aspect and behavior of Panic, the central character, and the issue of the politicization of this character. This created a problem for me simply because Panic became the unionist in a sudden transformation for which I could find no basis. I do understand that in history we have had leaders like Malcolm X who were criminals, who went to prison and then, through education they acquired while there, underwent transformation. The notorious South African prison, Robin Island, where President Nelson Mandela was incarcerated for many years has been termed the university of the marginalized because many of our political leaders who spent time there acquired experiences that transformed them into great leaders. We can easily pinpoint the basis for their transformation, but in *Mapantsula* everything is so obscured that I could not see where Panic's transformation originated.

I think Panic's sudden transformation came from knowing that the government oppressors had killed his brother or his friend. It was from there that he went looking for answers and later found himself (actually too late in the film) in the union movement. I think it is that killing of someone who was dear to him that culminated in the implausible transformation.

I believe, however, that you do not become politically conscious in isolation. There could have been a character who was an activist and associated with Panic to catalyze his transformation. It is in such a process that he would have realized he had been initiated into the people's movement against apartheid, although at this point he would not have been totally transformed because of his past criminal activities. Hence, when the situation reverses, he could then turn to that source of influence on his transformation. Those are the kinds of slow transformations that could have made that aspect of Panic's life more convincing. Mandela, Malcolm X, and our other great heroes did not emerge from prison transformed overnight.

You have been to FESPACO—what do you think about it and its role in the development and promotion of African cinema?

I have a problem presently with FESPACO. It is supposed to be an event that promotes African cinema and African filmmakers. The growth and development of African filmmakers in general has now become secondary because of this political maneuvering in terms of organization. First and foremost, the organizers attend to the needs of their country rather than the needs of the larger African filmmaking initiative. It has become an organization that caters to the politicians first, before the filmmakers are allocated whatever hotel rooms are left. I have come across filmmakers who will go to Ouagadougou, whose films are in competition, but are not allocated hotel rooms. Some filmmakers are not even invited. I think there is a problem in terms of what the objectives of the festival are today. Personally, I see FESPACO as a festival for promoting tourism and francophonie at the expense of African cinema.

Burkina Faso still remains the dominant force in the absence of other film festivals in Africa. Without it, there is no forum for us to see or discover African films.

I do not think it is important for me to be part of a forum of that grandiose scale if FESPACO does not develop filmmakers. After the festival, all the fanfare, what happens to our films? Filmmakers arrive at the festival with a copy of their film in a box, having paid for everything and labored to make it. After the festival they depart for home as they came, still holding that copy of the film in that same box because nothing has happened. In the future I am going to go to FESPACO with my film, and I can tell you right now that this festival will do nothing to get the film distributed.

What is being done to distribute Fools?

The film is going to be distributed in South Africa very soon. I will possibly tell you in the next year the outcome of the success of the distribution. But we have no room for failure. We have to succeed so that we can contradict the ideas propagated by the monopolies that African films or South African films do not do well at the box office. We have to fight against that. But we cannot just sit back and throw the film into the theaters without doing the things necessary to ensure audience turnout. This means we have to develop strategies to reach the people.

Do you have overseas distributors?

The film has been distributed in France, Belgium, Germany, and I think Switzerland. I suppose it is a question of time for the U.S.

Do you have plans to shoot films in other parts of Africa?

I would say that the need will come after some time. I believe at this point that there are too many South African stories waiting to be told.

Why did you choose filmmaking as a career?

I came into filmmaking from theater. I attended a theater school for three years or more. Thereafter, together with colleagues, I ran a theater in South Africa called the Dhlomo Theater, named after the first black playwright in South Africa who actually wrote plays, in the early part of the century. We ran this theater for about three years before we were closed down for political reasons. But to make the theater survive financially, we also ran a casting agency for the advertising world in South Africa. Hence, again, my slow entry into the movie world was involved with casting, but I did not think blacks were used correctly in some of the ads and films. When the theater was closed down, I decided to turn to film studies. I went to France and took some courses. I studied for a year and still was not satisfied. After that I went to London and studied at the London International Film School. My base in terms of moviemaking is theater. Theater for me is very important. Before my first feature film, I made some short films. Three of them were on Super-8mm using nonprofessional actors. One is a documentary and the other a fiction film made in London as part of my graduation thesis.

What is your take on the new technologies, such as the Internet, to advance the prerogatives of African cinema?

In discussing this revolution called the Internet, I think we are talking about two worlds. There is the world here in the United States and the world out there in Africa where we come from. No doubt this revolution is coming to us. We cannot negate its existence. It is there, but again, it is in my house because I was able to afford four thousand dollars to buy a computer and all the software for my daughter. She is into it, but what of other Africans? South Africa has 50 percent unemployment, 80 percent illiteracy, just as in most African countries, and it is even difficult to phone your neighbor in Africa. The important thing is that if they have a script they should film it with the format or system they can afford, and take the film out to the people and show it to them. At the moment, we African filmmakers are still lagging behind. We are still locked up in the old tradition of using Kodak film stock and less sophisticated cameras and sound and editing facilities. We are still trying to grapple with the perennial distribution problems, a nightmare for all of us. I am trying to see how this technology that you are talking about can be put to our advantage. I think it is cheaper, but how can it be made accessible to the people in South Africa or Africa in general?

Filmography

Secuba, 1985
Arouna, 1985
Ezikhumbeni, 1985
The Devil's Children, 1990
Fools, 1997

Jean-Marie Teno (Cameroon)

Jean-Marie Teno grew up in Cameroon, a country that has produced several prolific African filmmakers of international reputation, two whom are featured in this volume. Teno's filmography is impressive. Unlike some African filmmakers, he has been working consistently and producing at least one or two films every year. This is remarkable considering the perennial problems of funding that handicap African filmmakers' ability to make films on regular basis.

Teno graduated from the University of Valenciennes in 1981 in filmmaking and worked for fifteen years as an editor at the France 3 television network. In 1984, he made a short film, *Schubbah*, followed by *Hommage* (1985), which was well received. According to Teno, it is from "the process of experimenting with making short films [that] I learned about making real films." He had made several shorts before his first feature, *Bikutsi Water Blues* (1988), helping him to establish a trend that would mark his career. Today, he stands out as one who not only has advanced and popularized the African documentary tradition, but has made the medium an ideal communicative and educational tool for scrutinizing African developmental, social, and political issues. His feature-length documentary *Afrique, je te plumerai* (Africa, I will fleece you, 1992), whose structure deliberately mixes modes of address, remains a powerful example of unconventional narrative patterns. The film's construction perfectly exemplifies it as political manifesto. Its mode of interrogation stems from the juxtaposition of documentary with fictional images and from narrative discontinuity as well as oral tradition. Remarkable in this mix of cinematic and indigenous narrative codes is the manner in which what would seem on the surface to be a mélange of film styles (documentary, experimental, and narrative; montage editing, lighting, alternation of silence and sound) coheres to express significant, deep-rooted issues powerfully.

Teno experimented with fictional style in his next feature, *Clando* (1996). Although he is pleased with it, he does not consider himself a fiction filmmaker. Stating that he derives more fun from making documentaries, he declared, "I don't have the same emotional feeling for *Clando* as I do for *Afrique*, which required a different kind of hard work and intensive thinking."

I would like to thank Robert Lane Clark and Kathryn Lauten for assisting me in conducting this interview on April 7, 1996, during Teno's visit to the University of Michigan to participate in the film and video series "Screening Social Change," organized by Clark.

How did you launch your film career?

I did not start making films with the intent of becoming a professional filmmaker. I was in newspaper publishing with friends in Paris when I realized that the state we were living in had changed drastically and that we needed to record it. So I bought a 16mm camera and started recording events for posterity. That is how I made my first short film. In the process of experimenting with making short films, I also learned about making "real" films. Before this, I had done only still photography. At that time, I was working for television, and in my spare time would prepare short scenarios. During my one-month annual vacation, I went home to Cameroon and shot the film for which I had prepared the script during the year. That is how I started in filmmaking, but it was more for pleasure than as a career.

What is the title of your first film?

I started in 1983 with a film called *Schubbah*, which I finished in 1984. That same year, I went home with the intention of shooting *Yellow Fever Taximan*, but I could not get authorization to shoot it at that time, so I went into my village and shot *Hommage* [1985]. This film is an homage to my father, and it includes conversations we had when I was growing up. In 1986 I made *Yellow Fever Taximan*; in 1987, *La gifle et la caresse*; in 1988, *Bikutsi Water Blues*; in 1990, *Le dernier voyage*; in 1991, *Mister Foot*; in 1992, *Afrique, je te plumerai*; in 1994, *La tête dans les nuages*; in 1996, *Clando*.

Your film Hommage *is a documentary in fictional style. What inspired its making?*

Hommage is a personal film that was never intended for the public. When my father died in 1979, I could not attend the funeral. This film was a way of paying homage to my father and externalizes my own mourning. I went into my village and shot everyday images. Back in France, I wrote a dialogue between two people, one who stayed in the village and one who left. The conversation includes topics I discussed with my father, such as modernity and what he thought was progress. We had these conversations, but at the time I did not think we could really communicate because of our differences. It became a film with a voice-over of this conversation about everyday images.

Was this your inspiration? After this film, all your films seem to deal with political and social issues.

It is not really a source of inspiration; the question is more, "Why am I making films?" I grew up in a poor neighborhood in Cameroon, and we used to go and watch Indian films. But not everybody had the money to watch each film, so those who went commented on them to others. I grew up acting out films, retelling the stories in different ways.

When I was growing up, I wanted to be a journalist and write about things around me. Because of the strict censorship, however, I thought it would be easier to speak with images in a way that would not even be recognized as criticism—to speak out and attack the system by exposing what is wrong in the society. In 1975 a film called *Pousse-pousse* [Pedicab; Daniel Kamwa, 1975] really inspired me to work with images. That was the first time I saw a film that dealt with important social issues using humor and fantasy. Suddenly the issue of bridal dowries became very important. [The director] dealt with this issue in a very nice way, and people talked about it through this film. This made me realize that cinema is a way to get people to talk about and deal with issues. In Cameroon at that time, the national radio and press said continually that we were living in the most wonderful country in the world, and that everything was all right. The only problems, they said, were in apartheid South Africa, and that everything was perfect in Cameroon. But I came from a neighborhood where nothing was perfect. I saw what was going on and decided that cinema was a way to deal with these issues. That is how I started making films. The first issue I decided to attack was the problem of water supply. In 1988 I made *Bikutsi Water Blues*. The films I had done before, like *Yellow Fever Taximan*, were experimental, trying to understand how to make a film from beginning to end.

When I started working on the fictional documentary *Bikutsi Water Blues*, I turned to the social issue of water in Cameroon. People asked why I was talking about water, since it rains consistently and there is an abundance of water in Cameroon, unlike in other drought-ridden African countries. However, a doctor once told me that two diseases out of three come from polluted water. That was a shock for me. When I was younger, we all used the public water supplies in the neighborhood. As time went on, some people got wealthier and could afford private water supplies in their houses. The public water supply was not well maintained; when water pipes broke down, they were not replaced. People in the poorer neighborhoods did not have access to clean water. In these areas, as self-help projects, we dug wells to get water, but the latrines were just a few meters from the wells. In a town like Yaounde, these latrines polluted the water supply and, in some areas of the city, people were continuously ill. This affected, among other things, education. Because of illness, children had very low attendance at schools. Some would drop out and were later ashamed to return to school, realizing they were too old for the lower levels.

There are grievous cases of medical concern among the Cameroonian society.

One is the case of people in poor neighborhoods who drink polluted water and go to the hospital for medicine when they can afford it, but then return home and drink the same polluted water. They are permanently ill. This leads to the other problem in which uneducated children consequently remain in the same neighborhoods and turn to prostitution and delinquency since they cannot get good jobs. My idea was to attack the system and to explain that people need prevention and education. Cameroon was one of the richest countries at independence. Why didn't the government solve the water problem?

This issue is very important. It seems that such a film would have been shown by Cameroonian television. Is there any working relationship between Cameroonian television and independent filmmakers that would allow for such films to be shown for social enlightenment or education?

When I finished this film in 1988, I brought it back to Cameroon and tried to show it on television. It was impossible, however, because Cameroonian television wanted me to pay them to screen my film. I did, however, show the film a few times in a theater since it is a 35mm film. People were impressed. What interested me was the reaction of the audience. When I showed the film, I was in the theater and nobody knew me. I listened to comments such as, "We know all about these problems. What we need is entertainment and positive heroes when we come to the movies. This is not a real film with a strong Cameroonian hero who gives us dreams." Before my film, there were previews of the films shown regularly and commercially in that theater, violent foreign films with Sylvester Stallone, for example; and then we turned to my socially conscious film. You can guess what happened.

What was your response to the demand from the public for entertainment films?

My response is simple. I make films that I find the energy to make. I am not driven to please the public. If that were the case I would be making *Dallas*. People want only entertainment, but that is not my aim. Otherwise, I would not be a filmmaker. I would be a businessman. I make films to shake the African public from their apathy.

In Afrique, je te plumerai, *there is some entertainment. A viewer gets entranced by the political issues, but at the same time, he or she is offered relief from politics with humor and then returned to the hard issues.*

My main concern is always to encourage people to sit down and watch. For that to happen, I have to hold their attention. The cinema is also a place of emotion. You can elicit emotion with music or other things people like, but I also want people to realize the social situation. If the situation were not so bad, I would be making completely different films, but the situation is so traumatic that I cannot make only entertainment films and feel satisfied.

How do you respond to the audience members who say they want hope? Do you think, for example, there is a hopeful message in Bikutsi Water Blues?

When they say they want hope, they mean escape. That was not the whole audience, but just one negative response I heard. For me, there is hope when people start confronting an obvious problem to find a solution. For me, hope is people dealing with their problems, not searching for a scapegoat. Everything is getting worse, and we are waiting for the Messiah to solve our problems, but he is not going to come. The Providential man does not exist. No politician is going to do it on his own. People have to get conscious and really act. I also try to show how easy it is to blame the West, etc., but we must realize that we are in despair and must work to get out of it.

That is one of the main messages in Clando *as well. Why did you use the German woman, a European woman, as one of the main carriers of that message in the film?*

We say in our society that when you travel, you learn. When you go someplace, the people there can reveal your own situation to you. I chose this woman because she was politically active. Germany is a country where people are politically active. This woman happens to look at the situation in a very different way and forces the main character to look at the situation as well.

We did not see this German woman in Cameroon, where the man's Cameroonian wife is. Yet this white woman plays a dominant role in an African becoming politically conscious. Isn't the film alluding to the fact that someone has to remind Africans to wake up and deal with their problems?

Whoever reminds Africans to deal with their problems is welcome. It can be a white woman or man. I don't see people in terms of color. Some white people tried and left because the situation was hopeless. If a person goes to a neighboring country with a situation different from his own, he may meet someone who makes him face his own situation. Unfortunately, the situation seems to be the same in all of Africa. This character goes abroad and meets a white woman who is active and not complacent. She does not pretend she understands him. She doesn't understand, and this leads her to ask why the man doesn't do something about the problems in Africa.

You mentioned the influence of Pousse-pousse *on your work. What are your other African or foreign influences?*

My main influence is something that happened in Ouagadougou in 1983. I was working for a newspaper I had created with my friends, and I met an African filmmaker, Souleymane Cissé, with whom I started a conversation on African cinema. I was just a young man trying to understand everything about cinema. I didn't know much about the history of African cinema, but I had seen almost all the films in the African cinema library. We had a long discussion on his film *Baara* [Work, 1978]. He asked at the end of our conversation why I was wasting my time writing about cinema: "Why not make films?" he asked! He told me that I have read into his film things he had not consciously put into them. "You want me to explain," he continued, "but what do you want me to explain? You may read what you want to read. I am glad my films can have these readings." That is what really encouraged me to make films.

My major influences also include that of Djibril Diop Mambety's *Touki-Bouki* [The hyena's journey, 1973], whose style greatly influenced me to find my own way of editing. My concern is to deliver the message and still entertain people. I always want to keep the audience with me; while telling the story and dealing with the issues fully, I also want to keep the work entertaining.

That makes me arrive at a specific style. I work first with the idea and then decide on how to shape the narrative to integrate either documentary or fictional style, or both. It is, however, when I get to the editing process that I work on the form, which is very complicated on paper.

What kind of film is Afrique, je te plumerai? *The narrative style is a collage of different genres, such as satire, comedy, music, straightforward didacticism, and juxtaposition of opposites.*

I started this film knowing where I wanted to go, but the elements I had were so different. To really use them was difficult because I had so much archival footage of people saying ridiculous things. I also had people who had witnessed the opposite of what others said. In terms of montage, it was obvious to me to juxtapose one against the other. My narration was meant to lead people toward enlightenment. The sarcasm deployed in the film is to allow for humor, because without this humor, a film like *Afrique* would be very boring and hard to follow. When we were looking at the footage, we could not stop laughing at the commentary of the French in some of the archival footage. There was nothing to do but laugh. When you look at this footage, you can see that there has been no shift in the French colonial mentality—between that discourse and what is happening today. That is why the film is so unpopular in France. When I requested the archival footage, the authorities in France wanted to give it to me without the sound, but I needed the sound also. They tried to convince me that the sound was no longer relevant, but my response was that there has been no public statement denouncing what was said. I needed that footage to assess contemporary reactions.

This archival footage is very expensive. How did you finance its procurement?

The film was very expensive in terms of research and footage. The budget difference between this documentary [*Afrique*] and the feature film *Clando* is only fifty thousand dollars. *Afrique*'s budget was roughly three hundred thousand dollars. I was lucky that some of the footage came from left-wing organizations. The footage of Lumumba, for example, came from the DDR. Other footage came from the French army, and that required a lot of negotiating. In the end, they did not charge the normally high price since I am African. I think they felt a little guilty!

What are your funding sources?

For *Afrique, je te plumerai*, I got money mainly from German television, but some came from various nonprofit organizations. I got money from the Centre National de la Cinématographie in France. The Ministry of Cooperation gave about one-twentieth of the budget. (All the various sources are listed at the end of the film.) From Cameroon I got support from *Le Messager* [a newspaper] as well as various individuals. Cameroonian television did not want to work with me, though. Since I work in France as a television editor, I always approach Cameroonian television when I start a new project. I explain to them that other television organizations work in coproduction with independent filmmakers and that I want to work with them. I would appreciate equipment and technicians from their organization, but they never offer assistance. They say I do not want to be part of them, that I come from the *quartier* and shouldn't bother them with my problems. I explained how they can benefit from working with people from outside, because what they are producing locally is technically not very good. But they refused to listen. The only film I did with Cameroonian television is *Le dernier voyage*, because the producers in Europe made it clear they wanted me to direct the film and made that part of their funding conditions. That is my only film that has been shown on Cameroonian television.

Do you use African technicians for your films?

It depends on each film. *Yellow Fever Taximan* was shot completely with a local crew in Yaounde. Bonaventure was the cameraman. *Bikutsi Water Blues* was a big project, and I thought of using Bonaventure but I had a lot of problems with him when I shot *Yellow Fever*. Because he was the only good cameraman working with Cameroon television, he could be called upon at any moment for presidential duties. I could not take the risk of going to Cameroon to make the film not knowing if my cameraman would be on location. For my own security, I brought a camera operator and sound engineer from France. The rest of the crew was Cameroonian. When I shot *Afrique*, the situation was the same, so I again brought a cameraman and sound engineer from France but hired Cameroonians for the rest of the crew. When I made *La tête dans les nuages*, Bonaventure was on leave from television, so he shot it for me. We also made *Mister Foot* together.

Let us turn to some specifics of Afrique, je te plumerai. *What made you deviate from the original theme of* Afrique, *which was supposed to have been publishing?*

The original project was about writers throughout the century, but I also wanted to deal with the politics of writing books in Cameroon. However, when I arrived in

Cameroon in December 1990, there was an outbreak of violence. Celestin Monga had written his open letter to the head of state and violence broke out. The Berlin Wall had also just fallen and everyone in the country was enthusiastic. The newspaper *Le Messager*, which usually had a circulation of five thousand per month, went up to eighty thousand every week. People were reading and hungry to understand more about what was going on in the country and to know what was hidden from them. When we saw the images of the killings in Kumba, I said to myself that I had to really think about this violence. I could not understand how those in power could fail to solve the problems of the people when they had the means to do so. I wanted to investigate the minds of the leaders of the country and through that understand the culture and politics of Cameroon. I had dealt already with the flesh, the physical, and now I wanted to deal with the spiritual, what was in people's heads. This outbreak of violence was very much like that before independence. I also realized that this type of violence had always been used in Cameroon to crush political movements for change. Therefore, to deal with it required going into the history of the country in order to investigate how, from this violence, you can end up with people in their current state of apathy.

In the beginning of the film, you said, "Yaounde, cruel city." Is Yaounde still a cruel city?

Even worse. Yaounde is sometimes very deceiving. It was a cruel and arrogant city at one point. Now it has become a trash dump. It is painful to see this beautiful city become what I would call a sorrowful and pitiful city. It is gradually but steadily going downhill. You can see a trash dump grow for a whole year, get removed with some financial assistance, and then just start up again.

My students who saw Afrique *were so touched by the cruelty that one student said, "I don't think the filmmaker has been to Cameroon since he made this film," meaning that he did not think you would be allowed back in Cameroon after making such a revealing film.*

I said only obvious things. Everybody saw what happened. Everybody saw the images of people being killed in Kumba. Celestin Monga stayed in Cameroon for four years after he wrote the open letter. Pius Njawe still lives in Cameroon and still writes against the government. I have not done anything more than these people in terms of my political engagement. They fight the system every day while living in the country. What can the government do to me? People who I know are from the secret service came to my office in Paris to intimidate me. I spoke with them and they pretended they liked my work and wanted a video copy. I happily agreed to sell one to them, but that is not what they wanted. They asked where I live, and I gave them the address. I am not hiding. I am not part of a system which smuggles arms into the country to organize a coup. That is not my aim. I just say things that are obvious. People who write books say the same things. I want those in power to organize a debate with the people to see where our common interests are. I don't want people to just sit and watch them brutalize and loot the country.

Would you say more about the situations you referred to at the beginning of the interview that brought you to filmmaking? Were they specific to being a Cameroonian living in Paris?

Living in Paris made me more aware of what was going on in my country. Sometimes when you live in an environment, you don't have a critical mind about that place. I was living in France and going home almost every six months. I also had more liberty to speak at that time. You don't need to be in a system to attack it. When I was thinking about the issue of water, people in the system did not think it was important enough to talk about. When you are politically aware of a situation, you don't need to be physically present in the place to talk about it.

The way you talk about going to France and seeing things in a different way makes me think about how in Afrique *you juxtapose the past and the present, suggesting that you can understand the past better from the vantage point of the present. Do you see the historical stages Cameroon has gone through in terms of a continuous historical narrative or one with distinct eruptive breaks? With that in mind, do you look to possible solutions in terms of excising colonial influences from the present day, or is that period an inextricable aspect of the current Cameroon?*

I do not have a background as a historian or philosopher, but I just decided that I had to tell the story of the people around me. For *Afrique*, I went to the colonial period to understand the present. I have read books suggesting a kind of paradise in the precolonial period, but I do not buy that. Even in the villages some of the customs are oppressive. When talking with older people I sometimes disagree about this idea of an ancient lost paradise. The more I question how Africa is moving, the more I question our responsibility for its state. When you look over the past thirty years, there were many possibilities to reverse the course of things. Why did people in power not grab those opportunities? There is probably something within us, within our traditions, that we have to reconsider and question to really understand how we can be in this situation. My next work is an examination of what people say about precolonial times, to see what was good.

Would you talk about the reception of your films? Do you see a difference you could qualify between audiences who have seen it on different continents? Do you see a potential for your films to mobilize action that would bring about changes?

When I meet people who have seen the film, they give me their reactions, but I am more sensitive to some than to others. People say the film is great and that they learned a lot from it, and the conversation stops there. When people challenge issues, we argue and I keep more of these discussions in my mind, since they force me to see where there could be problems. When the film was shown in Cameroon through satellite, the people who saw it, who know me, told me that people got caught up in it and stopped their planned activities to see the whole film. They even called me in France to say that the film is wonderful and some asked how to acquire a copy of it. They appreciated seeing the events they had witnessed. I want people to be able to see the film on television so that they can discuss the issues. Change takes time, and this might help them start thinking of possibilities for change.

This raises the problem of distribution. You mentioned that the film was viewed in Cameroon by satellite, but Cameroonian television did not show it. People who have access to satellite programs are either the oppressors or the educated that know this history. There are, however, people who do not know the history and need to be educated in order to understand the importance of mass mobilization in trying to change the system. How have you reached the people that this film is intended to inform?

It is not my role to be sure everyone sees it. I have already spent three or four years of my life making the film. I cannot spend another three or four years trying to show it in Africa. This is the role of the people. Even if I do not reach those people today, the film will reach them one day. It is there; the film exists and is not going to disappear. One day the television system will change and people will see my films. I do not take this problem as something preventing me from working. If censorship exists, what should I do about it? I will not go on a hunger strike so that Cameroonian television will show my film; they would just let me die!

But what can be done about this problem?

Why should it bother you? It doesn't bother me.

Because with such a restricted audience for the film, how can you make enough money in order to create another film?

Even if people saw the film, though, would I make money? The television people wanted me to pay them to show the film, so even if it were shown on television I would not make money.

Have you made any money from Afrique*?*

I think I made about thirty thousand dollars, but it just went into the making of *Clando. Afrique*'s distribution in the United States brings in about one thousand to two thousand dollars every six months.

Are you optimistic about African cinema?

Of course I am optimistic about African cinema. There are many young filmmakers making new films. Also, there are older filmmakers who continue to make films. African cinema is diverse, fun, and enjoyable—if I may say so! I made films first for egotistical purposes, for fun. If I didn't enjoy making films I would just stop. Life is short. I have made my first feature and it was very difficult for me. Now I am going back to documentaries, because it is more fun to make documentaries. I am going to take *Clando* to Cameroon and other African countries to make some money. But I don't have the same emotional feeling for *Clando* that I do for *Afrique*, which required a different kind of work and intensive thinking.

What is it like, living and making films in exile?

It is difficult to live in exile. But are we really living in exile? When you see how situations are developing in Europe, we are not really in exile. Africa is more and more part of Europe. What is happening in Europe right now is a continuation of African history. The construction of Europe entails the exclusion of the African component in European society. They have almost managed to exclude Africa from the world economy. So living in Europe now, I am in the middle of the whole debate about Africa. The way people look at me, an African in Europe, is exactly how Europeans look at Africa. I have to fight this image in Europe. It is important to be there to remind Europe of history and of its own narrow-mindedness—to lobby and fight these attitudes about Africa.

Do you see that as a subject of a documentary at some point?

Yes, and a fiction too! I am going to make films in Europe, because Africa is in Europe and the situation of Africans in Europe is becoming dreadful. We are so much a part of the history of France, but it is easy for them to talk about us with disrespect. We cannot let them get away with that. We have to make films to enlighten them and to analyze what is happening.

Is it easy to show your films in France, especially given the critique of French imperialism?

No, *Afrique* had a lot of problems in France. People criticized the form; they said it is a collage and wondered if it was right to show the archival footage. It is always a strange dialogue, but we need to be there and fight. That is why I don't really feel like I am in exile. I am on the battlefield in France.

You mentioned that you are returning to documentary film style. Have you considered the use of video?

Yes, especially given the economy. The postproduction of *Clando* was done in video because the technology now exists. For my next project, even if I do not shoot in film, the postproduction will be in video. I might even buy a small video camera to do some documentaries. You can make very interesting films in video, and it is a lot cheaper than working in the 16mm format.

What is the situation in Cameroon today? Does television rely solely on programs from France, or do Cameroonians make their own programs?

Cameroonians make some of their own programs, such as video entertainment, music videos, and some soap operas, but most of the programs come from abroad. The quality of the production in Cameroon is poor, because they won't work with independents. The workers still have the mind-set of civil servants. They do not want to challenge anything or make their bosses unhappy, so they always tackle the same topics. Many of the programs are adaptations of the same novel written by the director of the National Television. There are now four adaptations of the same novel even though there are many other Cameroonian writers' works available.

The sequence in Afrique *where you went and spoke to the director of television was wonderful. His response was, why should he pay for your film if he gets foreign shows such as* Who's the Boss? and Dallas *for free?*

That was staged with an actor. The director would not have allowed us to bring in a camera and shoot him.

Yes, but it worked! The use of still photos in Afrique *is also a most powerful technique. There is fiction within the documentary and vice versa and, these two aspects reinforce each other. The eyewitness account of the old man who spoke about his son was also powerful. How did you conceptualize the structure?*

We interviewed Félix Moumie's father. He gave us photographs of his son, and we had the archival footage. We tried to follow the history while also keeping in mind the spirit of the time, which included what was in people's heads. We wanted to give an overview of how people in Cameroon were thinking and the overall state of mind at that moment.

Did you use professional actors at the end of Afrique, *and what is your view on the use of professional actors?*

The performer at the end of the film, Essindi Mindja, was going to talk about the theater in the original idea for the film. Because I departed from that project, I had him perform the elements that went into the actual film. This was a regular performance for him. He is a high school geography teacher who has acted in many Cameroonian films. After independence, the theater became a mode of expression, because people could not publish books without going abroad. Therefore, people wrote plays that are easy to stage. But the plays started being censored, and it became more expensive to stage a performance with many people. Therefore, the one-man show became popular in the mid-1970s. Mindja is one of the people who did a one-man show. He was going to tell that story, but in the end I just had him perform. That performance helped sum up the present situation.

The issues in his performance were specifically pertinent to your film. Did you write any of the lines for him?

No, that was all his own performance, but we did edit in only what was right for the film.

You question history a lot in this film. Could you comment on Sultan Njoya? Has that wonderful alphabet been completely obliterated?

It is still there, but at a very restricted level. The German missions did a great job putting it into a book, but unfortunately, for this at least, Germany lost World War I and had to leave the region. The sultan was forced into exile. Since then, the alphabet has been taught only in the palace of the sultan, but it is not in use today. However, some of the things he invented at the end of the century, such as the grinder, still have applications.

Regarding German relations with Cameroon, many people left their villages in Germany and came to Cameroon just before the Industrial Revolution and found Cameroonians at the same stage of development as themselves, for example, using animals for farm work. They built houses replicating German architectural designs. But when the Industrial Revolution came, the German government stopped any transfer of technology, even though Germans in Cameroon wanted to bring in modern products. After World War I, all of that was stopped because the French were not concerned with such things. However, some of the buildings built by the Germans still exist today.

Are there certain African codes or African ways of doing things that you can identify as influential in your narrative structure?

My films are edited in the form of traditional African storytelling. I put that part of Africa that I have into my films, and I think my way of telling stories is African. That is why I produce my own films—so that I don't have to listen to people tell me that my writing is not understandable because it does not follow classical Western forms. I produce my own work and go in the directions I want to go. I do not want to claim it is African or not African, for what is "African"? I don't even know.

In your own view, how Pan-African is FESPACO? What do you think about the French dominating influence at FESPACO?

If FESPACO were well organized I would be happy, but things are never well organized. I do not want to argue, however, over whether it is due to the French influence or the stupidity of the organizers. In addition to French influences, there are Dutch and Danish influences. If the British were to put more money into it, they would also have more influence. Whoever gives money has influence.

It is a matter of who sponsors the event. But in your view, does it have the Pan-African dimension it is meant to have?

I don't know. I have not looked into FESPACO. If someone wants to have a festival in Accra or Lagos, let him organize it. Whenever I make a film I subtitle it in English. If I had the money, I would dub it into English to be able to show it to the broader public. I would also dub it into other African languages if I had enough money. If there were more festivals or places where we could showcase our films, that would be fine. It is possible to create more possibilities if there are adequate resources. So, does it matter if French influence exists? If African films could be seen for one week in Ouagadougou and for another week at a different festival in another location wouldn't that be wonderful? It is a pity that the Mogadishu festival disappeared and that there is no festival in the anglophone countries. There is need for more festivals on the continent to show African films.

In making Clando, *what criteria did you use in choosing your actors?*

There were three professional actors. The lead male actor graduated from acting school, the German woman is a professional actress, and the old man at the end has played in many French films. The other people play themselves for the most part. The people in the film from Cologne are part of a commune, and I met them when I went to show my film at a festival there. If I had had more money for the film, I would have had the best actors in Cameroon. When I was filming there, however, a French producer was making a film. Most of the actors and technicians worked for him because he had more money to offer. When we talk about the solidarity of African technicians, we must realize that when faced with two possibilities, they choose to work with the French. While I was shooting, the man from France was making a stupid film called *The Master of the Elephant*, which takes place in northern Cameroon. He was using another Cameroonian producer who brought with him all the technicians we had trained together, since we are the two most active filmmakers in Cameroon. I finally made *Clando*, and the woman who plays the housewife was the script girl. She is from the National Television Organization, but Cameroonian television refused to give me coproduction materials for this film. The assistant cameraman and soundman are also from the National Television. These three people had to take their yearly vacation from work to help me make the film. They did this because they believe in the project. We had to train people to do the lighting.

Can you tell me what other Cameroonian filmmakers are doing now?

Daniel Kamwa recently made a film called *Le cercle des pouvoirs* [1996]. Now, he is preparing another film. Arthur si Bita is in Cameroon, but I do not know what he is doing. Dikongwe Pipa has not made a film in a long time, but he is also in Cameroon and working on a project.

Clando was shot in Cameroon and Germany. Why did you go to Germany?

For many reasons. The idea of the film started in Cameroon, and the man's story is almost all true. A man was arrested and spent two months in prison. When I was shooting the film, I met computer engineers who had been arrested under the same conditions at that period of time. The most famous of those arrested now living in the United States spent two years in prison. He had a computer company in Cameroon. In 1992, I was in Germany to show some of my short films at a festival. I was impressed by how many Africans I met who were well established in Germany. They told me that they had initially come for a weekend but had been living there for the last six years. They said that the city of Cologne has some kind of magic. I was impressed by that and by the fact that I met so many political groups and people who were politically involved in this city. People on the extreme left were very active. It is amazing that those working for the festival had the ability to mobilize ten thousand people in one weekend for political activities. I said to myself that I needed to make a film about their lives and to foreground the discussion I heard from them.

I was interested not only in their activism, but also in the women, who are not very politically active but who said things that were encouraging. One moment I wanted to show involves people asking lucid questions about a particular man. They wanted to know why no action had been taken in spite of all the problems they faced; his reaction was simply, "You don't understand." I wanted to show this—why someone would refuse to talk about a situation like that and could only respond, "You don't understand." Why not make others understand? Why only wait for things to change? I wanted to thread the two issues.

In the film, the white woman is the most active person, which is why I said earlier that if the lead actor's wife in Cameroon were more active, it would have highlighted women's involvement in the political struggle.

No, the wife in Cameroon would have been primarily concerned with her family. Everybody knows the kind of life we lead in Cameroon. The wife would have said that before getting involved, she must think first of her family. I am not inventing this. It is a big problem with most of the people at home. At the end, the wife follows because she cannot do otherwise, but the primary concern was if you challenge the state, where are you going to and how are you going to live?

In Clando *you use a lot of internal monologue that is reminiscent of Ousmane Sembene's* Black Girl. *You use voice-overs to articulate the man's thoughts and in some cases the music is almost subliminal, for example, in outside scenes.*

I use a lot of voice-over since I come from documentary filmmaking. I did not realize this is also the case in *Black Girl.* The Cameroonian saxophone player Ben Belinga composed the music, and Christiane Badgley did the sound editing.

Where did you do your postproduction work?

This time I did it in England, but next time I might do it in the United States.

Are you aware that there are ultramodern facilities available in Nigeria that will be relatively cheaper?

Yes, but I am skeptical about them. I need to see a film from there that has the quality I want for sound and other technical components. It is not only important to have the facilities but also technicians who have the experience and ability. Sound is a major problem in African films; there are problems in Zimbabwe, where there is also a lab. You need to go where people work regularly. I do not want to make any compromises about the quality of my work. If they want the lab to work, they need to produce regularly so we can see if it works. But I am going to Los Angeles for my sound mixing next time.

Filmography

Schubbah, 1984
Hommage, 1985
Yellow Fever Taximan, 1986
La gifle et la caresse, 1987
Bikutsi Water Blues, 1988
Le dernier voyage (The last voyage), 1990
Mister Foot, 1991
Afrique, je te plumerai (Africa, I will fleece you), 1992
La tête dans les nuages (The head in the clouds), 1994
Clando, 1996
Chief, 1999

Distributors of African Films in the United States

African Diaspora Images
71 Joralemon Street
Brooklyn, NY 11201
(718) 852-8353

Bullfrog Films
P.O. Box 149
Oley, PA 19547
(610) 779-8226
fax: (610) 370-1978
Web site: www.bullfrogfilms.com
e-mail: video@bullfrogfilms.com

California Newsreel
149 Ninth Street
San Francisco, CA 94103
(415) 621-6196
fax: (415) 621-6522
Web site: www.newsreel.org
e-mail: contact@newsreel.org

DSR, Inc.
9111 Gulford Road
Columbia, MD 21046
(301) 490-3500
fax: (301) 490-4146
e-mail: dsr@us.net

Filmakers Library
124 East 40th Street
New York, NY 10016
(212) 808-4980
fax: (212) 808-4983
Web site: www.filmakers.com
e-mail: info@filmakers.com

Films, Inc.
4411 N. Ravenswood Avenue
Chicago, IL 60640-5802
(800) 826-3456
fax: (773) 878-0416
e-mail: classics@homevision.com

First Run/Icarus Films
32 Court Street, 21st Floor
Brooklyn, NY 11201
(718) 488-8900
fax: (718) 488-8642
Web site: www.frif.com
e-mail: info@frif.com

Gris-Gris Films
17962 Valley Vista Boulevard
Encino, CA 91316
(818) 881-8725
Web site: www.grisgrisfilms.com
e-mail: grisfilm@ix.netcom

KJM3 Entertainment Group, Inc.
462 Broadway, Suite 510
New York, NY 10013
(212) 689-0950
fax: (212) 925-3191

Mypheduh Films, Inc.
P.O. Box 10035
Washington, DC 20018-0035
(202) 234-4755
(800) 524-3895
fax: (202) 234-5735
Web site: www.sankofa.com
e-mail: info@sankofa.com

New Yorker Films
16 West 61st Street
New York, NY 10023
(212) 247-6110
fax: (212) 307-7855
Web site: www.newyorkerfilms.com
e-mail: info@newyorkerfilms.com

Third World Newsreel
545 Eighth Avenue, 10th Floor
New York, NY 10018
(212) 947-9277
fax: (212) 594-6417
Web site: www.twn.org
e-mail: twn@twn.org

Nwachukwu Frank Ukadike is associate professor in the Department of Communication and the Program in African and African Diaspora Studies at Tulane University. He is the author of *Black African Cinema* and has published many articles in journals and anthologies. He is currently working on two book projects, *The New African Cinema: History, Narratology, and the Aesthetics of African Films of the 1990s* and *Video–Film Production: The Emergence of a New Cultural Art in Anglophone Africa.*

Teshome H. Gabriel teaches in the Department of Film/TV/New Media at the University of California, Los Angeles. He is the author of *Third Cinema in the Third World: The Aesthetics of Liberation.*